THE RHINE

ROLAND RECHT

THE RHINE

Culture and Landscape at the Heart of Europe

Thames & Hudson

Endpapers
Johann Ludwig Bleuler, *Source of the Vorderrhein [anterior Rhine] in Lake Toma; Mouth of the Rhine in the North Sea near Katwijk.* Aquatints from *Les vues les plus pittoresques des Bords du Rhin*, 1845.

Colour plates pp. 1–8
p. 1   'Father Rhine', sculpture in the gardens of Schloss Schwetzingen.
p. 2   Cologne master, *Martyrdom of St Ursula and her Companions in Cologne*, right wing of the St George altar at St Nikolai, Kalkar, c. 1480 (see p. 338).
p. 4   Friedrich Wilhelm Delkeskamp, *Panorama of the Rhine from Neuwied to Trechtinghausen*, c. 1840. Folding coloured aquatint, 20 cm (7⅞ in.) wide. Girozentrale, Westdeutsche Landesbank, Düsseldorf.
p. 6–7 Views of Rhenish landscapes from Johann Ludwig Bleuler, *Les vues les plus pittoresques des Bords du Rhin*, 1845 (Antiquariat Gerber, Basel).
p. 8   Hans Thoma, *The Rhine near Laufenburg*, 1870. Gemäldegalerie, Staatliche Museen Preussischer Kulturbesitz, Berlin.

Illustrations on pp. 86, 98, 118, 126, 142, 161, 167, 173, 190, 242–43 and 286
The historic views of different towns are based on copper engravings by Matthäus Merian (1593–1650) and appeared in Zeiler/Merian, *Topographiae*, 1650–88.

Translated from the German *Der Rhein: Kunstlandschaft Europas* by Francisca Garvie and Lorna Dale

This edition first published in the United Kingdom in 2001 by Thames & Hudson Ltd, 181A High Holborn, London WC1V 7QX

First published in the United States of America in hardcover in 2001 by Thames & Hudson Inc., 500 Fifth Avenue, New York, New York 10110

© 2001 Thames & Hudson Ltd, London
Original edition © 2001 Hirmer Verlag GmbH, Munich

British Library Cataloguing-in-Publication Data
A catalogue record for this book is available from the British Library

Library of Congress Catalog Card Number 2001088628

ISBN 0–500–51058–X

Printed and bound in Germany

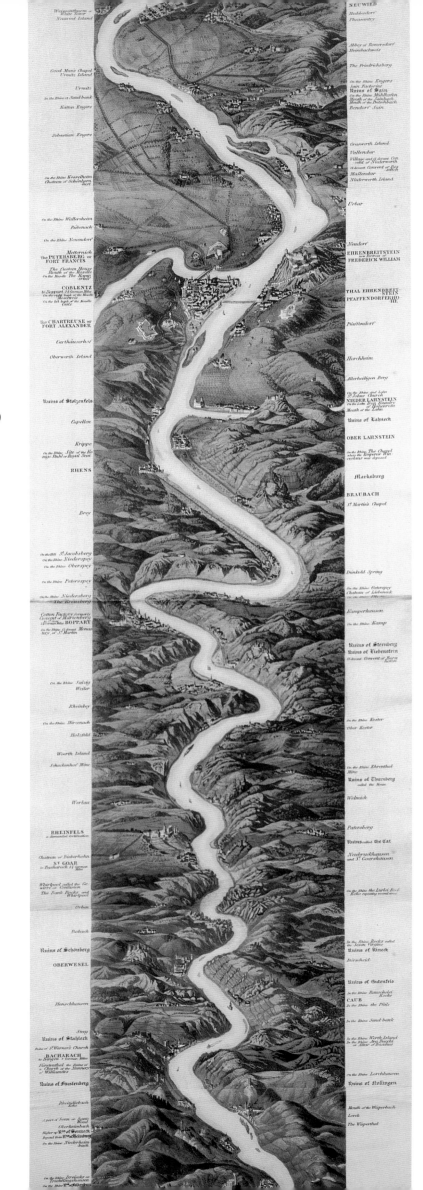

Contents

VUE DU COUVENT DE DISSENTIS, ET DE SES ENVIRONS,
PRISE PRÈS DE LA RÉUNION DE DEUX BRAS DU RHIN SUPÉRIEUR ET CELUI DU MILIEU.

1

VUE DU VILLAGE DE ZILLIS DANS LA VALLÉE DE SCHAMS, EN VENANT
DE VIA MALA, CANTON DES GRISONS.

2

RÉUNION DU RHIN ANTÉRIEUR ET DU RHIN POSTÉRIEUR A REICHENAU.

3

LE COURS DU RHIN PAR SA VALLÉE AVEC LA VUE SUPÉRIEURE DU LAC DE CONSTANCE.

4

VUE DE LA VILLE DE STEIN, CANTON DE SCHAFFHOUSE.

5

VUE DE LA CHUTE DU RHIN DE FISCHETZ.

6

VUE DE LA VILLE DE VIEUX BRISACH.

7

VUE DE LA VILLE DE BALE, PRINCIPALE VILLE DE LA RIVIÈRE RHÉNANE.

8

VUE DE LA VILLE DE MAYENCE ET DE SES ENVIRONS.

9

VUE D'OBERWESEL, DES RUINES DE SCHOENBERG, GUTENFELS ET OCHSENTHOURM.

10

VUE DES ROCHERS DE LOURLEY ET DE LA PÊCHE DES SAUMONS.

11

VUE DE BOPPART ET DU CHÂTEAU DE L'EMPEREUR.

12

VUE DE NONENWERTH.

13

VUE DE LA VILLE DE COLOGNE PRISE DE BAYENTHU.

14

VUE DE LA VILLE D'ANDERNAC.

15

VUE DE L'INTÉRIEUR DE LA VILLE DE LOUVAIN.

16

Preface

In this book the reader is invited to take a journey down the River Rhine, following its course from Disentis to Delft, from the High Alps to the North Sea, crossing four different countries. It is an artistic journey, during which the traveller will come across all kinds of works of art at the various stages and stopping places. The most striking elements are the great works of architecture, for it is these historic buildings, these cathedrals and churches, palaces and castle ruins, that have shaped the landscape of the Rhine and left their imprint on it. However varied the landscape, there remains a consistency of visual experience, to which the striking silhouette of a church spire or the splendour of a Schloss lend an unmistakable identity and colour. The various periods of human settlement and systems of rule are overlaid rather like a palimpsest, at whose original content we can only guess. Beyond all the ravages of war and deliberate acts of destruction, the works that remain are those that people have considered worth preserving. It is these works, however imposing or modest, the legacies of a long and deeply experienced history, that make us more keenly aware of the progress from chaos to order, from decline to renewal.

In 1919, just after the end of the terrible war that shook the entire Western world, Paul Valéry set the scene for his allegory of melancholy on the Rhine: 'And now – standing on a huge earthwork of Helsingör, stretching from Basel to Cologne, as far as the dunes of Nieuwpoort, the marshes of the Somme, the chalk cliffs of Champagne and the granite of Alsace, the European Hamlet sees a million ghosts.' In fact, the great valley of the Rhine offered Valéry's European Hamlet ideal standpoints for gazing into the heart of Europe, at the endless historical cycle of war and peace, reason and unreason, order and disorder, creation and destruction. There were many dreams of Europe along this arterial river, dreams that became reality, only to vanish again. Now Europe is being rebuilt, this time perhaps for good.

There can be no better way of gaining useful insights for the future than by looking carefully at the past. If we learn to know and understand the monuments and works of art that history has passed down to us, we may also acquire a keener sense of the resources and weaknesses of our times.

My warm thanks go to Hirmer Verlag in Munich, who first inspired me with the idea for this project and are responsible for its splendid presentation. I am particularly grateful to the editor Margret Haase for the help she provided from the outset. I hope that all those who read the text and look at the illustrations of this journey down a great and fascinating European river find the book equally rewarding and enjoyable.

Roland Recht
Strasbourg, summer 2000

For Marie

Introduction

The Rhine has many faces. When Hirmer Verlag in Munich suggested I write a book about it, I found the idea interesting but had some doubts at first. The image of the Rhine also brought back a flood of memories and impressions inspired by my personal experiences of the river and also by the associations it had with various works of art. To the music lover the Rhine probably means the E-flat prelude to Wagner's *Das Rheingold* or Robert Schumann's cheerful *Rhine* symphony, while the lover of literature and poetry will think of the *Rhénanes*, Guillaume Apollinaire's poems about the Rhine, or of the river depicted by Victor Hugo, Heinrich Heine, Alexandre Dumas, Gérard de Nerval or Christa Wolf. The mythical connotations of the Rhine are brought out in Clemens Brentano's Rhine fairytales or Hölderlin's hymn-like poem to the 'noblest of rivers', not forgetting the Rhenish landscape paintings by Turner, Hans Thoma and Max Slevogt or the woodcuts by Anselm Kiefer.

The river has so many associations that it has almost become a part of us. An analogy could be drawn between the river as metaphor for the passage of time and the continuous flow of history and of individual human destiny. Perhaps, if we contemplate the river long enough, we can retrace the course of history through it, a history in which we all play our part.

This book is concerned primarily with works of art, in accordance with the publisher's idea and the author's profession. Yet it makes sense to begin by looking at the geography of the Rhineland, as a landscape or sequence of landscapes linked by the river. The same waters pursue their steady course through the steep ravine of the Via Mala (evil way) the wide panorama of the mouth of the Alpine Rhine in Lake Constance and the banks of the romantic Middle Rhine studded with picturesque castles. More than any other landscape north of the Alps, the Rhineland reflects people's search for prosperity and power, for middle-class virtues. At the same time it reveals a highly developed sense of composition, of harmony and a love of life. These characteristics give the geometric patchwork of vineyards and towns along the Rhine their special rhythm. The Rhenish landscape acquires an almost musical form thanks to its regularly pronounced modulations.

This landscape is also made up of, and mirrored by, myths associated with particular times and places. Myths create a link between nature and people, people and heroes, heroes and gods. In the *Nibelungen* legend and its musical reconstruction by Richard Wagner, the ring made of gold from the Rhine becomes the epitome of wealth and power, the fateful object of desire. This myth draws on the fact that minute quantities of gold have been found in the sands of the Rhine since the beginning of the Christian era. In Wagner's *Ring* cycle, the form of the ring symbolizes the circular flow of both the water and human destiny. Wagner used the metaphor of the river, which can turn into a destructive force if it is too powerful, to show that owning wealth – the Rhine gold in this case – and love are diametrically opposed.

In this way the history of the Rhine can be viewed as a source of both good and evil. The link between the two is apparent in the artistic endeavours of the people from the Rhineland, whose love of art always remained alive and who were always a step ahead of other northern regions. This characteristic is coupled with a certain ostentation, which the Rhinelanders probably copied off the Italians, with whom the river brought them into constant contact.

The question is whether those who lived there managed to create a Rhenish art indigenous to this landscape. There is no doubt that they established the right conditions for it to develop. The important monasteries dating back to the Carolingian period and the richly endowed convents of the Ottonians, Salians and Hohenstaufens were intellectual centres that acted as catalysts. The great abbots and archbishops, often related to medieval rulers, the counts palatine, and the German princes of the 18th century tried to emulate their French and Italian models by attracting artists to their splendid courts and offering them attractive working conditions.

Creative art has always been influenced by changes of fashion. Artistic innovations first occur in places that favour them; neighbouring areas, however different the conditions may be, can then benefit from these achievements in their own way. Information about art and artistic models circulates as rapidly as goods and money, although the effect may not be quite the same. For art to be accepted, it is vital that people can recognize themselves in it. Moreover, artistic creation tended to be bound up with a kind of local patriotism, at least until the age of the Enlightenment. The centre and the periphery were linked in a dynamic relationship, producing a spirit of intense competition. The most obvious evidence of this competitive spirit can be found in architecture, which has helped to shape the urban environment and enhance the prestige of the centres of artistic production. However, it is as meaningless to speak of 'Rhenish art' as of 'Middle Rhenish art' or 'Upper Rhenish art'.

If Rhenish art has an identity, it is most perceptible in the towns, which is where artistic activity was concentrated from the 12th century. The importance and prestige of a town was due largely to the artists living within its walls. For instance, the records of a legal dispute between painters and sculptors in 1520 contain a reference to sculptors who enjoy a high reputation among kings, emperors, princes and lords and who make up 'the glory of Strasbourg'. In response to Vasari, who sang the praises of Florentine artists, Johann Fischart stressed the achievements of the painters working along the Upper Rhine, such as Grünewald, Baldung (Grien), Vogtherr and Weiditz, arguing that their art brought the people together and forged a community. When Christoph Scheurl gave an account of Albrecht Dürer's journey on the Rhine, he made a point of mentioning that the Nuremberg artist had visited the brothers of the deceased Martin Schongauer in Colmar and Basel. It was a matter of great pride and ambition for a town to attract important artists. Many workshops followed this tradition and experienced masters would help train a whole new generation of artists. Typically, the great sculptor Nicolaus Gerhaert von Leyden refused a first invitation to the emperor's court, preferring the clientele of patricians and clerics he had acquired in Strasbourg, Baden-Baden and Konstanz.

In the introduction to his masterly work on the Mediterranean in the time of Philip II, *Das Mittelmeer und die mediterrane Welt in der Epoche Philipps II*, Fernand Braudel explained how he approached this very broad subject matter. 'We have reached the stage of dividing history up into several levels and distinguishing between a geographical, a social and an individual time in history.' Geographical time is almost motionless and moves in constantly recurring circles; social time is measured by the yardstick of people and proceeds slowly; the third level is the history of events measured by the yard-stick of the individual.

Provided a sense of proportion is kept, the same method could be applied by taking a long-term approach to the historical landscape of the Rhine. In this case, however, the subject matter is art, so the third level will be concerned not so much with events as with the emergence and characteristics of specific individuals and styles. Art is only one of the 'symbolic forms' that people use to communicate, to express joy or to protest against fate, although it is without doubt the most powerful, because it helps to shape their visual environment, to enhance or expand the horizons of their daily life. The landscapes of the Rhine are marked by their variety and by their specific features. Here art becomes a kind of creative workshop that has conceived and shaped these landscapes.

Perhaps this is the moment not only to outline the artistic aspects and historical landscape of the Rhine but also to set out the limits of this project. Given the intention to consider the entire course of the Rhine and the huge number of monuments involved, it was also necessary to take a selective approach. The choice of monuments and works of art illustrated and artists discussed may, therefore, seem arbitrary. In order to do justice to every site and every monument in this geographical area that more or less clearly reflects the influence of artistic centres such as Cologne or Strasbourg towards the end of the Middle Ages, it would have been necessary to write a different book. This project is not so much concerned with specific aspects or periods but rather with an overview of the Rhine as a geographical and historical continuum. The aim is to highlight its importance as a vital centre of European culture and art, as reflected in the monuments of its cities and landscapes. The illustrations and the text, the visual impressions and the verbal explanations, are closely linked, the prime concern being to make this portrait as vivid as possible.

The River

Forces of Nature and Works of People: Origins and Development of the Rhine Landscape

Like people, so nature also has its history. The great geographer Alexander von Humboldt saw such close parallels between the two as to suggest a kind of 'physiognomy' of landscape. What distinguishes the history of nature from the history of people, however, is the length of time they each took to develop. Nature moves at such an infinitely slow pace as to appear not to move at all, whereas the brief, compressed heartbeat of a human life is easy enough to perceive. The emergence of the first human, or at least the first being biologically related to humans, *homo habilis*, goes back 1.8 to 1.6 million years, while the history of the earth dates back 2,500,000,000 years. Even that is a short space of time compared with the actual age of our planet, which is 4,500,000,000 years old. Within this span of history it is necessary to distinguish between slow-moving phenomena such as the movement of the continental plates (continental drift) and more recent events such as the appearance of rivers. At the same time, all these aspects are interrelated and can only be understood when they are considered in context.

The theory of plate tectonics came from an amateur geologist, Alfred Wegener (1880–1930), who explained how the world came to look as it does and what is likely to happen in future. When the plates drifted apart, oceans were born, and when they collided, mountains rose up. Yet the highest mountains are not the oldest ones; they are high because their relative youth has preserved them from erosion. The Black Forest in Germany and the Vosges in France are more than 200,000,000 years old. The Alps, however, which are fairly young by comparison, were created when the African plate pushed against the European plate in the late Tertiary period. That collision produced what is called a syncline, a basin-shaped fold of stratified rock in the surface of the earth with the younger rocks occupying the core and the older rocks the outer part. Throughout the Secondary period, enormous quantities of sediments accumulated there. The great central arc of the Alpine chain is formed of crystalline rock, while chalk sediments predominate in the north and west. In the course of the Oligocene epoch, in the mid-Tertiary period, long rift valleys formed between the mountains, although they had not yet become rivers. The main collecting channels of the Vorderrhein (anterior Rhine) and the River Aare, which gave birth to the River Rhine some 10,000 years ago, had not yet created the river bed and its channel.

The rift valley of the Rhine downstream from Basel is formed by an anticline, a fold in the form of an arch, with the older rocks in the core. This anticline is bordered by the sediments of the Paris region in the west, of the North Sea and Central Germany in the east. Waves of plate movement from southwest to northeast affected the base of the rift valley and produced the Vosges and the Black Forest, while at the same time opening up lateral breaches on either side of the rift – for example, the Porte d'Alsace and the Freiburg basin, the Col de Saverne and the Kraichgau, the valley between the Black Forest and the Odenwald. The Rhine valley did not take on its final form until the end of the Iron Age, so the birth of the river is a relatively recent event in the long history of the Eurasian continent.

This geological excursion would not be complete without a look at climatic conditions on the Rhine. The geographer Etienne Juillard noted the 'composite nature of this climate, which combines oceanic, continental and sub-Mediterranean features'. All along the Rhine axis, the winter climate is oceanic with rarely more than eighty days of frost a year; in summer the Lower Rhine enjoys an oceanic climate, while weather conditions in the south show stronger contrasts, because of the variations in altitude. A continental climate predominates from Basel to Koblenz. When the Föhn wind blows in from the Alps and melts the snow, some of the foothills of the Vosges prove to have a sub-Mediterranean climate, quite unlike the Black Forest, where the winters are particularly harsh. These climatic contrasts are one of the special features that make the Rhineland so attractive, while also favouring wine growing, first introduced there by the Romans, and hop growing.

In his book *L'Europe rhénane. Géographie d'un grand espace*, published in 1968, Juillard could still refer to this climatic variety as an 'ecological optimum'. However, a great number of factors linked to industrial progress have disturbed the original balance between the water, the land and the climate. Indeed, the situation will continue to worsen, not only for the surface water but also for the groundwater, which is no longer drinkable in many parts of the Rhine valley, especially around the industrial complexes of Basel and Ludwigshafen. The rivers are also being polluted by discharges of sodium chloride from the potash mines. This dangerous situation has been caused by major acts of intervention such as the canalization of the river in the 19th century in order to straighten its course, and events such as the environmental disaster caused by a Swiss pharmaceutical company in 1986. While many people still remember that accident today, the general public is less aware of the serious consequences resulting from the canalization of the Rhine.

In earlier years, the high waters of the Rhine ensured that the ecological system remained in a state of harmony. This natural balance was upset by straightening the course of the river. The alluvial forests of the Rhine, which owed their existence to the dynamic between high and low tides, have now come to be regarded as ecological models in the few areas where they have been replanted. The biological diversity characteristic of ecosystems of this kind 'contributes to the effectiveness of the natural purifying filter, which turns the alluvial forest into a bioreactor for the production of high-quality groundwater' (Roland Carbinier). These nature reserves are a unique reservoir of rare European plants – like the countless species of lianas – and animals. No less than eighteen species of amphibians have been identified between Basel and Lauterburg.

The river carries a variety of objects along with it. Pebbles and gravel can be seen sliding, rolling or bouncing about on the river bed. A journey of ten kilometres (six miles) can produce visible signs of erosion on the stones that are tossed and smoothed by the river because of the intense friction to which they are subjected. It is this friction – rather than the water itself – that digs the riverbed down deeper into the rocky ground. At the narrow pass of the Rock of Lorelei, the Rhine has dug its way down fifteen metres (fifty feet) deep. The stones are eventually deposited on shelves at a higher level, so the waters calm down and the erosion comes to an end. In this way lakes, such as Lake Constance, also act as dams.

While looking at the geomorphological aspects of the river, it is also necessary to consider the people who lived along its banks, who tamed its wild flow and who sailed on it in ships. Whatever early and more recent history seems to suggest, these people were certainly not 'archenemies' who were constantly quarrelling about who had ultimate control over the river. If so many people had not died, it would be easy to dismiss these past conflicts as having little historical significance and to argue that what unifies people is primarily a form of culture: not a conception of the world but a way of living, working and thinking that inevitably instils a sense of community, a sense of group identity, that has nothing to do with nationality or nationalism. The regional and ethnic groups living in the Rhineland were more or less united by their dialects and speech patterns, although the actual linguistic borders remained fluid. Yet they also shared characteristics. Robert Minder recently pointed out that the Franks regarded the Alemanni, one of the two large tribes living in the Rhine basin since early Christianity, as thinkers, while they saw themselves more as men of action. It is these kind of psychological traits that should be examined if we want to understand the Rhine and the people who make up the urban communities or grow wine along its banks and slopes.

River of History: Towns, Countries, Borders

According to archaeologists, the Celtic world was born along the Rhine, at the beginning of the second millennium BC. During the Iron Age, the river brought the Celts into contact with the Mediterranean basin. Etruscan objects dating from the 7th century BC have been found near Colmar. The Iron Age cemetery of Castaneda (Graubünden) has yielded amber pearls from the North Sea and Etruscan objects from the Bologna region, evidence of the importance of trade between north and south even at that time. The La Tène culture – so called after a settlement on the shores of Lake Neuchâtel in Switzerland that the Gauls used as a gateway for controlling the trade routes from the Rhône valley to the Rhine – also developed along the Rhine between the 5th and the 1st century BC.

However, a new situation arose when the Celts retreated under the pressure of the advancing Germanic tribes in the course of the 3rd and 2nd centuries BC, which led to a conflict between Germanic and Roman interests in Gaul. A passage from Caesar's *De bello Gallico* describes the background to this conflict: 'He [Caesar] realized that the Germans would gradually become accustomed to crossing the Rhine and that it would be a danger for the Roman people if a large number of them came to Gaul. If they ever managed to occupy the whole of Gaul, he believed nothing would stop these savage and barbarian people from taking over the province [Provence] and marching on from there to Italy, as the Cimberns and Teutons had done before them.' In 58 BC Caesar drove the Germanic tribes led by Ariovistus, who had reached the left bank of the Rhine, back to the right bank. The battle took place west of what is now Ottmarsheim. The Rhine, which the Romans viewed with trepidation – Lucian refers to *Rhenus gelidis undis* (the Rhine with icy-cold water) – was henceforth regarded as the border between the 'barbarians' and the Romanized world; it may have been a secure military front, but it was certainly not an ethnic border.

From 43 BC on, a Roman colony called *Augusta Raurica* (Augst) was established at the entrance to the Upper Rhine valley and used by the Romans as a military outpost. From this strategic base they embarked on expeditions into the hostile lands to the east. To protect their Gallic territory the Romans, led by Augustus, attacked the Germanic tribes east of the

14

Rhine and created an operational base on the Middle and Lower Rhine (Province of *Germania inferior*) by establishing military colonies. A long Roman road linked the fortified towns of Augst, Strasbourg (*Argentorate*), Mainz (*Mogontiacum*), Koblenz (*Confluentes*), Bonn (*Bonna*), Cologne (*Colonia Claudia Ara Agrippinensis*), Neuss (*Novaesium*), Xanten (*Colonia Ulpia Traiana*), Nijmegen (*Noviomagus*) and Utrecht (*Traiestum*). The colonies could also establish communications with the Mediterranean world thanks to an extensive road network. From Lyons, several roads led to the Rhine, two of them towards Basel and one towards Langres, with side-roads towards Trier and Mainz, and towards Cologne and Nijmegen.

In AD 275 Roman rule over the Rhine gave way on the Main to the invading Alemanni, although the Romans still managed to withstand their onslaught in Strasbourg in AD 357. After the end of the 3rd century, however, the Alemanni began to carry out more and more raids on the left bank of the Rhine and even penetrated as far as Champagne, while the northern Burgundians founded a short-lived empire between Worms and Mainz, which later formed the historical background to the *Nibelungenlied*. Yet it was the Franks who played the most important role in the history of the Rhineland. Two groups broke away from the main tribal grouping: the Ripuarians, who settled along the Middle Rhine south of Cologne and in the Mosel area, and the Salians, who settled northeast of the Schelde in the mid-4th century. The royal house of the Merovingians, who were descended from the Salian tribe, established the Frankish empire around AD 500. Yet first another, and far greater, threat appeared from the Russian steppes. It was heralded by the constant disputes and acts of reprisal between the barbarian tribes, which eventually led to their mass exodus. In AD 451 Attila and his

Huns crossed the Rhine to attack Metz, ravage northeastern Gaul and, a year later, invade northern Italy.

The barbarian invasions spelled the death of the towns and the decline of the first, basically urban Rhenish culture. The legacy of the Romans, who defended the Rhine line until around 400, passed down to the Franks, who had been united and Christianized by Clovis. They now rebuilt most of the Roman settlements, with the focus on religious buildings. In the 6th century, under the Frankish Merovingians and then also under the Carolingians, the Rhine no longer represented a political frontier. The same Alemannic and Frankish tribes inhabited its two banks. Under Charlemagne, the Rhine axis regained its cultural significance. The first Christian emperor of the west made Cologne an archbishopric, built a palace in Ingelheim near Mainz and founded the abbey in Lorsch. However, like the Merovingians before them, the Carolingians preferred to live in the valleys of the Maas and the Mosel. After the Treaty of Verdun in 843, preceded a year before by the Oath of Strasbourg sworn by Charlemagne's grandsons in Old High German and Old French – respectively the precursors of German and French – the Rhine formed the eastern border of the territories that went to Lothar. Renewed barbarian invasions temporarily upset the political equilibrium: the Normans sailed up the river as far as Worms, the Hungarians reached Basel. At a meeting on the Rhine in Bonn in 921 the two kings of the emerging French and German-ruled territories mutually agreed to recognize the German kingdom and French rule in Lotharingia (Lorraine) – the latter was of course, to remain a matter of dispute. In the late 10th century, however, major changes disturbed this balance of power in central Europe and created new conditions. In 987 the Capetians came

to the French throne and in 962 the Saxon Otto I (r. 962–73), supported by the combined wealth and spiritual power of the imperial German church, was crowned first emperor of the Holy Roman Empire of the German nation in Rome.

It soon became apparent how different the two sovereign territories were. France continued its efforts to establish and maintain a united kingdom, keeping a jealous eye on the stability of its borders. The empire, however, was split up into a great number of small feudal states and its claim to be a world power was weakened by its dispute with the papacy. Under the Ottonian and then the Salian emperors, the princes of the church grew ever more powerful, while the count palatine fortified his Rhineland territory by constructing numerous castles, expanding the fortifications built by Charlemagne. Under the Saxon emperors, only the kings and emperors were able to invest the bishops and abbots with the ring and staff of spiritual office. Now, however, after half a century of bitter fighting in what was known as the investiture dispute between the Salian emperors and the papacy, agreement was reached: under the Concordat of Worms dating from 1122 the emperor granted the spiritual authorities the freedom to choose and consecrate the bishops and abbots, confining himself to granting secular regalia. Yet the power of the church in the empire, and its many privileges, remained untouched by these political strategies – especially in the Rhenish dioceses.

At this time the urban centres founded by the Romans during the period of colonization began to flourish again. A 12th-century chronicle describes the region between Basel and Mainz as the heartland of the empire of the Hohenstaufen dynasty, which means that these rulers were even more Rhenish

15

Opposite: Samuel Harter and Nikolaus Müller, *Allegory of the Union of the Left Bank of the Rhine with France following the Peace of Lunéville (9 February 1801).* Copper engraving. Stadtarchiv Mainz.

than their predecessors, the Salians, who had settled around Worms and Speyer. Cologne can be taken as a good example of the general situation along the entire course of the river. Between the Roman walls of the city and the river lay an empty space that attracted merchants and traders during the 10th century and 'it was from the Rhine, the source of wealth, life and free activity, that prosperity flowed back to the city of ruins and brought it back to life' (Lucien Febvre).

The prosperity of the Rhineland was due largely to agriculture, which also made a major contribution to the growth of the towns. The inhabitants were fired by a new sense of their own worth and a new desire for freedom, and challenged the rigid structures of the empire. The organization of the church provinces, the vineyards, the growth of trade, and the founding of universities all contributed to the revival of the urban communities during the Middle Ages. The first free imperial towns were established at this time along the Rhine, starting with Hagenau in 1164, followed by Strasbourg in 1201 and Cologne in 1212. There were others that were smaller, but still powerful, such as Thann, Colmar, Turckheim, Barr and Rosheim at the foot of the Vosges, or Bacharach, Kaub, Oberwesel and Boppard between Bingen and Koblenz. In 1254, after the collapse of the Hohenstaufen rule, the first Rhenish league of towns was formed to protect local interests; the members included Speyer, Worms, Cologne, Mainz, Basel and Strasbourg. The arch-bishoprics of Trier, Mainz and Cologne and the bishoprics of Basel, Strasbourg, Speyer, Worms, Liège and Utrecht were linked along what came to be known as the *Pfaffengasse* (priests' road). Their power and ambition were reflected in the great Rhenish cathedrals. Four of the seven electoral princes responsible for

choosing the German king came from the Rhineland: the archbishops of Trier, Mainz and Cologne and the count palatine. In 1338, in what was called 'the Day at Rense', a small town on the Middle Rhine, the electoral princes managed to have the elected king recognized as Roman emperor, without requiring the assent of the Pope.

From the High Middle Ages on, the pattern of landownership along the 1,320 kilometres (820 miles) from the river's source to its mouth proved very varied and changeable. A new situation arose on the Upper Rhine in the course of the 13th century, when the family of the counts of Zähringen who owned land in the Black Forest and northern Switzerland died out (1218) and the royal Hohenstaufen dynasty lost its overlordship in Alsace, which disintegrated into a large number of politically autonomous fiefdoms and royal cities. A small, local royal family – the Habsburgs – now began to plan its territorial policy. Originally from south-west Germany, this dynasty came to rule the German empire and the whole of Europe. The Habsburgs held the position of Roman emperor from the 15th to the early 19th century. Yet their attempt to create a unified Alpine state met with bitter resistance in the west from the Swiss Confederation, with the result that the confederate cantons gradually dissociated themselves from the empire and formed an independent state. With the Peace of Basel (1499), the Rhine became a Swiss river from its sources as far as Basel, with the exception of the German enclave of Konstanz, forming a land border along the lower reaches of the Alpine Rhine, the west bank of Lake Constance and the High Rhine. The situation along the lower reaches of the Rhine also stabilized from the 16th century, when the Burgundian-Habsburg Netherlands (states general)

broke away and achieved independence under the Treaty of Westphalia in 1648.

The territorial situation along the Upper, Middle and Lower Rhine was more complex and unruly. From the 12th century on, the Rhine was bordered by the ecclesiastical territories of the electors of Mainz, Trier and Cologne, together with many church properties. Other landowners were the margraves of Baden, a family that was split into the Baden-Baden and Baden-Durlach lines from 1535 to 1771 as a result of the schism and whose domain became a grand duchy in 1803. The palatine domains of the counts palatine extended piecemeal on either side of the Rhine. The Palatinate, ruled by the Wittelsbach family since the 12th century, with its royal seat in Heidelberg (later in Mannheim), was next to the county of Nassau on the right bank of the Rhine in the region of Taunus and Westerwald. The Palatinate spread to the Lower Rhine at the end of the 17th century, with the succession of the Neuburg family who ruled the duchies of Jülich and Cleves. Their royal seat was in Düsseldorf, which also had some artistic implications (see Schwetzingen, pp. 224–27, and Benrath, pp. 324–25). Meanwhile, the count palatine of Brandenburg managed to extend his domain as far as the Rhine with the duchy of Cleves.

'The true power and true reputation of Germania lives around the Rhine.' This statement by Maria of Hungary, the sister of Emperor Charles V, describes the situation on the Rhine in the mid-16th century. However, because its territory was broken up, the Rhineland became, over the next few centuries, an even greater strategic bone of contention between the European powers. When the Dukes of Burgundy's vision of a new Lotharingian central kingdom came to nothing in 1477 and the Habsburgs

*Réunion de la Rive gauche du Rhin
à la République Française
le 18 Ventôse An 9.*

came into their inheritance in the Netherlands, a vacuum was created between the French and the German domains. The Reformation widened the political divisions in the empire even further, which inevitably whetted the appetite of others to intervene and annex territory. France, which was politically unified and stronger, dreamed of redrawing its borders to the Rhine. The 1648 Treaty of Westphalia gave France the government of ten imperial cities in Alsace, and with it the border of the Rhine, secured by the bridgeheads of Breisach and Philippsburg in order to protect the Rhine border. It marked the beginning of Louis XIV's policy of expansionism or 'Reunion', whose main object was to ensure French supremacy in Europe and end the rule of the Habsburg dynasty. The Sun King was supported by the Rhenish alliance of German counts in the anti-Habsburg party (Rheinbund, 1658–68). After the 'peaceful conquest of the Rhine frontier', France annexed Strasbourg in 1681. In 1689 Louis XIV's troops invaded the Palatinate, under the pretext of claiming their dynastic inheritance, and then systematically laid waste to the cities and territories of the Palatinate and Baden. They destroyed unique monuments such as Speyer Cathedral and the royal residences, including Schloss Heidelberg, which became a very picturesque ruin that touched many a romantic spirit (Ills. pp. 220–22). Under the Treaty of Rijkswijk in 1697, France retained Strasbourg and the Alsatian territory

gained from the 'Reunion'. The Rhine was established as the border. Louis XIV's policy of expansion along the Upper Rhine had terrible long-term repercussions on relations between the two neighbouring countries, effects that lasted well into the 20th century.

The political upheavals sparked by the libertarian ideas of the French Revolution, which later shook the whole of Europe and changed the course of history, also directly affected the Rhine. In 1794 the entire left bank was occupied and annexed to France (as confirmed by the Peace of Lunéville between France and Austria in 1801). Napoleon's political reorganization brought to an abrupt halt the fragmentation of Germany into a multitude of different states by denying recognition of the church territories or the status of most of the imperial cities. The *Reichsdeputationshauptschluss* of 1803, the last decision taken by a committee of the former Reichstag, established a new balance by creating viable central states and spelled the end of the Holy Roman Empire. French policy in Germany also paved the way for a new sense of German nationality that was fired by a romantically coloured and intellectually heated patriotism. This feeling inevitably led to further confrontations with France during the time of the Wars of Liberation and then the Restoration. The Rhine played a highly emotional role in these conflicts.

After the Congress of Vienna (1815), France had to withdraw to its earlier borders, while the former territory of the archbishopric of Cologne in Westphalia and the Middle and Lower Rhine became a Prussian province on the Rhine. Catholics and liberals violently objected to this new form of hegemony. At the same time the Rhineland experienced remarkable economic growth and prosperity. Prussia turned the Rhine into a 'German river', thereby fuelling French

hostility. Provoked by Bismarck's policy, Napoleon III declared war on Prussia in 1870. The French defeat at Sedan on 2 September 1870 led not only to the fall of the Second Empire in France but also to the Prussian king being proclaimed German emperor (18 January 1871), an event that took place in the historic setting of the Hall of Mirrors at the palace of Versailles. Under the Peace of Frankfurt in 1871, France ceded Alsace-Lorraine to the new German empire and the Rhine became more of a national barrier than ever. In 1919 the Treaty of Versailles restored the 1815 borders, which remained until the Second World War broke out, with a ferocity that had not been seen before, and once again turned the Rhineland into a battlefield and scene of devastation. The hopes that the founding of the Federal Republic of Germany after the war would gradually lead to closer relations with neighbouring countries again were eventually fulfilled. Robert Schuman, Konrad Adenauer – from the Rhineland – and Charles de Gaulle became the architects of a reconciliation between nations, which naturally and symbolically took place on the Rhine, to the benefit of not only the Rhineland but also Europe as a whole.

European Waterway: Roads, Bridges and Shipping

Seen from a bird's-eye view, the land along the banks of the Rhine describes a stable, complex pattern, rather like a patchwork, with the towns in the south tending to be more prosperous, those in the north more spread out. The river that flows through this landscape forms a natural transport route along which people and goods of all kinds are constantly moving. From Chur to Koblenz vineyards adorn the sunny slopes on either side of the Rhine. They were responsible for the remarkable flowering of the Rhenish civilization, economy and culture at the end of the Middle Ages. In the mid-16th century, between 700 and 800 Cologne families were making their living from the wine trade.

The Rhine valley is linked to the Mediterranean by Alpine passes: the Lukmanier (1,960 metres; 6,430 feet), owned by the abbey of Disentis, the San Bernardino Pass (2,065 metres; 6,775 feet) and the Splügen (2,115 metres; 6,940 feet), which lead from the Hinterrhein (posterior Rhine) valley to Lake Maggiore and Lake Como, the Septimer (2,310 metres; 7,580 feet), an old Roman mule track owned by the bishops of Chur, and the St Gotthard Pass. With the exception of the St Gotthard, all these Alpine passes lead to Chur, which explains the wealth of that diocesan town in the Middle Ages. The main north–south transport link was the route over the Hinterrhein valley to the Splügen. It led through the Via Mala, a wild and threatening gorge, up to 600 metres (1,970 feet) deep and at times just 3 metres (nearly 10 feet) wide, which was used as a pass even in Roman times (Ill. p. 80). In 1473 a path was opened along the side of the gorge and two stone bridges were then built. The Hinterrhein thunders down between the cliff walls and, before reuniting with the Vorderrhein (anterior Rhine), runs across the wide high-lying valley of Domleschg in the canton of Graubünden (Grisons), a cheerful, gardenlike mountain landscape dotted with castles, with villages huddled on the slopes to shelter from the unpredictable force of the river. In the 19th century the course of the river was channelled into a fixed bed and its sedimentary valley was prepared for agricultural use by 'integral improvement' measures – the soil was built up by the addition of river mud. Today mainline

railways and motorways cross the bottom of the valley.

The St Gotthard Pass (2,108 metres; 6,916 feet) built for merchants from Milan has linked Milan with Basel (the railway tunnel dates from 1882) and with the Upper and Middle Rhine since 1230. From Genoa, the merchants would travel to the Alps on mule-back, on to Basel by horse and cart, then by ship to Cologne, where they had international contacts via their offices in Venice, Antwerp, Brussels and London.

The Romans had already built solid bridges of stone and wood on the Rhine, in Augst, Mainz, Bonn and Cologne. In Mainz, a new pontoon bridge, supported by forty-eight ships, did not need to be built over the Rhine until 1661. During the Middle Ages, people usually crossed the Rhine by ferry. The bridge in Basel was built in 1225. The only fixed bridges further downstream were the bridges of Breisach (1225) and Strasbourg (1388). In his *Descriptio Sueviae* Felix Fabri describes the Strasbourg bridge as particularly expensive, not because of the material used, which was timber, but because it needed constant maintenance, repair and reinforcement work. The model of Schaffhausen bridge (Ill. p. 130), designed by J. U. Grubenmann in 1757 and destroyed in 1799, gives a good idea of what a very wide-span wooden bridge would have looked like.

People have used the Rhine as a waterway since very early times. The means of transport have ranged from the prehistoric pirogue and the Roman galley to the Norman drakkar, the local boats typical of the Upper Rhine (*Oberländer*), the Cologne region (*Cöllner*), the Netherlands (*Niederländer*) and Holland (*Holländer*), the Rhine clippers (*Segler*), the steam-driven paddle steamers introduced in 1816 and later the propeller-driven steamers, and finally

the 20th-century tug boat. High-risk, traditional forms of shipping with many stopovers have given way to today's radar and radio-assisted day and night traffic on the river.

'In the Middle Ages, the Rhine offered job opportunities for a population group that has now disappeared: there were fishermen and gold-panners, but also haulers, pilots and shippers, who used this waterway to bring in the goods traded by the merchants from Italian and Flemish towns, by the woodcutters and rafters from the Alpine forests, by the shipbuilders from the North Sea ports or even by the Rhenish or Burgundian wine-growers and the northern town-dwellers. The growth of maritime trade in the 16th century led to a decline in international trade on the Rhine, which was now confined to inter-regional goods: rafted timber, wine and cereals from the Rhine basin were traded for dried fish from Holland and the exotic goods that were landed at Antwerp, Amsterdam or Rotterdam.' This quotation by Pierre Carrière describes the economic importance of the Rhine, the 'mightiest river in western Europe', in the Middle Ages. It should be noted however, that in the mid-19th century, during the Industrial Revolution, the river once again became an important trade and transport route.

Until fairly recently, shipping on the Rhine was at the mercy of wind, rain, fog, low or high tides and banks of ice. Although the long history of Rhine trade might suggest otherwise, neither wars with their unpredictable effects on trade, neither the vagaries of the river's course nor looting by well-organized bands of robbers could weaken the boatmen's resolve. They organized themselves very early on. They founded the first corporation in Strasbourg in 1331, while the next one was founded in Basel in 1354.

Legend of St Ursula (from the Little Ursula cycle), *Stations of the Pilgrimage from Cologne to Rome and Back: Basel, Strasbourg, Mainz,* c. 1450. Wallraf-Richartz-Museum, Cologne (Ill. p. 287).

The boatmen carried people (traders or the many pilgrims), local products (wine, cereals, wood) and transit goods. After being loaded in the old customs house in Strasbourg, they reached the Rhine via the River Ill. Wines from Colmar were shipped on to Cologne and from there towards England, Scandinavia and the Baltic. North–south trade on the Rhine included goods from Italy (silks, spices and precious objects from the East, oil and salt) and cloth from Flanders, woollen fabrics from Lombardy and lead from England. In 1370 Emperor Charles IV (r. 1355–78) gave Strasbourg the right to levy a toll on the Rhine and in the 15th century Emperor Sigismund (r. 1411–37) granted the city the right to levy taxes on transit goods, as was the case in Cologne and Mainz.

There is very early evidence of customs privileges on the Rhine, dating back to 775 in the case of Strasbourg. In the 10th century the archbishops of Trier, Cologne and Mainz gained as much profit as they could from Rhine shipping by levying tolls in return for guaranteeing the ships' safety. The *Mäuseturm* (mice tower) downstream from Bingen (Ill. p. 256), which looks so romantic now, was once a customs post, like the so-called 'Pfalz im Rhein' (Ills. pp. 260 and 261). In the 13th century there were 44 customs posts, in the 14th century as many as 62 and in the second half of the 16th century the cloth merchant Andreas Ryff counted 31 customs posts on his journey from Basel to Cologne. The League of Rhenish Towns, founded in 1254 by Mainz and Worms, of which Basel, Strasbourg, Speyer and Cologne were also members, set up a river police of 150 armed boats to protect itself from the arbitrary tolls imposed by the rulers. Throughout the Middle Ages trade and shipping on the Rhine were hampered by monopolies and fiscal legislation, but after the Treaty of Westphalia

repeated attempts were made, mainly for economic reasons, to dismantle these privileges and guarantee free transport. In 1815 the Congress of Vienna laid down rules on Rhine navigation, yet taxes continued to be levied until the time of the Mannheim Act of 1868.

Tourism on the Rhine: Pilgrims, Artists and Travellers

During the Middle Ages, the relics of saints kept within the city walls had a major impact on the everyday life of the inhabitants of a town and the faithful believed that the more relics there were, the more the reputation of the saint in question would be enhanced and the more that saint would be led to intercede on their behalf. Images of especially beloved patron saints, who were

constantly called upon to intercede, were set up at street corners, in chapels and on altars in the form of paintings or sculptures. Knowing that these holy relics were so close at hand gave people a sense of security in their daily lives, or at least offered them support and refuge on the long road to salvation.

Cologne has a silver goblet belonging to St Elizabeth of Thüringen in the church of St Pantaleon, and a belt belonging to the same saint in St Maria im Kapitol, while the Dominicans have a garment of hers and the Franciscans have a chasuble sewn by her hand. Countless pilgrims flocked to view these holy relics, as shown by contemporary accounts. In fact, pilgrims made up the largest group of travellers along the Rhine in the Middle Ages. The history of the cult of relics reflects the great mobility of the faithful, for it was widely

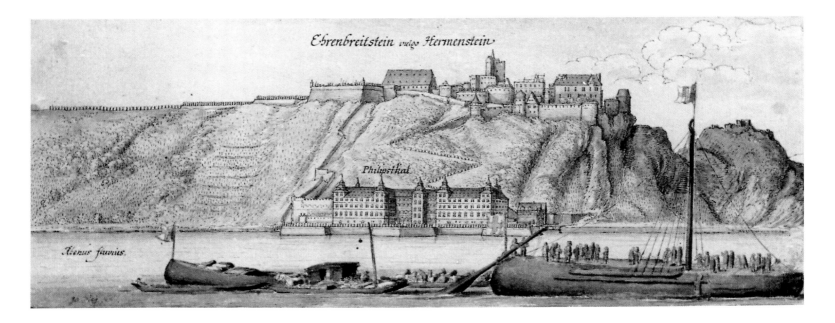

believed that human life was an earthly pilgrimage. Indeed, the magistrate of Ghent could choose places of pilgrimage according to the seriousness of the sin to be expiated. The possible places of pilgrimage between Basel and Utrecht ranged from the Collégiale St Thiébault in Thann to the cathedrals of Strasbourg, Speyer and Frankfurt, the cathedral of St Martin in Mainz, the St Werner Chapel in Bacharach, St Kastor in Koblenz and, of course, the holy city of Cologne, where more than one thousand masses were celebrated every day, and, last but not least of course, Aachen.

The legendary lives of the saints were in themselves a source of attraction for the pilgrims, like the legend of St Ursula. The daughter of a king of Britain, according to various sources, she, along with her companions, followed the same route as many merchant ships. She was instructed in a dream to sail up the Rhine to Basel and from there to make a pil-grimage on foot to Rome. On their way back she and her 11,000 companions were martyred in Cologne by the invad-ing Huns. The *Goldene Kammer* (golden bedchamber) of St Ursula in Cologne contains 122 reliquary busts of her companions (Ill. p. 315). The spread of the cult of St Ursula is reflected in the 15th- and 16th-century cycles of panels painted by the school of Cologne (Ills. pp. 2, 287). In the church of St Ursula in Cologne, a cycle of panels showing thirty scenes from the legend hangs near her tomb in the left aisle. Other depic-tions of the legend of St Ursula can be found in Spain, the Netherlands and Italy, including the monumental series of paintings by Carpaccio for the Scuola di San Orsola in Venice and Memling's panels of *The Shrine of St Ursula* in Bruges. It is evident that the painters greatly enjoyed rendering the picturesque scenery of the various stations in her pilgrimage. Like St Ursula, thousands of other pilgrims travelled along the Rhine, on their way to Einsiedeln or Zurzach.

In the 12th century the cult of St Ursula in Cologne faced competition with the relics of the Three Magi, which Archbishop Rainald von Dassel, a confi-dant of Emperor Frederick Barbarossa (r. 1155–90), had looted from Milan in 1164 and then brought to Cologne (Ill. p. 43). The archbishop, who was the imperial chancellor and driving force behind the policy of the Hohenstaufen, wanted the Three Magi to be perceived as prototypes of Christian rulers. This politically motivated propaganda reflected the revival of the idea of the *Sacrum Imperium*, as did the canonization of Charlemagne at that time. The Three Wise Men from the East – or rather their relics, kept in the most precious of Rhenish reliquary shrines (Ill. p. 295) – who had in a sense now been transformed into kings and patron saints of Cologne, became an important object of pilgrim-age until well into the 18th century. Year after year pilgrims from noble families converged on Cologne, joining the great 'hordes' from Hungary. The pilgrims from Slovakia and Croatia would often combine several visits: after Cologne they would go on to Aachen and later, from the 13th century on, also to Maastricht, Trier, Neuss, Cornelimünster and Düren. Wherever they went, the pilgrims were offered specific insignia, which were manufactured and sold by the clergy. In Einsiedeln in September 1466 the pilgrims acquired 130,000 such insignia in the space of a fortnight; and their distribution throughout Europe helps to reconstruct some of the pilgrims' routes. For instance, around a hundred casts of the insignia of St Quirin of Neuss were found on bells from Scandinavia to Slovenia, where they were believed to ward off evil. These insignia were not just 'badges' but 'representative relics' because they had been in contact with the authentic relics in the holy place and thus passed on the inherent power of those relics.

There were various means of making contact with the relics. Pilgrims were allowed to embrace the relics of St Mauritius, which Archbishop Albrecht of Brandenburg (1514–45) put on display in Mainz Cathedral. Sometimes the priest celebrating the Mass would touch the pilgrim with the relic to produce a more powerful effect; this custom was followed with the relics of St Theobald in Thann and in Konstanz Cathedral. In Mont Ste-Odile in Alsace, the pilgrims drank from the cup in which the saint was said to have received Holy Communion. The relics were also believed to give protection from danger; on the journey down the river towards Deutz, the pas-toral crosier – a relic Archbishop Bruno

(953–65) brother of Otto the Great, had acquired for the treasury of Cologne Cathedral – and the chains of St Peter were dipped into the Rhine, presumably to help prevent flooding. Apart from its 'magic' powers, the bishop's crosier also had a 'historical' significance, as an emblem of the Roman origins of Cologne. According to legend, its first recorded bishop, Maternus, was a disciple of the Apostle Peter, who had sent him to the Rhine.

The roads, unsafe and in bad repair, were less popular than the river. Besides the merchants and pilgrims, other travellers also began to contribute to the growth of navigation and inland shipping. The north–south axis was much frequented, thanks to the attraction of Italy, although these travellers were often interested not so much in the sites of pilgrimage as in the centres of art. For instance, the young Albrecht Dürer (1471–1528) left his home town of Nuremberg to begin his apprenticeship under Martin Schongauer (c. 1430–91) in Colmar. On finding that Schongauer had died before he arrived, Dürer went on to Basel and Strasbourg and eventually crossed the Brenner Pass to Venice. It was while crossing the Alps that he painted his first purely landscape pictures, which were no doubt adapted from nature and are devoid of any religious or mythological connotations.

The first landscapes inspired by the Rhine belong to a later period. In the early 17th century the Dutch painter Roelandt Savery enriched his imaginary landscapes with Rhenish motifs such as the *Mäuseturm* of Bingen and Ehrenfels Castle. Such precise and detailed topographical depictions of Rhenish towns and landscapes, drawing on a fixed repertoire of motifs, were highly valued. They included, for instance, the *Civitates orbis terrarum* by Braun and Hogenberg

and the admirable copper-engraved views by the cartographer Matthäus Merian, which also illustrate this book, and have great value both as documentary evidence and in aesthetic terms (Ills. pp. 86, 98, 118).

One pioneering Rhine traveller was the English diplomat, collector and lover of art Thomas, Earl of Arundel, who sailed up the Rhine to Frankfurt in 1636 on a political mission to the Viennese imperial court. He was accompanied by the writer William Crowne and by a pupil of Merian, Wenceslaus Hollar, who was commissioned to paint the landscape of the Middle Rhine. Hollar's pen and watercolour drawings are both topographical and painterly.

In the last decades of the 18th century, many people discovered the beauty of the Alps and embarked on journeys down the Rhine for both scientific and aesthetic reasons – to view the natural and historical sights. Among the pioneers of tourism on the Rhine were two clergymen, the Italian Giorgio Bertola and the English vicar John Gardnor, who travelled the Rhine independently of one another in 1787 but both recorded their personal impressions and reactions in their travel journals and watercolours. Georg Forster, who wrote *Ansichten vom Niederrhein* (Views of the Lower Rhine) in 1790, Alexander von Humboldt, the poet Friedrich von Matthisson and the young Goethe also travelled on the Rhine. Yet it was in the 19th century that Rhine tourism really

became popular. It is surprising to note that it was neither the French nor the Germans who prepared the way for the Rhine to become a symbol of the Romantic movement (see p. 25), but the English. One of the first was Ann Radcliffe, followed by Mary Shelley and, in particular, Lord Byron. Byron praises the almost therapeutic effects of the Rhenish landscape on his *Weltschmerz* in his epic poem *Childe Harold's Pilgrimage* (1812–18), a work that is in a sense his own poetic travel journal. Scores of English artists now evoked, if not invented, the picturesque qualities of the Rhine, a river viewed in terms of its ruins and its church spires. They included Samuel Prout, Clarkson Stanfield father and son, and William Callow. The 'pilgrims of the Rhine' described in Bulwer-Lytton's eponymous book (1834) are nothing but lay pilgrims in search of the landscapes and myths of the Rhine. David Roberts' illustrations for the book transform these sites into dreamlike visions. The English found in the Rhenish landscape the medieval atmosphere for which they yearned, the images of a nature that was sometimes wild and untamed, sometimes gentle and serene. As a landscape marked by bourgeois prosperity, while being a 'landscape of the soul', the Rhine satisfied the hunger of the Romantic sensibility for the picturesque and the sublime.

Turner's paintings of Rhenish and Alpine landscapes emphasize these two poles of the real and the ideal and

translate them into art. Turner's first journey to the Middle Rhine produced fifty-one small watercolours in 1817, from motifs noted down in his sketchbooks. Yet his best work using this technique is the series of visionary watercolours resulting from his journeys to Switzerland between 1841 and 1844, in which he combines broad areas of colour with precisely rendered detail to create harmonious studies. Referring to one of these watercolours, John Ruskin wrote in 1842: 'The Splügen Pass I saw in an instant to be the noblest Alpine drawing Turner had ever till then made.'

Shortly before, in 1840, the great French poet and novelist Victor Hugo (1802–85) travelled along the Rhine from Cologne to Mainz. This trip gave rise to *Le Rhin, lettres à un ami* (1842), a book that is far more an autobiography than a description of the Rhine. Jean Gaudon called it 'the book of lament, of old stones that never cease crumbling, of heroes who vanish over the horizon, of the evanescent memory of the peoples, and even, in a corner of the picture, of the passing of childhood.' Yet the river also assists people in their inner quest, for instance the German Romantics, such as the poet Clemens Brentano, born in Ehrenbreitstein in 1778 (see p. 25).

Between 1837 and 1849 the number of travellers recorded ranged from 150,000 to 1,000,000 a year. In 1829, 16,000, half the number of passengers on the stretch between Cologne and Mainz,

were English. The new steamboat companies now had their share in what had become a real form of mass tourism. The company that ran the steamboat line between Cologne and Mainz was opened in 1827. Hotels sprang up everywhere. The railway offered its own style of comfort; from 1844 on, trains ran between Cologne and Bonn, on the Upper Rhine along the Basel–Mulhouse–Strasbourg stretch and on the right bank of the Rhine between Offenburg and Karlsruhe. This tourism was closely linked to the world of the imagination, to the traveller's mental picture of these places as much as to the actual sites. Yet increasingly people did come to see the real sights, thanks to the appearance of printed guidebooks, of which the most famous are the Baedecker guides, and to other more subjective handbooks such as Aloys Schreiber's *The Traveller's Guide down the Rhine* (1819) or John Murray's *Handbook for Travellers on the Continent* (1837). The first Baedecker appeared in 1835, under the title *Rheinreise von Strassburg bis Rotterdam*; the first French translation followed in 1846, the first English translation in 1861. The Baedecker guides were aimed at travellers in a hurry, who just wanted to see the main sights wherever they went and did not want to spend too much money. For instance, two pages were devoted to the subject of 'tips', with suggestions about the appropriate amount to tip the guide, the porter, the waiter, and so on.

A trip down the river gave the passive spectators the chance to make innumerable discoveries, without any effort on their own part, while the printed guidebook helped them to place the sights in a specific time and space. It was like watching a panorama or diorama: huge, painted scenes that unwound before the eyes of the spectator between two great drums, often to the accompaniment of sirens and clanging bells – a great achievement by the tourist industry. In a sense, a boat trip was simply the translation of a panoramic spectacle into reality. In 1833, a pleorama show was put on in Berlin: some twenty spectators climbed into an artificially rocking boat for an imaginary journey on the Rhine from Mainz to St Goar, watching the course of the river and the landscape alongside it glide past on two long bands of fabric.

That same year, a cartographer called Jakob Dielmann produced twenty-metre (sixty-five foot) long strips of lithographs that depicted the banks of the Rhine between Mainz and Koblenz (the capital of the Rhenish province of Prussia after 1815) in the most painstaking detail. This show was a kind of home panorama, which showed the spectators the sights from the same angle as they would see them from the boat. The leaflet containing a bird's-eye view aquatint of the river by Friedrich Wilhelm Delkeskamp, of which several editions appeared between 1825 and 1850 (Ill. p. 4), offered another kind of panorama. While lithographic views of picturesque sites and monuments did not generally appear in editions of more than two or three thousand copies, the invention of steel engraving made it possible to print editions of 4,000 or 5,000 plates. The invention and rapid spread of photography allowed travellers to take home even more faithful images of what they had seen. In 1853 the Frenchman Charles Marville published *Les bords du*

Rhin – Monuments, Ruines, Vues pittoresques, the first collection of calotypes of the Rhine. The atmospheric pictures stressing the romantic aspects of the Rhine and its wines also added to the attraction of visiting the Rhine.

River of the Soul: Mystics, Humanists and Romantics

The Romantics discovered the Rhine, especially the Middle Rhine, as a 'landscape of the soul' in the 19th century and it then became a tourist attraction, helped by the transport facilities that came with the Industrial Revolution. Yet, long before that age, the Rhine was playing a vital historical role as the source and lifeblood of spiritual and intellectual currents throughout Europe. A particular kind of spirituality seems to have taken root on either side of the Rhine, inspired by a passionate desire to penetrate to the very essence of things and life. The examples range from Hildegard of Bingen via Master Eckhart to the philosopher Martin Heidegger in his hermit's retreat in Todtnauberg near Freiburg-im-Breisgau. Perhaps this spirituality was a kind of counterpoint, the *vita contemplativa* as opposed to the *vita activa* of the wine-growers, the merchants and the industrialists in the Rhineland. Perhaps this much-loved but also hated river had its own utopia. It is no doubt thanks to the coexistence of the two trends that the Rhine became the cradle of a fertile culture, a 'Nile of the West', as the French poet and historian Lamartine put it.

Born in the fertile soil of the cities, where bourgeois emancipation took place in the Middle Ages, mysticism developed as a spiritual movement in southern Germany, Switzerland and along the Rhine axis as far as the Netherlands during the first half of the 14th century. Two new monastic orders, known as mendicant orders, the Dominicans and the Franciscans, now established themselves in the urban centres and soon attracted a following, primarily among women of the nobility and high town dwellers. The pupils of St Dominic (Dominicus of Calaruega) settled in Cologne in 1221, in Strasbourg three years later and in Colmar in 1260. It was in religious and intellectual strongholds such as the Dominican convent of Unterlinden in Colmar, and in a climate of religiosity and piety, that German mysticism flourished, represented by Master Eckhart, Tauler and Suso. The more speculative form of Rhenish mysticism shows the decisive influence of Albertus Magnus, that 'most Rhenish' of all medieval thinkers, Bishop of Regensburg and Master of Theology at the University of Paris, who established the *studium generale* in Cologne in 1248.

Eckhart of Hochheim, born in Thüringen in 1260, entered the Dominican order of Erfurt, obtained his master's degree at the University of Paris and taught theology there. From 1314 he preached in Strasbourg and reformed the *cura monialium* of many congregations of women on the Upper Rhine; finally he taught at the *studium generale* in Cologne. He preached asceticism, renunciation of the self and the world, in order to attain union with God at the most profound level of being, at the source of what he called the *'fünkelin der sele'*, the divine spark in the soul. Master Eckhart did not live to see many of his theses definitively condemned as heretical by the Pope in Avignon. He died during proceedings initiated by the archbishop of Cologne and in this way escaped being burned at the stake.

Tauler, who was born in Strasbourg in 1300, was active as a preacher in his home town, in Basel and in Cologne. A disciple of Master Eckhart, he managed to communicate his teacher's message in a more understandable way. 'We must resist all will, all desire, all own action, leaving only simple and pure attention to God, without seeking in any way to be, become, or acquire anything ourselves; we must live solely and alone for Him and make room for Him in the highest and deepest way, so that He can accomplish His work and His birth in you without you hindering Him therein.'

Heinrich Seuse (Suso in Latin), born near Lake Constance around 1295, was also a disciple of Eckhart. He studied in Cologne and Strasbourg and taught in Konstanz. When he was forced to give up his chair, he became a kind of itinerant teacher, travelling around the Rhine valley and in Switzerland. The writings of Seuse, who has left fewer sermons than Eckhart or Tauler, reflect a rather emotive, sentimental spirituality, coloured by the spirit of chivalry and the *Minnesang*. Yet all three writers share a mysticism rooted mainly in the longing of the soul, freed from worldly temptations, to unite with God. Put in more colloquial terms, it is a turning inward into the self, philosophic endeavour par excellence. Alain de Libera correctly commented that the Rhinelanders had tried to 'think the thought' that inspired the Reformation two centuries later.

By the second half of the 14th century, the idea of the *unio mystica* had lost some of its force. In the north a form of spiritual life grew up that was geared more closely to people, placing the main emphasis on strengthening individual piety. It is a Carthusian monk from Strasbourg, Ludolph of Saxony (died 1377), who provided a *Vita Christi* that sought to impress a model of devotional life on the faithful, while Seuse, hailing from the Upper Rhine, placed greater emphasis on feeling. Gerd de Groote (Gerardus Magnus; 1340–84) from Deventer attracted the anger of the bishop

Hans Holbein the Younger, *Portrait of Erasmus of Rotterdam Writing*, 1523. Kunstmuseum, Öffentliche Kunstsammlung, Basel.

Opposite: Edward Jakob von Steinle, *Lorelei*, 1864. Schackgalerie, Bayerische Staatsgemäldesammlungen, Munich.

of Utrecht because he preached against the abuses of the clergy. He devised a form of devotion for his disciples, the 'Brethren of Common Life', which the chronicler of the Windesheim monastery (founded in 1367 near Zwolle) described as *devotio moderna* and which was to prove very popular throughout the 15th century. This movement also produced edifying literature, whose influence was felt until modern times: it was towards 1427 that a canon of Zwolle, Thomas à Kempis, wrote at least part of his *Imitatio Jesu Christi*, which presents Christ as the model for human behaviour.

The first German universities were founded in the ambitious cities along the Rhine axis: Heidelberg in 1386, Cologne in 1388, Freiburg in 1457, Basel in 1460 and Mainz in 1476. At much the same time, around 1440, Johann Gutenberg (?1398–1468) invented printing with movable type, again by the Rhine, and most probably in Mainz, his home town, rather than in Strasbourg, where he also lived for a while. His invention offered the cultured world and academic institutions a universal means of disseminating their

ideas through books. Humanism spread with the help of printers and publishers, of which there were a great many in Strasbourg and Basel, although the main centre of distribution was Frankfurt.

In the region from Rotterdam to Basel the most eminent of the humanists was without doubt Erasmus (1467–1536), a figure who stood at the crossroads of the *devotio moderna* and the stoicism of antiquity. A model of the European intellectual, tolerant, upright and honest, moderate in his actions, he devoted all his energy to the philological study of early Christian writings and to freeing them of the medieval textual glosses. Erasmus regarded his new edition of the writings of the Church Fathers as an incentive for his contemporaries to put into practice what he called the 'philosophy of Christ'. He was supported in this endeavour by colleagues such as Beatus Rhenanus and by the Basel printing works of Amerbach and Froben. As a scholar he prepared the way for the Reformation, yet he still remained true to his old faith.

Beatus Rhenanus (1485–1547) received his first training in the Latin school of the small town of Sélestat near Strasbourg. Later, in Paris, he studied under Lefèvre, who won him over to the teachings of Aristotle. In addition to his activities as a philologist, he also wrote historical works. His three volumes of *Rerum germanicum* (1531) tell of the old Germania after the Roman conquest, the people who lived there, the political and legal organization of the Franks and the topography of the medieval cities. Beatus Rhenanus proves himself a very modern historian, scrupulously consulting all the available sources while also attempting to evaluate them critically.

Two pre-Reformation humanists from Strasbourg also deserve a mention. Sebastian Brant (1457–1521), a jurist and teacher of ethics, published a satirical

moral poem – the *Narrenschiff* (Ship of Fools) – in German in 1494. Printed by Johann Bergmann in Basel and illustrated with woodcuts by the young Albrecht Dürer (Ill. p. 29), it ran into many editions. The preacher Hans Geiler von Kaysersberg (1445–1510) denounced the same follies and vices in the fiery sermons he preached in the vernacular for a period of thirty years from a pulpit in Strasbourg Cathedral specially constructed for him by the urban patricians.

Johann von Dalberg (1455–1503), the count palatine's chancellor, introduced the spirit of humanism into Heidelberg University by founding a scholarly society, the *Sodalitas litteraria*, which soon set an example to other Rhenish towns. One of its members, Jakob Wimpfeling from Sélestat (1450–1528), preached and taught in Speyer and Heidelberg. He believed that practical activity as a scholar and the reform of Christian life were equally important tasks for a humanist. After initially supporting Luther, he subsequently called for a return to the old faith.

Basel played an important role in this widespread movement for the renewal of spiritual life, thanks in part to the activities of Jean Heynlin von Stein (1430–96). He was prior of the University of Paris several times and an influential preacher in Basel, where he played a major part in the introduction of the printed book and belonged to the group of scholars who gathered round the famous printer and art collector Johann Amerbach (see p. 26).

It would be a mistake to place the humanists on the side of the Reformers. Erasmus did not follow Luther beyond what they both regarded as compulsory: the study of the Bible. By temperament, the Saxon monk was not inclined to tolerance or compromise. In 1521 he was brought before Charles V and church representatives in Worms. When he

refused to retract his theses, he was excommunicated and outlawed. Yet his ideas soon found sympathy among the German princes and some of the clergy. In 1521 Konstanz joined the Reformation, followed in 1523 by Strasbourg, in 1527 by Worms, in 1529 by Basel and in 1539 by Speyer, while the Rhenish archbishoprics of Cologne, Trier and Mainz remained loyal to the Roman Catholic Church.

Martin Bucer (1491–1551), a Dominican priest from the small Alsatian town of Sélestat, which became a centre of humanism, met Luther in Heidelberg in 1518. In 1523 he settled in Strasbourg, where he helped establish the Reformation and called for the churches to be cleared of images, altars and liturgical vestments. His doctrine centred on justification through faith – God's unconditional love for human beings – and called for reconciliation between all Christians. In later years he headed, from Bonn, a movement inspired by the Reformation that spread throughout the Lower Rhine.

At that time, Schaffhausen and Basel were more drawn to the doctrines of the Swiss religious reformer Ulrich Zwingli, as set out in Zurich in 1523, even though in many respects they were far more radical than Luther's ideas and even opposed to them. In 1536, during his

time in Basel, the French Protestant reformer John Calvin (1509–64) published the Latin version of his main theological work, *Christianae Religionis Institutio*, the most important dogmatic writing of the Reformation, which followed on from Luther's catechism. During his stay in Strasbourg, where the French version was published, he paved the way for another form of Protestantism, which eventually spread all along the Rhine. Like Zwingli, Calvin became a founder of the Reformed Church.

Two hundred and fifty years after the Reformation, the Rhineland once again underwent profound changes and reforms. At exactly the same time as France was seeking to spread the message of the revolution and impose its new order on Germany and Europe, the politically divided Rhine became the symbol of German Romanticism. This new vision of the Rhine landscape was inspired by its cities and monuments, which were seen as reflecting the chivalry and piety of the Middle Ages. The Romantics looked back in time for signs of their national identity in the language, the folk literature, the songs, fairy tales and mythology of the past, which were published as collections and became very popular.

The Rhine, particularly the stretch from Mainz to Koblenz, symbolized and satisfied the Romantic yearning for the infinite and the sublime, the search for a synthesis between feeling and understanding, experience and idea, nature and spirit, individualism and community. For the Romantics, the Rhine landscape, with its imposing and picturesque monuments, reflected the harmony between nature, culture and history. While the *Sturm und Drang* movement in the second half of the 18th century prepared the way for Romantic literature, poets were fired by the wars of independence and

transformed Romanticism into a popular political movement.

The 'discoverers' and main proponents of the 'romantic Rhine' include the poet Friedrich Schlegel, who went there in 1802, and the friends Achim von Arnim and Clemens Brentano, who travelled to the Rhine in the same year and experienced it as both a historic landscape and a source of myth. 'I really feel that an immense poem pervades the whole of nature, appearing sometimes as history, sometimes as an event of nature, of which the poet need perceive only a few weak echoes in order to penetrate into the deepest soul with infinite clarity,' wrote Arnim. Poets and scholars gathered in the University of Heidelberg, which came under the Grand Duchy of Baden in 1803 and at that time formed the spiritual nucleus of the Romantic movement.

The myth of the romantic Rhine also made an impact on Germany's neighbour to the west, France. In 1838 Alexandre Dumas (1802–70), the French novelist and playwright, was commissioned by two Parisian newspapers to travel to the Rhine in order to familiarize their readers with the picturesque landscape and sights of the Rhine, with its legends and, not least, with what the French regarded as the curious German way of life. 'We French find it hard to understand the Germans' deep reverence for the Rhine…. The Rhine is the symbol of everything. It means strength, it means independence, it means freedom…. However it is regarded, as an object of fear or hope, a symbol of hatred or love, the origin of life and death – it is a source of poetry for everyone.' The account of his journey, *Excursions sur les bords du Rhin*, which appeared in Paris in 1841, is an amusing piece of writing, pleasantly free of politics, that builds an international bridge of human understanding across the Rhine.

Art in the Rhineland

History of Art, Geography of Art

From around 1910, art historians have constantly endeavoured to make a connection between a particular region and the art it has produced, although at times the debate has been clouded by ideology. This regional approach is to be found even in the 'antiquarian' literature of the early 19th century. For example, the French art historian Arcisse de Caumont (1802–73) tried to compile a 'geography of styles' based on his research into Romanesque architecture. Indeed, the nature of the building material used can be a key to explaining certain formal characteristics and can therefore lead to the development of geographically distinct types. It has long been known that materials as different as slate, brick, granite and sandstone all satisfy different aesthetic requirements. Is it possible, however, to draw a clear distinction between the art of the Upper Rhine and that of the Middle Rhine? Or does the art of the Rhine have such distinct stylistic features, at least over a specific period, as to give it an unmistakable, clearly delineated profile of its own, making it different from other artistic landscapes, such as Swabia, for example? And once certain traditions have been defined within an artistic landscape, do they endure over a long period of time? Although this book does not claim to answer all the questions raised by this complex subject, it sets out to discuss the phenomenon of 'Rhenish art', by studying the actual works of art.

First of all, it is important to show that the conventional notions of 'schools' or regional styles of art are to a great extent determined by conventions in force at a particular time. For example, the art collections put together in Cologne around 1800 have formed the general view of late medieval Rhenish art. Canon Ferdinand Franz Wallraf (1748–1824)

rescued hundreds of liturgical objects and paintings from the churches of Cologne when the town was invaded by the revolutionary troops. Today they form the nucleus of several Cologne museums. The brothers Sulpiz (1783–1854) and Melchior Boisserée (1786–1851) also played an important role in collecting late medieval works of art at a time when these pieces were considered of little value. The brothers, who inspired new enthusiasm for Gothic art, adopted a very personal approach to art history, seeking to expand the collections they had put together from Cologne churches and private owners by purchasing early Dutch works in Brabant. Sulpiz wrote in a letter dated 1816: 'You know that we have saved a great many pictures from ruin by rescuing them from dust and damp, from attics and cellars, to the ridicule and laughter of our fellow-citizens.... But you do not know that we have only bought five pieces directly from churches, observing all the formalities...that it is precisely our most perfect paintings that have been increased in number by half as a result of the various journeys in Brabant.' Late Gothic painting in Cologne, known as the Cologne School, was in a sense invented by the Boisserée brothers, who first put it in a historical perspective. Sulpiz's interest in the medieval plans of Cologne Cathedral must be seen in the same context (Ill. p. 70). His ambition was to build a bridge between the present and the medieval past of his town, illustrating the unique nature of a specifically Rhenish culture through its works of art. In that respect the Boisserée brothers shared and encouraged a Romantic vision of the Middle Ages.

Rather than looking for formal artistic styles within a specific region, it is important to examine the background to the creation of works of art, the

place where they were produced (such as the masons' lodge or the individual artist's workshop), and the patron or client (such as the clergy, the nobility and the patriciate, or the merchant class). Yet these groups were not homogeneous: they belonged to different generations and could be subjected to outside influences. A bishop's court and a group of merchants who had made their money from trade would not have the same requirements when it came to works of art. At best, art historians can study written sources or objects that enable them to evaluate the activity of an artist, a workshop, an area or a 'school'. It is very rare for art historians to know anything about the possessions of a private individual or a family, for instance in the form of an inventory that not only lists the movable property but also provides information about the origins of the objects concerned. That knowledge can reveal the artistic inclinations and ambitions of a particular type of client.

In 1586 the lawyer and art collector Basilius Amerbach (1533–91), a professor at Basel University, member of the Council and the man responsible for starting the archaeological excavations in Augusta Raurica, owned sixteen paintings by Hans Holbein the Younger, Niklaus Manuel, Hans Baldung (called Grien) and Urs Graf the Elder, in addition to drawings and models of goldwork. His inventory dating from around 1650 lists 1,866 drawings, 525 woodcuts and 3,356 copper engravings, an impressive list, though it must be remembered that all these works dated back to the early 16th century. The collector's father, the jurist Bonifacius Amerbach (1495–1562), who acquired the paintings by Holbein the Younger, and his grandfather Johann Amerbach (1445–1513), who employed the twenty-one-year-old Dürer in his printing workshop, were much bolder and more resolutely committed to

26

collecting contemporary art. In contrast, Basilius Amerbach preferred what was already a past generation of artists, and showed a complete lack of interest in contemporaries such as Tobias Stimmer or Joseph Heintz. Besides the artists of the Upper Rhine, who made up a large part of his collection of drawings, Basilius Amerbach was also interested in the Strasbourg master, Hans Baldung, and the painter Hans Leu from Zurich. He owned a few works by the Danube School (Albrecht Altdorfer and Wolf Huber) and spent a long time searching for an authentic work by Dürer. The collector does not seem to have brought back much from his trips to Venice, Padua and Bologna. After reading Vasari, he instructed his nephew Ludwig Iselin to find him authenticated works by great masters such as Raphael, Michelangelo and Titian. However, this undertaking does not seem to have been very successful. His main source of supply was book dealers in Frankfurt, Lyons and Venice, who found him not only books but also engravings and medals. Overall, Basilius Amerbach's collection reflects a retrograde taste, combined with a strong sense of local patriotism. The city council of Basel bought the Amerbach collection in 1662 and today it forms a key part of the collection at the Basel Kunstmuseum.

When the term 'geography of art' is used, it is necessary to distinguish between the different levels of importance in the various geopolitical structures. As a political, administrative, legal and economic framework, the urban community played an important role in developing artistic work. The guilds and their rules gave the urban workshop protection from outside competition, which sometimes went as far as actual protectionism. In most towns, the people needed to have civic rights in order to follow a trade. The local clients were not always very keen on these rules, because they stopped them from turning to artists from outside town. During the Council of Basel, for instance, the clergy complained that the city of Mainz did not permit outside artists to be employed. The magistrate replied that employing outside workers would give rise to serious unrest and opposition. In the small but prosperous city of Colmar, the 15th-century painter Martin Schongauer appears to have had no professional contact with Kaspar Isenmann (c. 1410–85) who also lived there and was in fact very famous. Schongauer tended to look for his models far away, in the southern Netherlands.

The artists' clients, however, lived and were bound to meet one another within the city walls and their preference for one artist over another tended to encourage constant competition. There was as wide a range of cultural models within this urban context as outside it. The speed at which their influence spread depended not on geographical distance but far more on the demand within a particular social or professional group (nobility, religious orders, etc.) and their relationships with one another. The case of the sculptor Nicolaus Gerhaert von Leyden (active 1462–73/8) is revealing. It is said that the city council summoned him to Strasbourg and commissioned him to carry out the sculptural decoration of the portal in the chancellery. While working on this task from 1463, he also carried out a major commission for Konstanz Cathedral until his departure for Wiener-Neustadt in 1467, creating the monumental stone crucifix in Baden-Baden commissioned by the margrave's surgeon, Hans Ulrich Scherer (Ill. p. 211) and, again in Strasbourg, completing the memorial plaque of a canon of the cathedral (Ill. p. 200), until he departed for Wiener-Neustadt in 1467. With so many important commissions, it is highly unlikely that he had time to take on any other work during that period. This particular case does show, however, that Strasbourg was not as impressed by the outstanding talent of this out-of-town sculptor as the canons in Konstanz had been.

According to L. E. Stamm, a special feature of urban culture is the 'heraldic style'. Until well into the 14th century the workshops of the illuminators, fresco painters and decorators of the Alemannic regions of the Upper Rhine continued to follow the same tradition. They used stylized, geometrical forms and silhouette-like figures with no modelling, which go back to the kind of pictorial models that became popular at the beginning of the century with the dissemination of large collections of ballads (*Manesse* and *Weingarten*). These motifs from the past were repeated constantly, on wooden ceilings emblazoned with armorial bearings, in the secular painted decoration of bourgeois houses, on love caskets (*Minnekästchen*), on shields and even in the stained-glass windows of churches. Works of this kind tended to be commissioned by parvenus who had made their money from speculation and who regarded the references in these images to the age of chivalry as an expression of social rank, a sign that they belonged to high society, regardless of the fact that even the *Manesse* collections of ballads were no more than nostalgic reminiscences of the past.

The region of the Upper Rhine was divided into four dioceses: Konstanz, Basel, Strasbourg and Speyer.

Artists clearly did not regard these boundaries as impassable barriers, although there was a difference between architecture and other art forms. In the case of religious architecture, it was not just a question of typology; to some extent each cathedral had an exemplary function and influenced the style of the collegiate and parish churches. Yet there was no uniform architectural style within a diocese or 'regional' style that extended beyond its borders. For instance, the lodge of the parish church of Freiburg, which came under the diocese of Konstanz, was influenced more by the style of Strasbourg Cathedral than by the style of Konstanz Cathedral. In the case of the mendicant orders' provinces, the situation was different again. The Franciscan church in Würzburg played a key role in the Upper Rhine region in introducing the type of basilican church imported from Italy, with high aisles and slender round columns without capitals. The church constructed by the Franciscans in Rouffach in Alsace established a style specific to the Upper Rhine. The flat-ceilinged nave, a feature that was also adopted outside the mendicant orders, in Alsace, Switzerland, Lake Constance and Swabia, until well into the 13th century, is a characteristic feature of Upper Rhenish architecture, with the single exception of the (now destroyed) Dominican church in Strasbourg.

The bishop's court was another political authority, although it was less powerful than the town in the case of Strasbourg, Basel and Cologne. It had very different ambitions and the 'symbolic forms' chosen by an archbishop or bishop differed from those of the town dwellers. The princes of the church looked more to the courts of the kings and emperors and did not confine themselves in any way to the artistic potential of local workshops. Some of the artists working for the

religious and secular courts were summoned from far afield. This cosmopolitan quality was a feature of art throughout the Middle Ages and still predominated during the Renaissance and the 18th century. French models had a very strong influence on the Rhenish courts at different times, especially in the field of architecture.

As for the centres of artistic production, there was the masons' lodge. It took many generations to build a cathedral, so the lodge served as a constant framework for the development of an autonomous artistic tradition, within which long-term, historical references were perhaps more marked than contemporary trends. When the right-hand tower of Cologne Cathedral was built in the 15th century, the design was modelled on the 13th-century left-hand tower, without taking into account any stylistic developments that had taken place in the interim. One of the statuettes on the archivolt of the St Peter Portal is a copy of a sculpture in the choir stalls, which is three generations older. In Strasbourg, the statues in St Catherine Chapel are directly inspired by the sculptures of the west portals, which are over fifty years' older. An even wider time span separates the sculptor who, in the late 15th century, created the bust of a man leaning on the balustrade of the choir gallery in the southern transept sunk in contemplation before the pillar of the *Last Judgment* – a work dating from around 1230. In Mainz Cathedral, the series of bishops' tombs (Ill. p. 248) created between the 14th and 16th centuries obeyed a uniform pictorial typology that not only drew on convention but also corresponded to workshop practice. That does not mean that the lodges were resolutely conservative but simply that technical procedures, certain working methods and typological

models developed and became established within a particular production centre and continued to be followed over a long period of time.

However, the lodges were continually broadening their horizons. The leading masters of the Late Gothic period often worked in several different lodges at the same time; through their travels, these individual artists were mainly responsible for spreading new creative ideas. The links between Ulm and Strasbourg, for instance, can be explained by the fact that Ulrich von Ensingen was the master mason of both lodges. The existence of entire families of masons – with names such as Parler, Ensinger or, in the 18th century, Beer and Thumb – meant that artistic models could be disseminated systematically, regardless of any 'geography of art'. In the 14th and above all the 15th century, a new, healthy trend emerged; artistic work became more international and individual, and in this way counteracted the conservatism of the lodges.

It was not only the master masons who rose up the social ladder, but also artists from all sorts of fields. Nicolaus Gerhaert von Leyden arrived in the Upper Rhine around 1462 as an independent artist free to choose where he wanted to work, a fact made clear by his refusal to accept immediately the emperor's invitation to come to his court in Wiener-Neustadt. Mathias Grünewald (c. 1475–1528) was recruited by Guido Guersi, the Preceptor of the Antonine monastery of Isenheim in Alsace, having previously worked for the Archbishop-Elector of Mainz. He stayed on the Upper Rhine for some time, at least three years, where he probably came into contact with Rhenish artists and potential clients, especially in the two neighbouring centres of Basel and Strasbourg. Stylistically, the art of the

Upper Rhine had little influence on him, although the mystical intensity of his painting was entirely consistent with the spiritual climate of the region.

The artist's workshop was a production centre that was forced to consider economic factors, a fact that had considerable consequences for the development of art. One effect was the attempt to acquire a monopoly position, which meant that the workshop could take on commissions of all kinds and meet all sorts of different aesthetic requirements. It also had to try to export its work. It is safe to assume that a few workshops even specialized in the foreign market. One example could be the artist known as the Master of the Rimini Crucifixion (named after the work in the Liebieghaus in Frankfurt). A whole group of alabaster sculptures, scattered through the Netherlands, the Lower and Middle Rhine, as far as northern Italy and even Silesia, is attributed to him or his workshop. This master, who may have lived in northern France or the southern Netherlands and had come into contact with the work of the Netherlandish painter Robert Campin (*c.* 1380–1444) and the Flemish painter Rogier van der Weyden (*c.* 1400–64), evolved his own individual style, which was taken up by a whole network of subsidiary workshops. How such workshops were actually run from within remains a mystery. However,

it is possible to glean some idea of the way they were organized and the manner in which tasks were allocated from carefully studying the works themselves.

Generally, works of art, which were regarded as luxury goods, were marketed through the same channels as ordinary products. If some of these routes could be reconstructed, it would be possible to gain valuable insights into the taste and the economic function of the art market. It is known that events such as the Councils of Basel and Konstanz attracted thousands of scribes, copyists and illuminators, working full time to cope with the demand. Between 1414 and 1418, 72 goldsmiths and 1,400 artisans and traders visited the Council of Konstanz. Yet this intensive trade had no impact on the subsequent artistic production of Konstanz. The Council provided an opportunity to meet other artists, and at this time the town temporarily became one enormous market.

During the Middle Ages, as now, artists travelled widely, in order to broaden their own visual experience and to make contact with colleagues and potential clients. If the Rhineland offered ideal conditions for these travels, it also benefited greatly from all this mobility. The river formed a natural north–south axis, a route between northern Italy and the Netherlands, while also acting as a link between traffic from the east and west. Thanks to its geographical position, the Upper Rhine region came into contact with several places at the same time – the Alpine countries, Burgundy, central Europe and Italy. It was therefore particularly open to influences from these regions. Yet the artistic centres on the Upper Rhine were not all receptive to the same ideas at the same time. Early on, it became clear that certain people – clients and artists – played an important role. Clients did so even

though they were tied to a fixed social system, artists did so even though they were bound by the professional rules of their guild, at least until the 16th century.

Albrecht Dürer is a good example. At the age of nineteen he left Nuremberg to visit Martin Schongauer in Colmar, having seen engravings by him in the collection of his – Dürer's – father, a goldsmith, but the 'handsome Martin' had died by the time Dürer arrived. The family then sent the young artist on to Basel, to see the workshop of the goldsmith Georg Schongauer, who no doubt helped Dürer to find employment at the printing works of Johann Amerbach. Dürer was commissioned by him to do the woodcuts for the illustrations to Terence's comedies. After that he produced the illustrations for Sebastian Brant's 'Ship of Fools', for which no iconographic tradition existed at the time. Even before finishing that job, Dürer followed Georg Schongauer, who had married the daughter of the sculptor Nicolaus Gerhaert von Leyden, to Strasbourg, where he produced more graphic works, before returning home to Nuremberg in 1494.

Dürer's years of study on the Upper Rhine have always been regarded as a crucial stage in his career. In the catalogue to the Dürer exhibition in Nuremberg in 1971, Leonie von Wilckens wrote: 'This leading German artistic landscape of the time influenced him in artistic, stylistic and pictorial ways. With his own, personal way of synthesizing things, he was able at the same time to be entirely himself. Numerous studies from nature, to which the nude was added at that time, are evidence during these years of the artistic approach to the world around him that he continued to take throughout his life.' The artistic and intellectual climate around Dürer was enhanced in

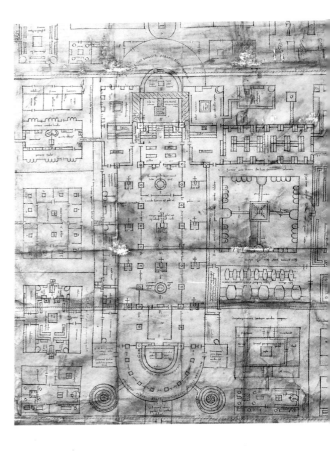

its turn by the presence of the young painter; the three stages of his artistic journey, Colmar, Basel and Strasbourg, each formed milestones in the rapid development of his art as he came to terms with the legacy of the Gothic period. The next milestone was Venice – beyond the axis of the Rhine.

It is clear that the artistic landscape of the Upper and Middle Rhine was remarkably receptive to movements from both neighbouring and more remote regions. This area became the site of intense interaction between artists, because of the links between the Upper Rhine and Burgundy, Champagne and even the Ile de France in the 13th and 14th centuries, and with the Netherlands in the 15th century, and also because of its position as a transit point from and to Swabia and Central Europe. There were similar links along the Middle Rhine, although they were often indirect and less intense, as though just following in the wake of the Upper Rhine. The ties that had existed with Italy since Roman times were never entirely broken, either in the pre-Romanesque and Romanesque period or in the Late Middle Ages. During the age of Enlightenment, French models dominated religious and secular architecture and the artists and workmen were recruited from France and Italy, as well as the Vorarlberg and various regions of Germany. The movements of artists and artisans always depended on their individual clients' tastes and on the means available, while factors such as prestige and competition largely determined the style of the princely building projects.

The Early Middle Ages and Romanesque Art

From the Romans to the Carolingians

The historical panorama of the Rhenish artistic landscape as seen today dates back to Carolingian times. The Roman cities along the Rhine paved the way for the political and cultural revival of the Christian kingdom of the Franks. In around AD 100, Emperor Trajan decided that the settlement situated on a branch of the Lower Rhine near a military camp used as the base for operations against the conquest of Lower Germania should be raised to the rank of *Colonia Ulpia Traiana* (Xanten). In accordance with the usual Roman town plan, Xanten had a right-angled road grid, occupying an area of 83 hectares (over 200 acres), a capitol, a harbour temple and an amphitheatre for 1,200 spectators. One of the factors that explains its continuity, even after the collapse of Roman rule, is the presence of local martyrs' tombs. The Christian settlement of Xanten sprang up around the tomb of St Viktor and his companions on the site of the present cathedral, where a memorial church had existed since the late 4th century (see p. 334). So here, as in Bonn, the cult of the saints was the link between the Roman settlement and the medieval Christian town.

The continuity of other Roman settlements, however, such as Cologne, Trier, Mainz and Chur, derived from their religious status as bishops' sees. In AD 50, the Empress Agrippina granted an early Germanic *oppidum* the status of *Colonia Claudia Ara Agrippinensis* (Cologne; see p. 286). This Roman town, of which the Roman tower and the northern city gate still survive, occupied an area of more than 96 hectares (237 acres). The medieval ground plan of the town still followed the main axes of the Roman road network and retained the open space of the central forum. Although the population had declined sharply, there was still much activity during the Frankish period, especially along the banks of the Rhine. There are records of a diocesan church being built as early as the end of the 4th century. Outside the city wall, new centres of worship appeared, in the form of memorial churches, such as the one at St Gereon, based on an oval ground plan with conches dating from the last third of the 4th century that can still be traced in the Hohenstaufen building (see p. 307). The ancient traditions of the glassmakers and goldsmiths also seem to have flourished under Frankish rule. Before the mid-6th century, a cathedral was built by the northern city wall to replace the first diocesan church (see p. 289). The later Carolingian building had a double choir, conforming to the famous plan in the library of St Gall in Switzerland that shows what an ideal monastery would look like. The ground plan was based on a square module, which determined the dimensions of the different sections – nave, transept and choir (without apses). This layout created the foundations for the 'alternating system' that later played an important part in religious architecture in the empire, especially in the construction of the vaults.

Traces of earlier, Christian buildings can also be found in the Alpine regions along the upper course of the Rhine: modest buildings made from rough materials, oratories or small churches, used as meeting or prayer rooms. The typical church with an aisleless nave, terminating in a semi-circular apse, soon evolved to include lateral symmetrical apses to house more altars. Three-apse churches constructed between the 8th and 10th century can be found in Disentis (see p. 76), St Luzius (see p. 91) and St Martin in Chur, as well as in Schaffhausen (remains found under the present abbey church). These apses are generally horseshoe-shaped. The crypt has played an important role in the development of religious architecture in the West. The early form of ring crypt has survived in St Luzius in Chur (Ill. p. 91) and in the abbey church of Disentis.

The *porta triumphalis* or gateway to the imperial monastery at Lorsch (Ill. p. 239) in the archbishopric of Mainz is an excellent example of Carolingian architecture. Dating from the foundation of the Benedictine abbey at the end of the 8th century, this Carolingian version of a Roman triumphal arch provides evidence of the survival and reinterpretation of the formal elements from antiquity. Although it is small, it creates an impressive effect and must certainly have had a religious function within the monastery complex. Its isolated position makes it all the more remarkable today. Lorsch Abbey also had an important library and several of the most valuable manuscripts it contained were incorporated in the Biblioteca Palatina in the 16th century and thus ended up in the Vatican. Pages from the Lorsch Gospels written around 810 in Charlemagne's court school in Aachen are now in Bucharest and in the Vatican, while one of the ivory panels of its ornamental cover is now in the Victoria and Albert Museum in London.

The reign of Charlemagne, which gave rise to the term 'Carolingian Renaissance', brought Western architecture two important benefits: interest in the civilization of Classical antiquity in the broadest sense, and the reinterpretation of this legacy to suit the requirements of Christianity. Towards the mid-8th century, the Classical architectural form of the basilica was introduced in the kingdom of the Franks. New solutions for the choir and the west façade were being sought in both west Frankish St Denis and east Frankish Lorsch at the same time, laying the foundations of Christian religious architecture that the Middle Ages later built on. Yet it was left to later periods, to the time of the Ottonian and Salian emperors, to create architectural systems from these precursors of medieval architecture. The octagonal church of Ottmarsheim, dating from around 1030, harks back to the central plan in Charlemagne's Palatine Chapel at Aachen, displaying a certain ostentation despite the simplified forms (Ills. pp. 154–55). Nijmegen in the Netherlands is another copy of the famous model (Ill. p. 340).

Little remains of the sculpture of that period; at least there are few extant works that can be said with any certainty to come from the Rhineland. The 'Priesterstein' or priest's stone in the diocesan museum in Mainz is a relatively primitive example. The head of a young man from a slightly less than life-size sandstone figure from Lorsch, (now in the Hessisches Landesmuseum Darmstadt), was dated to 800 after its discovery. It may, however, be considerably later. Another fragment, also found in Lorsch and now in the Darmstadt museum, is the only example of Carolingian stained glass; the head, reconstructed from numerous fragments in a way that has caused doubts about its authenticity, does nevertheless provide valuable evidence that glass painters were already helping to decorate churches during that period.

The Ottonian period

Historically this period lasted from the time of Otto the Great, who was crowned first Emperor of the Holy Roman Empire of the German Nation in 962, until the death of Henry II, which signalled the end of the Saxon dynasty in 1024. Given the continuity of artistic style, however, the date when the Salian period begins is fluid. Otto I's brother, Archbishop Bruno of Cologne, gave instructions in his will for the construction of St Pantaleon, which was begun after his death in 965 and continued by Empress Theophanu, the Byzantine wife of Emperor Otto II, who endowed it richly (see pp. 297–99). The imperial nature of this building is still reflected today in the interior elevation of the westwork, with its two-storey arcades that open up into wide tribunes on the upper level (Ill. p. 297). The rhythmic alternation of colour on the pillars and arches and the geometric patterns that

Left: Gero Crucifix. Oak, pre-976. Cologne Cathedral.
Below: The Golden Madonna of Essen, c. 1000. Cathedral treasury, Essen.
Bottom: Antependium from Basel Cathedral, c. 1000. Musée de Cluny, Paris.

cover the surface of the freestones are clear references to antiquity. Originally, the church had a single nave articulated by blind arcades. No doubt this literally outstanding place of worship in which the nave culminated had a special function, perhaps linked to the endowments and the tomb of Empress Theophanu.

The development of the 'westworks' goes back to the Carolingian era and represents an architectural innovation that did not draw on Classical or Early Christian models. The monastery church of Corvey on the River Weser is the best-preserved example. The real function of the westwork is still not certain; it was probably complex, sometimes used for the liturgy and sometimes for the cult of the emperor. These monumental structures, which lend the churches their characteristic silhouette, largely because of the vertical accents created by the one or more towers, soon took on different forms. Examples along the Rhine include St Pantaleon and St Ursula in Cologne and the churches of Reichenau-Mittelzell and Marmoutier in Alsace.

At about the same time that St Pantaleon was being built, another famous prince of the church, Archbishop and Chancellor Willigis of Mainz (975– 1011), began to rebuild Mainz Cathedral. Its ambitious design set an authoritative example, in spite of the changes made in the course of the 12th and 13th centuries (Ill. p. 245). The plan of a basilica with a nave and two aisles

and a very wide transept in the west was based on the Carolingian abbey church of Fulda, which was inspired by the Early Christian church of St Peter in Rome.

The crossing of nave and transept occupies a special place in the genesis of the cruciform basilica. Although it was a constant feature of medieval religious architecture, the origins and development of the various forms of crossing are difficult to determine. During the Carolingian period the continuous transept, forming a T-shape with the nave, predominated, but it still did not clearly define the area in front of the sanctuary, for instance by the use of four pillars and arches. There is a continuous transept in the church of the Holy Apostles in Cologne dating from around 1020, but it is situated not in front of the sanctuary but at the entrance side on the west. The treatment of the east end depends largely on the presence or absence of a crypt. At this time the earlier type of ring crypt began to be replaced by a uniform space, which was more suited to liturgical needs. These

hall crypts can in fact become real underground churches or undercrofts, as in Reichenau-Oberzell and Konstanz Cathedral (Ill. p. 103).

The structure of the nave also began to obey certain formal criteria. The usual support is the four-sided pillar or pier,

more rarely the column (such as at Reichenau-Oberzell). The alternating system commonly found in the Rhineland, consisting of one column between two square piers, was designed to reinforce the load-bearing structures and offered the advantage of rhythmic variations that produced an impressive monumental effect. The treatment of the upper wall must be studied in this context. The flat, timber ceilings leave a large, uniform space free on the upper wall for frescoes, as at Reichenau-Oberzell (Ill. p. 108). The external elevation is also articulated and enriched by decorative elements such as Lombard friezes and lesenes or pilaster-strips. Most of the buildings (such as the church of the Holy Apostles in Cologne) begun under the Ottonians were completed during the early Salian period, when architectural forms remained the same in theory but were taken further and began to acquire greater definition.

Ottonian sculpture and painting are more clearly defined and homogeneous than the architecture. In sculpture, which now tended towards the monumental, as in painting, the human figure began to be treated in a new way, which had no precedents in Carolingian art and did not draw on Classical sources. In such outstanding works as the Gero Crucifix in Cologne or the antependium from Basel Cathedral, Western Christian art achieved a degree of spiritual tension and intensity otherwise found only in Buddhist art. The Basel antependium, with its chased gold reliefs, shows archangels and St Bernard surrounding the hieratic figure of Christ, with the donors at his feet (Kunigunde and Henry II). The nobility of the figures and the clarity of the arcaded structure make this a masterpiece of Ottonian goldwork.

The magnificent Gero Crucifix (see p. 296) – named after Archbishop Gero – with its penetrating representation of suffering, was referred to again and again until well into the 11th century, as is apparent in the crucifixes from St Georg in Cologne (Ills. pp. 37, 305) and from St Margareta in Gerresheim (Ill. p. 326), although these two works are more than mere imitations. The wood-carvers of the Salian period employed an increasingly stylized formal language. Another typical subject of large-scale votive sculpture is the Madonna and Child, such as the precious example in wood entirely covered in gold leaf in the treasury of Essen.

During the Carolingian period, the large imperial abbeys such as Tours and Metz also produced illuminated manuscripts, but during the Ottonian period the scriptoria tended to be located further east, on the right bank of the Rhine. On the Upper Rhine, the island of Reichenau became the most important and productive centre of illuminated manuscripts, and it clearly also gave rise to subsidiary workshops elsewhere. The Reichenau scriptorium produced the *Egbert Codex* (named after Archbishop Egbert of Trier who commissioned it) around 980. It contains a pictorial cycle of fifty-two miniatures of scenes from the life of Christ, in a magnificent reworking and synthesis of Late Roman models (for example, the *Codex Virgile* in the Vatican, 4–5th century) and Byzantine influences. Although it shows marked Classical tendencies and affinities with the Carolingian illuminated manuscripts of Tours, the *Egbert Codex* is an important work. Like the Gero Crucifix, it set a new style and opened up new areas of exploration for medieval art, through its variety of tones, its dynamic pictorial composition and, particularly, its treatment of the figures, the expressive embodiments of a spiritual message. The illusionist pictorial space of Late Roman times is now replaced by an abstract, atmospheric background, against which the protagonists stand out.

Two other masterpieces among the countless liturgical manuscripts that came from the scriptoria of Reichenau

deserve mention: the *Gospel Book of Otto III*, and *The Book of Pericopes of Henry II*. In the *Gospel Book*, the monumental human figure now appears as 'gesture become form' (art critic Hans Jantzen). Here the illuminators of Reichenau have achieved a level of spirituality that goes beyond concepts such as time, space and physicality. In the *Book of Pericopes* (Codex lat. 4452, Munich), the gold ground acquires an almost sculptural dynamic of its own, which heightens the spiritual force of the weightless figure.

The illuminations produced in the monastic centres certainly have some affinities with wall painting, although the composition of the large frescoes in the church of St Georg in Reichenau-Oberzell (Ill. p. 108) is not modelled entirely on miniatures. What the two have in common is that they look back to Early Christian pictorial traditions. The wall paintings of St Georg are not as abstract in style as the Reichenau illuminations of the same period, although both attach the same importance to the expressive gesture. Unlike illuminations, however, in this cycle, which probably dates from the period in office of Abbot Witigowo (985–97), great care is taken in the treatment of the architectural framework within which the scenes unfold in accordance with a perfectly ordered spatial system. The influence of Byzantine art is apparent here. The decorative friezes framing the pictorial fields suggest a three-dimensional perspective based on Late Roman works, perhaps transmitted through Carolingian

models, which soon disappeared completely from Western painting until its rediscovery in the 14th century. Unlike the Carolingian frescoes in St Johann at Müstair in Graubünden, the fresco cycle of St Georg makes use of a carefully nuanced palette, showing that the painter was not only a talented storyteller but also a great colourist. All this confirms the fundamental artistic importance of the Carolingian period, without which the great achievements of Ottonian art would not have taken place.

During both the Carolingian and the Ottonian periods, precious objects made from valuable and rare materials were held in high regard. Gold, ivory and rock crystal were admired not only for their intrinsic value but also their apotropaic function, which made them seem particularly suited to the manufacture of liturgical and cult objects (for example, the comb of St Heribert in the Schnütgen Museum in Cologne, Ill. p. 306). These precious objects were produced in the same centres as the illuminations, in the monasteries of Trier, Reichenau, Regensburg and Hildesheim. The ivory reliefs that were used to decorate book covers are an art form in themselves. The cover of the *Gospel Book of the Abbess Theophanu*, Abbess of Essen and granddaughter of the empress of the same name, dating from 1050, contains an ivory relief depicting the Crucifixion, between the Nativity and the Ascension; the diagonally arranged, chased-gold bas-reliefs also show the donor kneeling below in a Byzantine attitude of humility before the Virgin.

In Carolingian and Ottonian times Lorraine was the leading production site for ivory carving, before Cologne took over towards the end of the 10th century. It does not seem, however, that any of the workshops, including Reichenau, developed a specific style for these book covers and each one tends to

be a separate, individual creation. One of the most admirable works of this type, the cover of a gospel book from Reichenau, came from the treasury of Bamberg and can now be seen in the Staatsbibliothek (state library) in Munich. The cover, which has an inset decoration of pearls and gemstones arranged around a central oval agate into which an Arabic amulet stone is set, has a surface of chased gold foil in the form of a cross with embossed figures of animals facing each other on either side. This plaque was probably created in Reichenau in the early 11th century, at the same time as the codex to which it belongs. In most cases, however, it is impossible to discover the precise place of origin of the precious objects collected or commissioned by rulers or high clerics. The famous empress' treasure found in Mainz and now in the Kunstgewerbemuseum of Berlin-Köpenick is a collection of jewels from the middle of the 11th century, some made by Byzantine and Italian goldsmiths, others by northern workshops working for the imperial court.

The double chapel of St Emmeram and St Martin in Speyer Cathedral, late 11th century.

The Salian period

Two buildings are essential to our understanding of 11th-century Western architecture: the abbey church of Cluny and Speyer Cathedral (Ills. pp. 228–32). In its two successive construction phases, Speyer expressed a new concept of architecture, which had considerable repercussions over the following decades. This cathedral, whose splendid proportions are evident even in the spacious hall crypt that survives from the original structure, is very closely linked to the Salian dynasty (1024–1125). The reconstruction (Speyer II) begun under Henry IV (r. 1084–1105) at the end of the century produced a system of formal and static coordination between wall and vaulting, which paved the way for the future development of Western religious architecture up to the Gothic period. With Speyer, ashlar blocks became an integral part of ambitious building projects. The motif of dwarf galleries running round the exterior at the top of the walls near the gutters, making the wall lighter while also while accentuating its decoration, was also introduced in Speyer. It then became a characteristic feature of Rhenish Romanesque, for instance in Mainz, Schwarzrheindorf and Bonn and in Great St Martin and the Holy Apostles in Cologne. The two chapels in the corners of the transepts were also built during the reconstruction work. The double chapel is found later in Mainz and in Schwarzrheindorf (Ills. pp. 272–73). The original ornamentation of the capitals and the frames of the transept windows reflect a return to Classical forms transmitted via Lombardy, which should be understood in relation to Henry IV's perception of his imperial status. He was also responsible for the major changes made to the eastern parts of Mainz Cathedral: the elevation of the apse and gable wall of the choir were modelled directly on

Speyer, while the architectural decoration is visibly influenced by northern Italy (Ill. p. 245).

The monastery church of Limburg an der Haardt founded by Konrad II (r. 1024–39) reveals a very different architectural style from Speyer Cathedral. The few surviving ruins (Ill. p. 233) still give some idea of the splendour of this building, one of the most successful examples of 11th-century monumental architecture, with its harmonious plan and rhythmic structure of blind arcades and apertures in the walls. Although this imperial building was no doubt regarded as a model of its type, in the end the aesthetic principle on which it was based did not become established. If most of the Late Romanesque buildings in the Rhineland are studied, it becomes clear that there was, during the last quarter of the 12th century, a tendency towards the decorative, while the great basilicas of Limburg and Speyer I, with their clearly

visible structures, bore within them the seeds of a great Romanesque architecture comparable to that which eventually emerged in Burgundy.

Another gem of Salian architecture is the collegiate church of St Maria im Kapitol in Cologne (Ills. pp. 300–303). This is another building begun by Abbess Ida (granddaughter of Emperor Otto II and Empress Theophanu) and it was largely completed when the eastern part was consecrated in 1049. It bears witness to the amazing ability of that period to innovate, by creating a synthesis between two opposing ground plans: the central plan and the basilican plan. The aisles, groin-vaulted as at Speyer, continue as an ambulatory in the conches of the transept and the choir, which means they run round the entire building, so that the nave fuses with the spacious triconch to form a monumental entity. But even a building as innovative as this one contains some references to

35

Top left: Herimann Crucifix,. Wooden core, copper gilt, pre-1056. Erzbischöfliches Diözesan-Museum, Cologne.
Bottom left: Holy water font from St Alban, Mainz. Bronze, 1116/19. Dom- und Diözesanmuseum, Speyer.
Below: Walnut pictorial doors at St Maria im Kapitol in Cologne (Ill. p. 303), pre-1065.

Opposite: Crucifix from St Georg in Cologne. Walnut wood, 2nd half of 11th century. Schnütgen Museum, Cologne (see Ill. p. 305).

the past, revealing that they must be interpreted as intentional on the part of the client who commissioned the work. The great arcade that opens the west-work on to the nave is an allusion to the Palatine Chapel of Aachen. The crypt seems to go back to the slightly earlier model of the imperial Speyer Cathedral.

The Merovingian cathedral of Reichenau-Mittelzell was expanded between 988 and 1048 and converted

into a three-aisled basilica with a western transept and tower with a high chapel (see p. 110). This tower harks back to the eastern part of Strasbourg Cathedral, consecrated in 1015, while the Lombard frieze on the outside wall shows the influence of northern Italy. All that remains of Bishop Wernher's original Romanesque building in Strasbourg Cathedral today is part of the crypt. However, it is known that it was a cruciform basilica with two symmetrical towers on the western façade, a system that was retained for the Gothic cathedral (although only the northern tower was actually built).

When the altar of St Maria im Kapitol was consecrated, Archbishop Herimann of Cologne, the brother of Abbess Ida, commissioned a Cologne goldsmith's workshop to execute a reliquary cross, in which the head of the crucified Christ is an antique lapis lazuli sculpture of the Roman Empress Livia. This gem was no doubt the property of the imperial family. The body of Christ, made in gilt bronze, is Byzantine in inspiration. This exquisite work, inscribed on the reverse side by the donors, is important evidence of not only the survival of works from antiquity but also the high regard in which the imperial court held Byzantine art. In the 11th century, Livia's head was viewed as a relic from the time of Christ. A similar example is the Roman cameo of the Emperor Augustus, which was given a new use as part of the Cross of Lothair in the cathedral treasury of Aachen.

In contrast, the pictorial wooden doors of St Maria im Kapitol in Cologne, completed no later than 1065, are an isolated work linked to local tradition (Ill. p. 303). It is tempting to look for models of these densely crowded scenes in ivory sculpture and the strongly modelled high reliefs do indeed look like miniatures that have been translated into sculpture and monumentalized.

The art historian Anton Legner attributed the uncomplicated narrative and popular pictorial style of these compositions to their didactic function at the entrance to the church, emphasizing the contrast with the 'grand style' of the crucifixes that 'express monastic culture, piety and reform'. The crucifix from St Georg in Cologne is an example of this more spiritual type: 'The tension between its unorganic physicality and the monumental stylization make it one of the most sublime examples of early German sculpture' (Ill. p. 305).

The Reichenau scriptoria stopped producing around 1100 and none of the many illuminated manuscripts created in the dioceses of Mainz or Cologne was particularly noteworthy. However, the fragment of a wall painting in St Gereon

is a remarkable work; the geometric stylization and priestly frontality are reminiscent of painting in Latium and Umbria around 1100 (Ill. p. 310).

The *Vita Annonis* (soon after 1100), referring to a fragment of the True Cross, shows that small pieces of relics were brought back from Byzantium and then mounted in reliquaries. The medieval goldsmiths often travelled widely and worked in a variety of places, as in the case of the monk Roger of Helmarshausen (died 1125). After spending some time working in the abbey of Stablo on the Meuse and in St Pantaleon in Cologne, he was active in Helmarshausen Abbey on the Weser from 1107. Roger is probably identical with Theophilus Presbyter, whose treatise *Schedula diversarium artium* discusses the techniques of painting, stained glass, goldwork and bronze casting.

One fine example of bronze sculpture, which is rarely seen along the Rhine, is the holy-water stoup from St Alban in Mainz, dating from 1116 to 1119, which has sides decorated with symbols of the Evangelists, personifications of the rivers of Paradise and hunting scenes. The

three bands of script encircling it give the names of the artist, Snello; the caster, Hartwich; and the client, Abbot Berthold.

The century of the Hohenstaufen

Between the mid-12th and the mid-13th century, architecture along the banks of the Rhine flourished in a way that it had not done before. In Cologne alone, twenty-eight new churches were built. When the Hohenstaufen dynasty came to the German throne in 1138 and renewed the empire with Frederick I, also known as Barbarossa I (r. 1155–90), the Rhineland once again became its centre. Frederick II (r. 1212–50) preferred the Upper Rhine, although the focal point of his empire, influenced by the great traditions of antiquity, lay in southern Italy, where the emperor himself can be regarded, according to Emile Bertaux, as the 'true architect and sculptor' of unique buildings such as Castel del Monte in Apulia. Yet the period of the Hohenstaufen did not break with architectural tradition. Flat-roofed basilicas continued to be constructed in the 13th century and at the same time the system of vaulting used in Speyer continued to be followed as a model.

The variety of influences at play in architecture around 1200 is particularly evident in Basel Cathedral (Ills. pp. 145–49). This is a unique example in the Upper Rhine of a nave triforium, copied from S. Ambrogio in Milan; the choir ambulatory (taken down to the level of the crypt here) is borrowed from northern France; while the polygonal plan of the chancel reveals the influence of Burgundian models. The St Gall Portal (Ills. pp. 38, 149) is reminiscent of portals in Petershausen and Zurich Cathedral, while the sculptural decorations are influenced by many different styles. Overall, the architecture of Basel Cathedral shows that its builders were receptive not only to the great Italian

traditions (of, for example, Milan and Modena), but also to the innovative trends from northern France. These two strands are particularly clear in the unconventional combination of pointed and rounded arches. The rectangular dimensions of the bays in the nave counteract the Lombard influence of the walls; the effect – together with the rather dense rhythm of the arcades – is to make the nave seem narrower.

Another example is Worms Cathedral (Ills. pp. 234–37). While the east choir, dating from the second quarter of the 12th century, adapted the monumental system of pilaster-strips and Lombard friezes, the western chancel, which was built before 1181, is the showpiece of a late Romanesque style that adhered to its own special aesthetic tradition, without taking account of the progressive currents in the neighbouring regions west of the Rhine.

The excessive love of ornament and the tendency to break up the walls reflect an almost anti-monumental principle, which seems to reduce the dimensions optically. Motifs inherited from Salian times, such as the dwarf galleries and the finely profiled mouldings of the windows and blind arches, make this architecture seem highly decorative. The ground plan of the west chancel of Mainz Cathedral in the form of a trefoil is also an original idea (see p. 247), although the exterior is still firmly anchored in the Romanesque tradition at the beginning of the 13th century, with its Lombard friezes and round openings.

The Romanesque style survived for an exceptionally long time on the Rhine, where architects managed to resist the attraction of new styles until the mid-13th century. The final break with tradition came in 1248 when the foundation stone was laid in Cologne for a new cathedral modelled on Amiens, at the initiative of

The two-storey central structure was no doubt based on the St Gothard Chapel in Mainz Cathedral (consecrated in 1137), for in both cases the upper storey was reserved to the princes, while their retinue remained on the ground floor. The church of the Holy Apostles in Cologne, dating mainly from the Ottonian and Salian periods, is another good example of Romanesque architecture during the Hohenstaufen period. The three-conch chancel in the east end, which uses the prototype of St Maria im Kapitol, is a spectacular achievement (Ill. p. 301). The almost contemporary building of Great St Martin in Cologne is also based on a trefoil system (Ill. p. 313).

Between 1219 and 1227 the Late Roman martyrium of St Gereon was transformed into a decagon. This new building was one of the most successful achievements of the time, not only because of the way it integrated the Early Christian edifice, treated here as a genuine architectural relic, but also because of the monumental effect of the four-storey interior elevation (Ill. p. 308). Like the trefoil plan of the east end of St Maria im Kapitol, followed by the east end of the church of Holy Apostles, the decagon of St Gereon is an extravagant variant of the centralized plan.

The Romanesque Bonn Minster, built in two stages before and after the turn of the 13th century and based on the ground plan of the earlier Salian building, reveals the influence of Gothic art in its references to the cathedral of Geneva (Ills. pp. 276–77). The abbey church of Maria Laach, which also took a long time to build, was only completed around 1200. While the church is still predominantly modelled on Speyer, the east chancel is more closely related to the one at Bonn Minster. With its strong silhouette, punctuated by six towers, and the motif of Lombard arches encircling the entire structure, Maria Laach is rightly regarded as one of the most beautiful and coherent examples of Rhenish architecture during the period of the Hohenstaufen (Ills. pp. 268–69).

With its triconch chancel plan, Neuss Cathedral, built between 1200 and 1250, is clearly based on the church of the Holy Apostles and Great St Martin in Cologne, while the introduction of

a francophile archbishop. Strasbourg proved less resistant to the new Gothic style from France, which influenced the architecture and sculpture of the southern transept of the cathedral as early as 1225. In fact the transept, which was begun in the Romanesque style before the turn of the century, is a striking example of the conflict between two different aesthetic tendencies, one from Worms, the other from Chartres.

In order to become familiar with the different types of Romanesque architecture along the Rhine, it is necessary to look at the Middle and Lower Rhine. The double chapel of Schwarzrheindorf is an exquisite example of courtly imperial architecture in the early Hohenstaufen period; its painted decoration is also perfectly preserved (Ills. pp. 272–73).

galleries in the central nave is an original, local feature (Ill. p. 333). Internal passages modelled on Reims run round the three conches, dividing the wall into two. The fan-shaped windows are characteristic of a Late Romanesque style that has been termed 'Baroque', while the stepped arcades of the west façade (Ill. p. 332) are reminiscent of the gabled façades of northern Italy (Pavia). Late Romanesque architecture along the Rhine showed a taste for profusely decorated façades, while both the components of this decoration and the general appearance of the façade still owed much to late 11th-century traditions, particularly to Speyer.

Romanesque architectural sculpture on the Upper Rhine also reflects a variety of influences. The Apostle pillars from the former rood screen of Chur Cathedral (Ills. p. 90) are related to the pillars of saints in St-Trophîme in Arles. The Romanesque St Gall Portal in Basel Cathedral clearly borrows from Ferrara and Verona in Italy in the arrangement of the figures, while the decoration of the capitals is reminiscent of Parma (Benedetto Antelami) and Burgundy. Inside Basel Cathedral there are, however, two reliefs showing, respectively, the life of an Apostle and the martyrdom of St Vincent (Ills. pp. 147, 148), which are far superior to the generally rather provincial quality of the St Gall Portal and still seem to echo the forms of Classical antiquity, perhaps transmitted via northern Italian Romanesque works. Throughout Alsace, late 12th- and early 13th-century sculpture was held back by convention, a situation that only ended with the epoch-making breakthrough brought about by the advent of the Gothic master in the lodge of Strasbourg Cathedral.

The limestone fragment of the Siegburg Madonna (Schnütgen Museum, Cologne), which takes up the Byzantine theme of the Hodegetria, is difficult to

place within the chronology of 12th-century sculpture in Cologne. It may date from around 1160. The sculptor may have been familiar with the sculpture of the west portals of Chartres, as the carvers of three slightly later wooden sculptures – the seated angel in Berlin, the Blessed Virgin in the museum of Esztergom (Hungary) and the Madonna and Child in Zülpich-Hoven – originally from Cologne, may have been. Works such as the tombstone of Plectrude – an ethereal figure, with a

shell nimbus and an inscribed band interrupting the regular flow of her drapery – and the tympana of St Cäcilien (Ill. p. 306) and St Pantaleon dating from the mid-12th century should be seen in relation to works from the Ile de France and Burgundy. All these examples show that the sculptors of Cologne were certainly receptive to the new ideas for sculpture in various western European centres.

The capital sculpture, probably dating from around 1220, in the 'paradise' of the church of Maria Laach (Ill. p. 270) is

Below: Fragment of a *Last Judgment* from Mariä
Himmelfahrt in Andernach. Limestone, *c.* 1210.
Rheinisches Landesmuseum, Bonn.
Bottom left and bottom right: Choir stalls with a
devil and an angel. Limestone, *c.* 1210. Bonn
Minster.

remarkable for the quality of its relief
carving, which is reminiscent of
bronze chandeliers of the same period.
Delicately chiselled acanthus foliage
artfully weaves between the animated
figures of animals and humans. The
sculptor, who was obviously inspired by
northern French models, is known as the
Master of Samson after the stone fragment of a torso kept in the monastery
(Ill. p. 270). However, his name probably
does not stand for an individual, but for
a group of sculptors sharing a common
style and using a technique and vocabulary that broke with local tradition. This
highly developed style is related to work
in the Meuse area and to the monumental sculpture of Mantes and Sens. The
inventive imagination shown in both
the two stone choir stall ends in Bonn
Minster and the fragments of a *Last
Judgment* from Mariä Himmelfahrt in
Andernach points in the same direction.
Much the same applies to the Master of
Naumburg, to whom the fragments of
the west rood screen of Mainz, dated
c. 1240, are attributed. Once again,
this name probably stands for a group

of sculptors, using the same workshop
practices and no doubt drawing on the
same sources (see p. 248).

There is a long tradition of goldwork
on the Rhine. In the late Middle
Ages there were close contacts between
the production sites on the Rhine and on
the Meuse, centred upon Cologne and
Liège, where the majority of the workshops were found. One name, which
pervades the entire Middle Ages, represents the very peak of this art form:
Nicholas of Verdun. This artist radically
transformed the great reliquary shrines of
the Meuse region with his monumental
shrine of the Three Magi in Cologne
Cathedral (Ill. p. 295), which can without doubt be attributed to essentially the
same master who created the ambo for
Klosterneuburg near Vienna, completed
before 1181. The traditional, formal decoration has given way here to a new
repertoire of forms drawn from antique
and Byzantine models, which reflect a
realistic approach to the human body
and physiognomy comparable only to
the early 12th-century baptismal font

in Liège. The Anno shrine at Siegburg
(Ill. p. 275) is another example of this
remarkable artist's wide-ranging style.

As discussed earlier (pp. 19–20), the
cult of relics was taken very seriously
in medieval times. For this reason many
sacred objects made out of rare and
precious materials have been found
from this era. In some cases, Byzantine
reliquaries were brought back after the
Sack of Constantinople in 1204, then
dismantled and reassembled in another
guise, such as the reliquary cross
from St Maria ad Gradus in Cologne,
founded by Archbishop Anno (now in
the treasury of Cologne Cathedral).

The crafts techniques developed in
the Meuse and Rhine area, as described
by the monk Theophilus (Roger of
Helmarshausen ?), included crystal
cutting. Because of its transparency,
crystal was often used as a magnifying
medium for looking into the reliquaries
and making the relics more clearly
visible. Reliquaries in the wider sense
of the word included portable altars,
represented here by the example
in Mönchengladbach. (There is a

Below: Cover of a gospel book showing Christ in
Majesty and busts of the winds. Chased and gilt
silver foil, *c.* 1170. Schnütgen Museum, Cologne.
Right: Tombstone of Abbot Gilbert from
Maria Laach. Mosaic, set in slate. Rheinisches
Landesmuseum, Bonn.
Bottom: Portable altar. Oak core, gilt bronze cast,
c. 1160. Cathedral treasury, Mönchengladbach.

similar one in the treasury of Siegburg
Abbey.) The lid is inset with a red and
green porphyry plaque, surrounded by
a sequence of pictorial scenes of the
Eucharist and enthroned apostles so
convincing that they seem to burst
out of their frames. The effect of the
polychrome enamelled ground against
which the gilded bronze engraved figures stand out is captivating. Further
evidence of the technical and formal
skill of the Cologne goldsmiths from
this period can be found in the cover of a
Carolingian gospel book showing a monumental Christ in Majesty in a quatrefoil
mandorla set with precious stones and
framed with enamel plaques.

The mosaic tombstone of Abbot
Gilbert (died 1152), once in the crypt
of the abbey church of Maria Laach, now
in the Rheinisches Landesmuseum, Bonn,
is unique. The portrait-like image, shown
with the insignia of the abbey, is accompanied by an inscription, which can be
translated as: 'Here lies Abbot Gilbert,
outstanding by his birth, outstanding
even more by his achievements, the
measure of virtue for all who officiate as

monks or abbots. He died on 6 August,
when the sun is ruled by Leo. Let him
rest in holy peace. Gilbert, first abbot
of this monastery.'

Unlike architecture, whose monuments still survive, little remains of the
painted decoration that formed an integral part of the Romanesque churches,
whether ornamental or figurative. Even
though its painted decoration has been
heavily restored, Schwarzrheindorf
remains a rare example of a monument
that integrates architecture and painting,
which are in perfect synthesis here,
enhanced by the changing light of day.
The figures of enthroned kings painted
on the arms of the Cross seem literally
to inhabit the niches in which they are
enthroned. The effect is comparable to
the stained-glass cycle of the kings and
princes of the Holy Roman Empire in the
north side aisle of Strasbourg Cathedral
(Ill. p. 199). In both cases the paintings
of contemporary rulers are inextricably
linked to the architecture.

An equally rare, yet very different,
example of Romanesque painting is the
wooden ceiling of Zillis dating from
the mid-12th century (Ills. pp. 78–79).
These paintings were aimed at the
masses of the faithful, which explains
their clearly intelligible language and
closely relates them, in didactic intention
at least, to the sculpted doors of St Maria
im Kapitol in Cologne. The 'picture

bible' of Zillis may have been inspired by the illuminated manuscripts of northern Italy. In any case, illumination no longer played the same role in the Rhineland as it had done in Ottonian and Salian times. The loss of the famous *Hortus Deliciarum* of Herrad of Landsberg (died 1195), Abbess of Hohenburg (Mont Sainte-Odile, Alsace), is therefore particularly sad. This manuscript was decorated with a cycle of 336 illuminations painted in glowing colours, which reflected the theological and philosophical world of the time. The manuscript, which was destroyed by fire in Strasbourg in 1870, is known only from earlier copies, but scientific analysis has shown that the iconography drew in part on Byzantine sources, and the same may be true of the style.

Two major cycles of stained glass demonstrate the quality of the work produced in the first half of the 13th century: one is in St Kunibert in Cologne, the other in Strasbourg Cathedral. One curious example of Strasbourg stained glass, the monumental, enthroned emperor from the old Cathedral (Ill. p. 209), together with a few fragments from the northern transept, can only be understood in

the context of the Byzantine influences of the *Hortus Deliciarum*. It is even possible that the same painters were responsible for both the illuminations and the cartoons for the stained-glass windows. In those with figures of emperors in the northern transept, the sparkle of the glass, cut into vertical, horizontal or diagonal ornamental bands, is almost comparable to the multicolour radiance of the mosaics in Byzantine churches (Ill. p. 199). Like the shrine of the Three Magi, with its stylized drapery, the stained glass of St Kunibert in Cologne dating from 1215 to 1230, of which eight figurative windows survive, is one of the most perfect expressions of Romanesque figurative art on the Rhine. As in Late Romanesque architecture, ornament plays a dominant role. The dynamic geometric and foliage motifs that frame the scenes and the large figures of saints already attain an almost Gothic idealism.

Gothic Art and the End of the Middle Ages

The end of the Hohenstaufen dynasty (1254) led to the Interregnum in Germany, which lasted until Rudolf of Habsburg was elected king in 1273. The territorial princes of the Holy Roman Empire exploited its collapse. The Rhenish archbishops supported the election of William of Holland in 1247 as German anti-king. The Confederation of the Rhenish League of Towns, which gave the towns, particularly those on the Rhine, new power and independence, was set up in 1254. The political and cultural climate in the urban centres, which encouraged individualism and creativity, paved the way for new artistic styles. This is where Gothic art, born in the urban centres of northern France, England and the southern part of the empire, found the right conditions

to develop, while at the same time reflecting a radical social change. For the individualism that accompanied this revival of the towns gave rise to competition: a combative and enterprising spirit in the commercial field, the race for profit, competition between towns and the adoption – and adaptation – of cultural and artistic models. The conquest of a market and the height of a church spire are two things which, if not identical, were certainly analogous in the eyes of these people, who felt a sense of solidarity with their town, while at the same time competing with one another. Because of the prosperity of the town and the security it provided, they managed to widen their horizons through trade and personal contacts. This urban context also provided the practical conditions for the emancipation of the artist, whose clientele included the clergy, the merchant class and the nobility.

Gothic art was the expression of a new sensibility and, above all, of the need to make visible. It was the artist's job to present the message of the Gospels and to 'represent' all the countless saints whom the faithful had known and worshipped only in the form of fragments of relics in the early Middle Ages. In sculpture and painting, the legends of the saints literally took form and became a concrete part of daily life: the Nativity, Passion and Crucifixion of Christ and scenes from the life of the Virgin.

The cathedral lodges:
Cologne and Strasbourg
Before 1248, there were no buildings in the empire that could measure up to the many great French cathedrals. Three buildings are, however, worth mentioning as precursors of the new style of architecture: the *'cappella speziosa'* (consecrated in 1222) Leopold VI built for his own use in Klosterneuburg; the centrally

The painted rood screen of Cologne Cathedral
(detail). Translation of the relics of the Three Magi,
1332–40 (see Ill. p. 293).

planned church of Our Lady in Trier
(begun before 1242); and the memorial
church of St Elisabeth of Thüringen in
Marburg (begun 1235). The last two
were strongly influenced by the architecture of the lodge at Reims Cathedral.
In Marburg, a trefoil chancel in the
tradition of Cologne adjoins a typical
three-aisled hall church.

The real break with tradition did
not come until 1248 when Archbishop
Konrad von Hochstaden (1238–61)
laid the foundation stone for Cologne
Cathedral. The cathedral is both a
sign of approval for French ideas and
a declaration of hostility towards the
Hohenstaufen monarchy. The choice of
a French design was therefore a political
act, just as when Charles IV (r. 1355–78)
built Prague Cathedral some time later. It
was echoed again in the construction of
the collegiate church of Xanten, begun
in 1263 by Friedrich of Hochstaden,
the archbishop's brother, who sought
to emulate the Cologne model. What
interests the art historian most, however,
is the way in which these French models
of High Gothic architecture, generally
known as the Rayonnant style – Amiens
in particular, but also Louis IX's Ste-
Chapelle in Paris and the nave of St
Denis – were adapted for German taste.

The vault of Cologne is only one
metre (about three feet) higher than
Amiens, yet that is evidence enough of
the ambition to surpass its model. In fact,
the architecture of Cologne Cathedral
gives an impression of completeness and
produces spectacular effects. The chancel
seems to open up on every side, the light
floods into the lower level through the
high windows of the radial chapels, into
the middle level through the glazed windows of the triforium (as in Amiens, but
not found systematically in France), and
in particular through the high, double-
lancet windows of the upper bays. The
wall is virtually dissolved, reduced to a

stone skeleton, a frame for the immense
areas of stained glass. The tracery of
circles and trefoils is characteristic of the
Rayonnant style of the Ile de France.

Master Gerhard, the architect of the
choir of Cologne Cathedral, was already
familiar with the construction processes
of a new style which hitherto, and especially in Cologne itself, had only been
partly adapted and was mainly confined
to formal elements. In fact, the building
methods used in Cologne were not modelled on Amiens. In Amiens, stones were
cut in series, meaning that all the stones
of a pier or wall were no longer cut in
relation to their specific function in a
particular place but hewn uniformly and
were therefore interchangeable. This
rational method, which saved time and
money, made it possible to prepare the
stones in the shelter of the masons' lodge
during the cold season, while the actual
construction work took place later.
Yet this new working method was not
imported to the Rhine. Clearly, the
workers recruited to build Cologne
Cathedral, most of whom must have
come from the west, were not yet familiar with this method, which involved
a totally different way of working.

Yet in Cologne, as also in Strasbourg
(see p. 45), there is eloquent proof that
the building process was organized in a
rational way. The architectural drawings
of ground plans and elevations were from
this time on drawn in ink on large strips
of parchment, showing the entire building and partial views. These drawings
had two functions. First, they provided
the workshop with a two-dimensional
view as a basis for drawing templates
on a 1:1 scale and, secondly, they gave
the client a practical idea of what the
finished building would look like. The
second function explains why these outline plans became so large in scale in the
course of the 13th and 14th centuries.
They played a fundamental role in the

genesis of Gothic architecture: they were
necessary because of the complexity of
the plan and construction of Gothic
buildings, while they contributed to the
linear, graphic side of the architecture.

A cathedral does not consist just of
monumental architecture. The sculptures, stained-glass windows, furnishings
and liturgical objects, reliquaries, tapestries and altar-cloths, together with the
choir stalls and the rood screen with
their sculptural decoration, all form an
integral part of the religious building.
Many of these elements have been
destroyed, while other works of art have
been moved from their place of origin
and are now scattered in museum collections over the world. Yet they were far
more than a means of superficial decoration: they formed an integral part of
the church, just as the pictorial cycles of
the lives of the saints are rooted in the
liturgy of a particular diocese or local
tradition. Cologne Cathedral still has

its original choir stalls, its painted rood screens (Ill. p. 293) and, not least, the cycle of the apostles on the piers of the chancel. The great surviving masterpiece is the reliquary shrine of the Three Magi

on the high altar, which attracted pilgrims from far and wide (Ill. p. 295). The design of the wide ambulatory allowed the faithful to circulate round the relics they venerated and gave them direct access to the radial chapels while the canons were celebrating the Mass in the liturgical choir. No money was spared to attract top sculptors to decorate this splendid sanctuary. The courtly ideal that had set the tone in sculpture in the Ile de France and Champagne from the mid-13th century was also adopted in Cologne, although no direct model has been identified west of the Rhine.

These masons' lodges can be regarded as enclaves within their local surroundings. However, it is not known how the sculptors were recruited; the works they have left merely suggest that they were not local artists. Nor did they leave any traces after they departed from Cologne. It is the same situation in Strasbourg. The extraordinary sculpture of the west façade has neither precursors nor direct successors. It is safe to assume that the masons' lodges were centres of innovation that attracted and encouraged unusual talents: craftsmen and artists headed by a master mason responsible for the overall conception. The creative climate of the lodge also acted as a challenge and inspired works that owed much of their originality to the socioeconomic, aesthetic and ideological context in which they came into being. It could be compared to a particular constellation that produces something unique, something that could never happen before and will never happen again.

While the Cologne Cathedral project shows how the Rayonnant style of the French cathedrals suddenly penetrated the empire, the situation in Strasbourg was very different. The

Opposite top left: Tympana showing the *Death of the Virgin*, sculptures on the south portal of Strasbourg Cathedral, c. 1230 (see Ill. p. 202).
Opposite top right: Tympana showing the *Coronation of the Virgin*, sculptures on the south portal of Strasbourg Cathedral, c. 1230.
Opposite bottom left and right: Ecclesia and Synagogue from the same portal at Strasbourg.

Pillar of the *Last Judgment* in the south transept of Strasbourg Cathedral, c. 1230 (see Ill. p. 197).

construction of Strasbourg Cathedral took a long time, interrupted by indecision and new styles that reflected the changing tastes of both the prelates and the local town dwellers. As the building progressed in time, starting with the east end and moving west, signs of a new architectural approach emerged west of the Romanesque chancel, marked by a search for lightness and naturalism, which became fully apparent in 1225 in the southern transept. Unlike some Middle Rhine churches, which only adopted the new Gothic style cautiously and within the context of traditional forms (for example, St Gereon in Cologne, Bonn Minster, Neuss Cathedral), Strasbourg refused to compromise from the outset and juxtaposed both styles. The unknown master mason who was responsible for the southern transept consolidated his authority by taking charge of the entire building project. He had nothing against sculptors who were still steeped in tradition working alongside supporters of the new Gothic style on the tympanum of the *Coronation of the Virgin* on the south portal, where the change of style is particularly striking. The statues of Ecclesia and Synagogue are clearly inspired by the Classical taste of Frederick II, yet stylistically they are inconceivable without a knowledge of French models (Sens and Chartres). At the same time, these two masterpieces of Strasbourg still seem to be isolated works, unique in their delicate, animated physicality, which is reminiscent of some of the figures by Nicholas of Verdun. There is no contradiction between the subtle handling of detail (hair, fabrics and folds of draperies) and expressive pathos. The pillar of the *Last Judgment* in the south transept, which resembles a monumental candelabra, is another sculpture that reveals the goldsmiths' craft, with its superimposed, relief figures that appear

fully three dimensional seen from the front and seem to revolve round their own axis. This sense of the theatrical was a characteristic of the Strasbourg masons' lodge until the 15th century.

There is a large amount of information about the origins of Strasbourg Cathedral. A lodge is mentioned here at the end of the 13th century, although its origins must go back much further. The lodge was both an instrument of church administration with a legal status, which owned property and received revenue and donations, while at the same time it was a workshop headed by a master mason, who was in charge of constructing the 13th-century building. By the end of the 13th century, the lodge was administered only by laymen, burghers of the town, who were also responsible for the financing. Strasbourg was the only imperial cathedral where the burghers alone shouldered the costs, instead of the bishop or the canons who were, after all, members of the nobility. In the 15th century, the cathedral lodge's income actually exceeded the expenditure for paying the workmen. The lodge was headed by an administrator and two or three curators. The master mason had the real responsibility for the construction, however, assisted by a foreman who took over in his absence and was also responsible for making the templates. The stonecutters made up the largest group in the lodge, followed by the blacksmiths, the masons, the carpenters who made the scaffolding, the lifting gear and the roof structure and, lastly, the labourers and crane-operators.

It is possible to reconstruct the different stages involved in building the west front of Strasbourg Cathedral to some extent by studying some important architectural drawings that have survived. Scheme B (Ill. p. 46), on which the 1275 façade project was based, is unique because of the inspired

Scheme B, the basis for the projected west front of Strasbourg, c. 1275 (detail). Musée de l'Oeuvre Notre Dame, Strasbourg.

architectural design and because of its exceptional artistic quality. The architectural drawings and façade decoration by the Strasbourg Cathedral lodge prove it to have been a real treasure house of tracery, more so even than Cologne Cathedral, that influenced not only other neighbouring or more distant lodges but also other craftsmen: glaziers, goldsmiths and illuminators, who adapted these formal inventions in their own techniques.

As in Cologne, the west façade of Strasbourg Cathedral was designed to have two towers. Only the northern tower was completed in Strasbourg, while in Cologne both towers remained unfinished until the 19th century. The principle of the twin-tower façade was restricted to cathedral churches: in Eglise St-Georges in Sélestat, Collégiale St-Martin in Colmar and St Thomas in Strasbourg the façade is surmounted by a single tower. Around 1280, however, instead of following the earlier prototype of the porch-tower (Ill. p. 163), a tall octagonal tower crowned by a pyramid of tracery was added to the parish church of Freiburg-im-Breisgau. The Freiburg tower is a bold act and a real

innovation. Although it may owe some of its details to the Strasbourg lodge, it is an original invention by the Freiburg master mason and could not have been conceived elsewhere, certainly not in Strasbourg, which had a twin-towered façade from Ottonian times. The strong contrast between the openwork of the upper levels of the tower and the almost Romanesque compactness of the lower levels has nothing in common with Strasbourg. On the contrary, a century later the Freiburg tower found an echo in the north tower of the Strasbourg façade. The height of the Strasbourg tower in 1439, which was not to be surpassed until the 19th century, is clear proof of its representative function, a symbol of the pride and prestige of the burghers who had financed the building. No other Rhenish town could compete with this ostentation.

When the Strasbourg Cathedral lodge was elevated to the status of supreme lodge of the empire in 1459, twenty years after the single tower on the façade had been completed, it acquired legal authority and could act as an arbiter. However, work on the site itself was now slowing down. Most of the master masons working on the cathedral during

that period are known by name and it has been recognized that their activities and reputation extended far beyond the regional context. One of them, Hans Hammer, who was the master mason on two occasions, has left a collection of drawings of vaults and lifting gear (now in Wolfenbüttel Library), that greatly improves visual knowledge of the techniques used at the end of the 15th century. Apart from Strasbourg, Hammer also worked in Saverne (lower Alsace) and in Fénétrange (Lorraine), as well as travelling to Hungary. Perhaps he is the same architect mentioned in the archives of Milan as being summoned to its cathedral lodge. Drawings of Strasbourg Cathedral can be found in Thann, Ulm and Vienna, while sketches kept in Strasbourg contain references to the cathedrals of Milan, Orléans and Paris.

It is tempting – but wrong – to assume that the rich tracery decoration was the preserve of cathedrals. In the parish church of Oppenheim, the complex tracery of the large lancet and rose windows creates a decorative façade that fuses graphic and architectural elements (Ill. p. 241). The love of ostentation is very obvious in this building. At the same time, it is worth noting that the formal repertoire circulated from one building site to another, transmitted through drawings or sketchbooks.

The architecture of the mendicant orders

The urban landscape of the late Middle Ages was not only made up of a cathedrals and parish churches. From the mid-13th century, two new religious orders established themselves in the towns, where they lived according to their rules and their mission. They were the mendicant orders of the Dominicans and the Franciscans. Originating in Italy, they devoted themselves mainly to the task of preaching the Gospel to an urban

The Blessed and the Damned, fragments from the former west rood screen of Mainz Cathedral, *c.* 1240. Bischöfliches Dom- und Diözesanmuseum, Mainz.

society that had turned away from religious practice as a result of the decline of the secular clergy. These young, dynamic orders soon enjoyed great success among the urban nobility, who supported them and founded churches for them. Like the Cistercians before them, the mendicant orders believed in the principles of austerity, avoiding any sculptural decoration or monumental emphasis in the form of towers. The roofs of their churches are flat; the only vaulting is above the choir and the sacristy. The Franciscan constitutions of Narbonne of 1260 also forbade any stained-glass windows, except behind the high altar. Two Franciscan provinces extended into the Rhineland from 1239, Colonia and Alemannia, while the Dominican province of Teutonia was established in 1239.

The mendicant orders endeavoured from the outset to create their own architectural style, to distinguish their buildings from the parish churches and the cathedral churches. The hall church, with its flat ceiling above the nave and its elongated choir with narrow, high windows was a type found widely along the Upper Rhine around 1300, although the Dominican church in Guebwiller in

Alsace is still a basilican structure. The innovative concept of the hall church inevitably influenced the system of supports and the way they related to the much-reduced upper wall. After 1250 octagonal pillars without capitals are found in the Franciscan church in Konstanz, while in the church of Rouffach (Alsace) the arcades and the pillars seem to merge into each other. One of the most original creations was the Dominican church in Strasbourg, built in the mid-13th century on a basilican ground plan and enlarged after 1307; apparently the choir was intended to surpass even that of the cathedral. This church, which was destroyed in the Franco-Prussian War (1870–71), was the largest Dominican building in the Rhineland and its engaged, concave-sided octagonal pillars represented a genuine technical innovation.

The Dominican church of Colmar is a flat-roofed hall church with a nave and two aisles (Ill. p. 178). Here, the supports, in the form of bare pillars, fuse perfectly with the rather reduced upper wall area, creating an impression of exceptional spaciousness. The original principles of austerity have given way

here to a different style. Architecturally, the church remains sober, but it is now enriched with sophisticated detail and an abundance of colourful stained glass (Ill. p. 178). Around 1300, the architecture of the mendicant orders was marked by an increasing contrast between the high chancel and the nave, which served as the lay church. This monumental type of chancel, raised higher than the nave, was first seen in the Dominican church of Cologne (destroyed in 1804), although this building had little depth. Between 1261 and 1269 the Dominicans adopted this system in Basel too, followed a little later by Colmar (Unterlinden) and Basel-Klingental. The choir of the Dominican church, built in Mainz between 1271 and 1314, extended the length of seven bays.

Sculpture in the 13th and 14th century
The southern transept of Strasbourg reflects the first flowering of a young art that looked to nature for inspiration. The capitals are now decorated with naturalistic foliage, while the figure sculpture reveals a concern to portray the anatomy of the human body in a realistic way. The capitals in Cologne are

similarly naturalistic, influenced in this case by Reims. Some of the sculptors belonging to a workshop that has been assigned the generic name of the Master of Naumburg probably came from Reims. This workshop was active in Mainz, Naumburg and Meissen, and probably also in Strasbourg. Fragments survive of a *Last Judgment* from the west rood screen of Mainz Cathedral, dating from 1237 to 1239. These most expressive figures, with their grimacing faces, are related to some heads from Reims, although they surpass their models in the intensity of their gestures and mimicry, ranging from the tragic to the extremely comic. The *Last Judgment* fragment, the head with the head band, which must also have come from the west rood screen, and the so-called Bassenheim Rider – St Martin cutting his cloak in two – attributable to the same workshop, are striking examples of the way models could be transposed and profoundly modified. Clearly the sculptors – and their clients – working in the empire attached special value to physiognomy and its characterization. The cycle of the Apostles and the *Virgin in the Rose Garden* (now in the Cloisters, New York) from the rood screen of Strasbourg draw on a different source of inspiration that spread from Paris to Reims and Strasbourg at the same time and bore no relation to the style that inspired the work of the Master of Naumburg.

Several sculpted tombs from the mid-13th century are evidence of other influences. The gilt bronze effigy of the archbishop of Cologne, Konrad von Hochstaden, portrayed with idealized features, could be inspired by the typology of the tomb of Evrard de Fouilloi in Amiens of *c.* 1240. Once again there is evidence that the archbishop who founded the new church looked towards France and adhered to a Classical aesthetic. The pillar statues in the chancel of Cologne, with their elegant, courtly gestures and rich draperies, are also related to this style.

The sculptors of Cologne seem to have enjoyed a kind of regional monopoly. The creator of the recumbent wooden effigy of Count Palatine Henry II in the abbey church of Maria Laach (*c.* 1270), which has recently been restored to its original polychrome colours (Ill. p. 270), comes from their ranks. The choir stall reliefs in Cologne Cathedral also reflect the great artistry of this Cologne workshop. A certain 'Magister Henricus de Colonia' is even mentioned as the creator of a bronze effigy in the collegiate church of St Catherine in Hereford in England.

The sculptor known as the Master of Erminold, after a stone tomb effigy of St Erminold in Prüfening near Regensburg, is not easy to trace. Once again the name probably stands for a workshop, which seems to have begun its activity on the Upper Rhine. The archivolt sculptures on the portal of Basel Cathedral (*c.* 1275) are characteristic examples of this backward-looking, highly expressive style, with its tense, unreal treatment of

the body. Certain other works, in Colmar,
Strasbourg and Konstanz, can also be
linked to the workshop of the Master
of Erminold.

A number of sculptors with different
stylistic approaches worked on the
façade of Strasbourg Cathedral, which
was begun in 1275. Some were familiar
with Parisian sculpture, such as those
responsible for the Wise and Foolish
Virgins (Ill. p. 192) on the right portal;
others were closer to Reims, such as the
creators of the statues of prophets on
the side walls of the central portal. Once
again, it would be pointless to suggest
that there were any strict, formal links.
Instead, the figures of prophets must be
regarded as individual creative achievements. The contacts between these
individual sculptors, brought together
by a high-ranking client to carry out an
innovative programme, were bound to
produce equally individual and innovative works. The profound mysticism of
the prophets was unequalled in its time,
with the possible exception of the work
of the Italian sculptor Nicola Pisano
(*c.* 1220/5–*c.* 1284) or the English
illuminations of the Oscott Psalter.
This Strasbourg community of artists
did not break up completely; some of
them went to Freiburg Cathedral to
work on the porch (Ill. p. 164), while
others contributed to the Gothic sculpture of Worms Cathedral.

The works of architecture and sculpture considered so far were created
within the lodges or in close contact
with them; but the situation soon
changed radically. The new forms of
private devotion and mysticism that
became established in the course of the
14th century, and particularly in the
Rhineland, gave rise to works of art
being produced in individual urban
workshops, which were already organized into guilds. The emotive formal
language of wooden devotional images,
such as figures of Christ with St John,
pietàs and the 'forked' crucifixes – of
which there is an early example in
St Maria im Kapitol in Cologne – spoke
very directly to the faithful. While the
monks and nuns regarded the groups
of Christ and St John the Apostle as an
example of mystical union during their
contemplation and devotions, the pietà,
the image of the Virgin with the body of
the dead Christ on her lap, was an object
of particular veneration and a separate
prayer was addressed to each of the
Saviour's five, bleeding wounds. In style,
these works are related to courtly art and
satisfy similar aesthetic requirements.
There are even some parallels with the
courtly art of the minnesingers, as
reflected in the elegant style of the *Manesse
Manuscript* of ballads illustrated in Zurich
and now preserved in Heidelberg. The
intensity of colour and the use of gold
enhance the sense of sumptuousness.

In the course of the 14th and 15th
centuries, a sculptural group also appears
in Germany that was used as a para-
liturgical cult image in connection
with the Passion: the Holy Sepulchre.

Left: Holy Sepulchre, *c.* 1340; tracery façade, 1578. Freiburg Cathedral.
Below: The Bearing of the Cross (surviving fragment). Terracotta, 1404. Skulpturensammlung, Staatliche Museen Preussischer Kulturbesitz, Berlin.

the Holy Sepulchre in Jerusalem. By contrast, the Entombment group in Mainz Cathedral (1495), corresponds to a type of monumental scene that was widespread in Burgundy and in Champagne in the late Middle Ages.

In the 14th century, a new type of sculpture developed, in the form of the carved, winged altarpieces that were very widespread until the end of the Middle Ages. The earliest examples can be found in Oberwesel (1331), Altenberg (1334) and Marienstatt (c. 1360). In some cases, statuettes are placed inside architectural niches within the shrines. Other altarpieces consist of narrative groups, such as the Bearing of the Cross from Lorch, dating from 1404 and executed in terracotta, a technique much favoured on the Middle Rhine and one that gave rise to works of a very high quality. Works from the same workshop active in the Rheingau include the Lamentation from Dernbach in Westerwald (now in the diocesan museum of Limburg), and the bust of Joseph of Arimathea from Mainz, now in the Hessisches Landesmuseum (1410–15). Even elements of architectural decoration could be

This typological model emerged in Strasbourg around 1340: the scene consists of the outstretched body of Christ on the tomb, with the three Marys bringing the ointments greeted by two angels, while the soldiers on watch are shown in the foreground asleep on the relief of the sarcophagus. This synchronistic contraction of two distinct events following the Crucifixion evokes a scene from a play, set within a niche surmounted by three funereal pediments. There are other, similar groups in Freiburg, Niederhaslach (Alsace), Thann, Vieux-Thann and Basel. The Holy Sepulchre in Konstanz, dating back to the 13th century (Ill. p. 105), adopts the same architectural form as the church of

Madonna and Child, central pillar of the west portal of Freiburg Cathedral, c. 1300.

executed in terracotta, such as the keystones of the cloister of St Stephan at Mainz. This material had the disadvantage of being fragile but the advantage of being fairly easy to reproduce.

From the 13th century on, the Madonna and Child became the most popular cult object and devotional image of all. The Madonna on the central pillar of the west portal of Freiburg Cathedral is particularly interesting because she is probably a replica of the sculpture on the main portal of Strasbourg Cathedral that was destroyed during the French

Revolution. In the course of the 14th century, a more mannered type of Madonna appeared, inspired by courtly taste, of which several examples exist on the Middle Rhine. The larger-than-life wooden figure of the Virgin in the church of St Gereon in Cologne, dating from the 1420s, reveals the influence of the 'Beautiful Madonnas' (*Schöne Madonnen*) of Bohemia, while the small sandstone statue of the Virgin from Zons goes back to works from the Brabant. These two works from Cologne are therefore evidence of the extensive artistic links between the Rhenish metropolis and centres elsewhere. There is still some debate about the origins of a whole group of pietàs (St Lambertus in Düsseldorf, St Alban and St Columba in Cologne). Were these works (like the Beautiful Madonna in the museum in Bonn) imported from central Europe, as suggested by their similarities with the pietà groups in what is known as the 'soft style', or were they executed in the Rhineland? The first hypothesis seems the more likely. Yet a contemporary source tells us that a Beautiful Madonna was imported to Strasbourg from Prague around 1400.

It is now time to return briefly to the cathedral lodges in the second half of the 14th century and examine some of the landmarks of monumental sculpture on the Upper Rhine, dominated by the Parler family. One of the most important representatives of the many branches of this family of masons and architects, found working first in Swabia and then on the Upper Rhine, was Heinrich Parler. He was responsible for the choir in Schwäbisch-Gmünd, the first Late Gothic church in Germany (dating from 1351). Yet the most famous of all was Peter Parler, whom Emperor Charles IV appointed to head the Prague Cathedral lodge in 1353, at the age of twenty-

three. The Parler family did not pursue a uniform architectural style, as is clear from the fact that both the choir of Freiburg and the rebuilt choir of Basel are attributed to them. In sculpture, however, some members of the Parler family developed a narrative style that is clearly perceptible in the triple tympanum of the Collégiale St-Thiébault in Thann in Upper Alsace (Ill. p. 157). The most impressive example of the art of the Parlers in the Rhineland is the console figure of a woman wearing a tall crown of foliage, inscribed with the mark of the Parlers (Ill. p. 306), in Cologne Cathedral. Stylistically, it certainly has some affinities with the lovely archivolt figures of the St Peter Portal at Cologne Cathedral (Ill. p. 289) and with the busts on the triforium of Prague Cathedral. Some conclusions can be drawn from this. In 1387 the architect and sculptor Heinrich Parler left his employment at Prague Cathedral and moved on from Brno to Cologne. It is therefore quite possible that he created both the console figure in Cologne and the Beautiful Madonna that originally surmounted it.

Illuminations and stained glass in the high Middle Ages

The loss of many illuminated manuscripts from the 13th century makes it difficult to give a historical overview of Rhenish painting. For the period with which this book is concerned, the Bonmont Psalter in Besançon library, which may have come from the diocese of Konstanz, is an important document. It contains a cycle of sixteen miniatures on a gold ground showing scenes from the life of Christ, which were executed in southwest Germany. The style is characteristic of what is known as the *Zackenstil* (zigzag style), an idiom sometimes also encountered in sculpture (the apostles on the buttresses of the nave

Bonmont Psalter, *Resurrection of Christ*, soon after 1253. Ms. Français 54, fol. 18, Bibliothèque Municipale, Besançon.

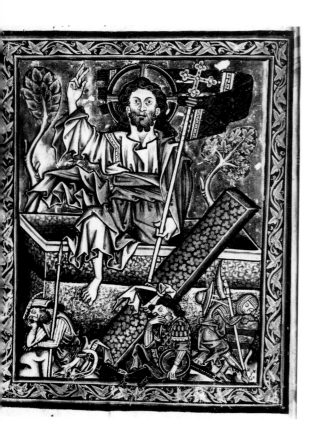

in Freiburg and the Master of Erminold followed a similar style), but more often in illuminations and stained glass. The figures have outsized heads and wear voluminous robes with damp-fold drapery broken up at regular intervals, lending them a gravitas and hieratic severity reminiscent of Byzantine models. The same retrogressive features are found in the gospel book from Mainz, now in the library of Aschaffenburg, while the Bonmont Psalter already reflects a new sensibility, responsive to the elegance of the Gothic style. The zigzag style that was adopted in glass painting in the period between 1250 and 1280 (in the aisles of Strasbourg Cathedral, chapel of the Three Magi in Cologne Cathedral, choir of St Veit in Mönchengladbach, Dominican church in Cologne, now in the cathedral) freed itself from the Late Romanesque formal language that continued to mark this style until the late 13th century.

The glass painters who worked on the nave windows of Strasbourg clearly did not come from the west, as the architect himself had, but lived along the Rhine. There is still some debate as to their number. Stylistically, there are signs of gradual modernization as the building work progressed from east to west. The sculpture workshops, which began with the work on the rood screen (1250–60), followed by the west portals (after 1280), influenced the formal development of the stained glass in the triforium and clearstorey windows. Around 1320, the Strasbourg workshops were inspired by the elegance of Parisian book illuminations, which were in turn inspired by the perspective achievements of Italian artists (Giotto). A major innovation was introduced on the Rhine, in the form of the monumental baldachins that surmount the figures as though they formed part of the actual architecture. The chapel of St Catherine in Strasbourg Cathedral, constructed around 1340, is a perfect example of this interaction between architecture and glass.

Besides working for the large cathedral lodges, the glass painters of the Upper Rhine also produced work for many of the mendicant orders' churches, in Strasbourg itself and in Colmar, Freiburg and Konstanz. The situation in Cologne was much the same. French Gothic painting did not make any real impact here for some time because of the strength of the Romanesque tradition. In the early 14th century, the creators of the stained glass in the cathedral and sacristy of St Gereon finally gave in to the elegance of the new Gothic forms, of which the first examples on the Rhine were the miniatures by the Minorite monk Johann von Valkenburg.

The most striking work in the field of painting in the early 14th century, however, is the monumental figurative and ornamental ensemble painted on the inner side of the rood screen at Cologne Cathedral, consecrated in 1322 (Ills. pp. 43, 293). All the formal experience gained from the treasure house of courtly art – the sophistication, the elegance and suppleness of the figures and, of course, the ornamental repertoire – is combined in this masterly work, whose genesis cannot be satisfactorily explained by its affinities with English or French illuminations, such as the art of Jean Pucelle, or with the painting of Normandy. It is a magnificent example of the complex symbiosis between the new stylistic movements that penetrated northwestern Europe in the early 14th century.

In the second part of the century, the painters from the Upper Rhine continued to be highly regarded. One of them was Nicolas Wurmser of Strasbourg, who was Charles IV's court painter in Prague and may have been responsible for the family tree of the Luxembourg dynasty in Burg Karlstein.

International Gothic
Towards 1400, a new formal language evolved in several parts of Europe, from Siena to Bruges and from Paris to Prague. Even though it was not a uniform style, there are striking similarities between the art produced in regions that were far away from one another. The main features of International Gothic are its extreme elegance and preciousness, derived from the courtly art practised in France since the 13th century. It was closely linked to social structures, so that works of art served as status symbols that reflected the life of ostentation and luxury enjoyed by many of the Western sovereigns. International Gothic was in a sense universal, for it was adopted in sculpture, painting and goldsmith's work, which all used the same idioms despite the different techniques and materials. The memorial gate of Mainz Cathedral (c. 1425), attributed to Madern

Master of St Veronica, *St Veronica with the Sudarium*,
early 15th century. Alte Pinakothek, Bayerische
Staatsgemäldesammlungen, Munich.

Gerthener (Ill. p. 246), with its almost
miniaturized sculpture and architecture,
is a clear example of this sophisticated
and polished formal language that probably originated in the architectural style
of the French courts (Berry, Burgundy).
The term 'soft style' was coined to
describe the preference for softly
flowing forms during this period.

Panel painting

In the 15th century, the main artistic
impetus no longer came from architecture. Painting, especially panel painting,
now came into its own. The painters
were faced with the challenge of satisfy-
ing the needs of private devotion and
the development of the winged altar.
In Cologne, after the overthrow of the
patricians and the introduction of a
democratic constitution in 1396, goldwork on altars was increasingly replaced
by small private altarpieces. The
Cologne illuminator Herman Scheerre
settled in England in about 1400. More
than fifty works have been attributed to
the Master of St Veronica, so-called after
a panel from Cologne. The painting of
St Veronica with the Sudarium reveals the
influence of the art-loving courts of the
Dukes of Burgundy and Berry. Goethe
gave a detailed description of this work
in his 1815 essay on 'Art and Antiquity
on the Rhine and the Main', written
after his stay in Heidelberg to visit the
Boisserée collection. He concluded:
'It exerts an incredible power over the
viewer, because it unites the dual elements
of stringency of thought and pleasing
execution, to which the contrast between
the terrifying, Medusa-like face and the
delicate Virgin and charming children
makes no small contribution.' In his collection of lyrics, the *Westöstlicher Divan*,
Goethe also remembers this icon of the
Lower Rhine as a 'happy image of belief'.
   The most important master of Late
Gothic painting in Cologne, Stefan

Lochner (died 1451), came from
Meersburg on Lake Constance and
worked in Konstanz before moving
down the Rhine and settling in Cologne
in about 1437. In 1442 he executed
various works for the celebrations to
mark the visit of Frederick III (r. 1442–
93), who stopped there twice on his way
to his coronation in Aachen. Lochner's
social status was confirmed by his election to the town council in 1447. That
position also gave him the civic rights
previously denied him as an immigrant.
One of his first works was the altarpiece
of the *Last Judgment* (now fragmented: the
central panel is in the Wallraf-Richartz-
Museum in Cologne, one wing in the
Städelisches Museum in Frankfurt, the
other in the Alte Pinakothek in Munich).
The altarpiece of the Patron Saints of
Cologne, also known as the altarpiece
of the Three Magi (*c.* 1440–45, now in
Cologne Cathedral; Ill. p. 294) is considered his masterpiece. Two opposing
styles come face to face in Lochner's
painting, one more traditional, the other
more progressive and realistic. While
his compositions are characterized by
balanced fields, a contrapuntal play of
lines and a rich palette, the painter has
also sought to give his figures individual-
ity and emotional expression. So there
are analogies with the Master of St
Veronica and with some of the works of
the group of artists active in Konstanz
(for example, the *Nativity* of 1415 in the
Rosgartenmuseum in Konstanz). At the
same time, Lochner was clearly familiar
with the naturalism of contemporary
Dutch painting. This dualism in the work
of one and the same artist was evidently
a deliberate stylistic choice, even if that
notion seems to conflict with the evolu-
tionary view of art history. It would
probably be easier to understand if more
was known about the clients involved
and the terms of the commissions in the
cases of both Lochner and Schongauer.

Late Gothic painting experienced a
remarkable flowering in Cologne. The
Master of the Life of the Virgin (active
between 1460 and 1480), named after a
cycle of paintings intended for the church
of St Ursula (now in museums in London
and Munich) was undoubtedly the most
important painter in Cologne after
Lochner. His work, clearly influenced by
Rogier van der Weyden and Dieric Bouts
(*c.* 1415–75), reveals a strong spatial
sense and a clarity of composition in the
staging of the scenes that mark him out
as an innovator. Noteworthy contemporaries of his include the Master of the
Lyversberg Passion (Wallraf-Richartz-
Museum, Cologne and Germanisches
Nationalmuseum, Nuremberg) and the

Master of the Altar of St Bartholomew (died 1515), who worked almost exclusively for the Carthusians, mainly in Cologne. In any case, Early Netherlandish painting had a direct and decisive influence on the painting of the 'school of Cologne' and was indeed physically present in the city. Around 1460 Rogier van der Weyden executed the altarpiece of the *Adoration of the Magi* for the church of St Columba in Cologne; the workshop of Dieric Bouts created the altarpiece for the church of St Laurenz, which was deconsecrated in 1803 (both works came to the Alte Pinakothek in Munich with the Boisserée collection).

At this time the Upper Rhine region was certainly a major artistic centre, receptive to new trends and responsible for spreading them. For example, the wall paintings in the former Augustine monastery church in Konstanz, dating from c. 1417 (known as the *Council* frescoes), show how Bohemian models influenced local artists. Meanwhile, in 1418 the town counsellors of Basel commissioned Hans Tiefenthal of Sélestat to do a painting, with the proviso that he modelled it on a work in the Carthusian church of Champmol in Burgundy. An artist named Haincelin von Hagenau (Hans Tiefenthal?) joined forces with a colleague from Brussels, Jacques Coene, to illustrate a bible destined for Philip the Bold, Duke of Burgundy. Evidence can also be found of contacts with Italy in the miniatures of the *Toggenburg Weltchronik* (Kupferstichkabinett, Berlin). Other painters in the forefront of artistic production on the Upper Rhine during the 15th century include Jean de Metz, Hans Tiefenthal, Konrad Witz, Hans Hirtz and Martin Schongauer.

The first of these, a contemporary of Lochner, was certainly an important master, although his works are little known (altarpiece of the *Passion* from St Leonard in Regensburg, *Mount Calvary* in the Historisches Museum in Frankfurt), but Tiefenthal was the more remarkable artist. He did part of his training at the court of the Duke of Burgundy and then, soon after becoming a burgher of Basel in 1420, settled in the Alsatian town of his birth, Sélestat. Summoned to Strasbourg by the patricians, he became a town counsellor there in 1444, while also working in Thann and Metz, assisted by his pupil Jost Haller. The famous *Little Garden of Paradise* in the Städelsches Kunstinstitut in Frankfurt has convincingly been attributed to Tiefenthal. This work, dated 1420–30, is a jewel of 'soft style' Gothic painting, harmoniously mingling the sacred and the profane, mystical piety and the atmosphere of the minnesingers. In the lyricism of its composition, it is comparable to a masterpiece of goldwork, the *Little Horse* of Altötting, executed early that century in a Paris workshop. Tiefenthal is also credited with the *Annunciation* in the Oskar Reinhart Collection in Winterthur.

Unlike Tiefenthal, Konrad Witz (1400/10–44/46) broke completely with the International Gothic style. He imbues his powerful figures with a strong sense of physicality, sensed beneath the broken folds of the draperies. These figures, either placed within the earliest examples of landscape painting in the empire, or isolated from the outside world in perspective 'boxes', herald the triumph of sculpture on the Upper Rhine in the second half of the fifteenth century. Witz's formal language presupposes a knowledge of Netherlandish art, in particular the works of Robert Campin, translated into more basic forms.

Very little is known about Hans Hirtz, who is mentioned in Strasbourg from 1421 and died there in 1462 or 1463, except that, according to Wimpfeling, a humanist from Sélestat, he was one of the great masters of the period, together with Schongauer and Dürer.

Konrad Witz, *Synagogue*, c. 1435. Kunstmuseum, Öffentliche Kunstsammlung, Basel.

The Karlsruhe Passion ascribed to him and originally destined for a church in Strasbourg marks the breakthrough to a new form of expression.

Martin Schongauer is rightly regarded as the outstanding 15th-century painter from the Upper Rhine. Born in Colmar around 1430, the son of a goldsmith, he worked both as a painter and an engraver; there are 116 known engravings by him, all monogrammed. It was as an engraver that he became famous and Vasari tells us that Michelangelo copied his *Temptation of St Anthony*. His masterpiece is the *Madonna of the Rose Bower* painted in 1473 for the church of St Martin in Colmar (Ill. p. 177). He imbued the Madonna in the *hortus conclusus*, a much-loved subject in the Rhineland, with a monumentality and presence that make the painting a real icon of Gothic art. Schongauer died in 1491 after completing the cycle of wall paintings in Breisach church (Ill. p. 168). His art was influenced by the Netherlandish masters, both Rogier van der Weyden and Dieric Bouts. No doubt Schongauer was also familiar with the work of Lochner and Tiefenthal. His

beautiful linear art, which can be evaluated by following the development of his graphic work, resembles the work of Lochner in its faithfulness to the traditions of the 'soft style' coupled with the use of a more realistic expressive vocabulary.

Schongauer occupies an important place in the chronology of Late Gothic engraving, after the anonymous Master E. S., who is known to have worked in southern Germany and the Upper Rhine until 1467 and to whom 317 engravings are attributed. Schongauer transformed the technique of engraving into an outstanding iconographic and stylistic medium, thus making a crucial contribution to the spread of this formal language to the workshops of painters, goldsmiths and sculptors. Thanks to Schongauer, copper engraving became more than just a typological vehicle and developed into an art form of its own, reaching its culmination with Dürer. It is also worth mentioning the Master of the Housebook (named after a set of his drawings), sometimes also referred to as the Master of the Amsterdam Cabinet (after his engravings held in Amsterdam), who was active on the Middle Rhine, especially in Mainz, between 1486 and 1500 and may be identical with Erhard Reuwich of Utrecht.

Stained glass and textiles
Stained glass developed along the same lines as panel painting during the 14th and 15th centuries. From 1477 on, the entire production in the southwestern part of the empire was dominated by a Strasbourg association of workshops. This association, centred around the workshop of Peter Hemmel, a native of Andlau born around 1422, was set up by the four glass painters Lienhart Spitznagel, Hans von Maursmünster, Diebold von Lixheim and Werner Störe. In Vieux-Thann as in Strasbourg, these large-scale compositions, with their rich

palette, splendid architectural decoration and great attention to detail, drew on the achievements of Netherlandish painting. The 'Strasbourg windows' became highly sought-after and stained glass from Strasbourg was exported to Lorraine, Swabia, Bavaria, Salzburg and even as far as Andalucia. This tradition was continued by Valentin Busch, creator of the stained-glass windows in Metz Cathedral around 1520, and by Hans von Ropstein in Freiburg.

Painters were also responsible for the cartoons of woollen tapestries, known as *Heidnischwerk*, which represent another form of art produced in the Upper Rhine area (Ill. p. 150). There is evidence of tapestry weaving in Basel and in Strasbourg. This craft tended to be the domain of women, whose clients were the merchant class, the patricians and the clergy. Unlike the great tapestries manufactured in the north, however, the products of the Upper Rhine were not marked and only rarely contained any heraldic motifs that would help to date and place them. Sometimes the dialect of the inscriptions is the only point of reference. The rather popular nature of the narrative scenes certainly gives these examples of secular art – a field in which little research has been carried out – a special charm.

Late medieval sculpture
Sculpture played a large role in the 15th century, in the form not only of monumental works but also of devotional statues and large or small portable altarpieces, then produced in increasing numbers. Most were made of wood. On the Upper Rhine the artists preferred soft wood, willow, while on the Lower Rhine they favoured the harder oak. There were many sculptors' workshops in the large art centres, such as Basel, Freiburg, Strasbourg, Mainz, Cologne and Xanten. Around 1468 a Strasbourg

Below left: Wall tomb of Archbishops Adolf II (left) and Gerlach (right) of Mainz, Counts of Nassau. Eberbach monastery church.
Below right: Strasbourg master, Dangolsheim Madonna. Walnut, *c.* 1460. Skulpturensammlung, Staatliche Museen Preussischer Kulturbesitz, Berlin.

workshop executed the reliefs for the choir stalls of the Frari church in Venice.

The new image of human beings fashioned by Gothic sculpture up to the beginning of the Renaissance is particularly perceptible in the double tomb of Archbishops Gerlach (died 1371) and Adolf II (died 1475) of Mainz, Counts of Nassau, in the monastery church of Eberbach in Rheingau, which was reconstituted in this form in 1707. The original tomb, attributed to the Master of Severi in Erfurt (Erfurt was the suffragan bishopric of Mainz), portrays the body symbolically as an incorporeal, spiritual being, while the Late Gothic tomb slab incorporated in it is a realistic image of a corpse with sunken, portrait-like features and open mouth: there is no idealization

here at all. The statuettes on the gables (the Virgin between St Peter and St Paul) and the reliefs (King David and the prophet Isaiah) are still executed in the soft style of the late 14th century.

Strasbourg's exceptional role in this field between 1460 and 1520 can mainly be explained by the arrival in town of the great sculptor Nicolaus Gerhaert von Leyden. Settling in Strasbourg in 1462 (at the latest), he worked there until 1467, producing a number of masterpieces that introduced an entirely novel, humanist dimension into the sculpture of the German empire. His outstanding work, marked by its formal mastery, inner dynamism and psychological insight (Ill. p. 210), had great influence, revolutionizing sculpture throughout southern Germany. As his winged altar for Konstanz Cathedral was destroyed during the Reformation, it is not possible to know what it looked like, although it certainly had a significant effect on the design of carved altarpieces in southern Germany. In Strasbourg, this sculptor's first work was the Crucifix for the Nördlingen altar produced in the local workshop of an eponymous master (Hans Jouch?). That master is known as the creator of the Dangolsheim Madonna in Berlin, a masterpiece that transcribes the formula of the Beautiful Madonnas of the early 15th century into an outstanding devotional sculpture, with voluminous draperies that go beyond the purely physical. At the same time the creative genius of Nicolaus Gerhaert von Leyden influenced three generations of Strasbourg artists.

Nicolaus of Hagenau, who created the striking figures of old men on the Isenheim altar dating from *c.* 1490 (Ill. p. 186), an altar (now lost) in Strasbourg Cathedral dating from 1501 and the tombstone of Bishop Albrecht of Bavaria in Saverne, may also be responsible for the Nativity group in the Rijksmuseum in

Amsterdam and for a few particularly beautiful statuettes in the chancel of Strasbourg Cathedral. The young Tilman Riemenschneider was familiar with his work, as was Hans Wydyz, the sculptor responsible for altarpiece of the Three Magi in Freiburg Cathedral. Another workshop was active in Strasbourg at the same time. It was headed by Veit Wagner, who created the main altarpiece of St Pierre le Vieux (*c.* 1500), the Mount of Olives for Nikolaus Roeder (1498), the Holy Sepulchre of Obernai and, last but not least, the magnificent Head of Christ in Sélestat (*c.* 1500; Ill. p. 189). These two masters, who were entrusted with a great many commissions, assimilated the innovations introduced by Nicolaus Gerhaert von Leyden, while

The chancel in Strasbourg Cathedral designed by Hans Hammer and completed in 1485 (in the background, the windows of the rulers of the empire in the north aisle, dating from the early 13th century).

developing their own individual style, mingling the trivial with the noble through the use of a very powerful sculptural language and a perfect mastery of its visual effect. A few of the sculptors belonged to the cathedral lodge: Nicolaus of Hagenau (Ill. p. 210) and Veit Wagner, as did Hans von Aachen and Conrad Syfer (?), who was involved in the sculptural decoration of the St Lawrence Portal (Ill. p. 203), and Bernhard of Worms. The lodge recruited craftsmen from neighbouring and remote regions, as the need arose.

The work of the mysterious sculptor and graphic artist known as Master H. L. is a special case. He may have been born in Austria and appears to have been influenced by painters from the Upper Rhine such as Hans Baldung Grien (1485–1545), whose altarpiece in Freiburg Cathedral (Ill. p. 166) clearly influenced the carved altar of Breisach (Ills. pp. 169–71). Yet the sculptural style of Master H. L. stands outside the traditions of Upper Rhenish art, even though willow, the wood commonly used in this region, was a most appropriate medium for his eccentric forms. This artist no doubt came to Breisach at the invitation of the town council.

On the Lower Rhine, Kalkar was an important centre for Late Gothic sculpture, which developed its own idiom there. During what was called the 'Dark Age' in Cologne, the period around the middle of the 15th century, neither Konrad Kuyn, a highly regarded sculptor in stone and master mason of the cathedral lodge since 1445, nor Tilmann van der Burch produced any significant works. The first genuine creative talent to emerge there was Master Arnt, mentioned in Kalkar from 1460 as *bildesnider* (wood carver), where he executed the altarpiece of St George around 1480 and the shrine and predella of the high altar in St Nikolai from 1488 to

Henrik Douvermann, Tree of Jesse from the altar
of the Seven Sorrows of the Virgin, 1518–22.
St Nikolai, Kalkar.

1492 (Ills. pp. 337–39). Like his contemporary Nicolaus Gerhaert von Leyden, he was receptive to the art of the great Netherlandish painter Rogier van der Weyden and familiar with the sculpture in Utrecht, while remaining more indebted than him to the elegant forms of the 'soft style'. Other works can be attributed to him, including the choir stalls in the Minorites' church in Cleves and the high altar with the shrine of St Viktor in Xanten Cathedral.

Another member of the Kalkar School was Henrik Douvermann, active in Cleves from 1510, who then became a burgher of Kalkar, where he executed the altarpiece of the Seven Sorrows of the Virgin for the church of St Nikolai (1519 to 1522). His virtuosity is apparent in his depiction of the Tree of Jesse, which is also the subject of his masterpiece, the altar of Our Lady in Xanten (Ill. p. 336). Douvermann's work combines Late Gothic idealized forms with a modern sense of physicality. Yet the real breakthrough to the art of the Renaissance only came with Arnt van Tricht, who came to Kalkar from Antwerp in 1540 (Ill. p. 339).

The art of the goldsmiths
Goldsmiths created unique works of art in the Rhine valley, within not only the empire but also Europe in general. The workshops carried out commissions for the clergy, producing liturgical objects such as chalices, patens, monstrances, reliquaries, as well as secular objects such as cups, bowls and cutlery in great numbers. Some goldsmiths, including Urs Graf the Elder of Basel, also made the moulds for medals, coins and seals. The precious materials with which they worked contributed to the high social status these artists enjoyed. In Cologne, where goldsmiths had been organized into guilds since the 12th century, they occupied administrative posts and became magistrates or town counsellors. Even the episcopal and princely authorities offered this craft and its representatives favourable conditions. In Konstanz, the goldsmiths' workshops were also commissioned to work for the monasteries of St Gall and Einsiedeln. In 1442 the city of Frankfurt commissioned Cologne goldsmiths to make goblets and vessels to mark the occasion of Frederick III's visit, and in 1477 the same emperor commissioned valuable presents for Marie of Burgundy, bride of his son Maximilian and heir to the Netherlands. In Strasbourg, one of the centres for goldwork, no fewer than 90 master goldsmiths are recorded between 1450 and 1530, while there were 80 in nearby Basel. The goldsmiths' workshops also flourished in the other regions of the Upper Rhine, in Konstanz, Speyer, Freiburg, Colmar and Heidelberg.

The Frankfurt fairs helped to market these luxury products. As in past centuries, the goldsmiths' craft still involved a lot of travelling: the goldsmith Erasmus Krug, who came from Nuremberg and settled in Strasbourg, also kept up his contacts with the silver mines of Graubünden and the canton of Uri. Georg, Paul and Caspar Schongauer came to Colmar from Augsburg.

Unfortunately, only a tiny proportion of these medieval works of art have survived today. Nothing at all remains of the treasures from Konstanz, Strasbourg or Speyer cathedrals. A book cover by a Strasbourg master around 1270, showing the influence of Parisian sculpture, was intended for the abbey of St Blasien in the Black Forest but now rests in St Paul in Lavantthal (Kärnten). The reliquary commissioned by Rudolf von Hallwyl before 1470 (Ill. p. 150) is the product of a Strasbourg workshop, while the reliquary by Peter Berlin in St Stephen's Church in Breisach is a fine example of the ornate Late Gothic style (1496; Ill. p. 172).

Hans Baldung Grien, *Death and the Maiden*, 1517.
Kunstmuseum, Öffentliche Kunstsammlung, Basel.

From the Renaissance to the Industrial Revolution

There is no real justification for referring
to 16th-century art as 'Renaissance'. In
fact, the northern European countries
were not looking back to antiquity, as
Italy and even Augsburg were. Augsburg
had close contacts with Italy because of
the Fugger family's love of all things
Italian. In towns such as Cologne and
Mainz, for instance, the legacy of antiquity meant old Roman ruins or everyday
Roman objects, which were not related
to any aesthetic ideal, as they were in the
case of the humanist circles of Florence
or Padua. Nor is the term 'Renaissance'
an apt designation for the innovations
that emerged in northern European
painting soon after 1500, and at a rather
later date in architecture. In fact, the
work of both Baldung and Grünewald
reveals a new approach to the traditional
iconography, marked by the use of bold
colours and a new way of treating nature
and the human figure. Master H. L., who
also belonged to this generation, was
discussed in the last section because
his sculpture was still anchored in the
traditions of the Late Gothic carved
altarpieces. However, in terms of formal
exuberance, he is closer to the Mannerists
or even to the pioneers of the Baroque.
Once again, the use of traditional termi-
nology and the dogmatic division of
art history into periods and styles is
intended merely to create a framework
and must not be taken too literally.

Painting during the Reformation
Hans Baldung (called Grien) was born in
1485 in the small town of Schwäbisch-
Gmünd. For many years it was assumed
that he trained in Strasbourg, although
today it seems more likely that he
learned his craft in a Swabian workshop.
He is unusual in that he developed a
personal style and freed himself from

the traditions of the Upper Rhine at
an early age. His travels took him to
Strasbourg and to Albrecht Dürer's
workshop in Nuremberg. Yet he mainly
worked in the Upper Rhine area: in
Strasbourg, which gave him citizenship
in 1509 and from where he ran his own
workshop, and in Freiburg, where he
executed his masterpiece, the altarpiece
for the cathedral, from 1512 to 1516
(Ill. p. 166), around the same time as
Grünewald was creating the Isenheim
altar. Baldung's paintings are inspired
by a strong feeling for nature and the
human body, features that are also apparent in his sketches. With the advent of
the Reformation in Strasbourg, which
he supported, and from the time that he
was no longer working for the clergy, he
began to develop his own, very personal
style. His palette became increasingly
intense and bold, while he also gave free
rein to his artistic temperament, to his
fascination with the demonic and the
irrational and with subjects mingling
Christian and pagan motifs. These
paintings, like his masterly woodcuts
for book illustrations, were clearly to
the taste of a sophisticated clientele,
who regarded art as an end in itself, with
no religious or secular function except
perhaps that of reflecting the artist's
inner world. Just as he used unusual
colour combinations in his paintings,
he employed inventive forms in his
graphic work. Baldung's oeuvre is
worthy of comparison with the work
of Grünewald and Dürer, a close
friend, and there is no question that
Schongauer's engravings also inspired the
young artist. Yet all these references are
overshadowed by Baldung's own unique
creative talent, which cannot be classi-
fied or interpreted simply in terms of
'German' or 'Upper Rhenish' features.
Links of this kind can only be identified
in rare cases, in relation to a specific
motif or characteristic form.

The works of the German painter
Mathis Nithart Gothart, called
Grünewald, reveal an entirely different
personality, even if they inspired
Baldung. Unlike him, however,
Grünewald, who worked not only as
a painter but also as an architect and
hydraulic engineer, was not seeking to
develop an artistic language of his own.
His art is inspired more by a spiritual
longing, a keen sense of emotion rooted
in the mysticism of the 14th century,
which is expressed with an extremely
heightened use of colour. Stefan Lochner
was also a great colourist, but he kept
within the conventions of naturalistic
lyricism and courtly poetry. Grünewald
is closer to Hans Holbein the Elder

Tobias Stimmer, *Self-portrait, c.* 1563. Museum
zu Allerheiligen, Schaffhausen.

(c. 1465–1524) in his artistic intention.
It is less a vision of art than a vision of
the world that he unfolds before the
spectator. After 1508 he painted and
drew seven Crucifixions. They are stages
in a continuous attempt, unique in the
history of painting, to comprehend
one of the oldest and most fundamental
subjects of Western and medieval figurative painting. In Grünewald's vision,
the martyred, cruelly distorted body of
Christ becomes a tragic symbol of evil in
a materialistic world, in which the pitiless
portrayal of the human aspect of Christ
in all its humiliation and ugliness in fact
enhances the Saviour's spiritual beauty.
In the 1510s, Grünewald worked as an
architect for the Archbishop-Elector of
Mainz, Uriel von Gemmingen, who lived
in Aschaffenburg, before creating the
great winged altar at Isenheim around
1512 (Ills. pp. 181–85). The altar was his
masterpiece, at the same time a continua-
tion and an enhancement of his earlier
attempts to depict the Crucifixion; he
surpassed himself and all others in the
extraordinarily dramatic panel of the
Resurrection, in the new feeling for
nature revealed in the landscapes and
in the scene of the Nativity.

By the time Emperor Rudolph II
decided he wanted to buy the Isenheim
altar around 1600, the name of this artistic genius had been forgotten. The altar
remained in southern Alsace, known only
to a small circle. Hans Holbein the Elder
(born in Augsburg) spent some time in
the winter of 1516 to 1517 in Isenheim,
where he seems to have worked for the
Antonines. During an earlier stay in
Alsace from 1509 to 1510 he had painted
an altarpiece for the Mont Sainte-Odile
convent in which, for the first time, he
placed the figures within an ornamental
Renaissance frame.

His son, Hans Holbein the Younger
(1498–1543), was also born in Augsburg
and his first works, executed for the

printer Johann Froben in Basel, date from
1516, when he was eighteen years old.
In 1519 he was accepted into the Basel
guild of painters; a year later he decorated the façade of the 'Zum Tanz' house
built for a goldsmith; and in 1520 the
town commissioned him to decorate the
council chamber. During his first visit
to London in 1526 he was introduced
to the humanist Sir Thomas More
through the Dutch humanist Erasmus
of Rotterdam. He remained in London
for eighteen months, returning to Basel
in 1528, a year before the outbreak of
iconoclasm inspired by the Reformation.
In 1532 Holbein went back to London,
where he was entrusted with numerous
commissions by the nobility and members of the court. Holbein, who was
employed by Henry VIII from 1536,
carried out a wide variety of tasks,
including engravings for book illustrations, projects in the applied arts, stained
glass, wall paintings, personal drawings
and paintings. His clients ranged from
parvenus, such as the merchant Jakob
Meyer who rose to become mayor of
Basel (a double portrait of him and his
wife dating from 1516 is in the Kunstmuseum, Basel) to the King. He excelled
in portraits (Ills. pp. 24, 27), managing
to penetrate the psychology of his sitters
and to create perfect harmony between
the architectural framework and the
figure posed within it. The society portrayed by Holbein is the generation of
patricians and intellectuals who, in the
name of humanism and the Reformation,
helped bring about a radical transformation of Europe. In 1543, shortly before
his planned return to Basel, Holbein
died of the plague in London.

In his self-portrait in the Schaffhausen
museum, the painter Tobias Stimmer
reveals both his gloomy temperament
and his remarkable talent as a portrait
painter. Yet his paintings are little known.
Only seven of them have survived; the

allegorical wall paintings in the palace of
Baden-Baden have disappeared and the
famous murals on the façade of the 'Zum
Ritter' house in Schaffhausen (1568–70)
can no longer be regarded as authentic
since being restored from 1937 to 1939
(Ill. p. 130). Only the painted decoration
of the Astronomical Clock in Strasbourg
Cathedral, where Stimmer lived from
1570 until his death in 1584, has survived,
confirming the Mannerist tendency
of his work. Stimmer also worked for
printers in Basel and produced a number
of engravings for book illustrations.

The 'Welsch' style
The Italian style known as 'Welsch' made
sporadic inroads into the architecture
and sculpture of the German Empire. On
Lake Constance, the façade of the town
hall at Überlingen (1490–94) is the first
example north of the Alps of this Italian
rustic style, although the actual architecture still adheres to Gothic traditions.
The first example of purely Renaissance
architecture in Germany appears, not
surprisingly, in Augsburg, which had
close contacts with northern Italy and

Venice: the Fugger family chapel in the church of St Anna (consecrated in 1518). The sculptor Hans Backoffen from Mainz played an interesting part during this time of stylistic change. His tomb for Archbishop Uriel von Gemmingen (died 1514; Ill. p. 248), commissioned by the very progressive art lover Cardinal and Archbishop Albrecht of Brandenburg, who also employed Grünewald, is an interesting mixture of Late Gothic elements (such as the baldachin) with a stylistic repertoire borrowed from the northern Italian Renaissance; here the figures already display a new sense of corporeality. The Renaissance reached Cologne via the Netherlands. The rood screen of St Maria im Kapitol (Ill. p. 300) is the work of a court artist from Mechelen called Jan van Romme (1523) and the epitaph to the canon of the cathedral, Jakob von Croy (died 1516), was also imported from Mechelen to the treasury of Cologne Cathedral.

While the Italian Renaissance first began to infiltrate the regions north of the Alps through the medium of painting, it was also gradually adopted in printed works, which employed the new ornamental vocabulary in the title pages and in the frames around the engraved illustrations. In the 1530s, stylistic features derived from Lombard and Venetian architecture became popular; it was not, after all, that remote from the exuberant spirit of Late Gothic art – one reason why the new Renaissance architecture was accepted in Germany. In France its acceptance depended on the taste and will of the sovereign; in Germany, however, this new style offered a wide spectrum of possibilities. During this first stage, in the period between 1520 and 1550, architecture was still very much under the influence of the Gothic tradition in both design and construction, while the new Renaissance forms were increasingly

adopted for the decoration (see the old guardhouse in Colmar, Ill. p. 174), although the figurative decoration still proved very troublesome. The same weaknesses can be seen in the volume published in 1537 by Heinrich Vogtherr the Elder (who was active in Strasbourg as a painter, ophthalmologist and printer), which describes the decorative repertoire of the Renaissance for the first time in Germany, even if in a very simplified form. Nonetheless, this 'strange and wonderful' manual for sculptors, painters and carpenters, entitled *Frembds und wunderbars Kunstbüchlein*, became very popular. The crafts, which had their own traditions, transmitted through the lodges, adopted these innovations with some reluctance and difficulty. They remained faithful to the aesthetic principles of the Gothic style and at times still showed an open admiration for the works of past centuries. Even such a scholar as the doctor and mathematician Walter Rivius, who published the German version of Vitruvius that appeared in Strasbourg in 1547, was full of praise for not only Milan Cathedral (like the Italian editor of Vitruvius, Cesare Cesariano, before him) but also one of the Gothic corbelled turrets of Strasbourg Cathedral. Tobias Stimmer wrote under the engraving of the Strasbourg Ecclesia, with a note of admiration: 'Here we can see the old art.' Hans Schweiner, who produced an early example of the new style with his octagonal tower in the church of St Kilian in Heilbronn (completed 1529), described the Romanesque churches of Frankfurt and Mainz as the works of 'the ancients'. Yet it was in the 1544 statutes of the Strasbourg carpenters' guild that the term 'Welsch' style appears for the first time. However, this theoretical interest in the new Italian style did not find an immediate response in the actual architecture of the Upper Rhine. As a

book, the illustrated treatise was regarded more as a vehicle of culture and science in intellectual circles than as an instrument of artistic practice. North of the Alps, therefore, there is a time-lag between the theory, usually drawn from foreign sources, and the actual practice of an art or craft. The only exception is found in urban furniture.

'German Renaissance': Schloss Heidelberg

Only in a second phase of building, beginning around the middle of the 16th century, were the theories of the Renaissance put into practice by architects. The period between 1555, the date of the religious Peace of Augsburg, and 1618, when the devastating Thirty Years' War broke out, was a time of intense building activity on the banks of the Rhine. There were examples of not only secular architecture – town houses for the merchant class and public buildings – but also palatial buildings inspired by foreign models that were commissioned by princes. The rivalry was certainly not as acute as it eventually became a

century later, but even at this stage there were signs that architecture was becoming the rhetorical language of power.

The palatine electors' residence in Schloss Heidelberg was a real showpiece of this innovative trend. The courtyard façade of the Hall of Mirrors built by Elector Frederick II from 1544 is evidence of the German prince's efforts to outdo the Italians, although the massive arcades, which were originally surmounted by another level of loggias, are more reminiscent of the Romanesque than of 15th-century Italian Renaissance.

The most original German Renaissance building, in terms of both inventiveness and aesthetic quality, is the wing called the Ottheinrich Building (Ill. p. 222) constructed between 1556 and 1562/66 and named after its initiator, the Count Palatine and Elector Ottheinrich. The name of the architect is not known, but he most probably came from the Netherlands, while the rich decoration of the façade is the work of sculptors from Mechelen – Anthoni and Alexander Colin and Hans Engelhardt. The sumptuous, richly articulated and

decorated red sandstone façade overlooking the courtyard shows little respect for the rules of Italian architectural theory as laid down by the 1st-century BC Roman architect Vitruvius in *De architectura* and updated by Sebastiano Serlio in the 16th century – despite the fact that the famous Biblioteca Palatina created by the humanist-trained count palatine contained both an Italian and a Nether-landish edition of Vitruvius. The sculptural programme was evidently designed to enhance its builder's personal prestige and emphasize his rank, as shown also by the inscription and coat of arms over the main portal, crowned by a portrait bust of Ottheinrich. Architecture becomes an affirmation of power, as shown by the fact that the elector ostentatiously included himself in the ranks of the illustrious men in this allegorical sculptural programme.

The Friedrich Building constructed by Elector Frederick IV (1583–1610) of Wittelsbach from 1601 to 1607 was intended for the same representational purpose. This northern façade of the Schloss has a good view of the town (Ills. pp. 220–21), while the façade overlooking the court adopts Ottheinrich's idea of glorifying the dynasty, here in the form of a row of ancestors going back to Charlemagne and leading up to Frederick IV himself. Unlike the earlier wing, however, the monumental statues do not form an integral part of the façade; instead they seem to stand out from their niches so that the architecture, however strongly profiled, seems merely to serve as a backdrop to magnify their importance. This time the architect, Johann Schoch, adhered to a strictly canonical system of elevation. Schoch had already designed the summer residence of Gottesaue (now in the urban precincts of Karlsruhe) for the margrave of Baden-Durlach and he may also have been responsible for the Hôtel du Commerce

The Waag, Nijmegen, 1612 (early photograph, see p. 341).

(former town hall) in Strasbourg (from 1583), although here the emphasis on the horizontal is very distinct from the vertical accents of the Friedrich Building. In its monumentality and strictly canonical order, the Hôtel du Commerce is without doubt a masterpiece of 'Welsch' architecture on the Upper Rhine.

At the same time as the Friedrich wing was being erected in Heidelberg as a splendid symbol of princely power, another building rose in 1606 on the right bank of the Rhine, not far from the mouth of the Neckar: the fortress of Friedrichsburg, with its mighty citadel and the royal seat of Mannheim, constructed on a chessboard plan (Ill. p. 64). The palatine elector, as head of the Protestant Union, founded this complex of buildings primarily as a strategic measure in anticipation of the political tensions between the two faiths, which sparked off the Thirty Years' War twelve years later.

Late Gothic and Early Baroque art
Germany was slow to accept innovations in religious architecture. Gothic traditions, mingled with traces of the Romanesque, still lived on in the Rhenish Jesuit churches, such as in Koblenz (1613–17), Molsheim in Alsace (1615–17) and the church of St Mariä Himmelfahrt in Cologne (1618; Ill. p. 319), and later still in Bonn (1686). All these buildings are marked by a historicist style inspired by the spirit of the Counter-Reformation, which sought to establish a direct link between the Middle Ages and the 17th century. The situation was very different in Konstanz, where the Jesuits began to build a church modelled on Il Gesù in Rome in 1604. The Jesuit church in Düsseldorf (now the parish church of St Andreas), begun in 1622 and based on the palace church of Neuburg on the Danube (the former residence of the new dynasty of rulers

on the Lower Rhine), marks the turning point towards Early Baroque, a style that later flourished in southern Germany. At the same time an individualist, Classical formal language gained ground in the Rhenish Netherlands: for example, in the Waag in Nijmegen market square (1612; Ill. p. 341) and in the town hall of Delft (1620; Ill. p. 348).

The overlap of stylistic elements between the Late Gothic and the Early Baroque period, evident in so much of the religious architecture of the time, was also apparent in sculpture. When the sculptor Jörg Zürn created his masterpiece, the carved high altar (1613–18) for the church of St Nikolaus in Überlingen in Lake Constance, he was clearly drawing on two sources. One was the restless style of Master H. L., the other was the bizarre architectural designs of Wendel Dietterlin (c. 1550–99) from Strasbourg, whose treatise on ornament, *Architectura von Austeilung, Symmetrie und Proportion der Säulen* of 1593 was extraordinarily successful. The architectural fantasies of the author, who also worked as a painter and façade decorator, were still rooted in the formal repertoire of the Late Gothic world.

Political events in Germany brought the prosperity of the 16th and early 17th centuries to an end. The new artistic style that appeared towards

the mid-16th century and came to such prominence in the architecture of Schloss Heidelberg was interrupted. The Thirty Years' War that dominated the first half of the 17th century, followed by the effects of Louis XIV's expansionist policy, made this century a sombre time for the Rhineland, which took a long time to recover.

The situation in the Netherlands was very different; the 17th century was a period of unequalled political, economic and artistic success there. So it is not surprising to find a great artist in the Rhenish part of the Netherlands. The outstanding work of Jan Vermeer of Delft (1632–75), whose genius was only discovered by later generations, marks a highpoint in the history of European art. His *View of Delft* (c. 1660; Ill. p. 352), which was praised by Marcel Proust, is a good example of his atmospheric art, revealing his sense of colour, light and form.

Baroque architecture: Rhenish residences
The Rhineland did not experience an artistic flowering again until around 1700, when the electors and margraves, who were keen to compete with the architecture of foreign courts, primarily of course Versailles, undertook a large building programme because of the prestige it gave them.

After the destruction of Baden-Baden, Margrave Ludwig Wilhelm (known as Ludwig the Turk; 1677–1707) founded the residential town of Rastatt, which was the first Baroque complex of buildings on the Upper Rhine. In the course of time the palace, based on plans drawn up by Domenico Egidio Rossi, grew from a simple hunting lodge into a huge, three-winged structure on the model of Versailles (Ill. p. 212). The town is linked to the palace by three converging roads, which are intersected by what is now the Kaiserstrasse, with the town hall and Catholic parish church defining the centre of the town.

In 1715, Margrave Charles William of Baden-Durlach followed the example of Rastatt by founding a new residence in Karlsruhe (see pp. 69, 216). His predecessor, Friedrich Magnus, had begun to build a summer residence in Basel in 1698, according to a plan based largely on the *Cours d'Architecture* written by the

French court architect and art theoretician C. A. Daviler published in 1691.

French architecture was very influential during the Baroque period, a time when the European princes went into a building frenzy, what Fénélon called a *'fureur de bâtir'* and what the Schönborn family ironically described as their special vice, the *Bauwurmb*. Robert de Cotte (1656–1735) played a key role in spreading the French style. At the age of eighteen he entered the service of the king, but had probably already worked for his brother-in-law Jules Hardouin-Mansart, the *premier architecte du Roi* or first royal architect. He became director of the Royal Academy of Architecture in 1699, was appointed to succeed Hardouin-Mansart as first royal architect in 1708 and became the intendant of royal buildings in 1719. He oversaw the completion of many commissions for the nobility and the court, as well as for the king himself, such as the

dome and esplanade of the Invalides in Paris and the chapel of the Palace of Versailles. However, he is best known for promoting the French architectural style during the transition from the splendours of Baroque to the age of Rococo. His high-ranking German clientele, no doubt found partly through the good offices of Hardouin-Mansart, included the archbishop and elector of Cologne, Joseph Clemens (1688–1723) from the Bavarian Wittelsbach family, who had begun to build a new electoral palace (now the university) in Bonn in 1697. Robert de Cotte's drawings, executed in 1714, transform the strict, Italianate concept into an open, Rococo arrangement with a formal garden. The work proceeded apace, initially directed by Benoît de Fortier, then by Wilhelm Hauberat, but always in close consultation with Robert de Cotte, who carefully followed its progress. Apart from the architecture, the choice of artists also reflects the supremacy of the Parisian style: the painter Claude Audran, the stucco-worker Oppenord, the ebonist Boulle, and the sculptor Rousseau, among others. At the same time Robert de Cotte was doing drawings for the palaces in Poppelsdorf, Godesberg and Brühl (see p. 65). Another major Parisian architectural project on the Rhine is associated with his name: Schloss Rohan, belonging to the prince-bishops of the Rohan family in Strasbourg (Ill. p. 207).

After being appointed archbishop of Strasbourg in 1704, Armand-Gaston de Rohan, a member of one of the most illustrious families of France, decided to build a new, noble residence, which would outshine even his palace in Paris. The bishop commissioned Robert de Cotte – who had already worked for him on the restoration of his palace in Saverne after it had burned down in 1709 – to draw up the plans. Schloss Rohan became an ideological symbol

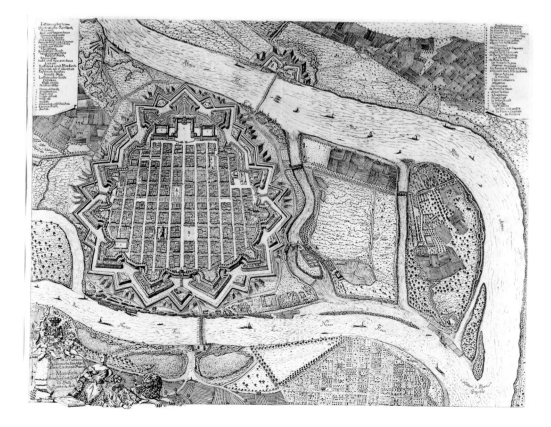

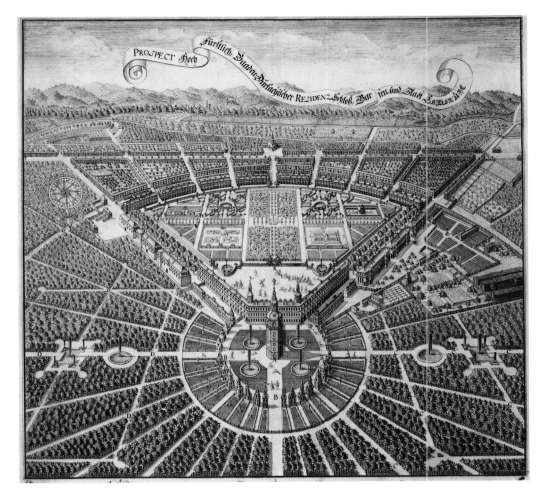

of French dominance in Strasbourg. The architectural plan drawn up by the first royal architect and executed by Joseph Massol starting in 1731, as well as the decoration created by such eminent sculptors as Robert Le Lorrain and Jean-August Nahl, are a perfect expression of the French taste and style. The royal chamber is remarkable for its Rococo decoration. Schloss Rohan situated on a narrow, irregular site between the river and the cathedral, dominates the old town of Strasbourg with its size and elegance.

Of the three religious electorates, Cologne, Mainz and Trier, Mainz is the largest, with about 400,000 inhabitants. The prince-bishops of the Schönborn family made it famous in the 18th century; one of the most impressive members of that family was Lothar Franz, who was both Bishop of Bamberg and Archbishop and Elector of Mainz (r. 1695–1729). A great amateur and passionate patron of architecture, he took part in designing his own projects. In 1704, he summoned the officer-cum-engineer Maximilian von Welsch to direct the work on the fortifications of Mainz and also to build a Rhenish replica of Louis XIV's Marly-le-Roy, in the form of the Schloss Favorite outside the city gates (destroyed in 1793).

Maximilian von Welsch was also responsible for the first plans for Schloss Bruchsal. This bishop's residence was commissioned by another member of the Schönborn family, Damian Hugo, prince-bishop of Speyer, and built from 1722 (Ills. pp. 218–19). The elegant staircase, however, is the work of the diocesan architect Balthasar Neumann, active in Würzburg, who modelled it on a design by his predecessor, Anselm Franz Freiherr von Ritter zu Grünstein. In both religious and secular architecture (such as the Hofkirche of Würzburg,

the pilgrimage church of the Vierzehnheiligen and the abbey church of Neresheim), Neumann revealed a strong sense of the play of light in space. In Bruchsal, the staircase, rising from a rectangular vestibule, sweeps up in two curved flights to the piano nobile, giving the impression of a gradual ascent from darkness to light. This theatrical quality is enhanced by the decoration, which is, unfortunately, only a replica now. The original *trompe-l'œil* painting in the dome of the stairway, which was the work of the fresco painter Johannes Zick and depicted the glorification of the bishopric of Speyer (Ill. p. 219), appears as a visual extension of the colonnades. By contrast, the wall painting of a rocky landscape by Giovanni Francesco Marchini makes the indirectly lit central ground-floor area circumscribed by the stairs look like a grotto. The drawings for the building of Ehrenbreitstein fortress (1739–48) and for Schönbornlust (1748–52), the palace near Koblenz of the elector of Trier, Frank Georg of Schönborn, are also attributed to Neumann. His masterpiece, the staircase at Brühl (Ill. p. 280), must not be forgotten.

The electorate of Cologne was ruled for five generations by archbishops from the Bavarian Wittelsbach dynasty. The great project of Augustusberg Palace in Brühl, for which Elector Clemens August (r. 1723–61) laid the foundation stone in 1725, after his predecessor Joseph Clemens had recruited Robert de Cotte to draw the plans (see p. 64), was initially built according to a design by Johann Konrad Schlaun. But after Clemens August's brother, the Bavarian Elector Charles Albrecht, criticized the project as not being modern enough and recommended the Munich court architect François Cuvilliés the Elder, a pupil of Blondel, the plans were radically altered and the project transformed from a castle surrounded by water to a French-style country residence. The staircase (Ill. p. 280) is by Neumann. As in Würzburg and Bruchsal, he again opted for a design that demonstrated his scenographic talent. Starting from the ground floor, the main flight of stairs rises up to a half-landing, where it divides in two and turns back on itself up to the piano nobile. The ceiling painting here and the painted decoration of the adjacent

65

the Palatinate entered a new phase of its
history. The new elector kept his residence in Düsseldorf because the war of
succession was devastating the Palatinate
at the time and Schloss Heidelberg had
been destroyed; so the focus of palatine
politics, culture and art now shifted to
the Lower Rhine. In the Düsseldorf
court, the eclectic taste of Elector Johann
Wilhelm (1690–1716; Ill. p. 328) now
led to the recruitment of Italian and
Netherlandish artists. Although he
admired the Sun King and the splendours of Versailles, he chose a Venetian,
Mateo de Alberti, as his director of
buildings. The elector was also an enthu-
siastic art collector and founded the
famous Gemäldegalerie in Düsseldorf.
Around 1710 he commissioned the
Walloon architect Jacques Du Bois to
build him a special gallery, accessible
from the palace, to house the paintings
his agents had acquired on his behalf.
Johann Wilhelm's brother and successor,
Karl Philipp (1716–42), initially moved
the residence back to the Palatinate.
Yet when the citizens of Heidelberg
resisted his attempts to return the city
to Catholicism, he dropped the plans
to rebuild Schloss Heidelberg and to
put new buildings on the banks of the
Neckar and abruptly moved the Schloss
to Mannheim. There he built a new
electoral palace on the banks of the
Rhine from 1720, in place of the
destroyed citadel, and rebuilt the
Jesuit church (Ill. p. 223).

Under the rule of Elector Karl
Theodor (1742–99), the influence of
France predominated and the elector
corresponded with Voltaire in perfect
French. In 1749 he appointed Nicolas
de Pigage (1723–96) from Lorraine his
'Intendant of Gardens and Waters' and
three years later appointed him 'Director
of Gardens and Buildings'. This architect,
who trained at the Paris academy of
architecture and admired Germain

garden room (1745–50; Ill. p. 281),
both the work of Carlo Carlone, glorify
the elector and his outstanding virtue,
Magnanimity, and the Wittelsbach
dynasty. The grandiose suite of rooms,
which take up the entire area of the
west wing, opens from the staircase
area, which thus becomes the central
point of reference. Both the clients and
the builders saw these spectacular stair-
ways as the quintessence of the Baroque.
For them, it was an architecture geared

to visual effect and movement, a brilliant
rhetorical gesture that set the scene for
the sovereign himself; in a sense it was
a secular equivalent to the Baroque high
altar that represented the spiritual heart
of the church; in both cases, there is an
apotheosis of light.

With the dynastic succession of the
Catholic Neuburg line, through
which it was joined in personal union
with the Duchy of Jülich-Berg in 1685,

Nicolas de Pigage, ground plan of the ground floor
of Schloss Benrath (detail of proposed plan),
1755–56.

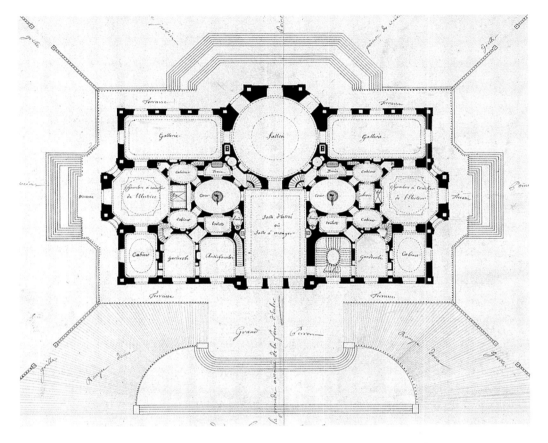

Boffrand (who designed the palace of
Lunéville and acted as advisor to the
elector of Mainz when he built his
Würzburg residence), has left two
major works on the Rhine: the gardens
of Schwetzingen and Schloss Benrath.
For the Schwetzingen gardens, Pigage
joined forces with two landscape garden-
ers from different generations, Johann
Ludwig Petri and Friedrich Ludwig von
Sckell. These gardens reflect the transition from the Baroque garden *à la française*
to the modern English landscape garden
during the second half of the century
(Ill. p. 226). Pigage's architectural
works, in the form of the Rococo theatre
(1752; Ill. p. 225) and other park buildings (the Classical temples – Ill. p. 227
– the bathhouse and the Turkish mosque)
reflect this same change of taste.

As for Schloss Benrath (see
pp. 324–25), between 1755 and 1765
Pigage was commissioned by Karl
Theodor to build a *maison de plaisance*, a
country seat, with room for a small court
but also equipped with all the facilities
necessary to a princely life style. Pigage
was a student of the latest French theories of architecture, as set out in Jacques
François Blondel's *De la distribution des
Maisons de Plaisance, et de la Décoration
des édifices en général* dating from 1737 to
1738 and Charles-Etienne Briseux's *L'art
de bâtir des maisons de campagne, où l'on traite de
leur distribution, de leur construction et de leur
décoration* from 1743. According to these
treatises, architecture must mirror the
lifestyle and the external decoration must
reflect the design of the interior. In this
search for harmony between external
and internal form, a rural site and the
domestic comforts of the princes, external features such as the gardens become
as important as the architecture itself.
Moreover, Benrath is an example of the
practical implementation of the theories
about separating the private rooms
from the public spaces, based on an

extremely effective and aesthetic organic
ground plan.

Pigage once again demonstrated his
mastery of the Rococo style with the
library of Schloss Mannheim (1751–58),
where he was assisted by a number of
very able interior designers; during the
1770s, however, he became increasingly
receptive to the Neo-Classical style,
which he liked to incorporate in his
Rococo architecture, as in Benrath. This
many-sided artist left engravings that
document the contents of the Düsseldorf
Gemäldegalerie, where Elector Karl
Theodor had the paintings rearranged by
'schools' in 1770 (Ill. p. 68). Like the collections of the Mannheim court, the
outstanding Düsseldorf
collection of the palatine counts came
to Munich in 1805 as the legacy of the
Wittelsbach family. There it was united
with the collection of the Bavarian
dukes and electors and now forms the

core of the Wittelsbach collection in the
Alte Pinakothek.

Painting, sculpture and applied arts in the Baroque period

During the 17th and 18th centuries, the
painting produced on the Upper and
Lower Rhine was rather insignificant
compared with other European regions.
Moreover, it followed the dictates of the
architecture and was basically decorative.
The artists concerned were mostly
recruited from abroad, mainly from Italy
and France. There were only a few
German artists. Januarius Zick (1730–97),
who was born in Munich, was court
painter in Ehrenbreitstein from 1760; the
style of his oil paintings was influenced
by Rembrandt and the Dutch masters,
while his painted ceilings (for example,
in the destroyed palaces of Mainz and
Koblenz) reflect the transition from
French Rococo towards Classicism.

CINQUIEME SALLE Troisieme Façade.

Gravé sous la Direction de Chr: de Méchel à Basle par M: G: Eichler en 1776.

Third façade, Room 5, Düsseldorf Gemäldegalerie. Engraving by Nicolas de Pigage, 1776.

Joseph Melling (1724–96) attended the Académie Royale in Paris as a pupil of Carle van Loo and came to the Karlsruhe court of Margrave Charles Frederick in 1758 to decorate the great hall and the gallery of the Schloss. Most of the artists entrusted with major projects had been trained abroad. Cosmas Damian Asam (1686–1739), who painted the vault of the chapel of Bruchsal (1728), was trained in Rome; he created a highly animated, theatrical and illusionist pictorial world, which reached its peak in Weltenburg on the Danube. Sculptors worth noting include Josef Anton Feuchtmayr (1696–1770), who has left some lovely examples of Rococo art in the Lake Constance region (Meersburg, Überlingen). The sculptor and stuccoworker Paul Egell (1691– 1752) worked at Mannheim court and is known for the fluid elegance and emotional tension of his figures. The architect, painter and sculptor Johann Christian Wentzinger (1710–97), originally from Breisgau, was the main exponent of Late Baroque and Rococo in Freiburg, where he settled in 1745 after a period of study in Italy

in 1731 and visits to Paris and Vienna. In spite of all his travels, which were the ideal training ground for a Baroque artist, his work remained inspired by his Upper Rhine home environment, as shown by his most important works, the Mount of Olives groups of Kenzingen (1734) and Staufen (1745) and the wall tomb of General von Rodt in Freiburg Cathedral.

In the applied arts, it is worth noting ceramics, which were highly valued by both the nobility and town dwellers as luxury articles. This craft enjoyed a real revival in two Rhenish towns, Delft and Strasbourg. The art of faience or majolica, which originated in Italy – where it developed into a separate art form during the Renaissance – did not reach the Netherlands until the late 16th century. It flourished there in the following century. Unlike the dominant blue tones and the chinoiseries characteristic of ceramics from Delft (Ill. p. 347), the pieces manufactured in Strasbourg, as well as in Hagenau and Frankenthal by the Hannong family (originally from Maastricht) in the course of the 18th

century display a diversity and decorative quality that explain the fame and popularity of Strasbourg ceramics throughout Europe.

The Vorarlberg school of architecture
From the 1680s on, architects, stuccoworkers and sculptors from the Vorarlberg made a considerable contribution to spreading a Baroque style that had freed itself from its Italian roots and had developed a profile of its own in Switzerland, Swabia and southwest Germany during the 18th century. The Benedictine abbey church of Weingarten is the most prominent example of what is known as the *Vorarlberger Münsterschema*, a hall church with its internal buttresses faced with pilasters and projecting so deep as to form chapels, connected above by a gallery (see also Disentis, p. 77). Peter Thumb II (1681–1766) was one of the most outstanding representatives of this school of architects. He settled in Konstanz in 1720, after completing the reconstruction of the Benedictine abbey church of Ebersmünster in Lower Alsace following a fire. When major projects of this kind were entrusted to foreign architects, it often meant that whole teams of workers had to move. Thumb came to Ebersmünster with a team of 200 workers but, as was the custom of the time, did not direct the work himself. While he was in Alsace, Thumb did not achieve the quality of his later masterpieces, which include the libraries of St Peter (Black Forest) and St Gall (1757), and the pilgrimage church of Birnau on Lake Constance (1746–49). Ebersmünster is, however, the most characteristic example of this architectural style on the Upper Rhine. By contrast, the church of Our Lady at Guebwiller, built by the architect Gabriel-Ignaz Ritter (1732–1813), also from the Vorarlberg, as the successor to the abbey church of Murbach (see pp. 159–60), is

based on plans that reveal the influence of French Classicism. As inspector of public buildings in Upper Alsace, Ritter was also responsible for the interior decoration of the churches of Marbach (choir stalls, now in the Dominican church of Colmar) and Masmünster.

From Rococo to Classicism

Two other architects working on the Rhine during the second half of the 18th century deserve mention. One is Pierre-Michel d'Ixnard (1723–95) from Nîmes, who also worked for Cardinal Rohan in Strasbourg. From 1775 on, he carried out a thorough remodelling of Konstanz Cathedral along contemporary lines (Ill. p. 101), designed the residence of the barons of Sickingen in Freiburg-im-Breisgau (1769) and, after the fire that destroyed it in 1769, reconstructed the monastery church of St Blasien in the Black Forest on a central ground plan, equipping it with an imposing dome and elongated choir. He was also responsible for the Koblenz palace of the elector of Trier, Clemens Wenzeslaus of Saxony (from 1777), the 'Spiegel' guildhall in Strasbourg (1782) and the library and auditorium of the Collège Royal in Colmar (1787). At times his work looks rather heavy and dry – Pigage once called it *colifichet galli-germanique* (Gallo-German frippery) – but it also reveals Classical elegance.

More interesting is another artist, Nicolas-Alexandre Salins de Monfort (1753–1838?), who was trained in the French Classical style and was directly influenced by Boullé's *Architecture parlante*. In 1779, when Salins was only twenty-six, Cardinal Louis-René-Edouard de Rohan-Guéménée commissioned him to draw the plans for reconstructing the Strasbourg bishop's residence in Saverne, modelling the architecture on Victor Louis's Palais Royal in Paris. In 1781 Salins drew the plans for the church of

St Stephan in Rosheim, giving it a monumental, Classical façade of columns.

Ixnard and Salins also worked in Karlsruhe (see p. 64). From the mid-18th century, under the rule of Margrave Charles Frederick (1738–1811) who had moved his seat here permanently, this Baden residence experienced its second great flowering. The architects involved in the designs for the reconstruction and extension of the former hunting lodge included the court architect of Württemberg, Pierre-Louis Philippe de la Guêpiere (from 1752), Joseph Massol who was in the service of the bishop of Strasbourg, Pierre-Michel d'Ixnard and Balthasar Neumann, whose plans formed the basis of the designs by Friedrich von Kesslau, the architect who supervised the work. The first plans for the town were based on drawings by Salins. When the margravate of Baden-Baden was affiliated with that of Baden-Durlach in 1771, many people settled in Karlsruhe and the town expanded southwards, beyond the circle within which the Schloss stood. The expansion of the town and the Classical accents of the *via triumphalis* leading from the Schloss to the town hall and Protestant church that represented the focal points of the town were the work of Friedrich Weinbrenner (1766–1826), who was very much influenced by the Palladian style. When he returned from Italy in 1797, he was appointed inspector of buildings for the margrave and, from 1806, when the margravate of

Baden became a grand duchy, he carried out a systematic town planning scheme. The order imposed on the urban space reflects the social structure of the community, dominated by the princes. Despite the lovely arrangement of squares and crossroads along the main road, Weinbrenner's town planning was authoritarian by nature, sacrificing content to form, thus bringing everything down to the same level. Weinbrenner was also responsible for the Kurhaus in Baden-Baden, with its Classical pillared entrance hall (1821–24).

Historicism

A pupil of Weinbrenner's, Heinrich Hübsch (1795–1863), played a significant role in German architecture in the next generation. He built the Orangerie (1853–58), the theatre (1851–54) and the art museum (1837–46) in Karlsruhe. In Heidelberg he constructed the Institute of Anatomy (1846–48; now the Institute of Psychology), in Baden-Baden the pump room of the Kurhaus (1839–42). Although trained in a Classical vein, Hübsch was convinced that the Classical style was not suited to the northern countries. In a commemorative essay written on the occasion of the Dürer celebrations in Nuremberg in 1828 entitled 'In What Style should We Build?' he called on architecture to show a 'vitality and variety' adapted to specific requirements, guided by 'the artist's talent and taste'. The pump room in

sensible, enlightened, impartial men confess that they could not help being impressed by a medieval building such as Cologne Cathedral, that proves just as much about Gothic architecture as it does about wine in that both can turn the wise man into a fool.' Thanks to the survival of medieval drawings from the time the cathedral was founded, the west towers could be completed according to the original plans, although there was no room for being creative. Nonetheless, the execution of this project under the architects F. A. Ahlert, E. F. Zwirner and R. Voigtel undeniably reveals the imprint of the 19th century.

Another Rhenish-Prussian architectural project was Schloss Stolzenfels near Koblenz, one of the most impressive examples of medieval secular architecture in the Rhineland. Based on plans by Karl Friedrich Schinkel and commissioned by the Prussian crown prince who later became King Frederick William IV, this Schloss was a jewel of Romantic, Neo-Gothic architecture, filled with the spirit of medieval chivalry (Ills. pp. 264–66.). The paintings are the work of Hermann Anton Stilke (1803–60), a pupil of Peter von Cornelius and Wilhelm von Schadow, and the Nazarene artist Ernst Deger (1809–85), who had trained at the Düsseldorf academy and had then taught historical painting there. Later, Deger also worked on the monumental frescoes of the Apollinaris church in Remagen, an important example of religious painting in Düsseldorf.

Besides Berlin and Munich, the leading German art centres in the 19th century, Düsseldorf gained an increasingly good reputation in the Rhineland with the opening in 1819 of the Royal Prussian Academy of Art. The first director of this institution (whose origins date back to the time of the electors), Peter von Cornelius (1783–1867)

Baden-Baden, with its elegantly curved, segmented arcades, demonstrates the very personal style Hübsch chose to adopt. He deliberately dissociated himself from the past and created a variant to the round arches that dominated the architectural style in Germany at the time. In the final analysis, he subordinated style to function. Hübsch was also responsible for a number of tombs. From 1846 to 1852 he restored Konstanz Cathedral and between 1854 and 1858 he restored the west end of Speyer Cathedral, which Franz Ignaz Michael Neumann had built from 1772 to 1778, only to be destroyed by French troops in 1793. In this building the architect was largely inspired by northern Italian Romanesque, though he attached too much importance to decorative detail, which detracted from the sense of monumentality. Yet Speyer remains an important example of architectural

restoration, comparable to the work Viollet-le-Duc carried out in Vézelay and Pierrefonds. It is an approach to restoration that is true to the spirit rather than the letter of the past style.

People had always lived in hope of seeing Cologne Cathedral, on which building work had stopped in 1560, finally completed. In 1816 the Berlin architect Karl Friedrich Schinkel took immediate measures to preserve the main structure, before the major works began in 1842, reaching completion in 1880. The project inspired an enthusiasm throughout the nation that infected the bourgeoisie as much as it did the intellectual elite (such as Boisserée and Görres), who saw it as a symbol of German unity. However, there were also some voices of protest, such as the anonymous south German who lectured the 'medieval fantasists' in 1844: 'If even

Städtisches Museum Abteiberg, Mönchengladbach.
Architect Hans Hollein, inaugurated 1982.

concentrated on monumental painting and became responsible for the revival of this style in the Rhineland, personally taking part in the decoration of Heltorf Palace near Düsseldorf. After Cornelius moved to Munich in 1825, Wilhelm von Schadow (1788–1862) took his place in Düsseldorf. When this great inventor of a new doctrine and new style came to the Rhine from Berlin, he was followed by a number of his pupils. In terms of content, Schadow called for absolute mastery of the human figure in the Classical tradition. One of the most original members of the Düsseldorf School was the landscape and historical painter Carl Friedrich Lessing (1808–80), director of the Karlsruhe art gallery from 1858, whose strongly expressive works reflect the transition from Late Romanticism to Realism. Another important figure was Alfred Rethel (1816–59), who painted the frescoes illustrating the life of Charlemagne in the coronation room of Aachen town hall and who also created a remarkable series of woodcuts. Johann Wilhelm Schirmer (1807–63) is regarded, along with Lessing, as one of the inventors of Rhenish landscape painting. Yet Schirmer's talent pales beside the genius of his pupil the Swiss painter Arnold Böcklin (1827–1901) from Basel. Böcklin's romantic and heroic landscapes and his mythological universe are paintings expressing mood, fluctuating between the grotesque and the sublime, between northern melancholy and an obsessive search for the harmony of the Italians.

One artist whose painting was shaped by the spirit of the Rhineland was Gustave Doré (1832–83) from Strasbourg. An inspired and inexhaustibly inventive illustrator and a virtuoso watercolourist, he assimilated every kind of influence: the epic Romanticism of Delacroix, the art of the English watercolourists, the satirical edge of Daumier, Granville and Töpfer, the Romantic vision of Victor Hugo and the sentimentality of Moritz von Schwind and Ludwig Richter. Doré was the most popular French artist of the 19th century.

The industrialization of the Prussian Rhineland in the 1830s encouraged the development of a new kind of architecture, which soon followed its own path, towards engineering. The bridges over the Rhine in Cologne are one of the early achievements of this technique, starting with the railway bridge (1855–59). The construction of the railway lines in the Rhine valley faced the builders with new challenges. The Baden architect Jakob Friedrich Eisenlohr (1805–55), who designed a Neo-Gothic funeral chapel in Karlsruhe, created an architectural style based on round arches for the railway stations of Mannheim, Heidelberg, Karlsruhe and Freiburg.

The economic prosperity enjoyed by the towns encouraged the flowering of culture, in particular the fine arts. The 'Kunstverein für die Rheinlande und Westfalen' was founded by Wilhelm von Schadow in 1829 with the aim of establishing direct contacts between citizens and artists. Art galleries also played an important role: as the sites of temporary exhibitions they familiarized the public with contemporary trends and stimulated and developed the taste and interest of amateurs and collectors, as in Basel, Baden-Baden, Mannheim and Düsseldorf.

In addition to the great museums of art from the past, there are now also important public collections of 20th-century art. Modern art museums, built in an equally modern architectural style, have sprung up in Schaffhausen, Basel, Strasbourg, Bonn, Cologne, Düsseldorf, Mönchengladbach and Rotterdam. On the Rhine there is a lively art scene, open to the progressive trends of the international art market. It is tempting to regard this strong commitment to contemporary art as a modern variant of the great collections accumulated by the princely patrons of art in the 17th and 18th centuries; it certainly demonstrates the long tradition of cultural variety and openness on the Rhine.

RHINE JOURNEY

ART, LANDSCAPES AND MONUMENTS

ALONG THE RHINE

The Alpine Rhine:
from the source rivers of the Vorderrhein and Hinterrhein to Lake Constance

The sources of the Rhine lie in the high Alpine region of the Rhaetian-Romansh Swiss canton of Graubünden (French Grisons). Its two headstreams, the Vorderrhein (anterior Rhine) and the Hinterrhein (posterior Rhine), are fed by a number of tributaries from the side valleys before meeting at Reichenau/Graübunden, 10 kilometres (six miles) from Chur. From here to Lake Constance the river is known as the 'Alpine Rhine'.

The Vorderrhein, whose source lies in the Toma Lake in the eastern part of the St Gotthard mountain range, runs along the bed of a long Alpine valley formed by glaciers towards Chur. The photograph shows the Vorderrhein valley near Ilanz with the Tödi mountains in the background.

Disentis

The impressive and monumental abbey of Disentis (a name stemming from the Latin *desertina*), dominated by the Baroque twin towered façade of the abbey church, stands on the slopes of a plateau above the Upper Rhine valley. This Benedictine monastery, the oldest in Switzerland, was built in the 8th century on the site of a hermits' settlement. The Frankish itinerant monk Sigisbert and the

indigenous martyr Placidus, who were venerated as local saints, are regarded as the founders of the abbey.

Archaeological finds and reconstruction work on the monastery have revealed that this remote site had a long Christian tradition. It seems that the earliest of the three adjacent, early medieval religious buildings, dating from around 700, was a simple hall. By 800 there were two churches, dedicated respectively to the Virgin and to St Martin, based on the three-apse plan often found in Rhaetia. Between the two was a St Peter's chapel. As early as 750 the church of St Martin had a ring crypt (see also St Luzius, Chur), where the relics of St Placidus were venerated (reconstructed in modern times). A narrow window opening was positioned in the vertex of the ambulatory so that once a year, on the feast day of the saint on 11 July, the sunlight could shine down into the hypogeum for seventy minutes. Ring crypts originated in late antiquity (for example, Hagios Demetrios in Saloniki) and were common in the area under Byzantine rule.

Opposite left: Votive altar of Castelberg, 1572.
Opposite right: Monastery church, Disentis.

Interior of the church looking towards the choir.

St Martin

The current monastery buildings date from the 17th century. An architect from Vorarlberg, Kaspar Moosbrugger (1656–1723), drew up the plans for the Baroque abbey church between 1683 and 1699, with the assistance of Franz Beer and Christian Thumb. Moosbrugger was also responsible for the reconstruction of Einsiedeln monastery, where he lived as a monk. The basic structure was completed in 1704 and consecrated in 1712. The ground plan is strictly rectangular and the spacious interior is built in the style of the pillared hall churches of the Vorarlberg school of architects: a front bay with an organ gallery, a three-bay nave with pilastered buttresses, between them chapels and open galleries, the whole crowned by lunette vaulting. The integrated transept that forms the centre of the space adjoins a recessed, raised choir and a rectangular altar area recessed even further.

One remarkable piece of church furniture is what is known as the votive altar of Castelberg in one of the chapels to the right, an exquisite, Renaissance-style wooden altar dating from 1572. Moritz and Jörg Frosch created the paintings on the altarpiece. The central panel, based on a copper engraving by Albrecht Dürer, shows the donor, the knight Sebastian von Castelberg, together with his son and St Michael, kneeling at the feet of the Apocalyptic Virgin on a sickle moon illuminating a lake-land scene.

The front bay of the church leads via a corridor and the 'rosary' staircase surmounted by a coffered ceiling, a replica of Bernini's *Scala regia* in the Vatican, to what is now the church of Our Lady, which was reconstructed between 1982 and 1983, while retaining the medieval hall church plan of a nave and two aisles terminating in three apses.

Zillis

A major axis of communication, the Splügen Pass, has linked north and south, the cantons of Graubünden and Ticino, since Roman times. It runs through the valleys of Schams and

Domleschg, through which the Hinterrhein (posterior Rhine) flows and which are separated by the ravine of Via Mala.

St Martin

This church played an important role in the religious life of Rhaetia throughout the Middle Ages. It is first mentioned in a Carolingian inventory of 831. In 1357 it was placed under the chapter of Chur Cathedral.

Its architectural history began around 500 with the construction of a square hall, adjoined to the east by a semicircular exedra. During the Carolingian period the Early Christian building was turned into a three-apse church, based on the customary Rhaetian plan, while retaining the outside walls (see also Disentis and St Luzius, Chur). During the third building stage, between 1130 and 1140, it was completely reconstructed and turned into a large aisleless nave church. In 1509 the architect Andreas Bühler from Thusis replaced the earlier square choir with the existing rib-vaulted Gothic choir. The painted, coffered ceiling above the nave and the attractive articulation of the square tower date back to the Romanesque period.

This ceiling, the earliest preserved example of an original Romanesque wooden ceiling, has made the church famous. It consists of 154 square panels each measuring about 90 centimetres (35 inches) on the side and 3 centimetres (over 1 inch) thick; most of them are made up of three pieces of wood. The 48 panels that serve as the perimeter depict fabulous monsters, illustrations of evil, which no doubt have some apotropaic significance. The inner cycle shows

Opposite top: View from the valley with fresco of
St Christopher on St Martin at Zillis.
Opposite bottom: View from the Gothic choir into the
Romanesque nave with painted wooden ceiling.

Part of the Romanesque wooden ceiling with scenes
from the childhood of Christ.

scenes from the life of Christ, ranging
from the Annunciation to the Crowning
with Thorns, together with scenes from
the legend of St Martin. The scenes
from the Passion are incomplete, probably
because the Romanesque choir has not
survived. The technique is tempera on a
chalk ground, on which the cartoons
were drawn in ochre. It is interesting
to note that the painter worked in two
stages, first preparing each panel before
putting them all together on the ceiling.
This is an example of panel painting
going hand in hand with wall painting,
for the meander frieze executed in the
fresco technique that serves as a border
for the entire wooden ceiling can be
attributed to the same workshop. The
main source of inspiration for the
painters of the wooden ceiling at Zillis
was illuminated manuscripts in the form
of codices that must have come from
either the Salzburg scriptorium, or, more
probably, a northern Italian manuscript
in the Ambrosiana in Milan. The stylized
manner of the master, and of his less
gifted assistants, the carefully regulated
design of the drapery folds (parallel
lines describing the same forms, V and
Y-shaped folds, etc.) and the narrative
tone, together with the clear and expressive pictorial language, show that this
work is like an illumination transposed
to a larger scale. This case suggests again
that many painters in those days were far
more able to master and combine different techniques than their counterparts
today. The relationship between different
art forms is particularly clear in Zillis.
The faithful, most of whom were illiterate,
could gaze at pictures of a theological
world that would otherwise have been
accessible only to the elitist circles of the
clergy or aristocracy in the form of precious illuminated manuscripts.

A monumental fresco of St Christopher
(*c.* 1300) outside the church is a sign for
Christians high above the Via Mala.

Via Mala

Below left: 'Haus Pedrun' at Andeer, with sgraffito decoration.
Below right: The Via Mala gorge in the Hinterrhein (posterior Rhine).

At the upper entrance to the Schams valley lies Andeer, which contains particularly fine examples of sgraffito façade decoration. This technique, characteristic of the Graubünden style, combines ornaments borrowed from the Italian Renaissance, such as diamond-shaped stone blocks, with rustic arabesques.

At the other end of the Schams valley, behind Zillis, the turbulent mountain river has forced its way through the cliffs. The gorge, 6 kilometres (over 3 miles) long and up to 600 metres

(1970 feet) deep, has long been known as the Via Mala (the evil way), reflecting people's dread of the black depths and terrible forces of nature.

The Hinterrhein leaves the dramatic ravine of the Via Mala to flow straight into the wide valley of Domleschg, a romantic place with its high mountain pass and many medieval castles, some of which still survive as ruins. Burg Ortenstein, poised on a steep cliff over the Rhine valley, is typical of Rhaetian feudal architecture.

Below left: Church of Our Lady, Thusis.
Below right: View of the choir at Thusis with
Late Gothic star vaulting.

Thusis

Church of Our Lady

Thusis owes its status as the capital of
the Domleschg valley to its key position
at the northern exit of the Via Mala.
When this gorge of the Hinterrhein,
once an area to be travelled only in fear,
was opened up to light goods traffic in
1473, the area began to flourish again,
which meant that the existing Lady
Chapel was no longer appropriate.
A local architect, Andreas Bühler from
Kärnten (inscription on the vaulting),
built the present church from 1491 to
1506, in a dominant position by the exit

to the gorge, and it was raised to the
status of parish church. Built entirely
in the Late Gothic style, it consists of
an aisleless nave, terminating in a choir
closed off on three sides. It boasts
a lovely stellar vault, culminating in a
complex pattern of ribs in the choir.

Rhäzuns

The north wall of the St Georg, Rhäzuns, with a
wall painting by the Master of Waltensburg,
c. 1340. To the right of the painting are St George
and the dragon. At the bottom the mass of St
Gregory and St George's legendary leap across the
Rhine are depicted.

St Georg (Sogn Gieri)

St Georg is situated outside the town
on a wooded hill overlooking the steep
bank of the Hinterrhein, is first mentioned in the 12th century. It is likely,
however, that it is the same church an
Ottonian source referred to as *in castello
beneduces et razunnes* (in the castle of
Bonaduz and Rhäzüns). Excavations
inside the church have confirmed that it
has stood here since the first millennium.
The aisleless nave is Romanesque, as
shown by some of the original parts
of the round-arched windows that have
survived. The square choir with ribbed

vaulting, however, is a complete reconstruction dating from 1325 to 1350, and
the interior wall paintings date from the
same period. Later alterations, such as
moving the entrance to the southwest
side, enlarging the windows and renew-
ing the wooden ceiling (signed 1731),
have not detracted from the basic
medieval character of the church.

The plain architectural style of the
hall church is particularly suited to wall
paintings. There are two distinct phases.
During the first stage, the choir, choir
arch and parts of the left wall were
painted. No doubt the artist known as

the Master of Waltensburg, who is
known to have worked here around 1340,
was the more talented painter, as his
treatment of the human figure and his
strong sense of composition reveal.
Only fragments have survived of the
original wall paintings in the choir: the
Annunciation on the left, the Crucifixion
on the end wall, the Coronation of
the Virgin on the right. The rib vault
contains tondi with the four Evangelists.
Outside this framework, the curious
foliage decoration on the spandrels lends
the sober architectural forms a certain
sophistication. There are three registers

View of the St Georg, Rhäzuns, looking towards the choir. On the triumphal arch there are scenes from the legend of St George, while at the bottom there are donors with the Madonna of the protective cloak.

on the wall of the choir arch, depicting the life and martyrdom of St George. On the bottom left, extending round the corner to the side wall, is the donor painting: a Madonna with a protective cloak, with a kneeling cleric and two women, surmounted by a large shield. The painting of St George and the Dragon, which dominates the wall by its size alone, dates from an earlier period.

During the second stage, towards the end of the 14th century, the remaining church walls were painted. This later artist decorated the upper register of the entrance wall with a cycle of scenes

from the Old Testament, starting with the creation of the world, which continues along the left side wall with three scenes from the story of Noah and Moses. The second and third-register wall paintings, which also overlap on to the left wall, tell of the lives of the Virgin and Christ.

The pictorial programme on the left wall is completed by two scenes from the legend of St Nicholas: the Archangel Michael weighing the souls, the feast day of Christ and the mass of St Gregory. It incorporates a local episode from the legend of St George, according to which

the early Christian knight escaped his persecutors by making his horse take an enormous jump over the narrow gorge of the Hinterrhein, landing exactly on the spot where this church was later erected. The right wall is devoted to a cycle of the Passion, up to the Pentecost, concluding with the Last Judgment.

The winged altar, dated 1522, was brought here from the parish church of Tamins in 1546 in the wake of the Reformation and has suffered some damage since then.

Domat/Ems

St Johann Baptist (Sogn Gion)
The church dedicated to St John the Baptist is situated in a prominent position on a hill between the little town and the river, near the place where the Hinterrhein and the Vorderrhein join forces and within sight of the episcopal city of Chur. It is the Late Gothic successor to a Romanesque fortified building, which played a strategic part

here in protecting the crossing over the Rhine. When it was converted between 1504 and 1515, both the Romanesque walls of the nave and the massive belfry were retained. The church has an aisleless nave, with fine rib vaulting and a recessed, raised choir above a crypt-like lower room.

The high point of the interior is the Late Gothic winged altar with five fully three-dimensional figures in the shrine. On either side of John the Baptist, against an engraved gold ground, are St Florinus and St Catherine on the left, St Urban and St Dorothy on the right. The inner panels of the wings contain high relief scenes: the Baptism of Christ in Jordan and the Beheading of John the Baptist. The Last Judgment is depicted on the back of the shrine. This remarkable work of art, dated 1504, has been attributed to the workshop of Jörg Syrlin the Younger because of its similarities to the altar in Bingen/Württemberg.

Within the enclosed churchyard on the hillside stands a chapel with pointed gables that was used as a charnel house. It dates from 1693 and contains an unusual medieval sculptural group: three almost life-size robed figures made of limewood representing the dead Christ and the two Marys grieving. It originally formed part of an Entombment group used in the Easter liturgy, in which the

Opposite left: Late Gothic winged altar, 1504,
at St Johann Baptist, Domat/Ems.
Opposite right: St Johann Baptist, Domat/Ems.

Two grieving Marys from a Holy Sepulchre
group, c. 1300, in the charnel house at St Johann
Baptist, Domat/Ems.

figure of Christ was symbolically buried.
Large-scale groups of saints, usually
carved from stone, became widespread
throughout the German-speaking
regions from the middle of the 14th
century (see the chapel of the Holy
Sepulchre in Freiburg Cathedral, Ill.
p. 50). These figures are a rare early
example, dating from around 1300
or even a few decades earlier.

Chur

The fortified town of Chur, known as *Curia Rhaetorum* in Roman times (French Coire), has always been an intellectual and economic centre of eastern Switzerland because of its location at the exit of major passes over the Alps. One of the earliest bishops' sees on the north side of the Alps, it is first mentioned by name in a letter from the synod of Milan to Pope Leo in 451. Archaeological finds have confirmed that an earlier, 5th-century building once stood on the site of the present cathedral. As the political focus gradually shifted towards Italy and this region became increasingly important in strategic terms, the Carolingian and Ottonian rulers of the new Western Empire began to make Chur larger.

The earliest evidence of a diocesan church in the form of marble slabs with interlace decoration (now used as panels on the altars of St Laurentius and St Fidelis) come from a medieval building dating from the 8th century. It has been attributed to the episcopate of Bishop Tello from the Viktoriden family, although it is not known what it looked like.

Chur Cathedral

The existing cathedral building is Romanesque. The choir and high altar were consecrated on 2 June 1178, but the final consecration did not take place until 1272. It is also known that the rood altar was consecrated in 1208. Given how long the cathedral took to build, its stylistic unity is astonishing. The west façade, with its window and portal, built just before the mid-13th century, still has a Romanesque round arch. This conservative approach and the general impression of strict architectural consistency can be explained by the influence

A. Der Hof zu Chur. B. Das Schloß. C. Die Bischoffliche Domkirch. D. S. Lucia. E. S. Martins Pfarekirch. F. Prediger Closter. G. Das Rahthauß. H. Das Kauffhauß. I. S. Regula Pfarekirch. K. Ploßur fluß. L. Der Rhein fluß. M. Schloß Haldenstein.

Below: Episcopal church with cathedral façade at Chur, with the tower of St Luzius in the background.
Bottom: View from St Luzius to the rear of the cathedral.

of Cistercian architectural ideas; both Bishop Berno of Mecklenburg-Schwerin, who consecrated the choir in 1172, and Adalgott, who was in office before 1160 and is considered to be the person who started this building project, belonged to that reformist order.

The architectural style of the cathedral reflects influences from various regions of Europe, Burgundy, southern France, Lombardy and Germany. It is a three-bay, piered, basilican church without transepts, with a crypt, a raised chancel and a recessed , rectangular termination. The crypt, with its anteroom below the upper choir, is the oldest part of the building. Originally this area was cut off from the nave by a screen with steps, rather like the *Pontile* in Modena Cathedral. One unusual feature is the irregular ground plan: the visitor becomes aware at once that the axis of the nave is out of line with that of the chancel, bending to the right.

The wealth of sculptural ornament on the capitals is in striking contrast to the sober architectural forms. In fact, this figurative decoration went against the ideal of simplicity advocated by St Bernard. The capitals of the nave are not of such a high quality, but the capitals of the crypt and the choir assume some familiarity with the great models of St-Trophîme in Arles or Milan Cathedral. The two friezes on the capitals of the choir arch pillars belong together. The northern pillar shows a man caught by a lion, by his side other figures of sinners hard-pressed by demons; its counterpart on the southern pillar shows Daniel in the lions' den as the incarnation of salvation, to which a bishop shown on the side points the way.

The four Apostle pillars at the entrance to the crypt were installed in 1925 (Ills. p. 90). Originally, they probably supported the lost chancel, both in physical terms and in a symbolic way as

The Gothic carved altarpiece by Jakob Russ of Ravensburg in the chancel of Chur Cathedral, 1486–92.

Opposite: View along the nave to the chancel of Chur Cathedral.

theological supports, rather like the Evangelists on the lectern of Freudenstadt. Following Lombard tradition, the Apostle pillars stand on the back of lions holding their prey between their paws and symbolizing sin, like the column set on a kneeling man now in the centre of the anteroom to the crypt. The incredible ornamental detail is remarkable when compared with the block-like figure, which cannot have been very up to date in its time (around 1208). This regressive style may, on the one hand, be explained by adherence to the original design, while it may, on the other hand, result from the lack of innovative trends in the 13th century. It is not unusual to find people clinging to past traditions in times of stylistic change.

The more recent stone sculptures include the tabernacle by Master Claus from Feldkirch, inscribed with the date 1484, and the sarcophagus of Bishop Ortlieb of Bradis (died 1491), created by Jakob Russ of Ravensburg. The bishop entrusted that artist with an important commission for the new high altar (1486 –92). The central panel of the altarpiece shows the Madonna and Child enthroned on a half-moon, flanked by the figures of St Lucius and St Emerita on one side, and by St Florinus and St Ursula on the other. The relief on the inside of the wings shows local saints. The statuesque arrangement of the figures in front of a drapery held by angels is based on a type of work by Swabian sculptor Hans Multscher. As patroness of the cathedral, the Virgin appears twice on the altarpiece: in the main scene of the Coronation of the Virgin, highly praised by Jacob Burckhardt, and at the top in the group of the Holy Trinity.

Among the valuable works housed in the cathedral treasury there is an outstanding example of Romanesque bronze sculpture: the gilt foot of a cross dating from 1130 to 1140 (Ill. p. 91). It shows the four Evangelists seated at their lecterns on a vaulted base supported by four paw-shaped feet. Below them, the four rivers of paradise flow out of spewing lion's heads. This 'Mount Paradise' culminates with Adam, climbing out of his tomb, flanked by two angels holding the actual foot of the cross. An inscription recounts that the crucified Christ awoke Adam to new life and that a

Romanesque Apostle pillars at the entrance to the crypt of Chur Cathedral.

Bottom: Vault of the Carolingian ring crypt at St Luzius, Chur.
Below right: Romanesque foot of a cross, 1130–40, in the cathedral treasury, Chur.

certain Nortpertus (Archbishop of Magdeburg from 1128) commissioned this work from an *artifex* (someone with a specific skill) named Azzo. The foot of the cross in the Kestner Museum in Hanover and the one in the Kunstgewerbemuseum in Berlin (mid–late 11th century) show parallel motifs.

St Luzius

According to tradition, St Lucius, who is venerated as first bishop of the diocese of Chur, was martyred here, uphill from the cathedral. The burial church of the saint that stood here in the 8th century had a ring crypt. The martyr's tomb was in the 'confessio' below the high altar, connected to it by an opening. A semicircular ambulatory allowed the faithful

to come to view the relics, while a rectangular vestibule regulated the flow of pilgrims. The raised choir terminated in three parallel apses, in accordance with the system customary in Rhaetia at the time. When the Premonstrasians took over the monastery around 1140, the Carolingian church was adapted. In 1252 the bones of St Lucius were housed in the shrine that is now in the treasury. Records show that in 1295 the enlarged church with its extended patrocinium was reconsecrated (vaulting dates from around 1500).

The structure of the Carolingian ring crypt within the renovated church has been restored at various times, from 1885 to 1889, from 1943 to 1945 and from 1951 to 1952.

Bad Ragaz

St Leonhard

The first reliable record of this pilgrimage chapel outside town dedicated to St Leonard of Noblat (near Limoges), a 6th-century Frankish abbot and missionary, describes the consecration of three altars by the bishop of Chur on 5 June 1412. On that occasion, visitors were granted indulgences, as confirmed by a document dated the following year. Pilgrimages to the church of St Leonhard, who was venerated as protector of the persecuted and the imprisoned, continued to be very popular, as the graffiti on the walls and frescoes reveals.

The walls and the groin vaulting of the square choir were entirely covered in a Gothic cycle of frescoes, which disappeared under a layer of new decoration in 1631 and was not rediscovered until 1945, when it was restored, although at times rather too excessively.

The walls are divided into horizontal bands of painting, unified by continuous arches in the lower and upper register. An exception is the votive painting in the southeast corner. It shows St Leonard dragging prisoners from a tower by a chain, interceding for a donor holding a banner who is kneeling before the Madonna and Child. Male and female saints are positioned below the blind arches of the lower register; above it is a framed sequence of scenes showing the Adoration of the Magi, the Flight into Egypt, the Murder of the Children of Bethlehem, the Presentation in the Temple and the Baptism of Christ. The upper register shows the Apostles with their attributes on benches below arcades, which produces a three-dimensional effect. The lunettes above contain prophets with banners. On the rear of the triumphal arch, David is depicted surrounded by the ancestors of Christ. The spandrels of the vault have a Coronation of the Virgin, St John and St Luke, St Matthew and an angel

making music and St Mark and two angels making music. The east window wall shows the Wise and Foolish Virgins. The entire fresco cycle dates back to the time of Abbot Werner of Reitnau (from 1415 to 1435) and the elegant forms are

indebted to the courtly International Gothic style of c. 1400, although this work juxtaposes traditional and more modern trends. The master of the workshop based in Bad Ragaz may have come from southern Tyrol.

The view across the Rhine valley to the Swiss mountains from Schloss Vaduz in Liechtenstein.

Vaduz

Romans, Ostrogoths, Franks, Alemanni and Swabians dominated the little principality of Liechtenstein on the right bank of the Alpine Rhine, along the old trade route from Italy to Augsburg. In the 14th century Liechtenstein became self-governing under the emperor, in 1719 it became a principality, in 1806 it was independent and today it is part of a triangle with Switzerland and Austria.

The medieval castle of Vaduz, in a dominant position overlooking the town and the Rhine valley, was reconstructed between 1905 and 1912 as the seat of the rulers. The 12th-century keep and the corner bastions overlooking the valley side added in the 16th century give it the appearance of a picturesque fortress.

Lake Constance Rhine: Konstanz and Reichenau Island

Within Lake Constance, its main inlet and outlet, the Rhine travels another 70 kilometres (43 miles) from its delta in Rheinau to Stein am Rhein. At Konstanz, it leaves the main basin for the Lower Lake (Untersee) and continues to the island of Reichenau. The length of the river is officially recorded from the bridge over the Rhine in Konstanz.

The photograph shows a view from the Altes Schloss Meersburg across Lake Constance to Switzerland and the Alps on the other side of the lake. From the Middle Ages, the Altes Schloss was used as the see of the bishops of Konstanz, who were responsible for building the picturesque central tower with its stepped gables.

Kreuzlingen

The Mount of Olives Chapel in the former monastery church of Kreuzlingen.

Opposite: View of the church of Kreuzlingen facing east.

Between 1120 and 1125 Bishop Ulrich I of Konstanz (1111–27) founded an Augustine monastery church near the town and dedicated it to the local Augsburg saints, Ulrich and Afra. That is where he moved the old hospice for the needy and the pilgrims, which had been set up by Bishop Konrad (934–75) and housed a fragment of the Holy Cross he had brought back from the Holy Land. The name of the church and of the subsequently built town of Kreuzlingen derive from the name of the relic, which was called *Crucelin* in the local dialect.

St Ulrich und Afra

After being destroyed in 1633 after the Swedish siege of Konstanz during the Thirty Years' War, this former Augustine monastery was rebuilt further outside town. The light and airy main structure with its very narrow aisleless nave dates from 1650 to 1653, while the collegiate church is somewhat later. The plans were drawn up by Michael Beer, a member of the same family of architects from Vorarlberg who, like the Thumb family, left their imprint on several generations of Baroque architecture throughout the Lake Constance area. Its present appearance is the result of Rococo reconstruction and refurbishing work carried out from 1760 to 1763 under Johann Ferdinand Beer. Andreas Moosbrugger was responsible for the stucco work. The illusionist ceiling paintings celebrate the church father Augustinus, patron of the church canons. They are the work of Franz Ludwig Hermann, the most important member of a northern Swabian family of painters, who worked as court painter for Prince-Bishop F. C. von Rodt in the 1740s in Konstanz. The ornate parclose choir screen (1737) is by the metal-worker Jakob Hoffner of Konstanz. After a major fire destroyed the vault in 1963 and caused other damage, the building was extensively restored in 1967.

On the north side of the nave, the Mount of Olives Chapel opens up behind a fine perspective Rococo grille by Jakob Hoffner. The ceiling paintings by Hermann, showing Moses and the brazen serpent, form a counterpoint to the monumental cross of mercy. The wooden crucifix (c. 1400), which came from an earlier church on the same site,

shows Christ with real hair, after a model that was widespread in south Germany towards the end of the Middle Ages.

The scene of the Mount of Olives, which fills the entire chapel, is depicted as a labyrinthine landscape within which more than 300 wooden figurines, probably carved in a Tyrolean workshop around 1720–30, enact the Passion.

Konstanz

A Roman settlement, mentioned in 525 as *Constantia*, once existed at the site where the Rhine leaves Lake Constance to enter the narrow stretch of the Untersee (Lower Lake). Around 600 the bishopric for the Alemannic region moved here. The first recorded bishop was called Gaudentius (died 613). The *Vita* of St Gall mentions a church dedicated to the Virgin in 615. The diocese, initially dominated by Alemannic and Frankish rulers, gradually gained more autonomy, especially during the Carolingian and Ottonian period. It was fortunate in being located so close to the abbeys of St Gall and Reichenau, whose bishops often served both the empire and the Church. Bishop Salomon III, a former abbot of St Gall, had coins minted in the early 10th century that bore the name of King Louis III beside his own. In an attempt to turn Konstanz into a 'second Rome', like the Roman patriarchal basilicas, Konrad, the pro-Ottonian bishop and later patron, founded the churches of St Johann, St Paul and St Lorenz and, later, the abbey of Petershausen on the Rhine. The Mauritius rotunda behind the cathedral choir, modelled on the Holy Sepulchre church in Jerusalem, also goes back to Bishop Konrad, who had made a pilgrimage to the Holy Land.

The name Konstanz is linked with the ecumenical Council held there between 1414 and 1418, with the aim of reforming the church and restoring its unity after the great schism in the West. The cathedral became a focal point, as the Council's assembly hall and the scene of liturgical ceremonies. The most significant events that occurred there were the condemnation and public burning at the stake of the reformer John Huss (1415) and the election of Martin V as Pope (1417). The conclave held its sessions in the 'Konzilgebäude', originally a warehouse. This building, with its imposing hipped roof, is a well-known landmark.

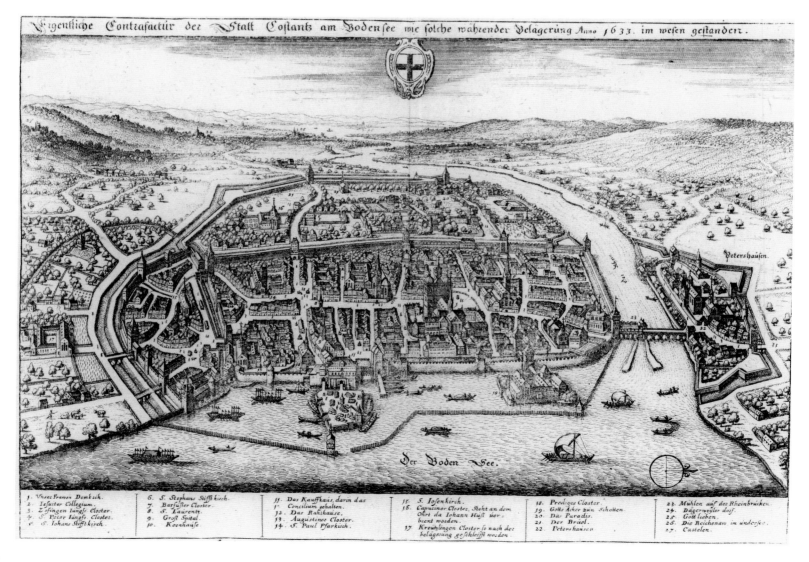

Below: The Rhine tower on the Rhine bridge in Konstanz, looking towards the cathedral.
Right: Konrad, patron of the bishopric. Gilt copper disc from the eastern gable of Konstanz Cathedral, 13th century.

The advent of the Reformation forced the bishop and the cathedral chapter to withdraw to Meersburg in 1527 (see pp. 94 and 95) and many works of art in the churches fell victim to the iconoclasts. However, in 1548, when it came under Austrian rule, Konstanz reverted to Catholicism. After Konstanz was joined to the Grand Duchy of Baden in 1803, the bishop's see was moved to Freiburg-im-Breisgau in 1821 and the diocese was dissolved in 1827.

With the conversion into a hotel complex (1874) of the Dominican monastery on the island adjacent to the old town, an outstanding example of an Upper

Rhenish 13th-century mendicant order church has been lost. The hotel has preserved fragments of the original basilican church, which reflect regional building traditions (see Konstanz Cathedral and St Georg in Stein am Rhein). It had a nave and two aisles, octagonal capitals, unprofiled arcades and an upper wall articulated by a cornice.

Konstanz Cathedral, SS Pelagius und Konrad

The oldest parts of this cathedral (now the Catholic parish church) and the crypt (Ill. p. 103) can be traced back to the late 10th–early 11th century. The

main area of the crypt, a groin-vaulted, rectangular space with a nave and two aisles, is flanked by six robust columns with capitals reminiscent of the 'Witigowo column' in the cathedral of Reichenau-Mittelzell (Ill. p. 111). The west wall of the crypt, below what was the site of the high altar, contains a small sarcophagus with the relics of St Pelagius. The choir, in three parts with a flat termination, and the wide transept were

Page 100: Tower façade of Konstanz Cathedral.
Page 101: Interior of Konstanz Cathedral looking east.

Left: Staircase, known as the 'Schnegg', in the choir of St Thomas at Konstanz Cathedral, 1466.
Below: Right-hand door of the double portal inscribed with the artist's signature (Simon Haider) at Konstanz Cathedral, 1470.

cathedral lodge, which reconstructed the Mauritius rotunda, St Konrad and the cloister and chapterhouse. Major works of sculpture were also created during this period. The decorative quality of this Gothic formal language, which could be regarded as a type of southern German 'Decorated style', is also apparent on the southern façade of the transept with its slender blind arcades, pinnacles, large tracery windows and bar tracery of pointed arches projecting from the gable wall. It is a horizontally designed system that has some stylistic affinities with the Cistercian church of Salem, although it is not known which was built first. The southern part of the two preserved wings of the cloister dates from 1300, the eastern part with its ornate tracery is one or two decades later. The anteroom below

reconstructed under the episcopate of Bishop Rumold (1051–69), making use of parts dating back to an earlier building stage under Bishop Lambert (995–1018). The same applies to the nave, reconstructed after the original Carolingian nave had collapsed in 1052. Bishop Gebhard of Zähringen consecrated this largely preserved Romanesque basilican church, with its nave and two aisles, crowned by a crossing tower, in 1089.

The large, round-arched arcades of the nave are supported by eight monolithic columns with octagonal capitals remarkably similar to those in the collegiate church near the Imperial Palatinate of Goslar. In fact, Bishop Rumold and his successor Otto I (1071–84) came from there. A profiled cornice draws the eye to the base of the clerestory. Originally it only had small window openings, although a Jesuit architect named Heinrich Mayer (1679–83) made changes, converting the church to the Gothic style and surmounting the nave with bossed rib vaulting.

Building work continued during the Gothic period, now headed by a

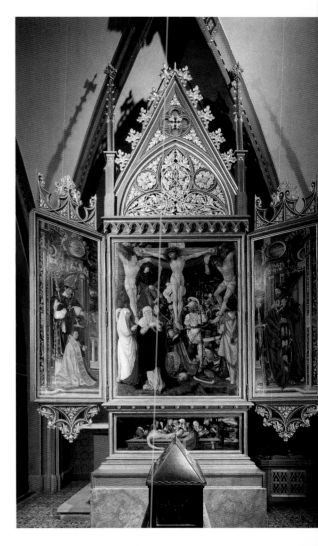

the northern choir and the adjoining St
Konrad to the east, consecrated in 1313,
are reminiscent of elegant Cistercian
architecture (Bebenhausen, Salem).

The Holy Sepulchre in the St Mauritius
rotunda (Ill. p. 105) donated by Bishop
Konrad and renovated around 1300 is
a model of Gothic architecture. The
delicately wrought sandstone tomb is
a twelve-sided central structure with
two storeys of tracery arcades, crowned
by triangular pediment gables. It is completed by a sculptural programme that
unfolds in three cycles. The groups of
statues surmounting the clustered piers
of the lower register are grouped in such
a way as to depict scenes from the childhood of Christ. Corresponding figures
relating to the funeral liturgy stand
inside. The twelve Apostles form a circle

between the gables. The affinities with
contemporary French sculpture and
the style of architecture suggest that the
Holy Sepulchre dates from around 1260.

The Gothic cathedral lodge also built
the west tower façade (Ill. p. 100). Work
on the north tower began as early as 1100,
while its southern counterpart was not
completed until 1378. The Romanesque
twin-towered façade was turned into a
three-part, block-like wall with mighty
projecting buttresses, between which
the main portal was inserted. In 1497 an
octagonal tower was built, a variant of
the Strasbourg one; the upper parts were
reconstructed after a fire in 1511. Other
Late Gothic additions are the side chapels,
built under the aegis of the architect
Vinzenz Ensinger of Bern, who was in
charge of the cathedral lodge (1459–89),

Wall painting in the Sylvester Chapel of Konstanz Cathedral, 1584. The Crucifixion and the Prophets Habakkuk and Jeremiah; Descent from the Cross; Pietà; Deposition.

Opposite: The Holy Sepulchre in the rotunda of St Mauritius, *c.* 1260.

and the Franz Xaver Chapel, built under Lux Böblinger from Esslingen (1490–1502). The Welser Chapel on the north side of the tower façade, a showpiece of Late Gothic architecture and sculpture, was restored in the 1920s; the gargoyles are modern.

From the north transept (Thomas choir), an artfully designed newel staircase, the famous 'Schnegg' (Ill. p. 102), leads to the cathedral chapterhouse area. Begun in 1438 by Master Antoni and completed in 1446, this staircase is modelled on examples from the French courts (Charles V's Louvre, the Hôtel Jacques Coeur in Bourges). Pairs of statues of prophets under baldachins stand at the corners of the structure, which is marked

by its ornate tracery. The reliefs on the balustrade tell of the life of the Virgin Mary, juxtaposing Old and New Testament scenes: Annunciation, Birth, Gideon and the Fleece, Burning Bush.

Many of the original wooden sculptures of the diocesan church fell victim to the iconoclasts during the Reformation, including the carved high altar dating from 1466 by the sculptor Nicolaus Gerhaert von Leyden. This work, destroyed in 1529, had a huge effect on the Late Gothic carved altars created by southern German masters in the next decades. The influence of the same great Netherlandish sculptor can be seen in the choir stalls (1467–71) and the panels of the main portal doors (1470), showing

scenes from the childhood and Passion of Christ. Both works come from the local carpentry workshop of Simon Haider, who signed his name in the frame at the top of the door (Ill. p. 102).

Among the preserved altars, it is worth noting the Late Gothic winged altarpiece in St Konrad donated by Bishop Hugo of Hohenlandenberg (Ill. p. 103), together with the relief of the Entombment made of calcareous slate by Hans Morinck (1580) on the retable in the Franz Xaver Chapel. The back wall of the upper chancel, which the Strasbourg architect Pierre-Michel d'Ixnard converted to a Classical style in 1775, is dominated by the Baroque wall painting of the Assumption (1701).

St Stephen

The church of St Stephen is the oldest parish church in Konstanz, dating from the time when the bishopric was founded. The Romanesque building of 1130, which had also been used as a meeting hall by the Council, was replaced by the existing Gothic church in 1428. At the same time, the original choir, which was rectangular in accordance with regional tradition and situated at the west end, was replaced by the long choir at the east end terminating in a polygon. The carved choir stalls, executed around 1450, contain components dating from around 1270 and 1300 taken from the stalls of the earlier Romanesque building. When the tower was finished in 1485, the Gothic building phase came to an end.

When the church was converted again during the Late Baroque period, the choir was given a stucco ceiling, for which bishop's court painter Franz Ludwig

Hermann painted the panel of the Adoration of the Lamb around 1770.

The basilican nave, which still incorporates Romanesque structures, is articulated by arcades of six high pointed arches on octagonal pillars (one Romanesque round pillar remains on the north side). The pillars are painted with a cycle of the lives of the Apostles (1572–83), while the upper wall contains other fragments of painting, together with a twelve-part cycle of scenes from the life of Christ dating from the early 20th century.

The tabernacle is the masterpiece of a sculptor from Konstanz, Hans Morinck, dated 1594. Made of calcareous slate, it is divided into several stories and contains a wealth of figurative reliefs (scenes from the Passion and the Resurrection of Christ). Other impressive works by this artist can be seen on the choir walls, including the epitaph of his wife Effrasina with a relief of the Lamentation (1591).

Opposite top: View of St Stephen, Konstanz, towards the east.
Opposite bottom: Lamentation relief by Hans Morinck in the choir of St Stephen, Konstanz, 1591.

St Georg, Reichenau-Oberzell.

Reichenau Island

Reichenau-Oberzell, St Georg

Abbot Hatto III (888–913), Archbishop of Mainz and Imperial Chancellor, is traditionally regarded as the founder of this former collegiate church. It is said that after going to Rome for the coronation of Emperor Arnulf of Kärnten, he brought back the relic of the head of St George. This Carolingian building, completed around 895 and still largely preserved in its original form in spite of some reconstruction work, is a pier basilica with a nave and two aisles. The transept is not visible from the outside; the rectangular choir rises above a crypt, whose cross-vault is supported by four massive round pillars. To the west, the nave terminates in a semicircular conch, to which a projecting porch was added in the first half of the 11th century. The height of the nave was increased as early as 990 and during the Gothic period the crossing was vaulted and the crossing tower with its pyramid roof was renovated. Another (again Gothic?) reconstruction completed the link between aisles and transept.

St Georg is most famous for the cycle of wall paintings in the nave, dating from around 990. At this time Abbot Witigowo, a close companion of Emperor Otto III, held office (985–97) and a special style of illuminated manuscripts was developed in Reichenau. Since the same artists were often responsible for wall paintings and illuminations, this cycle of wall paintings should also be seen in the context of the Reichenau scriptorium, although their monumental scale meant that special rules had to be observed in the arrangement and sequence of the scenes. The treatment of the stylized architectural background is evidence enough that this work of art dates from the Late Classical period, as Hans Jantzen said: 'A light shimmer of Late Classical art still glows on these Ottonian frescoes from Reichenau.'

Opposite top and bottom: Ottonian fresco cycle in the nave of St Georg, Reichenau-Oberzell.

Bottom: Fresco of the Second Coming in St Michael's Chapel at St Georg, Reichenau-Oberzell.
Below right: Fresco of devils holding a cow-hide at St Georg, Reichenau-Oberzell.

In contrast, the Last Judgment by a painter from Konstanz called Karl Mohr in the west conch of the nave dates from as late as 1708.

On the upper walls of the nave, between the arcades and the windows, a sequence of eight, large-scale paintings relate the miracles of Christ: the healing of the possessed man of Gerasa, the man sick of the palsy, the man born blind, the leper; the raising of the young man of Nain, the daughter of Jairus and Lazarus, together with the calming of the storm on the lake of Gennesaret. The unreal and almost supernatural quality of the space in which the protagonists act out these scenes is typical of Ottonian art, as are the exaggerated, expressive gestures, such as the raised hand of Christ working miracles. The perspective meander frieze running above and below the paintings is still part of the original decoration, as is the painted decoration of the block-like capitals and intrados, although these architectural components

have been much restored, unlike the wall paintings.

A Parusia (return of Christ) fresco dating from the first half of the 11th century covers the east wall (adjacent to the west conch of the nave) of St Michael's Chapel in the upper storey of the anteroom, which gives no direct access to the church. The figure of Christ enthroned on a rainbow within a mandorla is flanked by Maria/Ecclesia as the interceder and an angel bearing a cross, surrounded by the Apostles (c. 1080).

There is one highly original wall painting in St Georg, probably dating from the 13th century, beside the northern steps leading to the choir. It shows devils holding a cow hide rather like a banner with an inscription condemning the chatter of the two foolish women who are shown above as though on a balcony.

St Pirmin arriving at Reichenau and expulsion of the snake. Panel painting of 1624 in the south aisle of Reichenau-Mittelzell Minster.

Opposite: The nave looking towards the west crossing and the imperial loggia of Reichenau-Mittelzell Minster.

Reichenau-Mittelzell Minster

The history of the famous abbey of Reichenau goes back to the year 724. Summoned by the Frankish major-domo Charles Martel and local noblemen to impose a Christian peace on the Alemannic region, the Irish-Scottish itinerant monk Pirmin founded a monastic community on the island, which he himself headed for three years. From 736, Arnefried combined the offices of bishop of Konstanz and abbot of Reichenau. The abbey of Reichenau played an influential role as a political and cultural centre of the empire for centuries to come, producing a large number of prominent personalities and major works of art.

In its present form, the church is the result of numerous extensions and conversions. Pirmin's original building was

a simple hall church, which was soon extended and furnished with a rectangular choir. Records show that an extension in the form of a larger, cruciform basilican church was consecrated in 816 under Abbot Heito I (806–23), a confidant of Charlemagne. Its basic plan can still be seen in the eastern crossing and parts of the eastern transept, as well as in the design of the arcades. Under Abbot Witigowo, the nave was extended to the west and redesigned with the addition of St Michael's Chapel between two stair turrets. These early medieval building projects were temporarily completed in 1048 under Abbot Berno, with the addition of the western transept and the west tower and side entrances modelled on the Ottonian Strasbourg Cathedral. The Gothic choir was built four centuries later, between 1447 and 1477, although

its star vault was not completed until 1553. The upper walls of the nave were reconstructed in 1688. In 1970 restoration work began on the open, barrel-vaulted roof truss of the nave, making as much use as possible of the original oak timbers dating from 1236 and 1237.

From 923 on, the cult of the Holy Blood and the Holy Cross became the liturgical focus of the abbey. Initially, a round structure added to the square choir was used as the monumental shrine for the relic, replaced later by the Gothic choir. The legend of the relic of the Holy Blood and its veneration in Reichenau is depicted in the seven 18th-century wall paintings on the choir walls. The relic itself is now kept in the Baroque monstrance of the Holy Blood altar dating from 1739.

The Gothic rood screen terminating the nave was replaced in 1746 by an ornate, wrought-iron grille to separate the laity from the monks. The reredos of the high altar, dedicated to all saints, was painted by Master Rudolf Stahel, who was active in Konstanz, in 1498. The central panel shows the Coronation of the Virgin. On the floor behind the high altar lies a tomb with the portrait of Abbot Georg Fischer (died 1519) engraved in bronze; in front of it lies the tomb slab of Emperor Charles III, crowned in 881. In the eastern crossing, the oldest part of the abbey, the tomb slab of Count Gerold (died 799), brother of the Alemannic wife of Charlemagne, who donated a golden altar to the church, is a reminder of the Frankish origins of monastic life in Reichenau. A niche on the northern side of the chancel houses a Gothic sandstone Madonna and Child. It dates from around 1300 and is related stylistically to the sculptures in the narthex of Freiburg Cathedral. The wooden pietà in the northern aisle is essentially a late 14th-century work. An artist from Überlingen was responsible for the Renaissance wall

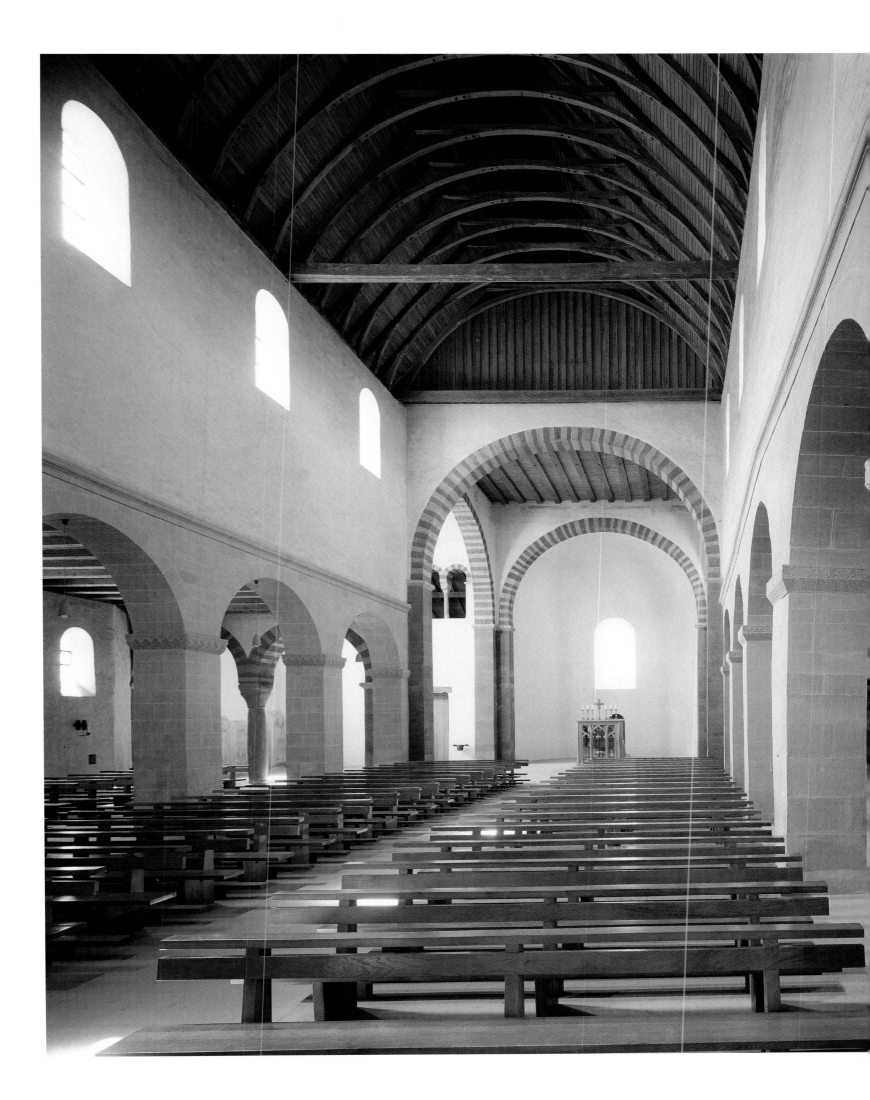

can only be dated from archaeological finds. It is supposed to have been founded by a Reichenau monk called Egino, Bishop of Verona, in 799. Excavations carried out around 1970 have shown that this original building took the form of an aisleless nave church with an eastern apse. Towards 1100 a new building was constructed on the existing foundation walls; the work progressed from east to west and was probably completed around 1134. Dendrochronological tests have proved that it was in that year that the last trees used to produce timber for the building were felled. The new basilica, with a nave and two aisles and without transepts, has a spacious sanctuary and three apses, terminating externally in a flat wall. The sober building, with a low western narthex added in the Late Middle Ages, is surmounted by a pair of Romanesque towers that rise up from the two lateral apses and dominate the eastern façade. In the mid-18th century, the church was converted to the Late Baroque style, which was superimposed on the medieval nave with its five round-arched arcades resting on columns with four-sided capitals, creating a curious contrast with the Romanesque wall painting in the main apse (uncovered around 1900).

This painting, executed between 1104 and 1126, is one of the last examples from the Reichenau School, which produced magnificent works for centuries in the form of both illuminated manuscripts and wall paintings. In the calotte of this apse the Pantocrator is enthroned in a mandorla, surrounded by the symbols of the Evangelists and the two patrons of the church, SS Peter and Paul. Below is an upper register of the twelve seated Apostles and a lower register of twelve standing prophets, in both cases holding books or scrolled parchments and surmounted by arcades. A meander frieze forms the lower frame.

paintings in the Gothic choir, inscribed 1555. The northern wall paintings depict the expulsion of the brazen serpent and the Crucifixion, the gathering of manna and the Last Supper, the sacrifice of Melchizedek and the sacrifice of the Mass. The southern wall paintings (dated 1558) show the sending out of the 72 disciples. A wooden relief of the stoning of St Stephen in the southern aisle, dated

1596, was executed by Hans Ulrich Glöckler, an artist from Überlingen.

The treasury is now in the former sacristy, a Late Gothic room dating from the mid-15th century. Although many works of art from Reichenau, especially the illuminated manuscripts from the world-famous abbey scriptorium, are scattered among various museums and libraries (Ill. p. 33), the treasury still houses some fine pieces, including several reliquary shrines, of which the most precious is the shrine of St Mark, in the form of a sarcophagus. The long sides depict scenes from the childhood and Passion of Christ, executed in chased precious metal. The trefoil-shaped enamel medallions with portraits of the prophets on the frame were originally complemented by gemstones. The short sides depict a miracle wrought by the relic of St Mark and the foundation of the church by the Habsburg royal couple, Albrecht I and Elisabeth. There are medallions of Christ, the Coronation of the Virgin and the Evangelists on the sides of the lid. The shrine of St Mark, which dates from 1303 to 1305, is the work of a goldsmith from Konstanz.

Reichenau-Niederzell, SS Peter und Paul

Because of the lack of any historical records, this former collegiate church

Schloss Arenenberg

The picturesque Schloss Arenenberg on the hilly banks of the Lower Lake (Untersee) played an interesting part in European history. After the fall of Emperor Napoleon I, Hortense de Beauharnais, his adoptive daughter and sister-in-law, took refuge in Switzerland with her son Louis-Napoleon, who later became Napoleon III. She bought this 16th-century manor house with its vineyard in 1817 and had the estate converted along the lines of Malmaison, her mother Josephine's last residence near Paris, turning it into a Classical country seat. Hortense de Beauharnais stayed in Arenenberg more and more frequently and her son spent much of his youth there; later it became a centre for the

Napoleon family who were driven out of France and who eventually established the Second Empire. When he was imprisoned in the fortress of Ham after a failed coup, Prince Louis-Napoleon had to temporarily give up the estate he had inherited from his mother, but managed to buy it back in 1855. In 1865, then Emperor Napoleon III, he visited it again with his wife Eugénie Arenenberg. After the fall of the Second Empire in 1870, Schloss Arenenberg became a favourite summer residence of the widowed empress who lived in exile in England. She also made some changes to the building and furnishings, before leaving the estate to the canton of Thurgau in 1906 to be preserved as a museum.

Two women, Queen Hortense and her daughter-in-law Empress Eugénie, have left their mark on Schloss Arenenberg. The museum has preserved much of this interior with its mixture of Empire, Biedermeier and Second Empire styles.

Queen Hortense's salon on the ground floor of the annex is preserved in its original, pure Empire style. Typical examples are the wall hangings based on a Napoleonic war tent seen in this and in some of the other rooms. Apart from the family portraits and mementos, there are two portraits by Felix Cottrau, one showing Queen Hortense at the piano the other depicting the young Louis-Napoleon climbing up to Schloss Arenenberg in winter, that give an idea

Right: Empress Eugenia's Second Empire salon at Schloss Arenenberg.
Below: Queen Hortense's Empire-style salon at Schloss Arenenberg.

of what it must have been like to live there. The lower salon, facing the lake, was originally an open pavilion, which Empress Eugénie incorporated into the suite of living rooms in 1873. It looks over the splendid panorama of the Lower Lake and beyond to Reichenau Island.

The Empress Eugénie's salon in the upper floor of the annex, decorated in the Second Empire style, reveals a lot about her. It is dominated by the large-scale state portrait of Napoleon III in his coronation robes; beside it hangs a profile portrait of the empress dating from 1861. Both paintings are the work of Franz Xaver Winterhalter. On the table stands a masterly bust of the empress by Jean-Baptiste Carpeaux.

The High Rhine:
from Stein am Rhein to
the Gates of Basel

From Stein am Rhein to Basel in Switzerland
the river, now known as the 'High Rhine',
flows gently through a picturesque landscape.
It is navigable up to Schaffhausen, but
soon after that it turns into a spectacular
cataract, 150 metres (490 feet) wide, that
thunders down from a limestone cliff. The
spectacular Rhine Falls in Schaffhausen
(Ills. pp. 132 and 133) is the largest water-
fall in Central Europe.

This aerial view shows the transition from
lakeland to riparian landscape near the
historic small town of Stein am Rhein,

Stein am Rhein

Below: 'Weisser Adler' house, Stein am Rhein.

Opposite top: The market square of Stein am Rhein, with the town hall (left) and the 'Zur Sonne' inn (right).
Opposite bottom: View over the Rhine to the monastery of St Georg, with Burg Hohenklingen on the ridge of the hill.

Thanks to its strategic position where the Rhine leaves the Lower Lake, protected by a castle with a stone bridge across the river in Roman times, the little medieval town of Stein am Rhein developed into a flourishing trade centre and was granted a town charter in 1267. Emperor Henry II (r. 1014–24) had paved the way in the early 11th century by moving the Benedictine monastery of St Georg here from Hohentwiel (near Singen) and granting it the right to mint coins and to trade. In an attempt to free itself from the authority of the abbot, the commune bought the castle of Hohenklingen, together with all its church advocate's rights, in 1457.

The history of this picturesque castle perched on the hilltop overlooking the small town, which was the seat of the major domo of the monastery, is closely linked to that of the Benedictine abbey of St Georg in Stein. It was first owned by the dukes of Zähringen, later it came into the hands of the barons of Klingen who had the original keep expanded and walled in the entire complex of tower, palace, chapel, kitchen and cellar vault. The wall paintings, dating from around 1440, in the northern choir chapel of the former monastery church of St Georg, where the Hohenklingen family was buried, tell of that ducal dynasty.

The medieval town, which has been preserved as a historic site, centres around three main areas: the town hall square, the monastery buildings and the landing stage. One good example of the picturesque old houses built to reflect

the prosperity of their inhabitants is the residential and business house 'Zum steinernen Trauben' at Rathausplatz No. 128. This 17th-century house, with its Renaissance façade and stone bay dating from 1688, belonged to the rich merchant's family of Etzweiler. The façade painting is a later addition, dating from 1900, as is the case of the pub next door (No. 127), the 'Zur Sonne' inn, where the wooden bay with the coat of arms of the builder Isaak Sulger and his wife Elsbeth Fahling was added in 1689 to the house originally built in 1659.

Former monastery of St Georg

The largely preserved columnar basilica without transepts probably dates back to an early 12th-century reconstruction of the monastery church. Side rooms adjoin the rectangular choir, which extends the entire breadth of the nave, from north to south. On the west front of the church, two square towers originally flanked a two-storey narthex. While the northern tower was rebuilt in the Late Gothic style in 1596 after it was struck by lightening, all that remained of the southern tower was the lower part.

The first four pairs of monolithic columns on the west side of the Romanesque nave, with their octagonally faceted capitals (see Konstanz Cathedral), date from around 110, while the three adjoining eastern columns were not added until the conversion work in 1583. The upper wall, with its round-arched windows reflecting the same rhythm as the arcades, is marked off by a cornice. The timber ceiling is a modern reconstruction.

There are wall paintings from three different periods in the choir. In its

Right: View from the cloister to the south end
of the church.
Below: Donor painting on the northern choir wall.

hieratic forms, the figure of St Christopher
dating from the second half of the 13th
century still looks entirely Romanesque,
while the pictures of the donors and
flanking saints date from the 15th century
and the paintings around the tabernacle
were executed around 1480. The donor
picture on the north wall shows Emperor
Henry II and his wife Kunigunde donating
a model of the Romanesque monastery
church. They are represented as saints,
wearing a crown and nimbus. The picture on the south wall depicts the earlier
church of Hohentwiel and the first pair
of donors, Burkhart II of Swabia and his
wife Hadwig.

One wall painting is still preserved in
the Lady Chapel, built on the north flank
of the choir in the 14th century as the

tomb for the Hohenklingen family. It
shows the *Volto Santo* and is known as the
'Sankt Kümmernis' (St Anxiety).

The church furniture also includes the
windows with coats of arms and insignia
of rank with, on the north side, in the
fourth window from the west, the coat of
arms of Johann Rudolf Rahn, magistrate
of the city of Zurich, dated 1607, and in
the third window the arms of Hans Maler
Seckel, dated 1600. The glass-painters
from Zurich, Christoph and Josias Murer,
had already executed a first cycle after
the renovation of the church between
1583 and 1584. The windows were
renovated again in 1679, probably by
the same donor families as before; fifteen
windows from that period have survived.

Little remains of the Romanesque
monastery buildings (in the west wing of
the cloister and in the parlatory). Yet the
existing cloister is based on the original
Romanesque structure. The whole complex is bordered by the church in the
north and the abbey buildings just by
the river in the south. The chapterhouse
on the east side of the cloister dates back
to the days of Abbot Johannes I Send

121

Page 122 and 123 and below: The great hall of Abbot David von Winkelsheim at the monastery church of St Georg, Stein am Rhein, painted with illusionist loggias, 1515–16.
Left: The medallion of St George and the dragon from the wooden ceiling of the abbot's room in the monastery church of St Georg, 1511.

Opposite top: View over the Rhine to Burg Hohenklingen.
Opposite bottom: Interior of the monastery church of Wagenhausen (Thurgau), facing the chancel.

(1413–44). The refectory was built at the same time. Abbot Jodokus Krum (1460–90) commissioned extensive building works, including the renovation of the cloister, the halftimbered building on the Rhine inscribed with the date 1481, the dormitorium and the predominantly heraldic wall paintings in the interiors. The most important client and patron, however, was Abbot David von Winkelsheim (1499–1525), under whose aegis the buildings completed the transition from Late Gothic to the Renaissance, thanks in particular to the influence of the painter Ambrosius Holbein. The most impressive building constructed during this period was the prelature (abbot's house), begun in 1506 and situated next to the half-timbered Jodokus building south of the monastery, with its bay-windowed gable façades facing the Rhine and the courtyard to the side (Ill. p. 119). The lower room of Abbot David von Winkelsheim overlooking the Rhine side has a wooden ceiling decorated with carved, hexagonal medallions (St George and the Dragon, symbols of Christ, 1511). The high point is the great hall on the upper floor. It is entirely covered with illusionist paintings of a loggia-like architectural framework and grisaille paintings of profane subjects: scenes from the story of Carthage and Rome (1515–16). This cycle of paintings, using the secco technique, is unique in Switzerland and shows that the abbot's taste was affected by the Italian Renaissance, although the style also reflects the direct influence of Augsburg painters such as Hans Burgkmair and Jörg Breu. While the prominent bay facing the Rhine side has delicate fan vaulting, the hall has a heavy, timbered ceiling of parallel barrel vaults, with carvings of Gothic and Renaissance motifs on the longitudinal beams and crossbeams (possibly by Peter Vischer from Stein).

Wagenhausen

On the other side of the river, within sight of Stein am Rhein and Burg Hohenklingen, lies the picturesque complex of buildings of the provost of Wagenhausen. Its origins date back to the 11th–12th century. Like Schaffhausen, this small Benedictine monastery was built during the time of the Hirsau reform. Founded by the abbot of the All Saints monastery church in Schaffhausen in 1083 and declared autonomous in 1105, the monastery flourished briefly before being subordinated to the parent monastery again in 1417 and then closed down during the Reformation.

The plain interior, a pier basilica, originally with a nave and two aisles and three staggered apses, still adheres to the strict structural design of the original Romanesque building, but it also contains remnants of Late Gothic wall paintings. Around 1600 windows were added to the main apse.

The eastern wing of the small cloister has also survived.

Schaffhausen

In 1045 Emperor Henry III (r. 1046–56) granted his cousin Count Eberhard III of Nellenburg the right to mint coins for *Scafhusun*, which was the equivalent to founding a town. The burghers, first described as *burgenses* in a record of 1190, originally came under the monastery church of All Saints, but soon managed to gain their independence. One key to the commune's prosperity lay in its position on the river, which encouraged marketing and trade. The historic corporative and public buildings and the splendid town houses reflect its former wealth, as also in Stein am Rhein.

Squire Hans Christoph of Waldkirch had the grand house of 'Sittich' in the Vordergasse built between 1653 and 1655 under the direction of the town's master mason Heinrich Peyer, to replace two earlier buildings. The façade was rebuilt in 1870 in the Neo-Renaissance style of a pupil of Semper, although the original portal and bay were not touched. The interior (Ill. p. 129) of this house, created by the master carpenter Conrad Mägis in 1655, reflects the wealthy lifestyle of the townspeople of Schaffhausen, tempered by sobriety.

The 'Goldener Ochsen' house (Vorstadt No. 17), reconstructed in 1608 by Hans Ulrich Hageloch, takes its name from an inn that once stood there. The ornamental façade has a round-arched portal of sandstone flanked by columns and a five-sided bay with interesting relief decoration. The painted façade includes a house sign dating from 1610 of a golden ox together with figures from Babylonian history and the Trojan War.

The Baroque buildings standing today, the 'Herrenstube' and the 'Fronwaagturm' (Fronwaagplatz Nos. 3 and 4), were based on plans by Hans Conrad Spengler from 1747, after the old tower had collapsed. The Herrenstube house, with its splendid Baroque portal, was used as a drinking and meeting place for the nobility in the 14th century. The gable of the original medieval tower, in which the market scales used to be kept (now in the All Saints Museum), houses an astronomical clock by Joachim Habrecht dating from 1561, which was taken over from the earlier building.

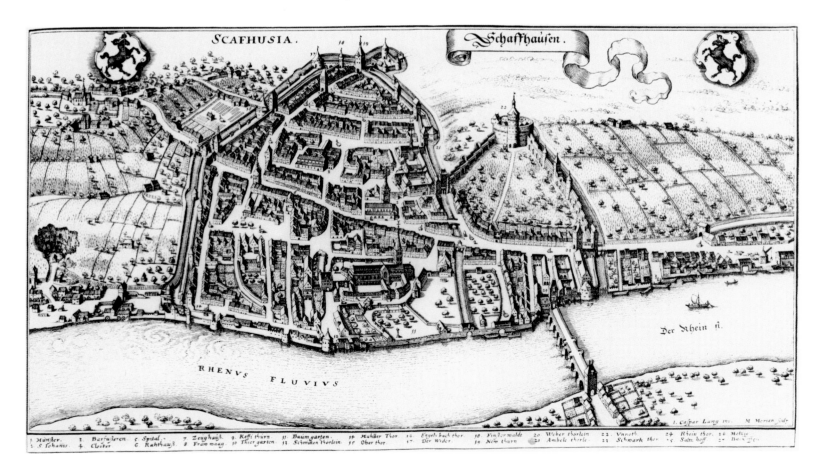

Opposite top: The 'Goldener Ochsen' house at Schaffhausen.

Right: Herrenstube and Fronwaag Tower on the Fronwagplatz in Schaffhausen.
Below: View across the Rhine to the fort of Munot.

'Zum Ritter' is without doubt the most important town house in Schaffhausen, both historically and artistically. The owner, Hans von Waldkirch, had the façade painted in the modern Renaissance style from 1568 to 1570 by the local artist Tobias Stimmer. The pictorial programme is arranged horizontally, following the alignment of the different storeys. It is mainly composed of large allegorical and mythological scenes, which allude to the owner's bourgeois virtues and heroism, such as the picture on the gable showing the Roman hero Marcus Curtius leaping into an open crevice. Unfortunately the painting has suffered badly over the years and been heavily restored. From 1937 to 1939 the painter Carl Roesch renovated the entire façade programme. Fragments of the original painting were housed in the museum (see Ill. p. 130).

The nave looking eastward in the former monastery church of All Saints, Schaffhausen.

All Saints

This former Benedictine monastery church was founded in 1050 by Count Eberhard III of Nellenburg (died 1078) and dedicated to the Saviour and All Saints. Until it was closed in the Reformation, it formed the spiritual centre of the area. Records show that in 1049 Pope Leo IX consecrated an altarpiece of the Resurrection, situated in what is now the St Anne Chapel, and the monastery grounds. Work began on the original church (Schaffhausen I) in 1050, under the direction of a certain Liutbald, the founder's chaplain and steward. It was consecrated in 1064 by Bishop Rumold of Konstanz. The small-scale basilica with a transept that terminates in a semicircular choir is modelled on the monastery churches of St Gall and Einsiedeln. The foundation walls of the choir were dug up south of the present cathedral.

Between 1080 and 1082, Wilhelm of Hirsau, third Abbot of Schaffhausen, introduced the Hirsau rule, a German variant of the Benedictine reform that

Right: The 'Schaffhausen Onyx'. Early Augustan cameo in a 13th-century setting. All Saints Museum, Schaffhausen.
Below: The 'Sittich' room. Interior designed by Conrad Mägis, 1655. All Saints Museum, Schaffhausen.

began in Cluny, into the monastery and then passed it on to his pupil Siegfried. The church was now too small to meet the requirements of the expanding order and was replaced in 1087 by a new, monumental building. At the instigation of Siegfried, that church (Schaffhausen II), which is largely preserved, was constructed on the model of the Hirsau church of St Peter und Paul consecrated in 1091. The choir was completed in 1093, while work on the nave began in 1100. Bishop Gebhard III consecrated them between 1103 and 1104. The square chancel and the massive tower with the northern chapel and the narthex are additions from the later 12th century.

Like the monastery church of Alpirsbach in the Black Forest, built at the same time, the abbey church of Schaffhausen is a perfect example of the architectural style of the Hirsau School. A flat-roofed colonnaded basilica based on a cruciform ground plan, with a staggered choir plan modelled on the monastery church of Cluny II, it reflects the search for simple structures and little decoration. In the front part of the lay church, the nave is articulated by six pairs of columns with plain cushion capitals, while the two eastern pillars mark out the liturgical area of the *chorus minor*, set back behind a screen. The entire east end of the church was reserved to the monks, forming the *chorus maior* with the crossing. A projecting cornice separates the arcades from the clerestory, where the rhythm of the windows reflects the

position of the round arches. The overall impression is sober, with a clear spatial arrangement of the different structures, particularly in the articulation of the transept. Outside, the only decoration is on the five-storey tower, with its blind arcades and the alternating colours of the sandstone ashlars on the corners. The pyramidal helm-roof is a later addition, dating from 1763.

HAVS „ZVM RITTER"
SCHAFFHAVSEN
AVFNAHME VON M=1:20
A. BRANDES 1907

FACADENMALEREI V.
TOBIAS STIMMER
ANNO · 1570

Left: 'Zum Ritter' house, façade by A. Brandes, 1907. All Saints Museum, Schaffhausen.
Below: Wooden model of the Rhine bridge dating from 1757, destroyed 1799. All Saints Museum, Schaffhausen.

All that has survived of the interior decoration is fragments of wall paintings (early 13th century) on the east wall of the choir, and a Credo frieze of intertwined medallions (*c.* 1450) in the southern side choir.

The spacious cloister built around 1100 was renovated in the late Middle Ages using Romanesque elements. Rows of epitaphs dated between 1582 and 1825 line the walls. In 1522 the Gothic St Anne's Chapel was built behind the former chapterhouse at the eastern wing of the cloister. It is a flat-ceilinged, aisle-less nave church with a polygonal, net-vaulted choir.

All Saints Museum

The monastery buildings were turned into a museum in the 1920s. Besides housing extensive collections of artistic and cultural works, it has also preserved some of the cloister rooms (see Ill. p. 129) in their original state. The tombs of the founder of the town and the monastery, Count Eberhard III of Nellenburg, his wife Ita and his son Burkhard (died 1105), now in the Erhard Chapel, are typical examples of Romanesque sculpture on the Upper

'Reitschnecke' tower at Munot, Schaffhausen.

Pages 132 and 133: The Rhine Falls near Schaffhausen.

Rhine. Other remarkable pieces of Romanesque sculpture dating from around 1200 are the fragmentary window lunettes of the abbey chapel, containing figurative images and inscriptions.

Most of the works in Abbot Siegfried's library, which came under Protestant control from 1529, have survived. They include manuscripts from Reichenau, St Gall and Hirsau.

The 'Schaffhausen Onyx' (Ill. p. 129) exhibited in the treasury is unique. It is a Roman cameo from the time of Augustus, representing the *Pax Augusta* as an allegory of the imperial peace regiment. The figure is shown holding a cornucopia in its left hand, a staff of Mercury in its right hand. This Classical work is mounted in a frame consisting of a triple row of pearls and precious stones, with inset figures of lions and eagles, which was probably made in Strasbourg in the 13th century.

Munot

This picturesque fort on the Emmersberg hill dominates the town of Schaffhausen (see Ills. pp. 126 and 127). Its name *unot* (*ohne Not*, without need) is first mentioned in 1460 in connection with a fortified tower built on the same site. When Schaffhausen joined the Confederation in 1501, the town needed an effective system of defence because of its isolated situation on the right bank of the Rhine. In 1563 it was decided to build a new, round fort, the only example of the type of round fortress described by Albrecht Dürer in his theory of fortifications, which appeared in Nuremberg in 1527. The citadel is linked to the Rhine by two walls and towers. Architectural historian Eugène Viollet-le-Duc, who described this impressive complex in detail, praised the defensive yet elegant nature of the architecture, which he considered far superior to comparable buildings in France or Italy.

131

Rheinau

Former Benedictine abbey church

Below the Rhine Falls, the river runs
through a picturesque landscape that
forms an island in the large loop at
Rheinau. This is the site of the impressive Baroque complex of the former
Benedictine abbey. The first monastic
settlement on this protected island dates
back to the 8th century. The Romanesque church, of which only a tympanum
in the narthex of the southern tower
survives, was consecrated in 1114. The
abbey owes its present appearance to
extensive reconstruction in the early
18th century. Franz Beer, a member of
the important dynasty of architects from
Vorarlberg, built the church from 1704
to 1710. The two belfries on the façade
come from the earlier Gothic church.

The interior, however, is characteristic of the Baroque style of the Vorarlberg School. It has a nave surmounted by barrel vaulting with lunettes, engaged piers linked by a gallery, a fairly short transept and a two-bayed, rectangular chancel. The uniform series of ornate altars on the engaged piers of the side chapels form a rhythmic counterpoint to the nave and produce an impressive spatial effect. In line with a custom that was widespread in southern Germany at the time (see Kreuzlingen, Ill. p. 97), the focus is on the ornate, perspective grille separating the lay church from the monks' choir. The high point of the interior decoration is the huge high altar, created by Judas Thaddäus Sichelbein, with the altarpiece of the Assumption of the Virgin. The monochrome stucco work on the vault is by Franz Schmuzer from the Wessobrunn School; the paintings of scenes from the life of the Virgin on the ceiling are the work of Francesco Antonio Giorgioli.

Zurzach

Below left: Arm reliquary of St Verena at the former collegiate church of Zurzach, 14th century.
Below right: Fresco of St Verena in the collegiate church of St Verena, Zurzach, late 15th century.

The town of Zurzach, fortified by a castle on the Rhine in Roman times, became famous in the Middle Ages as the site of the cult of St Verena, a hermit from Egypt who devoted herself to caring for the sick and was buried in Zurzach in 344. The Zurzach Book of Miracles, dating from around 1010, tells of the many pilgrims who flocked to her tomb. Such pilgrimages also promoted the economic development of the town. The regular markets held there became a kind of popular festival, known as the *Zurzacher Messe.*

Below: Zurzach market scene in the great hall of the monastery of St Georg in Stein am Rhein (see Ills. pp. 122–24).
Below right: The Gothic choir tower at the former collegiate church of St Verena, Zurzach.

Former collegiate church of St Verena

After the earlier church collapsed, a new Romanesque building was erected in the early 11th century above the Late Classical graveyard by the old Roman road. It took the form of a pier basilica with nave and two aisles. In 1294 it was largely destroyed by fire. The subsequent reconstruction produced the High Gothic choir, rising upwards like a tower. Queen Agnes of Hungary endowed the building, which was completed with its consecration in 1347. The elegant, tripartite lancet windows of the polygonal choir and the delicate masonry work of the Gothic celebrants' seat behind the high altar reveal stylistic links with some of the works in Strasbourg Cathedral dating from around 1300.

The church was converted to the Baroque style by the architect Giovanni Gaspare Bagnato between 1732 and 1734, with alterations to the upper nave walls and the construction of the splendid choir grille. This grille, which creates the effect of a central perspective space, contains the coat of arms of Prior Carl Joseph Ludwig Bessler. The mighty high altar was erected in 1742.

The choir rises above a three-bayed Gothic hall crypt with a nave and two aisles, which contains the tomb of St Verena, who is represented on the lid of the sarcophagus – as well as on the fresco in the choir – with her attributes of comb and jug, the tools of nursing.

Two precious works reflect the significance of the local cult of the saint. One is a Roman bronze vessel in a 15th-century setting and with a statuette dating from 1602. The other is an arm reliquary of the saint, an exquisite piece of goldsmiths' work dating from around 1294. The base is decorated with enamel plaques with scenes from the life of St Verena. The arm, inset with filigree and precious stones, has an opening at the wrist that provides a view of the relic; the fingers hold the golden comb.

Augst/Augusta Raurica

The Roman colony of Augusta Raurica on the left bank of the Rhine, twelve kilometres (over seven miles) from Basel, had already attracted the interest of the Basel humanists Andreas Ryff and Basilius Amerbach (see pp. 26–27) in the 16th century, when they carried out the first archaeological excavations north of the Alps on this site. The earliest timber buildings date from around 15–10 BC, the first stone buildings from AD 40–70.

The surface area of the Roman residential settlement with its main forum, temple and basilica extended as far as the 'castle' hill on the left bank of the Rhine. The impressive remains of the theatre built into the slope, the largest one north of the Alps, come from several successive building periods. The lower structure of a Corinthian podium temple has survived on the hill of Schönbühl on the other side of the river.

In accordance with Roman custom, the settlement was constructed on the basis of a rectangular road grid. The artisans and tradesmen lived in rather modest quarters, while the rich merchants lived in comfortable atrium houses, equipped with baths and decorated with mosaics.

Augusta Raurica, which must have had a population of around 20,000 during its golden age of 200, was burned to the ground by the Alemanni in 260. As the

Right: The centre of the 'Meerstadt' platter from the hoard of silver at Kaiseraugst. Römermuseum, Augusta Raurica.
Below left: Remains of a sanctuary at Augusta Raurica.
Below right: The curia at Augusta Raurica.

inhabitants began to feel increasingly insecure, they built a city wall. Augusta Raurica became part of the new province of *Maxima Sequanorum* under the Emperor Diocletian. Parts of the town were destroyed in the 4th century, while at the same time *Castrum Rauracense* on the other side of the Rhine gained importance as a military camp.

In 1962, the magnificent silver hoard of Kaiseraugst, which must have been buried there after 350 for safety reasons, was discovered near the fortifications. It consists of Roman imports of extraordinary quality. One is a round platter decorated in the centre with a medallion containing a highly original depiction of a sea teeming with boats, fish and people against an imaginary architectural setting.

The Upper Rhine:
from Basel to Mainz

The course of the Upper Rhine (Oberrhein), dropping gently from Basel to Mainz, used to flow naturally into irregular branches with stretches of marshland and meadow. Nowadays much of the river has been industrialized by canalization and barrage weirs and the landscape is much less picturesque.

The region between the Black Forest and the Vosges has always been in the mainstream of European history and culture, with Basel and Strasbourg (now the seat of the European Parliament) as the focal points.

The photograph shows the view across the Rhine to Basel Cathedral.

Basel

Archaeological excavations have proved that Basel's origins are Celtic. The nucleus of the settlement was the strategically sited hill sloping down to the Rhine on which the cathedral now stands. Here the Romans who had settled in Augusta Raurica, 12 kilometres (over 7 miles) up river, built a walled stronghold in place of the Celtic *oppidum* (town). When it came under attack from the Alemanni in the 3rd century, Augusta Raurica was increasingly abandoned in favour of Basilea. The Roman structure can be seen today in Basel's street layout.

The Romans retreated to Italy around 400 and were succeeded by the Alemanni. According to the *Notitia Galliarum* Basel was a bishop's seat from the beginning of the 5th century. Like Lausanne, the bishopric, which included the whole of the Sundgau (southern Alsace), came under the jurisdiction of the archdiocese of Besançon.

Basel became part of the Lotharingian Kingdom under the Treaty of Verdun in 843 and of the East Frankish Empire under the Treaty of Meerssen in 870. In 917 the city and the Carolingian minster were

totally destroyed by the Hungarians. Emperor Henry II took Basel over from the Burgundian King Rudolf II in 1006 and renewed the bishop's secular rule. In 1083 the bishop built the first ring of walls. The construction of the first wooden bridge across the Rhine after 1200 encouraged Basel's development as a trading centre and its citizens opposed the authority of the bishops with increasing success. The ring of walls enclosing all the suburbs and Lesser Basel on the right bank of the Rhine was completed just before 1400. The council convened

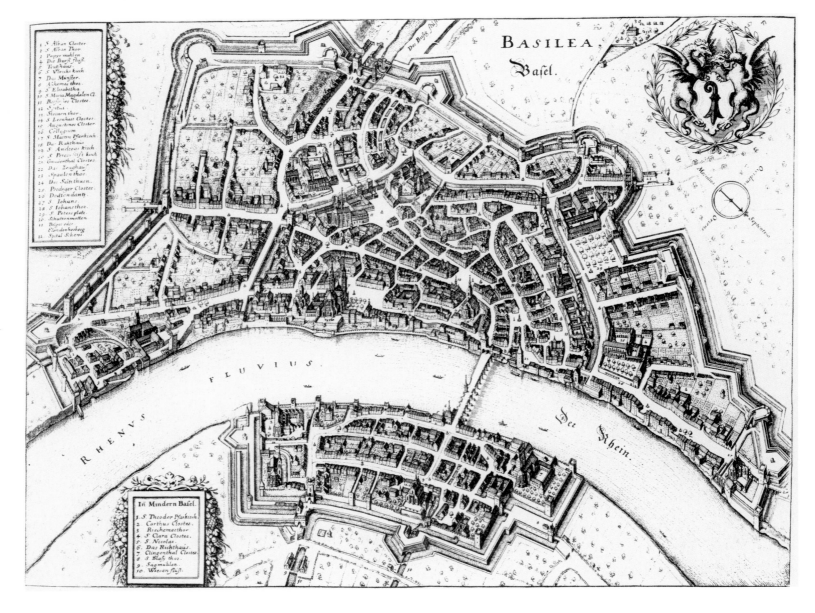

Spalentor, Basel, c. 1398.

to discuss the reform of the church met
in Basel from 1431 to 1448. In 1501 the
citizens won their independence in the
Treaty of Basel and joined the Swiss
Confederation.

In 1523 the city opened up to the
Reformation and numerous churches and
works of art were lost in the iconoclasm
that followed. Basel became a centre of
humanism and printing, associated with
names such as Erasmus of Rotterdam and
Johann Froben. The famous copperplate
engraver Matthäus Merian was also a
native of the city. His city pictures (some
of which appear in this book) were of outstanding artistic and cultural importance.

Spalentor

Between the 14th century and 1860 Basel
was surrounded by walls and the Spalentor
gate, built in 1398, was the main entrance
to the city and the end of the Sundgau
road. This imposing structure has been
well preserved. It consists of three towers,
a rectangular central block with a pointed
pyramidal roof flanked by two round
towers with octagonal upper stories
ending in a platform topped with battlements. The façade, which faces away
from the city, is notable for its important
sculptural decoration. On top of the
entrance is the city's coat of arms and
above that the Virgin (the city's patron
saint) and Child on a crescent moon,
flanked by the console figures of two
prophets (replaced by copies in 1932).
The statues now in the Historisches
Museum, Barfüsserkirche (the Franciscan
church museum), dating from around
1400, were made in the same workshop
as the west gable and St George Tower
of the cathedral, which was associated
with the Parler family.

Rathaus

Records refer to a town hall (*domus com-
munitatis*) as early as the 13th century.
From at least the beginning of the 14th

Basel Cathedral from the northwest.

century it was in the main market square, from which the Rhine bridges and the main traffic routes that converged there could be controlled. After the city joined the Confederation in 1501, the old building proved to be insufficient for its needs. Work on a new building in keeping with the status and pretensions of the citizens began in 1504 and all the phases up to 1611 are documented in detail. According to the records, Hans Holbein the Younger finished painting the 'great council chamber' in the rear building in 1530, having stopped work on it in 1522 (fragments are in the Kunstmuseum).

The imposing main section with its two façades on to the market and court-yard dates from 1504 to 1514 (the fine wrought-iron latticed gate was made in 1611). The market frontage was extended to the left when the 'front office' was added on the northwest side between 1606 to 1608. The flanking extensions to the tower and the bay façade are additions dating from around 1900, when the buildings at the back were also altered.

The original furniture and fittings of some rooms have been preserved. In the 'government representatives chamber', which has a magnificent wooden ceiling, there is an elaborate oak and precious wood portal frame made in 1595 by Franz Parregod (Grandfontaine), who had become a citizen of Basel two years earlier. As is confirmed by the key work on ornamentation published in 1593, *Architectura von Austeilung, Symmetrie und Proportion der Säulen* by the architect, painter and theoretician Wendel Dietterlin, this ceiling shows the influence of the Strasbourg group of artists.

Basel Cathedral

The origins of the Basel bishopric are obscure. In the early 7th century Ragnachar from the Luceuil monastery was appointed abbot of the churches of

Romanesque Apostle relief in Basel Cathedral.

Basel and Augst. The remains of a (possibly Carolingian) crypt with three apses have been found to the east of what is now the chancel. According to records, the ceremonial consecration of the church in 1019 by Bishop Adalbero (999–1025) was attended by the Emperor Henry II. The lower part of the north tower (the St George Tower) has survived from this 'Heinrich Building', which was a two-aisle basilica with a twin tower façade. The church was rebuilt after a fire in 1185. In 1200 Abbot Martin von Pairis preached the crusade and on his return five years later he donated a ceiling for the high altar, which indicates that the chancel had been completed. The ground plan of this Late Romanesque cathedral, largely preserved, was in the shape of a Latin cross and it had a polygonal ambulatory chancel that was unique in the empire at the time.

The nave has three massive double bays, with six corresponding bays in the aisles. The elevation is three storeys high. Above the pointed arches runs a gallery floor, semicircular like the upper clerestory window. Thus different building styles were juxtaposed, the pointed arch undoubtedly influenced by Burgundy, while the layout of the walls with the gallery opening comes from northern Italy (see S. Ambrogio in Milan). However, the appearance of the present building has been impaired by the removal of the original ribs and reinforcing arches still visible in the aisles, which corresponded to the three-dimensional arches, when the vaulting was renovated in the late 14th century.

The raised liturgical chancel above the crypt, with steps leading up to it from the crossing, has numerous counterparts in Italy, but the unusual layout of the chancel ambulatory, which originally went up to the level of the crypt (ground level), is somewhat obscured by the addition of a false ceiling. It was added

when the chancel was rebuilt in the Gothic style after collapsing in the 1356 earthquake. Johannes von Gmünd, a Gothic architect who also designed the chancel of Freiburg-im-Breisgau Cathedral after 1359, was called in for the reconstruction work and found an ingenious way of retaining the Romanesque structure of the cathedral church. Above the arcading of the ambulatory the wall of the chevet is broken up by pointed windows, their mullions also incorporating the gallery area pierced by rosettes, creating a sort of lattice. When viewed from outside, there is a clear link between the rosettes, a motif already used by the Romanesque architects in the transept, and the round shapes of the chancel ambulatory. The new Gothic chancel was consecrated in 1363.

Towers were often not completed until later, partly because they were used as a kind of lift shaft in which the building materials for the vaulting could be hoisted up on winches. In 1414 an

architect from Strasbourg, probably Ulrich von Ensingen, who was also head of the Ulm lodge, came to Basel and provided an outline plan for the towers. He also produced plans for the spires of Strasbourg and Ulm cathedrals, although they were never built. As in Basel, they were pyramid shaped with concave curved ribs. However, Ulrich died in 1419 and it was Johannes Cun who actually built the towers between 1421 and 1428. At the same time the gable on the façade with statues of the Virgin Mary, the Holy Roman Emperor Henry and his wife Kunigunde was restored. Work on the St Martin Tower on the south side did not begin until 1470. It was built by Johannes von Nussdorf, who became senior master of the lodge in 1475. Although modelled on the St George Tower, the St Martin Tower is more elegant.

Of the exterior statuary, the two groups on the tower façades are notable. On the left is St George fighting the dragon (after 1372; the original, which used to be painted in bright colours, is now in the Klingentalmuseum) and on the right St Martin and the beggar (19th-century copy).

The St Gall Portal in the north transept, possibly so named because the north cross-arm is known as the St Gall Chapel, is an important example of German Romanesque sculpture. In the tympanum is Christ enthroned with book and sceptre. Next to him are St Peter and the Emperor Henry with a model of the church and St Paul bringing in Kunigunde, assisted by an angel. On the architrave are the Wise and Foolish Virgins, with the Wise Virgins being received by Christ. In the bottom three niches of

the side pillar are works of mercy and above them figures of John the Baptist (left) and the Evangelists (right). At the very top are angels sounding the Last Judgment, which go with the reliefs of the dead rising from their graves in the spandrels. On the recessed doorposts, framed by inset columns, are relief figures of the four Evangelists with their symbols above them: Matthew and John (Ill. p. 38) on the left, Mark and Luke on the right.

The round-arched portal dates mainly from the late 12th century, although it is not in its original position and has been much modified since being moved to its present location in 1356. For instance, the structure of the frame was

a Renaissance addition, while much of the restoration work was undertaken in the 19th century.

Two works typical of the outstanding achievements of German sculptors before the emergence of the Gothic style have been preserved in the interior. The four-part composition of the St Vincent panel depicts the Spanish deacon's martyrdom in a series of eight scenes full of figures and action. The pictures at the top show him being interrogated, whipped, imprisoned and tortured on the grid. At the bottom are scenes of his body being taken out of the tower and protected by ravens against wild animals in the countryside, thrown into the sea and finally rescued by his followers, who

The Romanesque St Gall Portal in the north
transept at Basel Cathedral.

built him a mausoleum. On the Apostle
relief, which probably once had a counterpart, Peter, John, Bartholomew, James,
Simon and Judas are shown in pairs
under three semicircular arches, debating
in the manner of classical philosophers.
The design of the relief was undoubtedly
inspired by Early Christian sarcophaguses and possibly by the sculpture of
northern Italy.

The Gothic period is represented by
the west portal, which was originally
further to the east and led from the
narthex to the nave before being moved
to this position after the 1356 earthquake. The exaggerated gestures and
mime of the figures of prophets and
angels in the soffits of the archivolts
are in the style of an influential workshop that has left its mark in Strasbourg,
Colmar, Regensburg and elsewhere.
The scenes from the Passion, the life of
the Virgin and the Last Judgment that
used to be in the tympanum were lost in
the iconoclasm of the Reformation. The
statues of the Antichrist or Prince of the
World and a Foolish Virgin to the right
of the main portal are all that remain of
a late-13th-century Wise and Foolish
Virgins cycle in the porch. There is a
clear thematic and stylistic link with the
cycle in the right portal on the façade of
Strasbourg Cathedral (and the porch in
Freiburg), although the Basel carvings,
with their caricatured features, are not
of the same quality. The corresponding
figures of Henry II and the Empress
Kunigunde on the left of the portal are
from the same period.

Amongst the figurative monuments
inside the cathedral the monument of
Anna von Hohenberg, wife of King
Rudolf of Habsburg (died 1281), and her
infant son Karl is particularly striking.
The tomb of Duke Rudolf von Tierstein,
who died in 1318, is the oldest surviving
example on the Upper Rhine of a tomb
with the figure of a knight in chain mail.

Left: The Hallwyl reliquary from Basel Cathedral treasury. Strasbourg, before 1470. Historisches Museum, Basel.
Below: Woollen wall hanging depicting nobles with mythical beasts. Basel, c. 1410–20. Historisches Museum, Basel.

Opposite: The chancel of the Franciscan church in the Historisches Museum (sculpture collection). Historisches Museum, Basel.

On both tombs the recumbent figures on the lid are treated as if they are standing.

The stone pulpit dating from 1486 is an exquisite work by Hans von Nussdorf, who designed the St Martin Tower. With its purely ornamental profiled bars, reticulated tracery and pinnacles and miniature heads of prophets, it resembles goldwork, while the cup-shaped housing with its upswept lines suggests the organic shape of a flower.

Two medieval cloisters complete the episcopal church complex. The larger one, attached to the south aisle and transept, was modernized in the mid-15th century. The east wing was vaulted in 1442, the west wing between 1462 and 1467. The small cloister further to the east was completed in 1487. The walls are covered with numerous memorial plaques; one of the most interesting is the one erected by Bishop Christoph von Utenheim for his nephew Wolfgang who died in 1501, although it was seriously damaged in the Reformation. This plaque occupies a whole section of the wall in the large cloister and shows Wolfgang dressed as a knight, kneeling in prayer and looking up at Calvary.

Historisches Museum (the former Franciscan church)

In the early 14th century the simple church built between 1253 and 1256 for the Franciscan order, which had been established in Basel since 1231, was replaced by a new building, one of the most important mendicant order churches north of the Alps. Part of the church was already usable at the time of the Franciscan general chapter in 1332, although the chancel was still under construction in 1343. The structure of the wide two-aisle nave is reminiscent of the Dominican church in Guebwiller in Alsace. Even the profiles of the large arches are similar, but, with seven rows of arches, it is longer than the Guebwiller church. The most impressive feature of the Basel church is the monumental separate chancel, which extends across four bays with a five-sided polygon and projects over the nave. Much of the wall is broken up by tall triple lancet windows, giving the sanctuary the spiritual atmosphere of a light-flooded shrine. The contrast between this part of the church reserved for the monks and the simple mendicant order architecture of the nave used by the laity is particularly marked here.

Both the aisles and the façade had to be restored after the 1356 earthquake. A process of decline began with the Reformation in 1529. First the chancel and then the aisle were used as a store. From 1843 to 1845 the church was turned

Below: View of the Rhine from Basel, *c.* 1535. Pen-and-ink drawing and watercolour on paper. Historisches Museum, Basel.

Opposite top: Konrad Witz or his circle, Basel *Dance of Death.* Fragment of duchess. Tempera on plaster, *c.* 1435–40. Historisches Museum, Basel.

into a warehouse for the tradesmen's institute. Finally it was repaired between 1890 and 1894 and converted for use as a historical museum for the city of Basel.

The exhibits, mainly medieval, include fine examples of Late Gothic tapestry, which give at least some idea of the originality and diversity of a craft that was particularly flourishing on the Upper Rhine.

The chancel is the magnificent setting for the sculpture collection. The cathedral's treasures are kept in a side room. One of the old furnishings is the Hallwyl reliquary, a major work by an Upper Rhine goldsmith. It was donated to the cathedral in 1470 by a citizen of Basel, Rudolf von Hallwyl (Ill. p. 150), and the hallmark shows it to be Strasbourg work. It consists of a gilded silver shrine containing relics of the Holy Cross and the Sacred Blood, decorated with Gothic tracery and the founders' coats of arms with a gold Crucifixion group on top. With its detailed portrayal of the body

hanging on the wooden trunk, the wounds on the hands and feet represented by diamonds and the wound in the side by a ruby, the crucifix is above all an expression of the religious beliefs and devout reverence of mysticism, exemplified by the figures of Mary and John (see the stone cross by Nicolaus Gerhaert von Leyden in Baden-Baden, p. 211).

The museum also has nineteen fragments of the famous Basel *Dance of Death*, a series of paintings nearly 60 metres (197 feet) long in tempera on plaster depicting a procession to the charnel house. It was originally inside the cemetery wall of the Dominican church, which was demolished in 1805. The series, watercolours of which have been handed down, shows people of different classes, ages and characters dancing with death. An inscription under each pair shows Death's exhortation and the victim's reply. The name of the artist is unknown, but the piece has a number of similarities with the work of Konrad

Witz, suggesting that it was by him or a member of his circle. It must have been painted during the council; the *memento mori* iconography is possibly a reference to the plague epidemic of 1439. It was restored by the Basel painter Hug Kluber in 1568, but it has since then been somewhat disfigured by later restoration work.

The delicate pen-and-ink drawing of Basel measuring 9 by 40 centimetres (3½ by 15¾ in.) has been attributed at various times to two cartographers, Konrad Morand and Ambrosius Holbein. It is a faithfully detailed panoramic view of Lesser Basel across the Rhine on the built-up left bank, dominated by the cathedral. On the left the Klingental monastery stands out from the landscape on the right bank of the Rhine, which is then still empty. The old Rhine bridge links it to the old parts of town around the churches of St Augustine and St Martin on the right. This valuable drawing, combining topographical and artistic skill, records how the city looked in 1535.

Ottmarsheim

Nunnery church

This site, which lies about 30 kilometres (over 18 miles) north of Basel on the old Roman road from Milan to Mainz, was first mentioned in 881. Around 1030 Count Rudolf von Altenburg built an abbey for women on the site and the abbey church was consecrated by the Alsatian Pope Leo IX (Bruno of Egisheim) in 1049. It was founded by a close relative of Bishop Wernher of Strasbourg, a member of the Habsburg dynasty (which acquired its name later from the Habichtsburg in Aargau). Although he established the House of Habsburg in power on the Upper Rhine by assigning the church advocate's rights to his wife and daughters, he was not acting solely

for dynastic reasons. As patron, he was inspired by an ambitious concept of imposing architecture, at least so the comparison with Charlemagne's Palatine Chapel in Aachen modelled on the church of S. Vitale in Ravenna would suggest. The unusual central structure in Ottmarsheim soon prompted speculation; in fact the Sélestat humanist Beatus Rhenanus took it to be a heathen temple of the god Mars. It was not until the 19th century that the famous Basel art historian Jacob Burckhardt pointed out its similarities with Aachen.

The centrally planned structure of the church rises above an octagonal ground plan with the outside and inside in the shape of two concentric octagons

orientated to the rectangular front section of the tower and the two-storey square chancel. The internal octagon in the centre forms the actual church area. It has a domed vault and is surrounded by a two-story ambulatory opening in heavy semi-circular arches at ground level, while each of the tall rows of arches on the gallery story has an elegant arrangement of two columns one above the other with cubiform capitals. The upper clerestory is pierced by small round windows. The walls are of irregularly polychrome reddish and yellowish broken stone. In comparison with Aachen, all the components of this structure are simpler and more economical, making it extremely effective.

Wall elevation of the octagon at Ottmarsheim,
looking towards the chancel.

The outside of the building is also
clearly articulated. Some of its features,
such as the apertures in the lower storey,
the heavy rolled frieze on the edge of
the roof and all the stonework on the
north and south side of the octagon,
were added during 19th-century restoration. Changes had also been made in
the late Middle Ages; for instance wall
paintings were added in the ambulatory
and chancel around 1460, in 1465
Abbess Ursula von Andolsheim had
a chapel built at the southwest end and
in 1582 a chapel for the canonesses was
built on to the north side of the chancel.
A keystone in the Gothic vaults bears
the coat of arms of Abbess Agnes
von Dormentz, under whom the
Benedictine nunnery became a community of gentlewomen that remained in
existence until 1792.

In fact, there were other examples of
centrally planned buildings after 1000
(for instance in Nijmegen, Thionville,
Compiègne, Liège, Mettlach and
Germigny-des-Prés) and the architect
probably did not model Ottmarsheim
directly on the Palatine Chapel in
Aachen. The source of inspiration is
more likely to have been a building that
had already translated the imperial style
into Ottonian architecture, such as the
nunnery church in Essen, which has
the same elevation as Aachen in the west
part and retains the classical decoration.
In Ottmarsheim the forms are mostly
simplified and the polychromy of the
stonework comes into play instead.
Possibly the church was modelled on a
type of church dedicated to the Virgin
Mary rather than the Aachen Palatine
Chapel – although there was also a sort
of imperial palace in Ottmarsheim used
by the Habsburgs when they stayed
there – or the nuns' gallery in Essen
might have been the inspiration.

Thann

The legendary origins of the small town on the edge of the southern Vosges are connected with a relic of St Theobald, Bishop of Gubbio in Umbria, who is said to have performed miracles here in 1161. The first documentary reference to Thann was in 1225. In 1290 the place was designated an *oppidum* and it was fortified with a wall around 1360. Its rise is due partly to the local veneration of the saint and the associated pilgrimage and partly to its convenient position on the main trading route between Milan and Flanders.

Collégiale St-Thiébault

A church dedicated to St Theobald is recorded as early as 1287 but the collegiate church in its present form evolved over more than two centuries, suggesting that there were financial difficulties despite the revenue generated by pilgrims. Starting in 1389 a parish church was built in place of a simple pilgrimage chapel, with the Virgin Mary as its patron saint as well as St Theobald.

The south aisle, for which the lower floor of the tower preserved from the original church (now the St Theobald Chapel) served as a chancel, was built first of all in the early part of the 14th century, together with the lower part of the west façade. The Gothic chancel, which was three bays deep and terminated in a five-sided polygon, was started in 1351 but not consecrated until after 1423. The north aisle was built between 1430 and 1492. Its star-ribbed vault is the work of the Basel architect Remigius Faesch, who in 1495 also completed the four-bay nave with a ribbed vault aligned with the chancel and designed the gable façade. The citizens were so impressed by his work that they appointed him architect for life. Between 1506 and 1516 he built the filigree tower in the Upper Rhine tradition originating from Freiburg. The polygonal Lady Chapel, still with Gothic forms, was erected on the south flank between 1629 and 1631.

The church contains some exquisite late medieval statues. The processional statue of St Theobald with two founders at his feet was made in a Basel workshop around 1500. The sweeping folds of the cloak and the melancholy expression suggest that the statue of the saint in bishop's vestments in the St Theobald

Double portal on the west façade of the Collégiale
St-Thiébault, Thann.

Chapel, seated and holding the staff with
two angels hovering above him carrying
the mitre, was made at the Basel workshop of Hans Hoffmann in the 1530s.
The graceful *Virgin of the Winegrowers* in the
Lady chapel might have come from the
same workshop but was certainly made
shortly after 1500. The monumental
Christ bearing the cross in the north
aisle dates from around 1420.

The stained glass in the eight 15
metre (49-foot) high chancel windows
was made by various craftsmen between
1420 and 1460 and restored after the
First World War. It shows Genesis, the
Ten Commandments and the messianic
prophesies, the public life and Passion
of Christ, the life of the Virgin Mary,
the miracles of St Theobald and the
martyrdom of St Catherine. The last
was donated in 1422 by Catherine of
Burgundy, widow of the Habsburg duke
Leopold IV, Landgrave of Alsace, and
daughter of the Duke of Burgundy,
Philip the Bold (the town had been
under Habsburg rule since 1324).

The size of the double portal on
the west façade – 15 metres (49 feet)
high by 8 metres (6 feet) wide – and
its arrangement make it an outstanding
example of Gothic carving on the Upper
Rhine. The complex configuration, consisting of two tympana above the doors
spanned by another large tympanum,
results from a change of plan during
the construction and yet the style of
the figures on the three tympana seems
completely uniform. The plan was
based on the double portal, with the
Crucifixion (Christ and the two thieves,
restored in the 17th century) on the left
tympanum and the annunciation to the
shepherds and the arrival of the Magi
from the east on the right tympanum.
In the hollowed mouldings of the small
archivolts were scenes of martyrdom and
the whole was surmounted by two rows
of tall arches depicting Genesis and more

scenes of martyrdom. It was only then
that the idea of adding a Marian cycle
to the original design was conceived. It
would appear in the large arches above
the double portal. Three rows of arches

would be added to the existing two large
archivolts, with a row of prophets and
a double leaf frieze inside and kings
of Judea, Evangelists and Fathers of
the Church and a row of carved angel

Left: Star vault in the north aisle of the Collégiale St-Thiébault, Thann.
Below: Nave of the Collégiale St-Thiébault, Thann, looking towards the chancel.

musicians outside. An archivolt with figures of saints of the Basel diocese was accordingly added to each of the two small tympana. The pillar statues date from the 19th century. Above the portal are a deesis and early 15th-century statues of the Apostles. On the gable is St Theobald, patron saint of the town (late 15th century).

The north portal opposite the town hall was also magnificently decorated. In simplified form and translated into a modern style, it is similar in design to the west portal, with a large ogee (S-curved profile) arch above. Ulrich von Ensingen, the Strasbourg Cathedral architect, was obviously an influence, but the Middle Rhine (Frankfurt am Main) style is also visible. The date 1456 on the statue of John the Baptist, the counterpart to St Theobald next to the trumeau Virgin, shows when the sculptures were made. The heads of the mother and child are modern. The folds of the drapery, still soft but already sharper, are characteristic of the 'Dark Age' style.

Murbach

Abbey church of St Leodegar

All that remains of the splendid structure of the Romanesque abbey church is the towering fortress-like monumental east end with its prominent twin towers, testifying to the importance of this Alsatian abbey.

Around 726, itinerant Irish-Scottish monks settled at the end of the narrow wooded Murbach valley above Guebwiller. Pirmin, founder of Reichenau abbey, was also involved in the organization of the monastery founded and endowed by Count Eberhard vom Nordgau (died 747) and Murbach, like Reichenau, soon became a centre for the arts and sciences. Around 780 Alkuin paid tribute to the Murbach school for its part in the Carolingian Renaissance. Many church and monastic foundations originated in Murbach and it produced leading churchmen, such as Bishop Simpert of Augsburg and Bishop Landeloh of Basel. From 1228 onwards the abbots bore the honorary title of prince-abbot.

Very little is known about the appearance of the Romanesque church, which, according to records, was consecrated in 1134 (this date probably referred to the chancel). The Romanesque nave was demolished in the 18th century during a planned Baroque renovation of the abbey. However, work came to a halt in 1739 when the monks decided to give up the abbey and the Benedictine rule to settle in nearby Guebwiller as secular canons. Using materials from the old abbey the 'foundation of the knights of Murbach' complex was built there between 1762 and 1785, with a church dedicated to the Virgin Mary. Only the east end of the Murbach church was preserved and this building was handed over to the local community as a parish church.

Contemporary drawings show how the abbey church looked during the demolition phase. The mid-12th-century

founder. His recumbent figure can be seen on the tomb in a Gothic arch niche (late 13th century, traces of polychromy).

On the columnar portal with its sculptural decoration on the south transept arm is a tympanum with a stylized foliage pattern and two bas-relief lionesses facing each other which show Italian influences.

flat-roofed basilican nave was 20 metres (65 feet) high, the same as the Ottonian cathedral in Strasbourg. The nave was probably similar to those in the Rhine cathedrals (the first building of Speyer, Worms and Mainz).

The east end consists of a transept with two towers above and the square main chancel with two side chancels. All the vaulting, even in the side chancels, has squared built-up ribs. The rectangular crossing is flanked by square transept arms. Above the side chancels are galleries opening on to the main chancel in *bifore*, whose exact function is unknown. The triple chancel layout on the Cluniac model conforms to the Hirsau reform rules.

The east view of the church, the main façade, is impressively enhanced by a distinctive uniform division. Blind arches made of square stone blocks in alternating colours frame the six round-arched windows of the main chancel, placed one above the other in two groups of three. Above them is a blind gallery with half pillars. The gable and eaves are lined with arched mouldings. By contrast the figurative sculptures on the gallery and gable are fairly crude. It is the arrangement of the proportions that makes the whole structure so impressive. The chancel window set back in the wall is similar in design to the transept in Limburg an der Haardt (Ill. p. 233).

In the south transept wing is the wall monument to Eberhard, the secular

Freiburg

The medieval city of Freiburg was founded relatively recently by the dukes of Zähringen, an Alemannic noble dynasty named after the imperial castle of Zähringen im Breisgau, which gained control over the Upper Rhine in the late 11th century. A planned city with a coinage prerogative and customs jurisdiction grew up to the south around 1120 beneath the castle built by Duke Berthold II where the Dreisam valley emerges on to on the Rhine plain. With its easy access and the silver mining in the hinterland, it quickly began to flourish. Regular in shape and laid out on two main road axes, the city was dominated by the cathedral, whose Gothic tower became the symbol of Freiburg and the *Land* of Breisgau. However, it was not

until 1827 that it was upgraded from a parish church to the episcopal church in place of Konstanz.

Freiburg Cathedral

The first town parish church built on this site shortly after 1120, a two-aisle basilica with no transept, soon proved too small. Around 1200 work started on a new building that the dukes of Zähringen designated as their burial place instead of the Benedictine abbey of St Peter in the Black Forest. The crossing and transept and the substructure of the 'cockerel towers' on either side of the chancel were built in the first phase. These parts are very similar to the late Romanesque cathedral in Basel, suggesting a link with the Basel

lodge. Unlike Basel Cathedral, however, the Freiburg church had no choir ambulatory. The walled openings of the arches on the west walls of the transept wing indicate that the nave was planned with galleries, as in Basel. The first phase of work, still in the Romanesque style, was followed by a second phase with new models. The two eastern bays of the nave

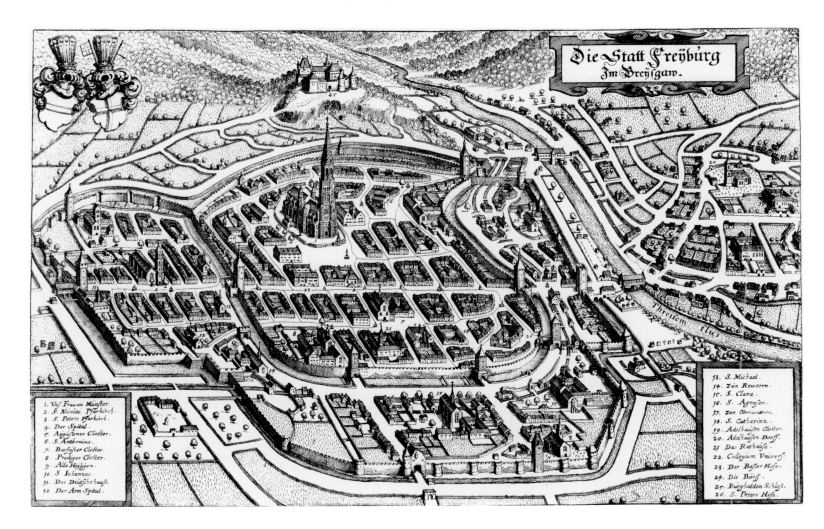

1. Vnf Frawen Münfter.
2. S. Nicolai Pfarkirch.
3. S. Peters Pfarkirch.
4. Der Spital.
5. Augustiner Closter.
6. S. Anthonius.
7. Barfüser Closter.
8. Prediger Closter.
9. Alle Heyligen.
10. S. Iohannes.
11. Das Deutsche Hauß.
12. Der Arm Spital.

13. S. Michael.
14. Zun Reweren.
15. S. Clara.
16. S. Agnesen.
17. Zur Oberwiedern.
18. S. Catherina.
19. Adelhausen Closter.
20. Adelhausen Dorff.
21. Das Rathause.
22. Collegium Vniuersi.
23. Der Basler Hofe.
24. Die Bürff.
25. Burghalden Schloßt.
26. S. Peters Hofe.

Page 162: The Gothic upper chancel of Freiburg Cathedral.
Page 163: View of Freiburg Cathedral from the castle hill.

Below: Cathedral porch with main portal.

appear to have copied the Burgundian Cistercian plan of the Tennenbach Cistercian monastery near Emmendingen. In 1240, obviously after a change of plan and architect, work began on the four

west bays of the nave. The central nave was vaulted and the west entrance façade started. The work was carried out under the supervision of a Gothic architect from the lodge that built the nave in

Strasbourg. It was this architect who introduced the idea of the single tower façade, common in parish churches on the Upper Rhine in the Carolingian tradition. Work on the tower façade was already under way by the 1250s. Around 1280 another Strasbourg architect built an octagonal superstructure and a tracery pyramid on top of the square foundations of the tower. They were finished around 1320. This architectonic solution completed and defined the shift from an originally Romanesque design to the Gothic style. Later in the 14th and 15th centuries similar octagonal towers with tracery pyramids after the Freiburg model were built all over the German empire. The work on the chancel towers also came to an end in the 1340s.

On 24 March 1354 the foundation stone for the new Gothic long chancel was laid, replacing the previous old-fashioned Romanesque structure. Externally it is similar in shape to the nave. As in St Vitus Cathedral, which was under construction in Prague at the same time, the ground plan was based on a wide ambulatory adjoined by thirteen radial chapels. It was designed by Johannes von Gmünd, a member of the famous Parler family of masons from Schwäbisch-Gmünd and cousin of Peter Parler, the architect working for the Emperor in Prague. From 1359 onwards Johannes, the architect of the new chancel in Basel Cathedral, worked exclusively in the Freiburg lodge. However, work had to be suspended around 1380 because of a shortage of money. In the meantime, the old Romanesque chancel was still open for public worship and it remained in existence until the beginning of the 16th century inside the slowly rising walls of the Gothic chancel. Between 1471 and 1491 the architect Hans Niesenberger from Graz continued the work according to Johannes von Gmünd's plan, except that he added ornamental

Tailors' guild windows in the north transept of
Freiburg Cathedral, showing the Virgin between
St Mary Magdalene and St Catherine, c. 1320–30.

features in the contemporary taste. He
was succeeded by Hans Niederländer,
who completed the vaulting of the
chancel in 1510. The church was consecrated in December 1513, with the radial
chapels still unfinished. The flying
buttresses on the outside were not added
until the 18th and 19th centuries.

The rood screens in the modern
Renaissance style, which have now been
moved to the end walls of the transept
arms, were made by Hans Böringer in
1579 and installed in the crossing. In
1620 Michael Glück built a Renaissance-
style vestibule at the front of the south
transept.

From the square in front of the south
end the four main construction phases
or styles are easily distinguishable.
Romanesque features can be seen not
only in the ground plan but also in the
transept arms and the substructure of the
west tower. The Gothic structures that
determine the general appearance of the
cathedral, such as the basilican nave with
its scaffolding of flying buttresses, the
upper parts of the tower and the raised
chancel with its radial chapels, are
designed for uniformity and continuity.
Freiburg, like Strasbourg, was originally
in the Rhenish tradition, but then
adopted French Gothic style and
later influences from the south east of
the empire, until the Renaissance style
took over. Through all the periods there
appears to have been one central aim,
to distinguish this building from the
large episcopal churches on which it
is modelled by simplifying the design,
either by leaving out the triforium or
by building a façade tower instead of
twin towers. A specific architectonic
style based on that principle evolved
in the 13th and 14th centuries, reflecting
the ideals of the merchant class and the
young and ambitious cities.

The two-door main portal in the
porch of the tower façade is framed by

a wide soffit. The Three Magi on the left
wall and the Annunciation and Visitation
on the right (the heads have been
restored) balance the Virgin and Child
on the central pillar. The allegorical figures of Ecclesia and Synagogue
face each other in the outside soffits.
The arrangement of the scenes in the
tympana seems somewhat confusing,
especially since the picture in the two
lower tiers is further divided horizontally. Starting from the bottom right,
they show the Nativity and the annunciation to the shepherds, then on the left
the Passion. On each side angels are
sounding the last trump and awaking
the dead, who are rising from their
graves above the scenes from the life
of Christ. The middle tier is dominated
by the central figure of Christ crucified,
with the Chosen on the left and the
Damned on the right. Above them is
a row of Apostles at the Last Judgment.
In the point of the tympanum is a deesis,
with Christ making the sign of the cross
between Mary and John the Baptist. The
moulding of the archivolts shows angels,
prophets and patriarchs. The iconographic theme is continued on the side
walls of the vestibule, with Christ as
bridegroom of the church and the Wise
Virgins on the left and further on Mary
Magdalene, Abraham and Isaac and John
the Baptist. The next two figures are
difficult to identify (possibly Zachariah
and Elizabeth). On the adjacent north
wall is the Prince of the World (the
tempter of the Foolish Virgins), turning
to a naked woman (an allegory of lust).
Next comes a warning angel with a
banner. On the right wall of the vestibule
are the Foolish Virgins and the seven
liberal arts: grammar, logic and rhetoric
as *trivium artes*, geometry, music, arithmetic
and astronomy (the last one on the west
wall to the south) as *quadrivium artes*.
St Margaret and St Catherine on the
west wall complete the series. These

sculptures concentrated on just one
portal and in the vestibule obviously has
no uniform theme and in fact some of
the sculptures predate the architectonic
design of the west façade. Stylistically,
they are clearly related to the statuary on
the west portal of Strasbourg Cathedral.
The beautiful *trumeau* Virgin and Child
(c. 1300; Ill. p. 51) reflects the influence
of French cathedral sculpture, exemplified by the Wise and Foolish Virgins on
the Strasbourg Portal (Ill. p. 192).

The statues of thirteen Apostles and
Christ on the clustered pillars of the
central nave date from between 1300 and
1310 and are reminiscent of the Apostle
cycles in the Ste-Chapelle in Paris and
the chancel of Cologne Cathedral.
The pulpit was made by Jörg Kempf
between 1559 and 1561. Compared
with the pulpit of Basel Cathedral, the
one in Freiburg Cathedral, with its Late
Gothic tracery decoration, has a slightly
heavy appearance.

Behind the Late Gothic tracery façade
with pointed arches and a balustrade
above (1578), the Holy Sepulchre chapel
on the south aisle contains a group of
statues depicting the body of Christ

stretched out on the tomb, the three
Marys and two angels swinging incense
(Ill. p. 50). The set, dating from around
1340, is copied from one in Strasbourg
Cathedral (fragments in the Musée de
l'Oeuvre Notre-Dame, Paris).

Much of the medieval stained glass
in the nave presented by citizens and
local notables to embellish the parish
church has survived. In the north aisle
are the early 14th-century guild windows
(Ill. p. 165) with the craftsmen's coats
of arms. The glass in the rose and lancet
windows of the transept, dating from
the early 13th century, is from
Strasbourg. The stained glass in the
chancel ambulatory and the radiating
chapels was made from cartoons by
Hans Baldung Grien and is a replica
of the original in the Augustinermuseum.
In the upper chancel are windows with
large figures of saints by Hans von
Ropstein and Jakob Wechtlin (1505–28).

The centrepiece of the upper chancel
is the altarpiece, a major German
painting from the Dürer period by
Hans Baldung Grien. The central scene
of *The Coronation of the Virgin* (1512–16)
has wings with groups of Apostles. In
the closed position the folding wings
show the Annunciation, the Visitation,
the Nativity and the flight into Egypt
on the outside. On the back of the
centre panel is a dramatic setting of
the Crucifixion. The entwined foliage
in the panel pictures and the adoration
of the shepherds group in the predella
are by the sculptor Hans Wydyz.

Another joint work by the two artists
is the altar from the Schnewlin Chapel,
now in the second imperial chapel in
the chevet with a group of statues
depicting the rest on the flight into
Egypt in front of a painted mountain
landscape with a rose bower. The
Locherer Chapel in the north chancel

ambulatory contains a magnificent
Late Gothic carved altar, the first authenticated work by Hans Sixt von Staufen
who worked in Freiburg from 1521 to
1524. It reveals the influence of the
Frankish masters, particularly Tilman
Riemenschneider.

Augustinermuseum

Very few features of the original
Augustine monastery founded in 1278
have been preserved. The transept was
built in the 14th century. The Baroque
cloister buildings and the church were
used as a theatre in the 19th century.
In 1923 the complex was converted to
a museum specializing in Upper Rhine
art and culture, original sculptures and
stained glass from Freiburg Cathedral
and major collections of religious art,
mainly from the Dominican monastery
in Adelhausen.

Breisach

The upper town is in a commanding position above the river on the slopes of the volcanic Breisachberg, which had already been fortified by the Celts and Romans to protect the Rhine crossing. The Hohenstaufens founded the site in 1185 and in 1200 handed it over to the dukes of Zähringen, who built a massive fortress on the north tip of the plateau and developed it into an imperial fortification. In its strategic position above the Rhine the town was repeatedly exposed over the centuries to large-scale attacks, by French revolutionary troops in 1793 and, more recently, in 1945, causing widespread destruction.

St Stephen's Church

At the beginning of the 13th century, work began on the construction of a vaulted basilica with a cruciform ground plan that had an alternating system on the southern edge of the upper town, replacing the smaller 12th-century church of St Stephen. The two eastern apses in the transept and the flanking chancel towers are fragments preserved from this first phase of construction, whose Late Romanesque forms – modelled on Basel Cathedral, which had been under construction from 1185 – are clearly visible. The chancel with its polygonal chevet and the upper storeys of the south tower were built in a second Gothic phase from around 1270. Yet the generally non-uniform appearance of the building is largely due to a radical change of plan between 1325 and 1350, starting in the west with the renovation of the nave as a Gothic hall church,

although, apart from the adjoining vaulted area, the conversion did not go further than the first bay. The historical divide is marked by the year 1422 in Gothic figures on the base of the more northerly of the two Gothic clustered pillars. The tower-like structure above the western bay was also unfinished. The sacristy was built from 1473 to 1494.

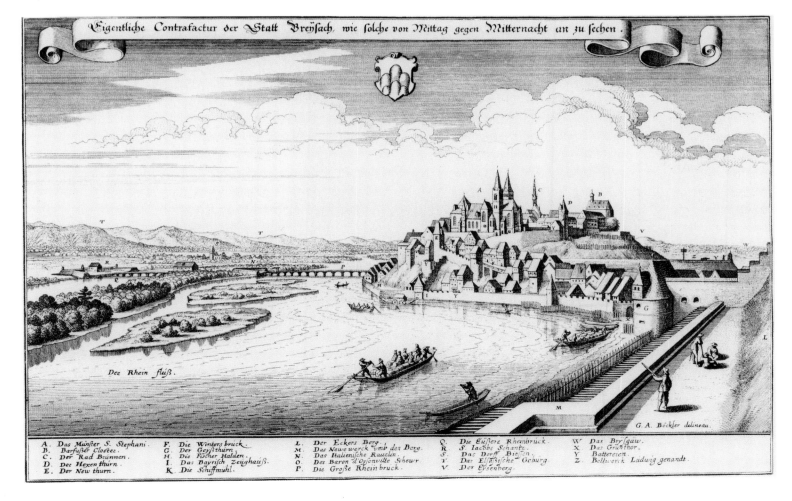

Eigentliche Contrafactur der Statt Breysach, wie solche von Mittag gegen Mitternacht an zu sehen.

Der Rhein fluß.

G. A. Böckler delineau.

A. Das Münster S. Stephani.
B. Barfußer Closter.
C. Der Rad Brunnen.
D. Der Hexen thurn.
E. Der New thurn.
F. Die Winters bruck.
G. Der Geyst thurn.
H. Die Fischer Halden.
I. Das Bayrisch Zeughauß.
K. Die Schiffmuhl.
L. Der Eckers Berg.
M. Das Newewerck vmb der Borg.
N. Das Italienische Rauelin.
O. Des Baron d'Oysonville Schewr.
P. Die Große Rhein bruck.
Q. Die Eußere Rheinbruck.
R. S. Iacobs Schantz.
S. Das Dorff Bisßen.
T. Das Elsäßische Geburg.
V. Der Eysenberg.
W. Das Brysgaw.
X. Das Grünthor.
Y. Battereien.
Z. Bollwerk Ludwig genandt.

167

end of the 15th century. A set of figures with local associations has been added to the delicate five-bayed baldachin structure consisting of radiating ogee arches and a balustrade ending in filigree tracery, topped with alternate finials and tabernacle towers. On the front are statues of St Stephen, Joseph and Mary next to the Three Magi, on the north side St Gervase and St Joachim, to the south St Anne and St Protase and on the back an Annunciation group. According to tradition, the relics of the Three Magi were kept overnight in the Breisach church in 1164, when they were being transported from Milan to Cologne. Protase, Gervase and Stephen are the church's patron saints. The style of these rather heavy sculptures with their curious drapery shows the influence of Strasbourg. There is a similarity with the work of Master V. S., who sculpted a memorial plaque in the St Catherine Chapel of Strasbourg Cathedral.

By contrast the altarpiece, made between 1523 and 1526 and bearing the initials H. L., is an outstanding example of south German woodcarving. The centre shrine, which ends in a trefoil, has an animated scenic illustration of the Coronation of the Virgin, with the figures of St Stephen and St Lawrence, St Protase and St Gervase almost completely in the round on the wings. In the predella are half-length figures of the four Evangelists with their symbols. Other figures appear in the traditional Gothic superstructure, which soars up over 11 metres (36 feet) with the Man of Sorrows at the top. Most of the altar is not polychromed. Only the flesh tints, hair and jewelled ornaments of the main figures are varnished to contrast with the warm tones of the lime wood.

It is still a mystery who H. L. was and nothing is known about his origins or the background to his work on the Upper Rhine. Of the sculptures

In 1932 a severely damaged monumental wall painting of the Last Judgment by Martin Schongauer covering three walls was uncovered in the west hall. Started in 1488 when the master from Colmar became a citizen of Breisach, the painting must have been completed at the time of his death (2 February 1491) and it is, so to speak, his artistic testament. In the centre Christ is enthroned on the rainbow, surrounded by Mary and John the Baptist, groups of prophets and Apostles, angels with the instruments of the Passion and the trumpets sounded for the Last Judgment. The side walls show Heaven and Hell. The painter was clearly familiar with the *Last Judgment* altar painted by Rogier van der Weyden for the Hôtel Dieu in Beaune. Schongauer skilfully translated the iconographic scheme of the composition, integrated into the existing architectural style, into his own personal 'soft style' with larger-than-life figures.

The rood screen separating the chancel is Late Gothic stonework dating from the

Opposite: Master H. L., carved altar at St Stephen's Church, Breisach, 1523–26.

Right: Master H. L., carved altar, showing God the Father on the central shrine (detail), at St Stephen's Church, Breisach, 1523–26.
Below: Master H. L., carved altar, showing predella with the four Evangelists (detail), at St Stephen's Church, Breisach, 1523–26.

associated with him, the Breisach high altar is his undisputed masterpiece. The initials also appear on copper engravings and woodcuts.

In the centre panel the forceful body language and gestures of the three protagonists and the turbulent throng of angels around them intensify the composition to a scene of remarkable excitement and vitality. The *putti* on every level of the relief are a high-spirited and playful crowd, romping about irreverently in the folds of the robes. The ornamental draping of the materials and the skilfully crafted locks of the beard and hair add to the impression of passionate unrest. H. L. has one – and only one – characteristic in common with Mathias Grünewald: he makes no attempt to imitate nature but leads the spectator into the unreal world of art. Every form has a decorative function, which ultimately even takes precedence over the iconographic theme.

The emphatic 'Baroque' stage of the Gothic style reaches its peak with the Breisach high altar. It is a work that marks the turn of an era, the inspired creation of a restless spirit already seduced by the 'expressionistic' forms of Mantegna, with whose graphic work

the artist must have been familiar. He has literally taken the creative possibilities of wood reliefs to their limits. Indeed, it is surprising to find such a progressive work in this otherwise rather conservative field of architecture and sculpture.

The two hallmarks show that the shrine with the relics of St Gervase and St Protase now enclosed in the base of the altar table, which has the signature Petrus Berlin de Wimpfhna and the year 1496 on the gable side above the view of Breisach, was made in one of the many famous Strasbourg goldsmiths' workshops. The silver embossed casing

is in the shape of a church nave, with round niches containing the figures of saints. On the long sides, next to the Crucifixion framed in a tall arch, are two pairs of statues, the martyred brothers Protase and Gervase on one side and Paul and Peter on the other side with their parents, Vitalis and Valeria. In the three niches on the short sides are Andrew, John the Baptist and Ambrose, together with an unidentified saint, Stephen and Philip. The reliefs on the sloping roof with scenes from the legends of the two patron saints (from Jakobus de Voragine's *Legenda aurea*) show off both the craftsman's narrative style and the architectural decoration.

Apart from the stylistic affinities of the statuettes on the reliquary and those on the rood screen, which are cruder in style, the many references to Strasbourg art are evidence of a common background, noticeable both in the architecture (see the St Lawrence Chapel) and the sculpture (see the chancel in Strasbourg Cathedral).

Colmar

The nucleus of the community in Upper Alsace to which Frederick II of Hohenstaufen granted the privileges of a free imperial town in 1212 was a Carolingian *thing* court belonging to the Crown, first mentioned in a document by Ludwig the Pious in 823 (*ad fiscum nostrum nomine columbarium*). In Colmar, as in many other cities in the Middle Ages, the aristocracy and the burghers (organized into guilds) were in open conflict before the burghers managed to assert their rights in the municipal decree of 1360. Colmar's prosperity was based on agriculture and the wine trade and, as well

as being a centre for the arts and sciences, the city had a flourishing intellectual life. The Dominican monasteries (Unterlinden, St Catherine) were strongholds of mysticism and an exalted ideal of piety. A monastic reform of the Dominican order leading to stricter observance spread from Colmar to the whole of Europe.

The old part of Colmar has been preserved largely intact as a historic group of religious and public buildings, manor houses and mansions and the picturesque half-timbered houses of the burghers. The elegant Renaissance loggia and the

portal underneath make the old guardhouse built in 1575 on the site of a charnel house opposite the south transept of the Collégiale St-Martin, an anomaly amongst the medieval buildings, standing out from the otherwise unadorned façades (Ill. p. 174). The impression given by this elaborate structure is that the owner and the architect, whose initials 'A. M.' appear on the keystone in the vault of the loggia, were parading their cultivated modern taste at a time when all the other buildings in the region were in the medieval Gothic style.

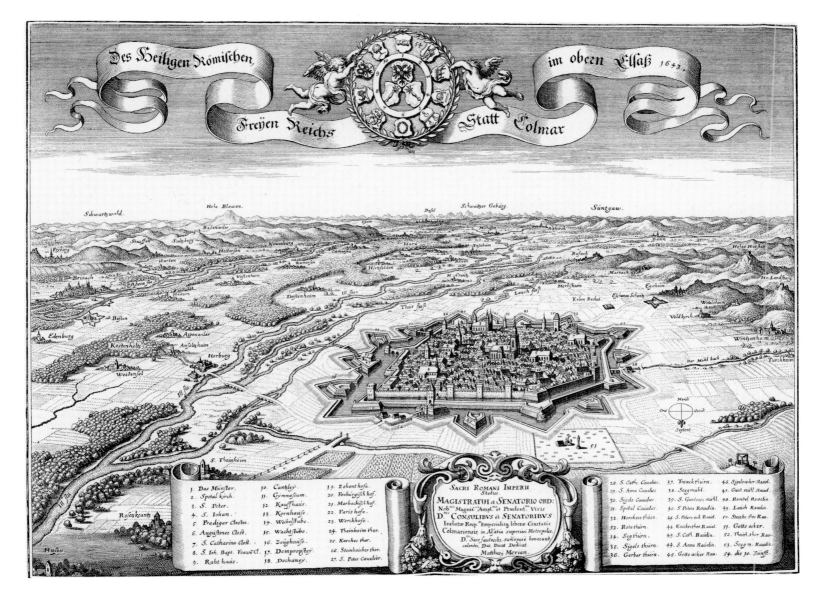

Left: The old guardhouse, Colmar.
Below: St Nicholas Portal on the south transept of the Collégiale St-Martin.

Opposite: The nave looking towards the chancel of the Collégiale St-Martin.

Collégiale St-Martin

Excavations around this collegiate church have uncovered traces of an Ottonian building that was extended in the late 12th century. However, the present church is more recent. The collegiate chapter founded in 1234 and the aspiring burghers wanted a new collegiate church built to replace the parish church that had stood since the Carolingian period. A series of letters of indulgence in the period 1282 to 1344 point to intensive building work, although the lack of documentary evidence means that the chronology can only be worked out from the structure itself. There was probably not enough money for a full building plan. The transept, nave and west façade were built in the first phase. The transept is made up of the three equal-sized squares of the crossing and the two cross-arms supported by struts. Five rectangular bays divide the central nave, which has square aisle bays. Solid sectioned round pillars with eight engaged shaft abutments mark the entrance side and crossing, while the nave supports have only four engaged shafts, an arrangement copied not from Strasbourg but from Amiens and Reims. As in Freiburg-im-Breisgau, the wall elevation has two storeys and no triforium, but this is a less elaborate version, no doubt partly due to lack of funds.

Outside, the nave is surrounded by supporting arches that show the influence of Strasbourg. The north transept opens in a double portal with trefoil arches. On the St Nicholas Portal of the south transept the legend of the saint is illustrated in the lower round arch of the tympanum. In the pointed arch above is the Last Judgment. On the left, underneath the small statues in the outer archivolts, is a picture of an architect with a square and the inscription *Maistres Humbret*, who was, presumably, the designer of the transept and nave. He appears from his name to have been French. The still formal style of the sculptures, modelled on the rood screen sculptures in Strasbourg Cathedral, suggests that the transept was built in the 1260s and the nave in the next decade.

The construction of the chancel is much better documented. The revenue from benefices had been earmarked for the new building from 1315, but it was not until 1350 that the canons acquired the land for a new Gothic long chancel

topped with baldachins, an arrangement used in Gothic mendicant order architecture. The Colmar chancel cannot have been influenced by the Schwäbish-Gmünd chancel started in 1351, since it had already been planned a year earlier. In fact, it was built by Wilhelm von Marburg, who died between 1363 and 1366. He also built the St John Chapel in St-Pierre-le-Jeune in Strasbourg and the progressive features are attributable to the bold innovations in Strasbourg art since the beginning of the century rather than to direct Parler influence. However, the console figures on the engaged shafts of the vaulting in the upper chancel and on the outer gallery of the south transept point to contact with the Schwäbisch-Gmünd lodge.

With its façade divided vertically by massive buttresses the west end, built between 1310 and 1350 and largely modelled on Strasbourg, shows a careful treatment of individual form, although the style is plain. The bottom of the tympanum on the main portal depicts the Adoration of the Magi, with the Last Judgment above. On the pediment is St Martin on horseback (the original is in the Musée d'Unterlinden). The two side chapels in the nave were built at the same time. The vaulting of the transept, dating originally from 1491, and the chapels in the east chancel were replaced during 19th-century restoration work.

Few of the furnishings survived the disturbances of the Revolution. The chapter was abolished in 1792 and the church was turned into a 'Temple of Reason'. The altarpiece of the old high altar by the Colmar painter Kaspar Isenmann dating from 1465 is now in the Musée d'Unterlinden (Ill. p. 180). The middle chapel in the chancel contains a magnificent 14th-century crucifix. One of the chapels houses the 15th-century Virgin of Colmar, a painted lime-wood carving. The choir stalls and statues were

with radial chapels. The remains of the old building can still be seen in the east walls of the transept. Although records refer to the chancel in 1358 (hinder dem Nuwen Kor ze Sant Martin), by 1365 it was still unfinished. The ground plan and elevation are similar to south German buildings by the Parler school, such as the Heiligkreuz church in Schwäbish Gmünd, Freiburg im Breisgau and Münster. Its three rectangular bays lead

into a 5/8 polygon. Down below the outer buttresses of the upper chancel form the dividing walls of the radial chapels, connected to each other by a passageway with pointed arches which is a chancel ambulatory and opening only on to the chevet in arcading. Outside, the severe socle area of the radial chapels contrasts with the elegant symmetry of the triple lancet window and the buttresses of the upper chancel

Schongauer workshop, *Noli me tangere*, from the winged altar of the former Dominican church in Colmar, late 15th century. Musée d'Unterlinden, Colmar.

Opposite: Martin Schongauer, *Madonna of the Rose Bower* in the chancel of the former Dominican church in Colmar, 1473.

made by the Neo-Gothic sculptor Theophil Klem in 1870. The glass in the chancel was restored as a uniform set in the early 20th century, using old fragments from the Strasbourg firm of Ott. The frames of the three west windows on the north side and the first and third windows on the south side are old fragments from the nave of the Dominican church (pre-1330).

The glass windows on the west side of the church are particularly interesting. In front on the left are ten 14th-century panes originally from a *speculum humanae salvationis* cycle. Above the southwest side portal there is a small round window with a fragmentary head of Christ, probably early 13th century.

Former Dominican church

Apart from the fact that the foundation stone was laid by King Rudolf von Habsburg in 1283, it is difficult to establish the precise construction dates of this church built for the Dominican order, which had been established in the city since 1260. It is undoubtedly one of the most advanced examples of mendicant order architecture. The central section is in the shape of a spacious hall with a sloping wooden ceiling in the two aisles, which are slightly lower. Six arches reaching almost to the ceiling rest on tall, slender, unbroken columns. This part of the church was only completed after the Dominicans were banished from the city (1330–46). Work on the vaulted chancel reserved for the monks had started before that, around 1310. It extends across four bays, terminating in a five-sided polygon. Outside there is an elegant arrangement of alternating buttresses and lancet windows with variegated tracery.

By about 1300 decorative features such as wall painting and stained-glass windows had become common, even in mendicant order architecture which followed strict aesthetic rules and had no towers or decorative sculptures.

The brilliantly coloured stained glass with pictorial motifs and tapestry patterns is amongst the most important in Alsace, the oldest dating back to the first half of the 14th century. The window with Solomon on the baldachin throne above the main portal on the south side of the nave has an interesting iconography. The lions at his feet symbolize the twelve tribes of Israel. Beside him are prophets and the Virtuous, above him the Virgin and Child, flanked by Ulrich of Strasbourg and Agnes of Herkenheim, founder of the Unterlinden convent.

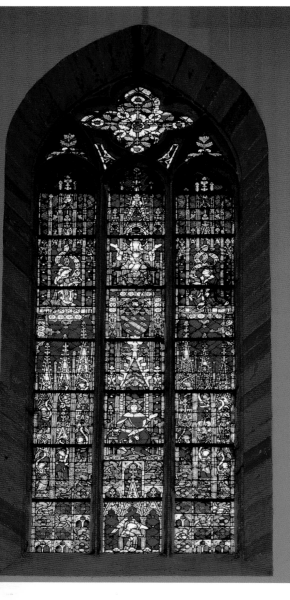

Left: Stained-glass window on the south side of the nave depicting Solomon on the baldachin throne.
Below: The nave in the former Dominican church of Colmar, looking towards the chancel.

Martin Schongauer's *Madonna of the Rose Bower*, now displayed in the centre of the chancel, was also not originally from here. It might have come from Collégiale St-Martin, which, according to the Sélestat humanist Wimpfeling, had a collection of several of Schongauer's works.

The *Madonna of the Rose Bower*, painted in 1473, is the most important of the

Below the Virgin is the coat of arms of the Upper Alsatian landgraviate. The theme and composition of the stained glass are modelled on the pediment of the centre portal on the façade of Strasbourg Cathedral, combining architecture and sculpture (Ills. pp. 194–95).

The church was secularized in 1791 and after that was used to store corn before being repaired at the end of the 19th century and restored to a place of worship.

The high altar used to have a winged altarpiece made by the Schongauer workshop (Ill. p. 176). The Crucifixion panel in the museum dating from around 1410–20 (Ill. p. 179) probably also came from this church.

The choir stalls by the Guebwiller sculptor and architect Gabriel-Ignaz Ritter are not part of the original furnishings. They came from the former Cistercian church in Pairis and the monastic church in Marbach.

Crucifixion panel from the Collégiale St-Martin,
c. 1410–20. Musée d'Unterlinden, Colmar.

few panel paintings by the great Colmar master to have survived. The monumental and iconic character of the Virgin in the red cloak is partly due to the fact that it used to be a triptych, but the edges of the panel have been cut and the wings lost. The Virgin in the *hortus conclusus* is in a long-standing iconographic tradition (see Stefan Lochner in Cologne; Ill. p. 292). The figure of the Virgin with the rosebush appeared in the rood screen sculptures in Strasbourg Cathedral as early as 1250. However, there is a strong element of mysticism in this late medieval work from Colmar. The influence of Rogier van der Weyden, especially his *Virgin and Child* in the Prado, can be seen in Schongauer's work, but the intensity with which the Virgin is painted is incomparable. She wears the sorrowful expression of a mother who already knows about her son's sacrificial death and the natural beauty of the setting is portrayed in rich detail.

The mid-18th century convent buildings were extensively restored between 1948 and 1951 and now house the city library. The transept dates from the second half of the 15th century and the wall-painting cycle, with scenes of the Passion by Urban Huter, from around 1495.

Musée d'Unterlinden

The Dominican convent of St John the Baptist 'under the lime trees' was founded in 1232 and sanctioned by Pope Innocent IV in 1245. The church was begun in 1252 and in 1269 Albertus Magnus consecrated the chancel. The transept was completed twenty years later. According to records, the architect was Brother Volmar. The chronicle of Abbess Catherine of Gueberschwihr testifies to the high standard of teaching and intense spirituality in the monastic community.

The convent buildings were ruined during the Revolution, but partly rebuilt in the 19th century. When the Schongauer society was founded in 1847 city, librarian Louis Hugot was able to repair the convent buildings and the church with the aim of starting a school of drawing, a graphic art gallery and a collection of religious works of art from the former Musée National de Colmar (from 1852).

Kaspar Isenmann, *The Mourning and Resurrection of Christ*, panel from the old altarpiece in the Collégiale St-Martin, 1465. Musée d'Unterlinden, Colmar.

Opposite: Mathias Grünewald, *The Crucifixion, St Anthony and St Sebastian, Entombment on the Predella*, Isenheim altarpiece, c. 1512–16. Musée d'Unterlinden, Colmar.

The aisleless, flat-roofed church used to have a south aisle. The vaulted chancel extends across seven bays, ending in a polygon. An upper storey was added to the four-sided, well-proportioned transept with its fifty-four arches in the 18th century.

Of the museum's magnificent collections, only a small selection of the pieces from churches and monasteries in and around Colmar will be mentioned here. They include the former altarpiece from the Collégiale St-Martin by the local painter Kaspar Isenmann (c. 1410–85), authenticated by the contract dated 1465 that has been preserved. However, the composition of the winged altar, which was removed, dismantled and dispersed in 1720, is difficult to reconstruct. In the closed position the wings showed St Catherine, St Lawrence and St Martin on the left, St Barbara on the right (the other two figures were lost). The left inside wing showed the Entry into Jerusalem and the Last Supper, the Mount of Olives and Christ's Arrest, the right wing opposite the Mourning and Entombment of Christ, the Resurrection and, possibly, the women at the tomb. The central shrine of the altarpiece probably had a Crucifixion group, especially since the work is described in old documents as a 'cross altar'. Yet the space seems too narrow, suggesting that the altarpiece was larger and, possibly, that it had double wings.

Isenmann's work is an outstanding example of Upper Rhine art. He is clearly influenced by Dutch painting, particularly Rogier van der Weyden, whereas his contemporary Konrad Witz takes after Petrus Christus and the Master of Flémalle. The figurative and scenic representations in the relief from the Carthusian monastery in Strasbourg (in the Musée de l'Oeuvre Notre-Dame), showing the influence of Brabant on the art of the Upper Rhine, might be cited as a comparison. Isenmann is unique among the German painters of his period, not least because

of his vivid and detailed portrayal of landscapes.

A particularly fine panel picture of the Crucifixion from the Collégiale St-Martin certainly does not originate from there because the founder, kneeling at the foot of the cross in prayer, is a Dominican. With its bold composition and handling of colours, the elegant use of form and sensitive portrayal of the faces and robes, this work is a gem of Upper Rhine painting from that period in the style known as International Gothic. The painting (1410–20), has recently been attributed to the painter Hans Stocker who worked at the court of Friedrich zu Rhein, Bishop of Basel, and had links with the pre-Eyck school of painters in Bruges.

The winged altar from the Dominican church (see Ill. p. 176) was made in the late 15th century in the local studio of the painter Martin Schongauer. When closed the wings show, from left to right

and bottom to top, the Mystical Pursuit, the Visitation, the Nativity, the Adoration of the Magi, the Presentation of Christ in the Temple, Jesus among the Scribes and the Coronation of the Virgin Mary. When opened, it has four scenes on either side of a lost middle section, which possibly depicted the Crucifixion. The left volet has scenes from Christ's Passion, from the Entry into Jerusalem to Christ carrying the Cross. The right volet continues the theme, from the Descent from the Cross to the Effusion of the Holy Spirit. Thus the two series of pictures showed the Joys of Mary on the outside and the Passion on the inside. It might seem surprising that Schongauer left it to his studio to produce such a large work, at least 4.6 metres (15 feet) wide and 2.3 metres (7½ feet) high, especially as it was such an important commission. However, this way of working was normal practice for artists' studios in the 15th century. The master

might merely sketch the composition of the whole or individual scenes and hand it over to assistants (like the mysterious Master A. G.) to execute. The Passion scenes were certainly completed before the engraved Passion cycle, a major work by Schongauer of masterly clarity and 'legibility'. For all its artistic weaknesses, the Dominican winged altar is an important preliminary stage in the artistic development of this outstanding painter and graphic artist.

The panel pictures from the world-famous Isenheim altar come from the monastic church of the Antonine hospital order in Isenheim, not far from Colmar. They were painted between 1512 to 1516 by Mathias Grünewald, about whom very little is known. While the design of the monumental polyptych undoubtedly dates from the time of the teacher Guido Guersi (1490–1516), it was executed at two different stages. The Strasbourg woodcarver Nicolaus of

Pages 182 and 183: Mathias Grünewald,
The Incarnation of Christ (first position)
in the Isenheim altarpiece, *c.* 1512–16.

Below left: Mathias Grünewald, The Annunciation
in the Isenheim altarpiece, *c.* 1512–16.
Below right: Mathias Grünewald, The Resurrection
(wings in first position) in the Isenheim altarpiece,
c. 1512–16.

Hagenau, whose association with the Antonines in Strasbourg is well-documented, had already produced the sculptures for the shrine around 1490 (the sculptures for the high altar of Strasbourg cathedral were to follow in 1501). In the deep central niche of the shrine (Ill. p. 186) St Anthony, the patron saint of the order, is sitting on a throne. The two small figures at his feet are bringing offerings, the farmer a cockerel and the country squire a piglet. On the left, in the flatter side sections of the shrine, is St Augustine (whose rule the Antonines adopted in 1298), with the kneeling figure of the donor, Jean d'Orliac; on the right is St Jerome, the first biographer of St Anthony. The figure of Christ on the predella is also the work of the master, while the Apostles were an early 16th-

Below left: Mathias Grünewald, St Paul the hermit and St Anthony in the Isenheim altarpiece, c. 1512–16 (wings in second position).

Below right: Mathias Grünewald, the Temptation of St Anthony in the Isenheim altarpiece, c. 1512–16 (wings in second position).

century addition. In a second phase of work the reliquary altar, which had been put up temporarily, was turned into a complex polyptych by the addition of the panel pictures. However, it was another twenty-two years or so before the work was commissioned from Grünewald.

On the closed wings is the central theme of the Crucifixion (Ill. p. 181), with the group of mourners (Mary Magdalene, John the Disciple and the Virgin Mary) on one side and the solitary figure of John the Baptist on the other. Pointing at Christ and holding the

inscription *Illum oportet crescere, me autem minui* (He must increase, but I must decrease), he is the bearer and interpreter of the theological message. On the fixed outside wings are the figures of St Anthony and St Sebastian on plinths. The predella, painted by a different

colours that express Mary's dual nature. By contrast, in the tragic setting of the temptation and even more so in the atmospheric landscape of the meeting between St Anthony and St Paul, the painter uses a very distinctive range of colours to portray the richness of earthly creation.

Like no other artist of his time, north or south of the Alps, Grünewald presents, on the Isenheim altar, the mystic vision of the Saviour on the cross with a superhuman intensity of passion. Beside this broken and bloated, body, with twisted limbs nailed to the cross and bleeding wounds, Mary's dazzling white robe stands out against the dark background.

Yet Grünewald is not only an outstanding colourist, he also composes almost musical harmonies when he links the different scenes by analogies of form. For instance, the aura of light in the Resurrection is a counterpart to the Gothic vaulting in the Annunciation scene. Other such parallels are to be found in the two landscapes in the second position. With a strong feeling for dramatic presentation and passionate expression, the painter uses every register to make the scene even more intense, for instance the three figures at the foot of the cross and the soldiers thrown to the ground as if by lightning at the sight of the transfigured Christ. Where pain and grief are taken to their limits, the concepts of beauty and ugliness become irrelevant. Art follows its own laws, which transcend the physical. Grünewald draws the observer into the autonomous world of art.

artist, shows the Entombment. The main theme of the first position is the Incarnation, divided into a heavenly and an earthly sphere (Ills. pp. 182 and 183). On the left volet is the Annunciation, on the right the Resurrection (Ills. p. 184). The third position, when the altarpiece is fully open, shows the reliquary with its carved figures. St Anthony's visit to St Paul is on the painted wing on the left, the gruesomely illustrated Temptation of St Anthony on the right (Ill. p. 185), both scenes set in fantastic landscapes.

Grünewald was an artist of such genius that he was able to use new creative techniques to translate his patron's ideas, rooted in the mystic visions of medieval religion, into a supernatural scene of high drama and burning passion. His use of colour is particularly striking. The illuminated face of the transfigured Christ transcends physical boundaries and the colours Grünewald uses to illustrate the traumatic temptation scene are appropriately gruesome. In the Nativity scene the Virgin appears in two guises, once with a halo in a heavenly circle of angels as a being chosen by God and once in her earthly guise as a mother holding her child. Here again it is the

Sélestat

Sélestat grew up around a small port on the Ill and as a Hohenstaufen estate had privileges conferred on it several times. In 1216 Frederick II fortified the little market town with a wall and elevated it to the status of a free imperial town. It already had a royal court in the Carolingian period and Charlemagne celebrated Christmas there in 775.

Eglise Ste-Foy

Around 1087 Hildegard, duchess of Swabia, widow of Friedrich von Büren, had a rotunda chapel built on the model of the Church of the Holy Sepulchre in Jerusalem. Remains have been found under the crossing of the present church. In 1094 the duchess founded a Benedictine priory, to which monks from Conques abbey in Rouergue were summoned. The priory adopted the abbey's patron saint, St Faith, a youthful martyr from the time of the Emperor Maximian.

The impressively simple Romanesque priory church (a parish church since 1803) was built in the 12th century with an alternating system. It has three square bays in the central basilican nave and six bays in the aisles, supported by alternating sectioned pillars and quatrefoil columns and spanned by heavy reinforcing arches and ribbed vaults. The impost area at the start of the clerestory is decorated with a rolled frieze running right round the church. The projecting transept opens to the east in three apses with a front bay, the middle one (the main chancel) being deeper.

The east end of the church is dominated by a pyramidal octagonal crossing tower, similar to the one in Paray-le-Monial in Burgundy. At the west end are two square towers with a narrow gable façade and an open portal vestibule between them (the spires are 19th century). This twin tower façade is common in Alsatian Romanesque churches (Andlau, Lautenbach, Guebwiller).In many ways the architecture of Ste-Foy is similar to buildings in Lorraine such as Notre-Dame in Saint-Dié and Vicherey.

Of the furnishings, the magnificent pulpit built in 1735 with scenes from the missionary work of the Jesuits is worth

The nave of Eglise Ste-Foy, Sélestat, looking east.

Opposite left: View of the west tower of Eglise
St-Georges, Sélestat.
Opposite right: Veit Wagner, Head of Christ from
Eglise St-Georges, c. 1500. Bibliothèque humaniste,
Sélestat.

noting. Archduke Rudolf of Austria had
handed Ste-Foy over to the Jesuits of the
Mainz diocese in 1614 for them to set
up a college.

Eglise St-Georges

During late 19th century excavations, a
rotunda 22 metres (72 feet) in diameter
was found on the site of what is now the
sanctuary. A document by Ludwig the
Pious dated 836 confirms ownership of
the chapel by the Bishop of Chur. The
parish church was obviously built when
Sélestat was made a free imperial town
around 1216 and became independent of
the priorate's authority. The outer walls
of the aisles were built in this first phase
in about 1220. The capitals on the south

side are reminiscent of the Romanesque
capitals by the builder of the crossing
in Strasbourg Cathedral. A three-apse
chancel was built in a second phase.
Only the two side apses in the corner
of the cross-arms have been preserved.
Semicircular chapels opening into an
arch in the middle are connected with
the transept and the raised chancel by
a passageway. The ingenious double-
shell walls (the late Gothic tracery on
the balustrade is 19th century) link them
to a group of buildings in Soissonais and
Burgundy and a similar arrangement can
be found in a church on the Marne,
Rieux near Montmirail.

After the chancel section had been
built between 1230 and 1235, work

began on the construction of the nave.
First of all two square double bays with
six-part vaults were built in the east,
adjoined by two rectangular bays on the
west side. The piers are similar in structure to those in Freiburg Cathedral. It
is clear that there was a further delay in
carrying out the building work towards
the west because the influence of the
Strasbourg Cathedral façade is already
apparent, so this part could not have
been built before 1290–1300. A real west
transept in the tradition of Carolingian
westworks, it is used as an entrance with
the main portal moved to the south because of the church's position in the town.
By the mid-14th century the building
had been completed up to the vaulting.

In 1415 the patriarch of Aquileia issued letters of indulgence, the proceeds from which were to be used to build a splendid new chancel. This phase of construction is better documented than before. Even the names of the builders are known: Hans Obrecht, mentioned in 1410 as a council member and mayor; Erhard Kindelin, recorded as the foreman at Eglise St-Georges from 1410 to 1422, a member of the Strasbourg guild of bricklayers and stonemasons and appointed by the city authorities as expert for the Strasbourg tower project; Medern Gerthener from Frankfurt; and a Master Georg from Württemberg. Kindelin probably oversaw the work on the Gothic chancel, which must already have been under construction around 1400, but he did not draw up the plans. The west tower was completed in the late 15th century.

The stained glass in the Gothic chancel is impressive. It includes the cycle of the legend of St Catherine in the central north window (c. 1430), the cartoon for which was drawn by the painter Hans Tiefenthal. He is believed to have

painted the famous panel picture of the *Little Garden of Paradise* in the Städelsches Kunstinstitut in Frankfurt (Ill. p. 54). The more recent St Agnes cycle in the first south window (c. 1460–70) is in the style of Peter Hemmel's Strasbourg workshop. Another window shows the legend of St Sylvester.

Original stained glass has also been preserved in the west transept. The rose window on the south side presented to the parish church (around 1400) by the knight R. von Eckerich and his wife, a member of the Blotzheim family, shows the Ten Commandments. Other windows portray the Evangelists, the Annunciation and the Presentation in the Temple.

The Head of Christ, a fragment of the church's triumphal cross (c. 1500, now in the Bibliothèque humaniste), is a moving piece of work by Veit Wagner, who also made the Mount of Olives group from the churchyard of St Thomas in Strasbourg, which can be seen in Strasbourg Cathedral.

The library's impressive collections of manuscripts and incunabula reflect the town's spiritual importance as a centre of humanism. The 670-volume set of papers that Beatus Rhenanus bequeathed to his native town can also be seen here.

Strasbourg

Strasbourg's history, like that of other cities on the Rhine, begins with the Romans, who built a *castrum* (encampment) on the island in the Ill in 12 BC. Traces of the Roman settlement, referred to on a milestone as *Argentorate*, can still be seen in the layout of the old town. It was not until the Frankish period, which began in 496 when King Clovis I (?466–511) defeated the Alemanni, that it became known as *Strateburgo* (fortress on the roads). In the Middle Ages the Latin form *Argentina* was common. In the Frankish period the bishop appointed himself ruler of the city and took control of trade and traffic. When Charlemagne's Carolingian empire was divided, Alsace and Strasbourg first became part of the Lotharingian Middle Kingdom and, when this was split up in its turn under

the Treaty of Meerssen in 870, part of the Holy Roman Empire. The Strasbourg Oaths sworn in old French and old German in 842, which sealed the alliance between Charles the Bald (r. 875–77) and Louis the German (r. 843–76), are not only early evidence of the linguistic difference between West and East Franconia but also a historical record of Strasbourg's role in the meeting of these two great European cultures.

In the Hohenstaufen period Strasbourg blossomed spiritually and culturally, a flowering reflected in the conversion of the Romanesque building into a Gothic cathedral. The illuminated manuscript of the *Hortus Deliciarum* written by Abbess Herrad of Landsberg (1167–95) in the nearby monastery of Mont Ste-Odile was a key work in medieval religion and

philosophy. Gottfried von Strassburg wrote *Tristran and Isolde*, a courtly verse epic in the French style based on Celtic legends, in Strasbourg around 1210. At about the same time the city was enclosed in a ring of walls built all round the island. King Philip of Swabia had already granted Strasbourg rights as a free imperial city. Rudolf of Habsburg renewed this status after the citizens had won a decisive victory over the bishop in 1262. At the end of the 13th century the cathedral building was brought under the city's administration. Patrician families, corporations and guilds gained control of the council.

In the late Middle Ages Strasbourg developed not only as a focal point for spiritual movements like mysticism and humanism but also as a centre for the

arts. The eminent sculptor Nicolaus
Gerhaert von Leyden and the painter
Hans Baldung (called Grien) worked
there and in 1440 Johann Gutenberg
(?1398–1468) from Mainz started a far-
reaching cultural and political revolution
with his printing press, which contributed directly to the spread of reforming
ideas. As an outpost of south German
Protestantism, the city offered asylum
to Calvin in 1538. In 1621 the emperor
elevated the academy to a university.

In the Thirty Years' War the citizens
were initially able to preserve their status
and religion. The Treaty of Rijswijk,
signed in 1697, in which Louis XIV
of France asserted his claim to Alsace,
brought to an end the War of the Grand
Alliance (1689–97) between Britain, the
Netherlands and Austria against Louis XIV
after his invasion of the Palatinate in
1688. For Strasbourg the French administration meant a return to Catholicism
and restoration of the bishop's office,
which was occupied by four cardinals
of the Rohan family between 1704 and
1803. Goethe studied in Strasbourg from
1770 to 1771 and his tribute to Erwin of
Steinbach paved the way for a revalua-
tion of Gothic architecture.

The French Revolution met with
a strong response in Strasbourg. The
cathedral was turned into a 'Temple
of Reason' and seriously damaged, but
spared from demolition. In 1871 Alsace
once again became part of the German
empire. The new part of Strasbourg was
built in a planned extension. In 1872
the university was refounded and rebuilt.
In 1918 Alsace was returned to France,
except for a period in the Second World
War from 1940 to 1944.

Today Strasbourg has a new international role as a European capital, the
seat of the Council of Europe and the
European Parliament and a geographical,
historical and cultural bridge between
France and Germany.

Strasbourg Cathedral

Strasbourg has had a Christian community since the 4th century, but it is not certain whether a church already existed at the end of the Roman period in 406, nor is anything known about an episcopal church in the time of Clovis I, who made the establishment of the Roman Catholic Church in France a cornerstone of his policy and consolidated its power. The first definitely contemporary reference was by the Frankish chronicler Ermold in a poem of praise to the

Emperor Ludwig the Pious around 826, although even then it is not clear what form the church took, for instance whether it had a double chancel (as in the St Gall monastery plan) or apses arranged next to each other at the east end. The Carolingian building was damaged when it was sacked in 1002 and soon after that completely destroyed in the great fire of 1007. Bishop Wernher, a member of the Habsburg dynasty, then laid the foundations for a new building, to be financed by revenue

from St Stephen's abbey. This Ottonian structure, built in 1015, was a large basilica 103 metres (338 feet) long with a projecting transept and a crypt, above which was a raised flat-ended chancel adjoined by two lower side chapels (see Reichenau-Mittelzell). With its twin tower façade on the west the building probably had some similarities to the Salian monastery church at Limburg an der Haardt. The measurements of the transept, which have been retained in the present building, show the scale of Bishop Wernher's ambitious undertaking.

The appearance of the Ottonian building changed when the façade was altered between 1130 and 1140 and the east crypt between 1110 and 1120. The west part under the present transept only dates from the middle of the 12th century. The east transept walls had to be repaired after a fire in 1150 and after another fire in 1176 the transept was completely rebuilt. The successive and sometimes abrupt transformation of the flat-roofed basilica into a vaulted room left visible traces on the interior brickwork.

Around 1190 a remarkable architect appeared on the scene when the St Andrew Chapel was built on the south flank of the chancel. He is also believed to have been responsible for the polygonal design of the inner chancel (Ill. p. 196), the large double arches to the side of the crossing supporting the dome carried on squinches and the plan for the vaulting of the transepts. The north transept was completed in a subsequent phase (1220–25). The powerfully monumental character of this architecture is still in the Late Romanesque style of many of the buildings on the Rhine (see Worms and Mainz cathedrals). It was not until the arrival of the 'master of the south transept', who designed the building in the new Gothic style between 1225 and 1240, that a radical

The middle portal of the west front of Strasbourg Cathedral.

Page 194: The west front of Strasbourg Cathedral.
Page 195: The portals and rose window storey of Strasbourg Cathedral.

change came about. He was responsible for the completion of the St John the Baptist Chapel and the construction of the chapter house above it on the north side of the chancel and, in particular, for the south transept (Ill. p. 197).

His innovation was the highly ingenious visual design of the central pillar supporting the vault. Instead of a massive cylindrical shaft, as in the north transept, he built a sectioned pillar copied from Chartres, with eight alternating stronger and weaker engaged shafts. On the four thinner shafts he put a set of sculptures depicting the Last Judgment in three tiers. At the bottom are the four Evangelists with their symbols, above them four angels blowing trumpets and at the top Christ in Judgment making the sign of the cross and three angels with the instruments of the Passion. From the positions of their bodies most of the figures under the baldachins seem to be standing away from the pillar, although they are actually part of it (Ill. p. 45). The classical beauty of the faces, the linear arrangement of the folds in the drapery and the suggestion of a circular movement, as if around an axis, hint at the genius that inspired the architect and sculptor – possibly the same person – in this masterpiece. The art historian Johan Huizinga refers to the 15th century as the 'autumn of the Middle Ages'; this could be described as the spring of German Gothic, in which the seeds of stylistic developments are sown. On the south portal (Ill. p. 202) the sublime figures of Ecclesia and Synagogue (c. 1225) and the tympanum with the death of the Virgin show the same creative power as the models in Chartres with which they have rightly been compared (Ill. p. 44).

Soon afterwards, around 1240, work also began on the two-aisle nave (Ill. p. 201). Although similar to the previous building in its relatively solid proportions, the architecture is obviously

inspired by High Gothic buildings in the Ile de France and wall articulations such as those in St Denis and Troyes. Above the pier arches runs a pierced triforium, integrated into the large window area with the posts of the tracery going down to the base of the triforium. The clustered piers in the nave consist of a square core surrounded by sixteen round engaged shafts of three different strengths, each fitting into the ribs of the arches and the vaulting. The seven bays in the nave were built in vertical sections

from east to west. 'Scheme A', a design drawn up in 1250, shows the first plan for the façade. Only one of the sets of sculptures from the rood screen built at the same time has been preserved (in the Musée de l'Oeuvre Notre-Dame) and this to some extent suggests the influence of the Reims lodge. The gables of the pediments were decorated with the works of mercy and a Madonna in the rose bower was surrounded by statues of the Apostles (The Cloisters, Metropolitan Museum of Art, New York).

In 1275 excavation work began for a new double tower façade. 'Scheme B' for this project, 2.74 metres (nearly 9 feet) high and drawn on parchment, is a unique masterpiece demonstrating exceptional skill in projecting a complex architectonic system on to the two-dimensional surface (Ill. p. 46). The foundation stone was laid in 1277 by Bishop Konrad of Lichtenberg, who only a few years before had levied his troops against the citizens of Strasbourg. As a result of the conflict between the episcopal and city authorities in the last two decades of the 13th century, a cathedral lodge was set up under the city's administration.

The two lower levels of the façade were completed in 1340. The inventive-ness of the architect (possibly Erwin of Steinbach) is most evident in the portals and the shape of the large rose window. Against the bare façade wall is a delicate pattern of mullions and tracery, with hidden passages behind. Above this another layer unfolds, with pierced or carved pilasters and lofty pinnacles. It is unlike any other French façade and even in the Germanic region it remained unique. The Strasbourg façade marks the triumph of Gothic architecture. This principle of transparency, which in Louis IX's Ste-Chapelle in Paris filled the chapel with a supernatural light, has the effect here of removing the barriers of spatial observation. On both sides of the rose window on the second level of the façade, not completed until after Erwin's death in 1318, it is already clear that this system is dying out.

In 'Scheme B' the towers started from the third level of the façade, but this idea was abandoned and instead the twin tower façade was replaced by a block-shaped façade ending in a platform, with the belfry between the towers. Michael of Freiburg, the architect in charge of this work phase, which began in 1385,

Page 196: Romanesque upper chancel of Strasbourg Cathedral.
Page 197: Pillar of the Last Judgment (*c.* 1230) and astronomical clock (1574) in the south transept of Strasbourg Cathedral.

Below: Stained glass in the St Catherine Chapel on the south aisle of Strasbourg Cathedral, *c.* 1340.

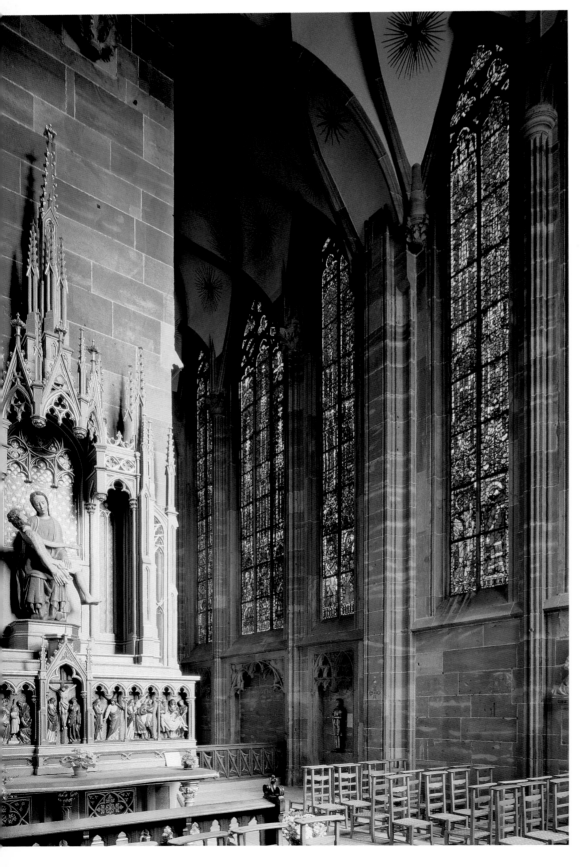

was a member of the Parler family (who also worked in Basel, Freiburg and Thann). In a final phase the plan for a tower façade on the Freiburg and Ulm model was reinstated. Ulrich von Ensingen, who was called to Strasbourg in 1399, built the octagonal base of the north tower, flanked by four polygonal stair turrets. His successor, Johannes Hültz from Cologne, took over the project in 1419 and finished the tower with a pyramidal spire. The work was completed in 1439. At 142 metres high (about 466 feet) Strasbourg Cathedral was the tallest building in Europe until the 19th century. At the exit from the octagon steps eight statuettes were added as an expression of civic pride in this city landmark (fragments can be seen in the Musée de l'Oeuvre Notre-Dame). They included, besides the architect Ulrich von Ensingen, St Catherine and St Barbara who are kneeling and looking up towards the spire.

The key to understanding this magnificent façade, impressive for the clear iconography of its message, lies in its sculptures. On the walls of the central portal a double row of prophets welcomes the faithful, while Christ's Passion spreads across the four sections of the tympanum, with a deesis above. In the archivolts are scenes and figures from the Old and New Testaments (Ill. p. 193). The Virgin Mary is on the large pediment with angel musicians. Underneath is King Solomon with twelve lions representing the twelve tribes of Israel on the steps of his throne (Ills. pp. 194 and 195). Some of these sculptures have been replaced, others preserved in the museum, but most have been kept *in situ*. The cycle emphasizes the typological connection between the Old and New Testaments – Solomon as the prefiguration of Christ, the prophets as his heralds – and the central motif is redemption from sin by Christ's Passion. On the tympanum of the left portal are

Rulers of the Holy Roman Empire: Otto III and Conrad II with a young prince. Late Romanesque stained-glass cycle in the north aisle of Strasbourg Cathedral.

scenes from the childhood of Christ, on the jambs the Virtues fighting against the Vices. On the right portal the Wise Virgins are following Christ, their bridegroom, while the Foolish Virgins on the left are turning to the Tempter or Prince of the World (Ill. p. 192). The tympanum depicts the Last Judgment. The overall theme is therefore moralistic, proclaiming the significance of Christ's sacrifice for the idea of salvation. The side tympana have been extensively restored (the original figures of the Virgins are in the museum). The statues are stylistically diverse; for instance, the rhetorical gestures and expressiveness of the prophets are completely different from the sophisticated style of the Virgins. The statues on the portal probably date from after 1280.

Above the rose window runs a gallery with figures of the Apostles, Mary and the risen Christ (restored in the 19th century). The decoration of this magnificent façade is rounded off by the protagonists in the Last Judgment underneath the platform on the belfry.

The cruciform cathedral has several extensions. In 1340 Bishop Berthold von Bucheck had a St Catherine Chapel built between the south transept and the nave in a sumptuous architectonic style. The chapel, which had a double bay and a star-ribbed vault with hanging keystones (replaced in 1542 by an intricate ribbed vault), used to contain the tomb of a saint (1340, fragments in the Musée de l'Oeuvre Notre-Dame). The pietà on the altar dates from 1350.

Jakob of Landshut built the extravagant St Lawrence Chapel, which is almost non-architectonic in its ornamentation, in front of the end wall of the north transept, right at the end of the Gothic period between 1495 and 1505. The sculptures on either side of the portal, attributed to Hans von Aachen, are of the Adoration of the Magi (Ill. p.

199

Left: Nicolaus Gerhaert von Leyden, memorial plaque of a canon at Strasbourg Cathedral, 1464.
Below: The tomb of Bishop Konrad of Lichtenberg.

Opposite: The nave of Strasbourg Cathedral, looking west.

Konrad of Lichtenberg (died 1299), surrounded by elaborate tracery in three sections, is in the French style and similar in form to the sculptures on the west façade. On the same wall are remnants of the epitaph of a canon (possibly Konrad of Busnang), shown in the outlines of a Gothic chapel in front of a balustrade in adoration of the Virgin and Child. Dated 1464 and signed 'N. v. L.', this masterly Late Gothic work by one of the greatest sculptors of the period, Nicolaus Gerhaert von Leyden, is already imbued with the spirit of humanism (see pp. 210, 211). The naturalism of the lifelike faces and gestures and the intimate atmosphere are reminiscent of a painting by Jan van Eyck from the 15th century. The coats of arms that used to hang under the Gothic framework were removed in the Revolution and the *transi* figure on the tomb slab has been lost.

203). On the right is the patron saint of the chapel with other saints. The martyrdom of St Lawrence under a baldachin, originally by Master Konrad, has been restored in modern times. The canons' sacristy on an octagonal ground plan adjoining the chapel on the east side was built in the French Baroque style by Joseph Massol, architect of the bishops' palace, in 1744. The old St Martin Chapel built in the north side aisle in 1515 (now the St Lawrence Chapel) was symmetrical with the St Catherine Chapel and had net vaults and carved keystones based on a plan by Hans Hammer, who designed the pulpit.

Johann Lorenz Goetz built the external Gothic style arcades on the north and south sides of the cathedral between 1772 and 1778 to hide the stalls that had been set up there (Ill. p. 203).

Of the internal furnishings, two major works of medieval funerary sculpture in the St John the Baptist Chapel are worthy of note. The tomb of Bishop

The south (Last Judgment) portal of Strasbourg
Cathedral depicting Solomon enthroned (modern),
Ecclesia and Synagogue, the Death and Coronation
of the Virgin on the tympanum (see Ill. p. 44).

Opposite left: Adoration of the Magi on the
St Lawrence Portal of the north transept of
Strasbourg Cathedral (original in museum).
Opposite right: The north aisle with Neo-Gothic
screen for stalls and transept at Strasbourg.

Two of the plastic works in the north
transept are notable, the font in the altar
niche on the east wall made by Jodokus
Dotzinger in 1453, covered with ornamental tracery, and opposite it on the
west wall a Mount of Olives made by the
sculptor Veit Wagner in 1498, which was
moved from the graveyard of St Thomas.
On one of the north pillars in the central
nave is the famous stone pulpit, a two-
storey structure on a ten-sided ground
plan, designed by Hans Hammer for
the cathedral preacher Hans Geiler von
Kaysersberg and completed with the
assistance of various sculptors in 1485
(Ill. p. 57). The artistically pierced
architectonic design with baldachins,
columns and about fifty figures in
the round give it the appearance of a
monumental piece of goldwork. Around
the pulpit is a Crucifixion scene with
Apostles and angels carrying the instruments of the Passion. The astronomical
clock in the south transept next to the
Last Judgment pillar, which dates from
1574 (Ill. p. 197), is also interesting.
The mechanism was designed by the
scholars Konrad Dasypodius and David
Wolkenstein and made by the Swiss
clockmakers Isaac and Josias Habrecht.
The outside was based on designs by
Tobias Stimmer. The present clock
was restored by Jean-Baptiste Schwilgué
in 1838. Of the old high altar made
by the Strasbourg sculptor Nicolaus
of Hagenau in 1501, only a few fragments have been preserved.

Strasbourg Cathedral also has some
of the finest and most important stained-
glass windows to have survived from
the Middle Ages. The three medallions
in the north transept, showing the

judgment of Solomon, date from around 1200. The glass picture of an emperor on a throne is even older, dating from after 1175 and possibly from the chancel of the old building (Ill. p. 209). The rose windows in the south transept contain stained glass from between 1230 and 1240, with similar iconography to the sculptures of Ecclesia and Synagogue on the south portal. In the north aisle is a cycle with emperors and kings of the Holy Roman Empire, the oldest of which were probably moved around 1210 and the others between 1250 and 1270 (Ills. pp. 57, 199). The clearstorey window in the nave was glazed when the cathedral was built, apart from the fifth and sixth windows which were added between 1330 and 1350. The stained glass in the south aisle, dating from between 1330 and 1340, depicts a kind of *Biblia pauperum*, with subtitles in everyday language. The stained glass in the narthex was added in the mid-14th century. The coloured glass in the tall narrow lancet windows in the St Catherine Chapel (Ill. p. 198), dating from 1340, shows Apostles and standing saints in variously shaped tower-like baldachin structures.

Below: The tympanum with Doubting Thomas
at St Thomas, Strasbourg, 1125–30.
Bottom: The sarcophagus of Bishop Adeloch
in St Thomas, Strasbourg, 12th century.

St Thomas

St Thomas, one of the oldest and most
important in the city, has been a stronghold of Alsatian Protestantism since
1524. The monastic church is believed
to have been founded by St Florentius,
a Strasbourg bishop, who encouraged
the settlement of Scottish monks and
was buried here in 693. The translation
of the saint's venerated relics to Haslach
in 810 deprived St Thomas of a rich
source of revenue and triggered a dispute
over their ownership that continued
for the next hundred years. The church's
history is reliably documented from the
time of Bishop Adeloch (786–823), but
nothing is known of the pre-Romanesque
and Romanesque period, except that the
Emperor Frederick Barbarossa confirmed
its privileges in 1163.

Around 1196 work began on a new
building, which was paid for with funds
from an indulgence granted by Bishop
Henry I (died 1190). The oldest part of
the present church is the rectangular
west end with its rose window. Built
around 1230, it originally opened on
to the nave with a portal on three levels

(still clearly visible under the round
arches of the façade) and an anteroom
with tribunes.

As the church was built in several
stages, the present building is a mixture
of different styles. The exterior is dominated by the massive west end with its
square central tower and the box-like
body of the nave. By contrast, the

interior is light and spacious, with the
hall-like nave extending across four
bays. This was one of the earliest hall
churches after St Elisabeth in Marburg
and in its turn it strongly influenced
the restoration of the Dominican church
in Strasbourg and the Heiligkreuz
church in Schwäbisch-Gmünd started
in 1308.

The chancel, terminating in a 5/8
polygon, was built first, around 1270,
after which there was obviously a change
of plan from the basilican structure to
the hall church – evident not only from
the proportions of the west end but also
from the consoles at the beginning of
the aisles. In the early 14th century the
north side of the nave was extended by
a row of chapels and the south side
by a projecting aisle, so that the church
had four aisles. It was vaulted in 1330,
possibly by Hans Erlin who was appointed
foreman in 1328 and later worked as
vicar-general for Bishop Berthold von
Bucheck, founder of the St Catherine
Chapel in the cathedral. The contrast
between the central supports in the form
of sectioned round pillars (see Collégiale
St-Martin in Colmar) and those on the

The nave of St Thomas, Strasbourg, with a view of the chancel.

south side, whose elegant ogee moulding profile continues seamlessly into the ribs of the vault, shows the different stages of construction. After the nave had been roofed over, another storey was added to the west tower in 1366 and in 1521 the Late Gothic Evangelists' Chapel was added on the south side of the nave.

On the choir screen of the south transept is the tympanum from the old portal with the figure of Doubting Thomas by a sculptor who worked on the Last Judgment pillar in the cathedral around 1225–30. An Atlas of the same school is behind the choir stalls. In the middle of the south transept is the tomb of Adeloch, the church's founder. It is a stone casket in the style of the Alsatian arched tombs from the workshop that carved the capitals of the cloisters in Eschau (now in the Musée de l'Oeuvre Notre-Dame). In the middle of a row of seven arches on the long side is the half-length figure of Christ, with the bishop and an angel with a stole. The narrow side shows an investiture scene. On the sloping sides of the lid is a monumental inscription in Carolingian capitals.

The chancel apse is dominated by the monument to Maurice of Saxony (1698–1750), *maréchal* of France and son of the elector August II, a Protestant who won brilliant victories for France and was honoured by Louis XV with this magnificent white marble monument. Made by the royal sculptor Jean-Baptiste de Pigalle before 1750, the monument is an outstanding example of 18th-century French sculpture. The hero, crowned with a laurel wreath, fully armed and holding the baton of the *maréchal*, is in the centre of the extravagant Baroque scene, about to descend into Hades. Death is opening the lid of the splendid tomb awaiting him there, while on the left Hercules remains in the gesture of mourning, promising eternal glory. The female personification of France tries in

enemies in the shape of animals – the Habsburg eagle, the English leopard and the lion of Flanders – are left behind, defeated, on broken flags.

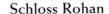

Jean-Baptiste de Pigalle, the tomb of Maurice of Saxony, *maréchal* of France, in the chancel of St Thomas, Strasbourg, pre-1750.

vain to ward off death, while the spirit of victory under the proud standards of the *grande nation* has already lowered the torch of life. On the other side the hero's

The church also has an organ made by the famous organ builder J. A. Silbermann in 1740, often played by Albert Schweitzer.

Schloss Rohan

Between 1731 and 1745 a magnificent archbishop's residence was built on the site of the medieval bishop's court south of the cathedral for Cardinal Armand-Gaston de Rohan-Soubise, who then settled in Strasbourg. The building was designed by the first royal architect, Robert de Cotte, and Joseph Massol supervised the work. During the Revolution the palace was occupied as a town hall and then used as an imperial residence under Napoleon. After 1870 it became the university and, in 1899, a museum of decorative arts. The complex was extensively restored after being damaged in the Second World War.

The imposing building, modelled on the great palaces built for the nobility in Paris, was laid out *entre cour et jardin*, between the *cour d'honneur* aligned with the south portal of the cathedral and a large terrace above the Ill in place of a garden. The main entrance is formed by the concave inset portico topped with a balustrade between two square pavilions with a mansard roof. Walls divided by blind arches separate the *cour d'honneur* from the offices and service quarters. The façade of the *corps de logis* on the courtyard side with the small apartments has two storeys and projecting wings at the side serve as vestibules.

The main façade on the river side extends across seventeen axes. It has a rusticated lower storey where the ground slopes away and is divided symmetrically by a central projection with four colossal columns and a triangular gable that contained the reception rooms. The library building, opening up on to the river in a portal-style window frontage, is to the left, immediately on the façade.

Right: The Salon d'Assemblé in the Schloss Rohan, Strasbourg.

Below: View of the south façade of Schloss Rohan, Strasbourg, across the Ill.

The splendid ornamental sculpture on the outside of the palace, in particular the elaborate decoration of the window frames, was by the royal sculptor Robert le Lorrain, assisted by Paul de Saint-Laurent, known as Paulé, and Jean-Auguste Nahl.

The interior is in the aristocratic taste of the time, although the wall decoration is only an approximate reconstruction of the original furnishings and now takes second place to the display of the works of art.

Maison Kammerzell

The Maison Kammerzell in the Place de la Cathédrale, named after its 19th-century owner, is an outstanding example of domestic art and one of the sights of the city. The three projecting half-timbered storeys with high hipped roof and two façades were built for a wealthy merchant called Martin Braun on top of an arcaded 15th-century stone ground floor after 1571. With its elaborate carvings, the house is a secular counterpart to the adjacent Gothic cathedral. The west façade is decorated with a cycle of heroes and heroines and a row of musicians. Personifications of the theological virtues on the corner posts (from top to bottom charity, hope and faith) connect with the gable façade aligned with the

cathedral, which is covered with allegorical images. Right at the bottom are the five senses, above them the seven ages of man and the signs of the zodiac on the window consoles. There are parallels with the sculptures on the south and west façade of the cathedral, but the contemporary themes are shown

in a humanistic rather than a religious context. The interesting wall paintings inside were done in 1905 by the Strasbourg painter Leo Schnug, whose traditional old German style was clearly inspired by Upper Rhine artists like Urs Graf and Hans Baldung Grien. He also worked in Haut-Koenigsburg.

Opposite far left and left: Views of Maison Kammerzell, Strasbourg.

Below: Head of Christ from Weissenburg. Glass pane, 11th century. Musée de l'Oeuvre Notre-Dame, Strasbourg.
Below right: Enthroned emperor. Stained glass from the old Romanesque cathedral, after 1175. Musée de l'Oeuvre Notre-Dame, Strasbourg.

Musée de l'Oeuvre Notre-Dame

The former administrative buildings to the south also belong to the cathedral, including the 'Oeuvre Notre-Dame' responsible for building work, from which the museum on the site takes its name. The complex, built between the 14th and the 16th centuries, is an appropriate setting for the medieval and Renaissance works, which include 17th-century furniture, paintings and decorative art from Strasbourg.

Among the museum's treasures are architectural drawings from the 13th to the 16th centuries, second only to the collection in Vienna in importance. 'Scheme B' (Ill. p. 46), dating from around 1275, is the original plan for the cathedral's present façade. The original sculptures from the cathedral, including the famous figures of Ecclesia and Synagogue (Ill. p. 44), and fragments of the destroyed rood screen are particularly interesting. The highlights of the medieval stained-glass section are a head of Christ from Weissenburg, one of the oldest pieces of stained glass in existence, and the enthroned emperor dating from after 1175, probably made for the middle chancel window in the cathedral. Like the famous *Hortus Deliciarum* of Herrad of Landsberg, this stained glass shows Byzantine influence.

Late medieval sculpture is represented by a rare masterpiece made by the great Dutch sculptor Nicolaus Gerhaert von Leyden during his time in Strasbourg (1462–67), although it has never been established exactly where and when it was produced. The bust of a man sunk in contemplation is probably a sort of personal testimony, which breaks abruptly into the Gothic-inspired vision of an idealized world and confronts the spectator with an image that is the very first portrayal of a person's frame of mind in sculpture north of the Alps. The man's meditative mood is emphasized by the realistic gesture of the hand cupping the chin. Leaning figures like this were a common motif from then on in southern Germany, although they never achieved the same psychological intensity as the two busts attributed to Nicolaus of Hagenau. The artist, who worked in Strasbourg from the 1480s, also produced the shrine sculptures on the Isenheim altar (see Ill. p. 186).

Baden-Baden

SS Peter und Paul

The first record of this former collegiate church, built above the foundations of the Roman baths, is in 1245. Between 1453 and 1477 the 13th-century Romanesque building was converted into a Late Gothic hall church with a long chancel. The church is dominated by the splendidly Baroque monument to Ludwig Wilhelm, known as 'Ludwig the Turk', under the tombs of the margraves of Baden.

Today the chevet houses the 6½ metre (21 foot) high cemetery crucifix in pink calcareous sandstone that Hans Ulrich Scherer, surgeon to the Margrave of Baden, commissioned from the eminent Dutch sculptor Nicolaus Gerhaert von Leyden when he was working in Strasbourg. On the back it is inscribed '1467 *niclaus von leyden*' and the founder's coat of arms appears on the front above the stone pedestal. The figure of Christ crucified represents a new iconographical type that later became the convention, particularly in south Germany. The stretched-out body is nailed to the cross rising from Golgotha, portrayed as the Tree of Life with the stone imitating the wooden structure of the crossbeam. Yet Christ's face shows no sign of pain; instead it is calm and peaceful. This spiritualized portrayal was undoubtedly influenced by metaphysical concepts of mysticism. With its superb anatomical detail the body seems to exude power and strength and the chisel has been used with remarkable skill to fashion the naturalistic crown of thorns and the curve of the loincloth. The Baden-Baden crucifix is the last work by this master on the Upper Rhine after the lost high altar in Konstanz Cathedral. From then on he worked at the imperial court in Vienna until his death.

Rastatt

View of the *corps de logis* at Schloss Rastatt across the *cour d'honneur*.

Opposite: The ancestral hall of Schloss Rastatt with portraits of the margraves of Baden.

Schloss Rastatt

The palace, town and castle in Rastatt, the first new Baroque residences on the Upper Rhine after the destruction caused by the Palatine War of Succession in 1689, were founded by Margrave Ludwig Wilhelm of Baden-Baden, known as Ludwig the Turk because of his spectacular feats in the Turkish wars. A hunting lodge under construction since 1698, under the supervision of Domenico Egidio Rossi, was soon superseded by new plans for an imposing residence, also built by Rossi. The exterior was completed by 1702. The interior decoration was carried out by the painters Paolo Manni and Giuseppe Roli, with stuccowork by Giovanni Battista Artano. The brilliant centrepiece is undoubtedly the ancestral hall, an impressive Baroque ensemble of royal iconography. The ceiling fresco shows the apotheosis of Hercules, an allusion to the heroic owner of the Schloss, while portraits of the margraves of Baden hang on the walls.

The *corps de logis* (main building) is unmistakably modelled on Versailles, which epitomized royal might and absolute power and was much imitated in the German residences. The church of the Schloss (palace), with a staircase designed by the architect Michael Ludwig Rohrer, is one of the extensions built for the margrave's widow Sibylla Augusta after 1707.

The Schloss, which is the largest Baroque residence in southern Germany after Mannheim, completely escaped being bombed during the Second World War. It is remarkable that it has scarcely been altered since the Catholic line of Baden-Baden died out in 1771, even in the 19th century, and is largely preserved in its original 18th-century form.

Opposite: The central room, designed as a sala terrena, at Schloss Favorite, Rastatt.

Right: The Hall of Mirrors at Schloss Favorite, Rastatt.

Below: View of the grounds and lake in front of Schloss Favorite, Rastatt.

Schloss Favorite

Michael Ludwig Rohrer built this summer residence between Rastatt and Baden-Baden for the margrave's widow Sibylla Augusta from plans by Domenico Egidio Rossi between 1710 and 1712. A double-sided flight of outside steps leading up from the park to the *piano nobile* accentuates the main part of the house, which has three wings and a central projection. The nucleus of the symmetrically planned building is an octagonal central hall stretching up three storeys and ending in a cupola.

The furnishings, which have been well preserved, reflect the fondness of the Bohemian-born margravine for the royal lifestyle and magnificent surroundings. A devout Christian, she also had a hermitage built in a wooded area of the grounds, an original design by Rohrer in the form of an octagonal central room.

Karlsruhe

After the royal residence of the margraves of Baden-Durlach was destroyed in the Palatine War of Succession in 1689, Margrave Charles William had a new town built as his official residence on a hunting ground near the Rhine in 1715. The layout of the Schloss area and the town are still based on the original plan radiating out from an octagonal tower, probably designed by the engineer Friedrich von Batzendorf (Ill. p. 65).

In 1718 the court was transferred to Karlsruhe. The first Schloss, a simple half-timbered building, soon proved inadequate as a residence and in 1749 Margrave Charles Frederick began planning a new building in the grand style. For this project he called in the Italian architect Leopoldo Retti, who was working in Stuttgart, Balthasar Neumann from Würzburg and, from 1752, Pierre-Louis Philippe de la Guêpière, the court architect of Württemberg. It is not surprising, therefore, that the design of the *corps de logis* has similarities with Schloss Stuttgart, which was being built at the time. The construction work began in

1752 under the supervision of Friedrich von Kesslau, who used some of his own ideas, particularly for the interior. The exterior was finished in 1770, the whole of the spacious Schloss, which combined late Rococo style with elements of early Classicism, in 1785. During the Second World War, the building was badly damaged, but the façade was rebuilt and the interior refurbished to make it more suitable to house the Badisches Landesmuseum. The landscaped park that replaced the Baroque gardens in 1790 has been partly preserved.

In the original plan a circle separated the three-wing structure of the Schloss, with the Schloss yard in front on the south side, from the town, which radiated out in a fan shape. In the 18th century the two moved closer together. The architect Friedrich Weinbrenner left his mark on the town, which became the seat of the Grand Duchy of Baden in 1803. His Classical buildings in the Marktplatz, including the town hall, the Protestant church and the pyramid monument in the centre (Ill. p. 69), are on the main axis of the Baroque plan.

Opposite left: Rear view of Schloss Karlsruhe, with the tower marking the centre of the town layout.

Below: View of Schloss Karlsruhe from the town side.

Bruchsal

Below: View of the staircase at Schloss Bruchsal, from the vestibule with the lower grotto.
Bottom: View across the *cour d'honneur* of Schloss Bruchsal, which was ruined by bombing in 1945. It has since been restored to its former glory.

Opposite top: Staircase dome with restored Johannes Zick frescoes (allegorical pictures illustrating the history of the Speyer bishopric) and stuccowork by Johann Michael Feuchtmayr.

Schloss Bruchsal

Apart from Schloss Rohan in Strasbourg (Ill. p. 207), Bruchsal is the only large ecclesiastical residence on the Upper Rhine. Like the palaces of the temporal princes in Baden-Baden, Durlach and Heidelberg, the bishop's palace in Speyer had become a ruin. It was the prince-bishop of Speyer, Damian Hugo von Schönborn (1719–43), who decided to move the seat to the area on the right bank of the Rhine under Speyer's jurisdiction and have a new Schloss built. The work started in 1722. The building, based on plans by the Electorate of Mainz architect Maximilian von Welsch, was a pavilion with three wings and a large *cour d'honneur*. Anselm Franz Freiherr von Ritter zu Grünstein from Mainz was commissioned to work on the middle section, the *corps de logis*, and he drew up the original plan for a central elliptical staircase. However, the work came to a halt because of high-handed interference by the prince-bishop, who dabbled in architecture himself. It was not until the architect Balthasar Neumann was called in from Würzburg in 1728 that an ingenious solution was found for the staircase (1730–31). It is now regarded as a masterpiece of Baroque architecture in Germany. The painted decoration is a tribute to the owner and his successor, Franz Christoph von Hutten.

Heidelberg

Schloss Heidelberg

The first reference to a *castrum* was in 1225. The building was laid out in the time of the Elector Ruprecht III (1398–1410). It is set around a large inner courtyard and protected on three sides by a moat. Round fortified towers mark its boundaries. Under the Elector Ludwig V (1508–44) the medieval seat of the Palatine Wittelsbachs was fortified by a solid rampart to the west and by the 'Thick Tower' on the town side.

However, it was his successors who turned the fortress-like structure into an imposing residence befitting the status of the counts palatine of the Rhine as the highest-ranking secular princes of the empire. Their ambitious projects included the Hall of Mirrors (1544–46; Frederick II), the Ottheinrich Building (1556–59), the Friedrich Building (1583–1610; Frederick IV) and the English Building (1610–23; Frederick V). Under Frederick V the French land-scape gardener Salomon de Caus also designed the *hortus palatinus*, a magnificent Renaissance garden with spacious terraces stretching to the slopes southeast of Schloss (castle) Heidelberg.

The whole building was severely damaged in the Thirty Years' War and the War of the Palatine Succession. It was also struck by lightning in 1764. In the Romantic period the ruins came to symbolize the unity of history, art and nature. The structure, in particular the Friedrich Building, was reinforced and restored in the second half of the 19th century.

Schloss Heidelberg is made up of various parts built in different periods and styles. It opens up from the inner courtyard, entered from the south through the gate tower. On the left (west) side are the oldest part of the Ruprecht Building and two buildings dating from the time of Ludwig V: the library, still in the Gothic style, and

View of the town side of Schloss Heidelberg from the north.

the Bower (King's Hall), the half-timbered upper storey of which was replaced by an over-heavy roof in the 18th century.

Johann Schoch's Friedrich Building, which dominates the north façade, copied the decorative pattern of division by columns and in particular the idea of an allegorical and historical set of sculptures (Ill. p. 62) from the façade of the Ottheinrich Building on the east side of the courtyard, which was erected half a century earlier.

The two façades represent an original concept of Renaissance architecture, quite distinct from the Italian models. The façade of the Ottheinrich Building, more restrained and balanced in its proportions, is one of the most remarkable examples of the new 16th-century style north of the Alps influenced by the Dutch Renaissance. The humanist patron, the last representative of the older palatine electoral line, has built himself a monument. An outside flight of steps leads up to the splendid portal. Above this is a eulogistic inscription referring to the elector, crowned with his portrait in the medallion so that he takes his place amongst the Old Testament and mythological heroes whose statues decorate the façade.

This function of architecture as a symbol of royal power is further enhanced by the sculptures on the Friedrich Building. The row of Rhine palatine counts and electors, from Charlemagne to the building's patron, the Elector Frederick IV, glorifies the dynasty. The narrow squat-arched section containing the Hall of Mirrors, which prefigures the 'German Renaissance' (Ill. p. 62), is fitted in between the two magnificent façades.

Outside the courtyard, between the Bower and the Thick Tower, is the austere back of the English Building. Its façade, divided by pilasters, faces the town. The eminent English architect Inigo Jones stayed briefly at the Heidelberg court at the time of the English Electress Elizabeth Stuart, which might explain the Palladian-influenced style of this section.

Opposite: Courtyard façade of the Ottheinrich
Building at Schloss Heidelberg.

Below: The interior of the Jesuit church at
Mannheim, facing east.

Mannheim

The city, which developed from a minor settlement in a strategic position at the confluence of the Neckar and the Rhine, is mentioned in records as early as the 8th century. The Friedrichsburg fortress, named after its founder the Palatine Elector Frederick IV, was built in 1606. It consisted of a citadel aligned with the Rhine and the adjoining city. The centre of Mannheim is still laid out on the same chessboard plan (Ill. p. 64). After it had been completely destroyed in the War of the Palatine Succession, Elector Johann Wilhelm began rebuilding it in 1698, but without the citadel. A huge Baroque Schloss complex was built on the site after the Elector Charles Philip (1716–42) transferred the electoral seat from Heidelberg to Mannheim from 1720. Mannheim's brief period of glory as a royal capital ended in 1777, when the inheritance of the Bavarian Wittelsbachs passed to the Elector Karl Theodor and he moved to Munich. In 1803 the city and the Palatinate on the right bank of the Rhine became part of Baden. After the city was bombed in 1943, only the outside walls of the Schloss Mannheim were left standing. The interior was restored and it is now a university and district courthouse.

Former Jesuit church

In 1727 the Elector Charles Philip called the Jesuits to Mannheim and allocated them a site near the palace to build a college and church. The church, considered the most important Baroque building in the southwest of Germany, was started in 1738 and consecrated in 1760. The architect Alessandro Galli Bibiena built a cruciform pier basilica modelled on Il Gesù, the order's mother church in Rome. It has side chapels linked by passages, with tribunes above. A row of tall pilasters runs right round the church. The most striking feature is the lofty crossing cupola. The exterior is dominated by the elaborate twin tower façade, more German than Italian Baroque. The relief on the gable was by the palatine court sculptor Paul Egell, who also designed the high altar built by his successor Peter Anton Verschaffelt. The church was extensively restored after the Second World War.

Schwetzingen

Schloss Schwetzingen

The Schloss, a residence that used to belong to the palatine electors, became a seat of the grand-dukes of Baden under the jurisdiction of the Heidelberg and Mannheim residences in 1803. As it has not been modified since the Wittelsbach succession, which forced Elector Karl Theodor to move his seat to Munich in 1777, it is an authentic example of a German, Late Baroque royal residence.

After the medieval castle surrounded by water had largely been destroyed in the Thirty Years' War, work began under the Elector Karl Ludwig (1648–80) to convert the rural hunting lodge of the palatine rulers into a Baroque summer residence, which is the nucleus of the present building. The Schloss was sacked in 1689, a fateful year for the Palatinate, and rebuilt by the Heidelberg architect Johann Adam Breunig for Elector Johann Wilhelm between 1700 and 1708. It was then extended between 1710 and 1717, in accordance with plans by the building supervisor Matteo Albert Sarto. The

Opposite top: Overgrown pergola in the grounds at Schloss Schwetzingen.
Opposite bottom: The garden side of Schloss Schwetzingen with large parterre.

Below: Nicolas de Pigage, Rococo theatre in the grounds of Schloss Schwetzingen, 1752.

imposing *cour d'honneur*, with wings and connecting buildings, was built on the east side, while a four-storey projection, whose massive corner pavilions still emphasize the severity of the façade, was added to the garden side of the middle section. The wrought-iron Baroque gate at the entrance to the *cour d'honneur* on the town side was also added. The bases of the pillars on both sides bear the fine coats of arms of Elector Johann Wilhelm and his wife Anna Maria Luisa de' Medici, who had their residence in Düsseldorf.

Elector Charles Philip made Mannheim his main seat and had a garden with an exotic orangery built in Schwetzingen. However, it was his successor, Karl Theodor of the Pfalz-Sulzbach dynasty, who was responsible for the magnificent park for which Schwetzingen is famous. A lover of the arts, the elector planned a complete reconstruction of the old Schloss in the grand style. The young Lunéville architect Nicolas de Pigage was involved in drawing up the plans. The semicircular building to the north

was built first, in 1748, followed by another to the south in 1753. In 1752 Pigage, by then architect to the elector's court, built the Rococo theatre, which, after extensive renovation, is now once again an elegant setting for plays and concerts. However, the War of Austrian Succession disrupted the project and it was never completed.

Johann Ludwig Petri from the Zweibrücken court was also involved in the design of the gardens in the 1750s. The centrepiece of the ingenious

Below: The Turkish mosque in the grounds of
Schloss Schwetzingen.
Bottom: Semicircular building on north side
by circular flowerbed.

Opposite: The temple of Apollo in the grounds
of Schloss Schwetzingen.

Sckell, a landscape gardener who later
worked in Munich. On Karl Theodor's
behalf he went to England to study the
new style of landscaping inspired by
the spirit of Enlightenment and met its
leading exponents, William Chambers
and Capability Brown. For this English
garden, with its curving paths and natural
plantings of trees, Pigage designed the
temple of botany (1776–79), the picturesque ruins of the temple of Mercury
and, lastly (starting in 1780), the exotic
Turkish mosque area in the south.

As a historic example of a landscaped
garden in which two contrasting periods
and styles complement and enhance
each other in a harmonious whole,
Schwetzingen is one of the outstanding
achievements of 18th-century court
culture. Thanks to the conservation work
that has been carried out, its ingenious
design and natural beauty can still be
appreciated today.

landscaping is the circular French-style
parterre, bordered by the two semicircular
buildings and pergolas and intersected
by double pathways on the main axes
(Ill. p. 66). The Arion fountain is the
symbolic and geometrical centre of
the parterre and at the end of the garden
opposite the Schloss is a group of deer,
beyond which the eye is drawn to the
Haardt hills along the main visual axis.
On both sides of the main axis are low
symmetrical shrubberies, flanked on the
north side by the rectangular orangery
garden and the grove of the temple of
Apollo, laid out as a natural theatre.
Other buildings in the Baroque garden
designed by Pigage include a bathhouse
and the Roman temple of Minerva.

The new ideas that were brought
to Schwetzingen when the park was
extended to the west in 1778 soon
spread to the rest of Europe. The plans
were drawn up by Friedrich Ludwig von

Opposite: Aerial view of Speyer across the Rhine.

Crypt of the imperial cathedral, facing east.

Page 230: The nave of Speyer Cathedral, facing east.
Page 231: View of Speyer Cathedral from the northeast.

Speyer

Speyer Cathedral

Speyer, like Limburg an der Haardt (p. 233), was founded by the first Salian Emperor Konrad II, who had, by about 1030, drawn up the plans for the huge new imperial cathedral and designated it the burial place for his dynasty (see Worms, p. 234). The cathedral was still a building site when Konrad was buried at the end of the nave in 1039. Konrad's son and heir Henry III continued the work on the original building (Speyer I) and the cathedral was consecrated in 1061. Yet it did not take on its final form until Henry IV made radical changes between 1082 and 1106. In its majestic beauty and its formal achievements this largely preserved Late Salian building (Speyer II) represents a landmark in western religious architecture, heralding the age of monumental Romanesque vaulted buildings in Germany.

The imperial cathedral did not escape the systematic destruction by Louis XIV's troops in the Palatinate and Upper Rhine in 1689. The whole of the western half was reduced to rubble and the ruins deteriorated further over the next few years. The restoration work did not begin until 1772 and was never completed in the west block. In the disturbances of the Revolution and the Napoleonic era the plan to demolish the cathedral completely was only just prevented by an imperial decree when Bishop Colmar of Mainz intervened in 1806.

Extensive restoration work was carried out between 1819 and 1854 after the Palatinate on the left bank of the Rhine, formerly Wittelsbach territory, had passed to the Bavarian monarchs in 1816. The westwork (1854–58) that was then rebuilt by the Karlsruhe architect Heinrich Hübsch certainly gives some idea of the original medieval appearance but the style is unmistakably Neo-Romanesque. The cycle of pictures

(1845–53) by Johann Schraudolph on the upper walls in the nave was donated by King Ludwig I of Bavaria. The cathedral was restored again between 1957 and 1972.

With an overall length of 133 metres (436 feet) – the nave is 70 metres (nearly 230 feet) long – Konrad II's building has the monumental dimensions of the cathedral and the ground plan of a

two-aisled pier basilica with a raised transept, separate crossing and chancel above a projecting crypt. The walls of the nave in Speyer I, which was flat roofed in the style of an Early Christian basilica, were divided by a sort of colossal order with blind arches rising from the massive pillars and framing the clearstorey windows. One of the most crucial changes made under Henry IV was the vaulting of the nave. For this, every second wall pier had to be strengthened with an abutment and semicircular engaged shafts to support the blind arches, ribs and reinforcing arches of the vaulting compartments.

The main feature preserved from Konrad II's original structure is the crypt consecrated in 1041, which occupies the whole area beneath the transept and chancel. It is a real undercroft, spanned by a network of groined vaults whose reinforcing arches rest on pillars with solid cushion capitals. As in the church above, massive pillars divide the hall-shaped room into four square sections, extended in the east by a semicircular apse (Ill. p. 229). The magnificence of the crypt shows the importance that was attached at that time to these places of worship used for the preservation and veneration of relics (see Cologne, St Maria im Kapitol, Ill. p. 302).

Especially in its outward appearance, the cathedral heralds the new Romanesque style, expressed most clearly in the layout of the east section. The various parts – transepts, upper chancel and apse, with stair turrets and domes projecting above them – are clearly separated from each other and at the same time brought together by an innovative dwarf gallery running round the cathedral. The pilaster-strip motif was also found in Ottonian architecture (St Pantaleon in Cologne), but here it is developed into a distinctive system. Ornamental carving is also a feature. Palmettes and arabesques with fabulous animals, attributed to stonemasons from Lombardy, decorate the window frames in the transepts.

Speyer II introduces a new austere and monumental style of building, leaving behind the Early Christian tradition that had shaped early medieval architecture for centuries. Whereas before the upper walls in the nave had been treated simply as flat surfaces whose sole function was to divide the space or separate interior from exterior, in its organic connection with the vaulting the wall now had a structural purpose, aligning loads and load-bearing surfaces.

The invention of the compound pier, a support consisting of a core, an abutment and engaged shafts now used in Romanesque buildings and later a basic component of Gothic architecture, was part of this process. Thus a new chapter in the history of western architecture began in the second half of the 11th century, not at the beginning of the Salian dynasty but later on under Henry IV, at the time of the investitures controversy between the Emperor and the Pope and the loss of imperial power.

The square double chapel dedicated to St Martin and St Emmeram in the corner between the transept and the south aisle was built at the end of the 11th century. The finely crafted scroll capitals of the four supporting pillars at ground level were the work of Lombard stonemasons, imported or made on the spot, as were the original capitals with carved monsters in the St Afra Chapel in the corresponding position on the north side, where the excommunicated Emperor Henry IV was initially buried in 1106. The aisleless four-bay chapel had been under construction since 1100 and was not yet consecrated when he died. It contains a 1470 relief of the Annunciation influenced by Nicolaus Gerhaert von Leyden (see pp. 200, 210, 211).

Empresses and later kings were buried in the imperial vault in Speyer Cathedral, together with the four rulers of the Salian dynasty. The cathedral is therefore important not only as an example of the new Romanesque architecture but also as a historical monument. Next to the unadorned imperial tombs the tombstone of King Rudolf of Habsburg (r. 1273–91) now on the end wall of the vault is a striking example of medieval tomb carving. The sculptor is said to have portrayed the effects of ageing on the king's features very accurately.

Limburg an der Haardt

Benedictine monastery church

After his accession Konrad II, the first Salian on the German throne, turned his family's ancestral castle (see Worms, p. 234) in a mountain range on the edge of the northern Vosges into a Benedictine monastery and Limburg was founded. The church, started in 1025, was built much more quickly than Speyer Cathedral, which Konrad also founded. According to records, there were already three altars in the crypt by 1035 and the church was consecrated in 1042. Henry III's first wife, Gunhild, had already been buried in the nave in 1038 (her tombstone is now outside). After the church and monastery were sacked and burned in 1504, only the chancel was restored and partitioned off with a wall before the monastery was abandoned in 1574 and allowed to deteriorate. In the 19th century the first steps were taken to reinforce the deserted ruins. As an important example of 11th-century Salian architecture, the abbey is still majestic even in its fragmented state.

The ground plan is a two-aisle cruciform basilica. Each of the arches in the nave was supported by eleven columns. The east part, which has largely been preserved, consists of a projecting transept with a separate crossing and square cross-arms, opening to the east in a semicircular apse, and a square chancel. Underneath is the crypt, supported on four columns. The dominant octagonal crossing tower is balanced by two symmetrical square towers on the west façade. The architectonic design of the early Salian building is impressive in its balanced proportions and the clear articulation of its parts. The walls are divided by flat niches, pilaster-strips and blind arches both inside and out, while the windows are simply cut into the wall. Limburg an der Haardt appears to be one of the earliest, and certainly one of the

most influential, examples of a system often found on the Upper and Middle Rhine, in which the walls play a structural, and also decorative, role.

233

Worms

Former Worms Cathedral, now parish church of St Peter

The Merovingian queen Brunhildis, who died around 613, had a royal palace and an episcopal church built on the cathedral hill, which in Roman times was the site of the forum with public buildings and temples. However, it was not until Bishop Burchard's time (1000–25) that an ambitious church was built. It was consecrated in the presence of the Emperor Henry II in 1018. Its arrangement as a cruciform pier basilica with an alternating system was also a model for the present 12th-century cathedral. Bishop Burchard was buried in the west chancel in 1025.

As the family seat of Duke Konrad the Red (died 955), son-in-law of Otto the Great and founder of the Salian dynasty that succeeded the Saxon emperors, Worms was one of the most favoured places in the empire. The Salian emperors endowed the cathedral, the burial place of their ancestors, whereas they built the new cathedral in Speyer themselves. In 1122 the Concordat of Worms ended the investitures controversy between the Emperor and the Pope. Three years later the Salian dynasty died out with Henry V (r. 1111–25). The period of Hohenstaufen rule that began with the election of Konrad III in 1138 ushered in a new style that influenced many important religious buildings on the Rhine. Worms Cathedral is one of the finest and most typical examples of this Hohenstaufen architecture.

Bishop Burchard's Late Ottonian cathedral was completely rebuilt in the 12th century, step by step from east to west. Only the foundation walls were retained. The initial phase began around 1130 with the construction of the east end. This consisted of the chancel (semi-cruciform inside, straight ended outside), with staircase turrets at the sides and transept divided into three with a separate crossing, above which was a cupola on squinches. The five-bay nave, balanced by ten bays in the aisles, was built between 1160 and 1170, followed by the extended west chancel. Bishop Konrad II consecrated the Hohenstaufen church in 1181.

It is remarkable that at a time when the radical transition to the new Gothic architecture was already under way in

France, important buildings like Mainz and Worms cathedrals clung so firmly to the traditional plan with alternating supports and a second chancel in the west. While the exterior is generally impressive, some irregularities are noticeable in the interior as the style evolves. Every second pillar in the nave is reinforced by a wall abutment with half-columns in front carrying the reinforcing arches and cross-ribs of the vaults, while squared built-up ribs span the transept arms and front chancel. Under the clearstorey windows the wall is divided by blind arcading and pilaster-strips; below them runs a profiled moulding that incorporates the imposts of the wall abutments. Profiled pilaster-strips divide the lower

walls of the front chancel in the east, with three arches corresponding to three niches in the apse. A new tectonic and decorative concept is particularly evident in the west chancel, the newest part of the building. The wall is treated as a kind of pattern book of architectonic forms and tiered on several levels in traditional Rhenish style (see Cologne, p. 291). A similar feature can be seen in the north transept of Strasbourg Cathedral.

In Worms the Rhenish style is especially noticeable on the exterior. Like the larger cathedrals of Speyer and Mainz, Worms is a magnificent example of Rhenish architecture – with its two crossing towers and four stair turrets, the double chancel arrangement that

shifts the main entrance to the side and many other features that give the cathedral (downgraded to a parish church in 1803) a striking and indeed picturesque silhouette. The monumental ensemble of east chancel and flanking towers, designed as a frontage on to the town and the Rhine, is remarkable for its strict system of division in the form of structural pilaster-strips and arched mouldings in the Lombard style and the clear articulation of the storeys. The triple arrangement of the profiled windows and the dwarf gallery counteracts the solid weight of the lower section so that the façade appears optically lighter towards the top. By contrast, the interplay of structural components and ornamentation gives the west chancel a fairly delicate appearance. It might be described as a Romanesque 'Mannerism', which makes the style less monumental.

Apart from the imaginative sculptures on the east façade, with animals in the round on the window ledges and demonic masks as consoles, and the carved columns of the dwarf gallery with the figure believed to be a portrait of the architect, a few fragments of sculpture complete the picture of the Romanesque cathedral. The Gothic tympanum on the south portal shows Christ making the sign of the cross between Mary and a bishop (possibly St Nicholas) on one side and St Peter on the other side, holding a book with a passage from John 14:6, 'I am the way, the truth and the life'. On the back is a relief of various figures including Christ enthroned amongst saints. This was a tympanum on the Hohenstaufen cathedral and was reused the other way round on the Gothic portal. Three original fragments, showing Daniel in the lions' den, Habakkuk and the three angels and three lions, now in the wall in the St Agnes Chapel, are probably also from the old south portal.

A few valuable sculptures from the cloisters built in 1484 date from the Late Gothic period. In the St Nicholas Chapel is the large relief of the Tree of Jesse made for Bishop Johann von Dalberg in 1488 (the date is at the base of the trunk), whose ornamental arabesques look like a mysterious calligraphy. The composition seems to have been influenced by contemporary carved altars. A four-part cycle of reliefs shows the Annunciation, the Nativity and the Entombment (from the workshop of Hans Syfer) and also the Resurrection. The Late Baroque high altar, filling the whole of the east chancel, was designed by Balthasar Neumann and built between 1738 and 1742, while the sculptures are by Wolfgang von der Auwera.

Synagogue

The synagogue in Worms is one of the most important Jewish cultural monuments in Europe. The first synagogue was built in 1034 (founder's stone plaque on the portal) and destroyed in 1146. The main building used for worship, now the men's synagogue, was built from 1174 to 1775. The women's extension was added at the side from 1212 to 1213 and in 1624 the Raschi Chapel was built at the front. Of this complex, only the underground baths built from 1185

to 1186 have been preserved in their original state. The rest of the building was burnt down in 1938 during the persecution of the Jews by the Nazi regime and the ruins were blown up in 1942. It was rebuilt between 1959 and 1961, using parts of the original structure.

The 12th-century men's building is a hall with two aisles and groined vaults. The two (restored) central pillars are topped with magnificent foliated capitals, pointing to a connection with the cathedral lodge. One of the impost slabs

decorated with palmettes bears a Hebrew inscription and the years 1174 to 1175. Between the columns is the pulpit (bima) where the Torah is read. The fine Romanesque portal on the north side was salvaged from the debris and rebuilt.

Dominican church

The two narrow sides of this former collegiate church founded by Bishop Burchard in 1015 were rebuilt in the Romanesque style in the Hohenstaufen period, although they have been extensively restored since being destroyed in the Second World War. The 11th-century building already ended in a kind of westwork, of which only the lower storeys of the flanking stair turrets have survived. However, the present transept-like west section with its octagonal tower and the rectangular east chancel ending in a polygon were only added when the church was rebuilt after a fire in 1231. The nave of the Hohenstaufen columnar basilica was converted into a hall with a stucco ceiling between 1706 and 1716.

The chancel can be seen as a smaller replica of the west chancel of the cathedral church, on which the division of the apse by profiled pilaster-strips and friezes of semicircular arches and the shape of the dwarf gallery are based.

The division outside is the same as inside the chancel. The apse has five semicircular niches cut into the lower part of the wall, with semicircular windows above. The west end, which might still retain some elements of the earlier 11th-century church, is divided into three by arched buttresses. The central section is emphasized by a portal with whorled pillars in the walls and semi-circular archivolts and by an elaborate rose window.

Below and right (detail): Gatehouse of the Benedictine abbey at Lorsch.

Lorsch

Benedictine abbey

The abbey church was consecrated by Archbishop Lulle of Mainz in the presence of Charlemagne and his sons in 774. It was used to house the relics of St Nazarius brought from Rome by Chrodegang, Bishop of Metz, and other furnishings were added under his successors in the Carolingian period. For instance, the head of a man in the Hessisches Landesmuseum in Darmstadt, one of the few surviving examples of Carolingian sculpture, comes from Lorsch. The freestanding rectangular 'gatehouse', a kind of triumphal arch, was built towards the end of the 8th century and has been remarkably well preserved. It was originally inside the large atrium in front of the church to the west, its axis aligned to the church entrance. The lower floor consists of an open hall with three arches on each of the two façades. On the floor above is a room about 10 metres (32 feet) long with stairs leading up to it in the extensions of the narrow side. The original liturgical purpose of this room is not clear; a cycle of wall paintings dating from about 1400 suggests a Marian iconography and it was not until the 18th century that St Michael was recorded as the abbey's patron saint.

The arch is a uniquely important architectonic relic of the early Carolingian period. Its shape and function as a *porta triumphalis* and its division and ornamentation are proof of both the survival of the Romanesque architectural tradition and its reinterpretation in the Carolingian Renaissance.

Oppenheim

View of St Catherine's Church, Oppenheim,
from the north across the Rhine plain.

Opposite: Nave/south side of the façade of
St Catherine's Church, Oppenheim, facing
the town.

St Catherine's Church

This multiform church dedicated to
St Catherine, regarded as one of the
finest Gothic churches in the Rhineland,
is in a picturesque position on the slopes
of the Oppenheim castle hill with a
sweeping view across the Rhine plain.
It was founded when the town started
to expand after Emperor Frederick II
had granted it a town charter in 1226.

Only the two west towers have been
preserved from the first Late Romanesque
basilica completed in 1240. After 1258
or 1262 the construction of a new
church in the contemporary Gothic
style had already begun. The east end,
consisting of the chancel and transept,
was built in the first phase. At right
angles alongside the rectangular chancel
ending in a five-sided polygon are lower
side chancels in the shape of half hexa-
gons connecting with the chancel and
the square transept arms.

The construction of the High Gothic
two-aisle nave began in 1317. It is of
medium height – 19 metres (62 feet)
– and, with its four rectangular bays,
rather wider than it is long – 15 by 24.5
metres (49 by 80 feet). Above the pier
arches the wall is almost completely
broken up by quadruple lancet windows,
balanced by tracery windows with six
lancets in the aisles. Underneath, the
room extends into chapels situated
between the arched buttresses.

Because of the slope on the south
side aligned to the town and the
Rhine plain, this nave is designed as
the main façade. The church is famous
for this unusual arrangement and the
remarkable diversity of its forms. The
range of motifs in the tracery of the
windows and pediments, rhythmically
divided by arched buttresses topped
with pinnacles, is so varied that it all

but obscures the architectonic structure. Even the remaining wall surfaces are covered. This church is a real corpus of 14th-century Rhenish tracery forms, inspired by not only the Cologne Cathedral lodge (Master Johannes) but also contemporary work like the front of Strasbourg Cathedral. The south front was built after the parish church was elevated to a collegiate chapter after 1317 and was completed in 1328. The gable latticed with mullions and tracery windows in the transepts and the

crossing tower were not built until the mid 14th century.

The towering chancel reserved for the clergy was built in 1415 and consecrated in 1439. It has no side aisles and adjoins the Romanesque towers on the west side. Huge 17 metre (55 foot) high windows with six panels, narrower in the chevet, make the room seem light and spacious. The stained glass has been restored in recent times and the Late Gothic net vaults have been rebuilt. Madern Gerthener from

Frankfurt is recorded as the architect (see Mainz Cathedral, pp. 246 and 248). The chancel contains a collection of medieval and Renaissance monuments.

With its striking silhouette, the church shows the influence of three architectural periods, Romanesque, Early Gothic and Late Gothic. The façade on the south side is a particular work of art. The geometrical decorative shapes blend with the tectonic structures so that the architecture looks almost like a drawing.

Mainz

The *Moguntiacum* encampment set up by Emperor Augustus's son-in-law Drusus on the strategically sited hill opposite the mouth of the Main around 16 BC was the nucleus of the civil settlement that developed into the capital of the province *Germania superior* in the first century and was first mentioned as a *civitas* in 297. By the end of the first century it was already connected to the fort on the right bank of the Rhine by a permanent bridge. There has been an episcopal church on the site of St John's Church behind the present cathedral since Constantinian times. In fact, St Irenaeus mentioned a Christian community even around 200. The priest

Albanus, who was martyred in Mainz in 406 in the onslaught of Alemanni, Vandals, Huns and Burgundians during the mass migration, has always been venerated there as an Early Christian martyr.

A new era began with St Boniface, who founded the archbishopric between 746 and 747 and made Mainz the 'Holy Seat' of the German province with fifteen suffragan bishoprics, including Worms, Speyer, Strasbourg, Konstanz and Chur on the Rhine and also Prague.

Mainz enjoyed a privileged position under the German kings and emperors from Carolingian times. The episcopal authority was at its most powerful under Willigis, who acted as regent while Otto

III was a minor. The Pope granted him the right for the Mainz archdiocese to crown the German king, making him the highest-ranking spiritual prince in the empire. The construction of the first cathedral on the present site was a tangible expression of that political power. Willigis also laid the foundations for future electors of Mainz by acquiring land on the other side of the Rhine.

In the 12th and 13th centuries conflict broke out between the burghers fighting for their independence, and the archbishop, who as grand chancellor of the empire also had a leading political role. When Archbishop Arnold was murdered by citizens of Mainz, Emperor Frederick I

The Gutenberg memorial in Mainz. Bronze casting after a model by Bertel Thorvaldsen, 1836.

(Barbarossa) dismantled the walls and withdrew the city's privileges as a punishment in 1163. Nevertheless, the emperor continued to hold court there. In 1244 Mainz was a leading member of the Rhenish Town League. A golden age of economic prosperity was followed by a decline in the 15th century. In 1462 all civil liberties were finally lost and the archbishop gained control of the city.

Mainz is particularly associated with the name of Johann Gutenberg, whose invention of printing in c. 1440 opened the door to a new era in the history of western culture and made his native city the birthplace of typography. In 1476 the episcopal ruler Dieter von Isenburg founded the university. By his forced sale of indulgences the humanist Elector Albrecht of Brandenburg provoked Luther into nailing up his theses and so became a key figure in the Reformation and the ensuing religious struggles. As a patron of the arts, he brought the painter Mathias Grünewald to his court. Grünewald's work for the cathedral was removed and destroyed when Sweden was defeated in the Thirty Years' War. In 1688 the French easily captured the city.

Mainz still has many fine Baroque mansions built in its final heyday in the 18th century, which was brought to an abrupt end by the French revolutionary troops and the collapse of the empire.

Mainz Cathedral

The history of the cathedral begins with Archbishop Willigis. Soon after being appointed by the Emperor Otto II in 973, he commissioned a massive new building that was meant to reflect Mainz's status and pretensions as a religious and political centre of the Holy Roman Empire. The imperial foundation building, modelled on the Constantinian church of St Peter in Rome, was a two-aisle basilica with a projecting transept and chancel on the west side and stair turrets to the east. An atrium in front terminated in a small church dedicated to the Virgin Mary. On the day of its consecration in 1009 the Willigis cathedral was destroyed by fire. It was reconsecrated under Archbishop Bardo in 1036 and burned down again in 1081.

The present cathedral is the result of renovation work commissioned by Henry IV around 1100, based on the ground plan for the Willigis cathedral. The nave and east chancel cannot have been completed before 1137, the year in which the St Gothard Chapel in front of the north side of the west transept was consecrated. The construction work began in the east with the apse, which, as is clear from the division by a dwarf gallery and semicircular niches on the gable, is based on Speyer II. Inside, the square chancel is vaulted with a cupola and treated as a crossing. However, the partition walls at the side make a proper transept impracticable. The two pseudo-transepts flanked by the original stair turrets are actually entrance halls for the two east portals.

The 11th-century nave had a flat roof. It was probably Archbishop Adalbert I of Saarbrücken (1110–37) who had it converted to a vaulted structure with an alternating system. Once again Speyer is the model, although the Mainz building is not as high as Speyer. The upper wall is supported on square pillars, every second pillar reinforced by an engaged shaft with archaic cushion capitals. The reinforcing arches and cross-ribs support one of the five vaulting compartments, while the blind arches on the imposts of the pillars form another monumental row of arches under the paired windows of the inner walls. The vaulting in the nave and aisles was renovated between 1200 and 1239 and the east part replaced by a new building in contemporary style. The final consecration, by Archbishop Siegfried III of Eppstein, was in 1239. In the Gothic period the aisles were extended by a row of chapels (1279–91 on the north side, 1300–19 on the south side). With their

Madern Gerthener, memorial portal at Mainz Cathedral, *c.* 1425.

Opposite: The nave of Mainz Cathedral, looking towards the west chancel.

varied tracery on the large windows and dividing walls, they are one of the cathedral's most distinctive features.

The Hohenstaufen transept is a legacy of the Willigis plan. Inside, the main chancel has three polygonal apses so that it forms a triconch. The elaborately divided west tower rises above the crossing with its octagonal cupola. Only the lower storeys of the tower are 13th century; the upper section is late 15th century. The upper sections of the west stair turret were rebuilt after the 1767 fire.

Between the Gothic chapels on the north side of the nave is the early 13th-century tiered market portal flanked by pillars with a *maiestas domini* on the tympanum. It now contains the bronze door moved here when the Lady Chapel was demolished in 1804 (Ill. p. 244). With its Latin inscription and profiled frame mouldings, this magnificent monument to the Willigis period is reminiscent of the Palatine Chapel in Aachen. The name of its maker, Berenger, is recorded for posterity. Another inscription appears on the upper panels of the two wings, the confirmation of a privilege for the citizens of Mainz by Archbishop Adalbert in 1135, here commemorated in bronze. The early 13th-century Late Romanesque Leichhof portal in the west wall of the south transept, with its artistic arabesque decoration in the jamb, archivolt and capital area, has a deesis on the tympanum flanked by two half-length figures of bishops (St Martin and St Boniface). A frieze of Corinthian-style foliated capitals with human and animal figures decorates the Romanesque Our Lady portal dated 1137 on the east side. The deesis group on the tympanum is attributed to the same workshop as the west rood screen (see below). The double-sided memorial portal on the south aisle, topped with an ogee arch, is an exquisite Gothic work of art. A row of ornamental statuettes under baldachins forms the archivolt in the hollow moulding of the pointed arched frame. Right at the bottom on the jambs are the patron saints Martin and Stephen. Opposite, in pairs, are St Catherine and St Barbara, St Alban and St George. The ensemble, which has the grace and elegance characteristic of the soft style, was clearly made by several craftsmen of varying degrees of skill. The overall design

Bishops' tombs in Mainz Cathedral:
Far left: Siegfried III of Eppstein (died 1249).
Left: Peter von Aspelt (died 1320).
Below far left: Uriel von Gemmingen (died 1514).
Below centre: Damian Hartard von der Leyen (died 1678).
Below right: Cathedral provost Heinrich Ferdinand von der Leyen (died 1714).

was by Madern Gerthener, a Frankfurt cathedral architect (c. 1425).

The St Gothard Chapel in front of the north transept was built by Adalbert I as a chapel for the archbishop's court. While the idea of the double chapel had already been used in Speyer (Ill. p. 35), Mainz became the model for the Hohenstaufen palatine chapels – such as Schwarzrheindorf (Ill. p. 273) and Goslar – in which rulers and people were separated. The square two-storey room divided by four pillars forms an apse to the east. A dwarf gallery runs round the outside.

The fragments of the west rood screen pulled down in 1681, which were found in the floor when work was being carried out between 1926 and 1928 (now in the

Hans Backoffen, crucifixion group beside the church of St Ignaz in Mainz Cathedral, after 1519.

Bischöfliches Dom- und Diözesanmuseum, Mainz; Ill. p. 47), are key examples of the Gothic style in the Rhineland. They are part of a body of work historically associated with the name of the Master of Naumburg, a French trained itinerant artist who moved on from Mainz to Naumburg, where he created his major works, the west rood screen and the statues of the founders in the cathedral. This group, however, combines an innovative approach and a direct human appeal rather than stylistic uniformity and for that reason it is no longer attributed to him, although there is an obvious connection with some of the works in Reims Cathedral (inside the northwest tower). Like the Mainz head with the headband and the Bassenheim Rider (Ill. p. 48), the rood screen fragments of the Last Judgment dating from around 1240, with their expressive body language and mime, mark a significant step in the development of Gothic sculpture in Germany.

Mainz Cathedral is also important as the burial place of the spiritual rulers. The collection of tombstones and imposing monuments vividly illustrates sculptural trends from the mid-13th to the late 18th centuries. The tombstone of Archbishop Siegfried III of Eppstein on the first pier in the nave to the south, which combines archaic and modern styles, depicts the coronation of two kings, an unusual subject for a tombstone.

The coronation iconography, this time with three kings, is repeated on the gravestone of Archbishop Peter von Aspelt, which introduces a new element into funerary sculpture, the architectonic frame. Towards the end of the century the frame was extended into a niche and the medieval type of tomb with recumbent figures on top was replaced by the upright wall monument. In later monuments the niche takes on the more elaborate shape of a portal, with small sculptures on the pillars.

One of the most original works of Late Gothic funerary sculpture is undoubtedly the monument to Archbishop Uriel von Gemmingen. It shows St Martin and St Boniface, intercessors and patron saints of the diocese, at the foot of the crucifix before which the archbishop is kneeling humbly. This memorial statue, a masterly combination of monument and epitaph, is believed to be one of the later works of the court sculptor Hans Backoffen. The style is a mixture of Gothic and Renaissance, while Baroque touches are already evident in Christ's fluttering loincloth and the heavy draperies of the saints. The centrepiece of the composition is the strongly modelled figure of Christ, which has similarities with the figure by Nicolaus Gerhaert von Leyden on the Baden-Baden crucifix (see Ill. p. 211).

Johann Mauritz Gröninger's monument for cathedral provost Heinrich Ferdinand von der Leyen, erected in the provost's lifetime, is the largest and most important of the Baroque monuments. The provost is portrayed as a man of

St Stephan

The collegiate chapter abolished in
1802 was founded in the late 10th century. The present Gothic parish church
was built in the early part of the 14th
century in three stages, firstly the east
chancel, followed by the transept with
its two adjoining nave bays and lastly the
rest of the nave, west chancel and tower.
However, the top part of the tower was
not erected until 1495. The church has
been rebuilt after suffering extensive
damage in the Second World War.

Although this parish church – an
early example of a Gothic hall church
– is modern in concept, the traditional
design of the previous building is still
visible in its ground plan, with a transept
and a second chancel to the west. In
fact, the combination of hall church and
transept is a somewhat unusual arrangement, reminiscent of buildings in Hesse
(St Elisabeth in Marburg). The circular
piers of the rectangular nave bays are
divided by slender columns. The east
chancel ends in a 5/8 polygon opening
into tall double lancet windows. Towards
the west the tracery becomes increasingly intricate, reflecting the order in
which the church was built. The west
chancel, with its square bay and tribunes
at the side, is in the tradition of
Carolingian and Ottonian westworks.

Amongst the furnishings, the
tabernacle made around 1500 and the
slightly later stone figures of St Mary
Magdalene and St Stephen are noteworthy. The atmospheric cloister, built
after 1450 and rebuilt since the Second
World War, contains a fine relief of the
Crucifixion dating from 1485.

The stained glass in the five windows
in the east chancel based on a design by
Marc Chagall was added between 1977
and 1980 and is now the church's main
attraction. The brilliant blue colouring,
imaginative design and poetic narrative
of the windows convey a message of

the world, with the allegorical figures
of death and time. The theatricality of
the composition is emphasized by the
different sizes of the figures and the
catafalque.

The tribunes in the transepts were
added in 1683 when the west chancel
was redesigned by the architect Clemens
Hinck. He was also responsible for the
massive oval of the choir stalls in the
triconch of the west chancel with its
magnificent Rococo decoration (1683).

In one of the north chapels is a life-
size burial group of a type common in

Champagne and Burgundy, similar to
the Holy Sepulchre groups in Germany.
It is probably the work of the Master of
Adalbert (named after the monument
to the administrator Adalbert of Saxony,
who died in 1484), identified as the
stone carver Master Valentius from
Friedberg. The tombstone of Bernhard
von Breidenbach, dean of the cathedral
(died 1497), unusual in its realistic
portrayal of the deceased, is by the
same artist.

Interior of the parish church of St Ignaz, Mainz, facing east.

peace and international understanding, faith and hope and, in the imagination of the Jewish artist, symbolize the common ground between Judaism and Christianity. The pictures in the three centre windows are scenes from the Old Testament, while the theme of the three side windows is 'praise of creation'.

St Ignaz

This parish church, built from plans by Johann Peter Jäger between 1763 and 1774 after a previous Gothic church was demolished, is a cruciform hall with a crossing dome and half domes in the cross-arms and in the altar area. The narrow three-storey façade with its Classical arrangement of pillars is modelled on St-Gervais in Paris. Combined with rocaille features, the clear-cut architectonic style of the light and well-proportioned interior, whose uniform furnishings have been preserved, reflects the transition from Late Baroque to Classicism. The stucco decoration was by Johann Peter Metz, the ceiling frescoes by Johann Baptist Enderle (1773–74). The high altar in the shape of a semicircular baldachin with columns was based on a design by Johann Jakob Schneider (1779–86).

The remarkable tufa Crucifixion group (Ill. p. 249) next to the church is in the Late Gothic style, with Mannerist touches. The legacy of the Mainz court sculptor Hans Backoffen, it was put in place after his death in 1519. Although the master himself designed it, most of the work was probably done by his workshop. Even so, his originality comes though in the composition and expressive power of the piece.

The Middle Rhine:
the 'romantic Rhine' between
Mainz and Cologne

Beyond Mainz the river bends west, bordered
by the gentle, hilly landscape of Rheinhessen
and the Rheingau. On the stretch between
Bingen and Koblenz the Middle Rhine has
hollowed diagonally through the Rhine slate
mountains, forming the narrow winding river
valley between Hunsrück and Taunus. This
is the 'romantic Rhine' discovered in the early
19th century, with its terraced vineyards
and the striking Rock of the Lorelei. After the
confluence with the Mosel near Koblenz the
landscape widens out to the Neuwied basin.
As it flows on to Bonn, the river runs past
the foothills of the volcanic Eifel on the left
and the slopes of the Westerwald and the
Siebengebirge on the right.

The Pfalz im Rhein, with Burg Gutenfels
towering above it, is a typically romantic
Middle Rhine castle (see pp. 260 and 261).

Eberbach monastery church

Eberbach monastery in the Rheingau.

Opposite above: The monks' dormitory at Eberbach.
Opposite below: The nave of the monastery church, looking towards the chancel.

The monastery, in a secluded valley in the Rheingau, was settled first by Augustine canons and later, in 1136, by Cistercians from Clairvaux in Burgundy. Next to Maulbronn, Eberbach is the best-preserved Cistercian monastery in Germany. The monastery buildings adjoin the rectangular transept on the east side and opposite them on the west side, separated from the cloister area by an alley, are the quarters for the lay brothers who provided the monastery with its daily supplies. The church dedicated to the Virgin Mary and John the Baptist is at the south end of the complex. It has a cruciform ground plan with a projecting transept, flat chevet and three rectangular chapels on the east side of each cross-arm. The monumental building was started in 1145. It was originally modelled on Clairvaux I and Fontenay and was intended to have barrel vaulting, but after a change of plan the present Romanesque structure was begun in 1170 and consecrated in 1186. A massive groined vault on strong reinforcing arches spans the central nave, which has an alternating system (five and a half bays, corresponding to eleven in the aisles). The imposing interior is in keeping with the Cistercian ideals of ascetic severity and clarity of form. A series of Gothic chapels was added to the south aisle between 1313 and 1335.

The monks' dormitory, completed in 1270, is a light hall 73 metres (240 feet) long with two aisles. Its cross-ribbed vaults are supported by round columns with foliated capitals emphasized by ogee moulding. The elegant star vault of the High Gothic chapter house (*c.* 1345) on the ground floor below rests on a single support in the centre of the room.

The church contains many important tombs, including those of Gerlach (died 1371) and Adolf II, Duke of Nassau (died 1475), both archbishops of Mainz. Their figures epitomize concepts of the human form in different periods (Ill. p. 56). The memorial stone of Wigand von Hynsperg (died 1511) in the first side chapel was made by the Mainz court sculptor Hans Backoffen during the transition from the Gothic to the Renaissance style.

Left: St Roch Chapel, Bingen.
Below: The *Mäuseturm* on the Rhine near Bingen, with the ruins of Ehrenfels on the right bank.

Opposite: Gothic carved altar in the chancel of St Martin, Lorch, 1483.

The picturesque and majestic landscape of Bingen, where the river enters the Rhine slate mountains, marks the beginning of the romantic Rhine valley. Originally a Frankish royal estate, the town had belonged to the Mainz archdiocese since Ottonian times. In the 14th century a watchtower for the Mainz electorate's Ehrenfels toll fortress on the right bank was built on a rocky ledge in the river in front of the mouth of the Nahe. Its name, *Mäuseturm* (mouse tower), comes from the word *Mautturm*, meaning toll tower. The crenellations were added in the 19th century when it became a signal station for shipping going through the infamous Binger Loch.

St Roch Chapel

'From Bingen a hill close to the river slopes up to the flat land above. It might have been a foothill in the old days when the waters were higher. At its eastern end is a chapel dedicated to St Roch.' That was how Goethe described the scene when in 1814 he attended the traditional church dedication festival held on the first Sunday after 15 August. In his account of his journey he painted a vivid picture of the Festival of St Roch in Bingen, a Christian public festival in the Rhineland style with 'marvellous religious and secular events'. The pilgrimage church founded in 1666 in honour of the plague saints had just been repaired at the time after the unrest of the Napoleonic era. The present picturesque Neo-Gothic complex was built after the previous church was destroyed by lightning in the late 19th century.

Lorch

St Martin

This fine Gothic parish church is on a
terrace in the middle of the little town
on the northern edge of the Rheingau.
The oldest part is the tower, built on the
site of a Roman watchtower and cutting
irregularly into the ground plan. The
Rhenish Early Gothic chancel was built
at the end of the 13th century, followed
by an aisleless nave. A north aisle was
added around 1400.

The most interesting feature is the
15.2 metre (50 foot) high carved altar
donated by noble families in the area
and erected in the chancel in 1483.
Sculptures are arranged on the shrine in
two tiers. Surrounding the Madonna and
Child are St Barbara and St Catherine on
the left and St Margaret and St Dorothy
on the right; above is the church's patron
saint, St Martin, giving his cloak to
the beggar, flanked by St Matthew and
St Wendelin, St John the Baptist and
St Anthony. All the figures are in niches
in the shape of a Gothic chancel with
lancet windows and tracery. The artistic
carvings of vine leaves and grapes on
the baldachins above them add a local
touch. The superstructure is dominated
by a Crucifixion group. The inner sides
of the wings, originally decorated with
reliefs, were painted in 1719. They
were repainted in the 19th century,
but the paint was removed when it
was realized that the altar was not polychrome. Predating Riemenschneider's
Münnerstadt altar by nine years, it is
probably the earliest known example
of this type of pre-Reformation altarpiece, which was left plain and unpainted
to heighten the spiritual effect. At the
feet of the Virgin Mary are two busts
holding inscriptions, the one on the
left 'All art and industry in honour and
praise of God' and the one on the right
the date of the altarpiece.

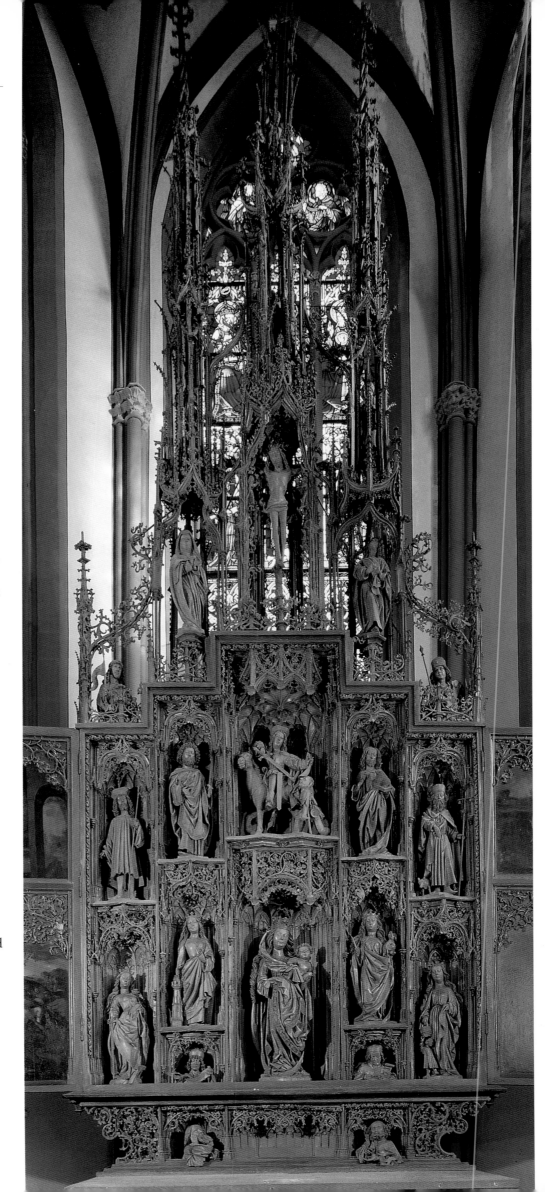

Bacharach

The old wine-growing centre of Bacharach is the quintessence of the romantic Rhine admired by travellers, poets and painters. It is surrounded by a largely preserved medieval ring of walls, stretching uphill in a semicircle from the riverfront and enclosing Burg Stahleck, a castle that has played a key role in the Palatinate's history. As the seat of the counts palatine of the Rhine from 1143, it was, with Pfalzgrafenstein (see p. 260), the northern outpost of the Palatine electorate's territory. The imposing Hohenstaufen site on the Rhine, with ring and inner walls, round keep and great hall, was destroyed in 1689. Rebuilt on the foundation walls in the 1920s and converted into a youth hostel, it now has a picturesque view of Bacharach.

While the present evangelical parish church of St Peter, dating from 1225 to 1250, is one of the last major examples of the Rhenish Late Romanesque style, the ruins of the Werner Chapel are in the new High Gothic style influenced by the Cologne Cathedral lodge. The chapel commemorates, and derives its name from, a boy who, it is said, was killed by Jews in Oberwesel in 1287, thrown into the Rhine and drifted ashore here. The pilgrimage chapel built over his grave was begun in 1297 and the chancel consecrated in 1337, although the chapel was not finished until 1437. The trefoil ground plan with a rectangular bay on the west side was possibly inspired by the church of Our Lady in Trier. The delicate tracery on the narrow lancet windows is typical of early 14th-century Middle Rhine Gothic. The nearby derelict building was demolished in the 18th century.

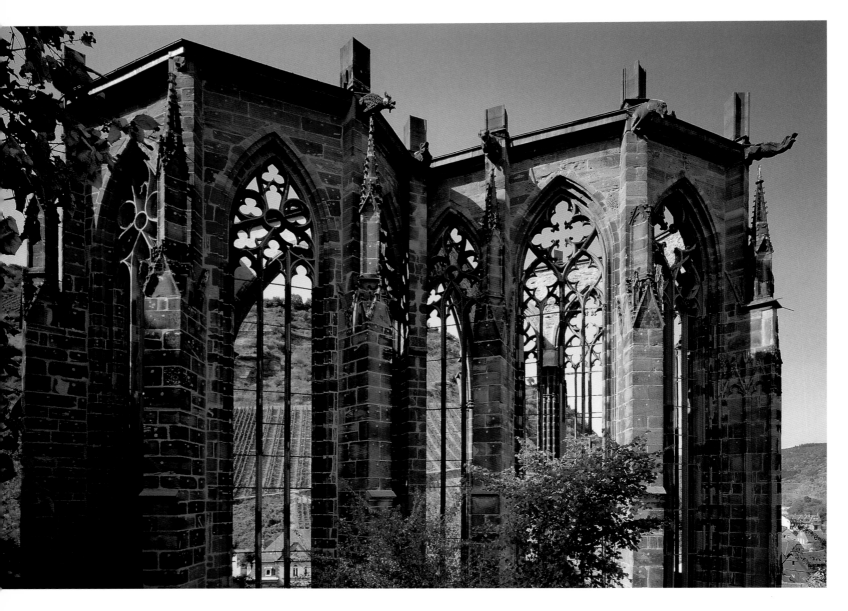

Kaub

Below: The inner courtyard of Pfalzgrafenstein with battlements.

Opposite: The Pfalz im Rhein near Kaub, on the right bank of the Rhine above Burg Gutenfels.

Pfalzgrafenstein

With the hillside castles in the romantic Rhine valley the Pfalzgrafenstein, a medieval castle on a rocky island in the Rhine near Kaub, occupies a special position. The island fortress was bound up with the political and economic interests of the counts palatine of the Rhine, who ranked amongst the most powerful princes of the Holy Roman Empire after Count Palatine Konrad (r. 1156–90), brother of the Emperor Frederick I (Barbarossa), unified the former Salian estates around Speyer and Worms and on the Neckar and the original estate around Burg Stahleck. In 1214 the Palatinate and the Heidelberg residence passed to the Bavarian ducal family, the Wittelsbachs. In 1329 Ludwig the Bavarian ordered the separation of the Bavarian territories and the Palatinate and soon afterwards the Palatinate became a Palatine electorate. It was only after the Elector Karl Theodor succeeded to the Palatine electorate that the Palatinate and Bavaria were again reunited dynastically and territorially in 1777.

In 1327 Ludwig the Bavarian, count palatine, duke, king and emperor, built a customs post in the shape of a five-sided tower on the rocky island on the Rhine, which was on a strategic axis with Burg Stahleck and Burg Gutenfels. Ten years later it was surrounded by a 12 metre (39 foot) high ring wall and turned into a stronghold. The two-tier arcade in the inner courtyard was added in 1607 when the building was enlarged by Elector Frederick IV and the south side, which was particularly at risk from floods and floating ice, was reinforced by a pointed ashlar wall shaped like a ship's bow, with a bastion in front.

Massive defence works are hidden behind the picturesque silhouette of the building with its irregular roofline, to which the Baroque top of the keep was added in 1755. The customs post remained in operation until the Palatinate was abolished in 1803. The palatine lion with the shield indicating the historic function of the island castle can still be seen on the bow of the south bastion.

Boppard

St Severus

The seal of Bruno, Archbishop of Trier from 1102 to 1124, found in the north side altar of this parish church gives an indication of the date of the towers incorporated in 1200 into the new galleried basilica with a nave and two aisles, originally flat-roofed, which was consecrated in 1225. The long chancel, closed on three sides, and the unusual 'webbed' vault were added in the mid-13th century. The wall elevation of the remarkably dark and lofty central nave with its low aisles is still in the Rhineland Romanesque style, set off by the heavy pillars of the arches and galleries, with the emphasis on horizontal lines. The contrasts in this last 'transitional' phase of the Romanesque are reflected in the picturesque exterior, particularly the imposing east end aligned with the market. While the massive towers, articulated by trefoil and round arched friezes, arches and accentuated edging, are still in the Rhineland Romanesque style, the chancel, with its blind arches and gallery, shows clear indications of the shift towards the Gothic, although it still retains some more traditional features.

Former Carmelite church

The convent was founded in 1265 and around 1300 work began on a Gothic church in front of the medieval town wall, starting with the chancel, which was closed on three sides (1330). The nave, originally flat roofed but later vaulted, was not completed until 1420 or 1430. Between 1439 and 1444 it was extended on the north side with an aisle of the same height.

The austerity of the architecture, in keeping with the rules of the order, is slightly softened by the fine tracery windows. The precious stained glass was sold off in 1818 and is now in museums in Darmstadt, Cologne, Glasgow and New York. However, the church still has

Right: Loy Hering, tomb of Margarete von Eltz in the former Carmelite church of Boppard, 1519.
Below: The nave, looking towards the chancel in the former Carmelite church at Boppard.

some fine pieces, notably the carved oak Gothic choir stalls with original figurative and ornamental motifs (second half of the 15th century). The interior is dominated by the projecting Baroque high altar, made in 1699, which stretches up to the vaulting of the chancel. Fragments of wall painting have been preserved on the south wall of the nave, including a cycle depicting the legend of St Alexis in fourteen framed panels, which, according to the inscription, dates from 1407. One of the most remarkable of the many epitaphs and wall monuments of local aristocrats is the Solnhofen limestone tomb of Margarete von Eltz on the north wall of the chancel, with a signed work by the Eichstätt sculptor Loy Hering dating from 1519 showing the Trinity (after Dürer's 1511 woodcut of the Trinity). There is also a fine early 15th-century wooden pietà.

Opposite: Schloss Stolzenfels, Koblenz.

View from the pergola area, looking towards
the arcade and courtyard at Schloss Stolzenfels,
Koblenz.

Koblenz

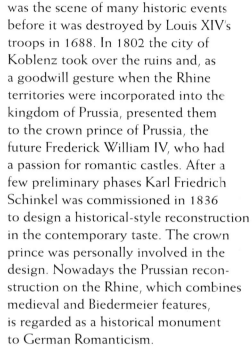

Schloss Stolzenfels

The fortification built by Arnold II of
Isenburg, archbishop of Trier from 1241
to 1259, opposite the mouth of the Lahn,
south of the confluence of the Mosel and
the Rhine, was originally a strategically
important customs and border post for
the Trier territory. Extended into a splendid residence for the electors of Trier at
the end of the 14th century, the Schloss
was the scene of many historic events
before it was destroyed by Louis XIV's
troops in 1688. In 1802 the city of
Koblenz took over the ruins and, as
a goodwill gesture when the Rhine
territories were incorporated into the
kingdom of Prussia, presented them
to the crown prince of Prussia, the
future Frederick William IV, who had
a passion for romantic castles. After a
few preliminary phases Karl Friedrich
Schinkel was commissioned in 1836
to design a historical-style reconstruction
in the contemporary taste. The crown
prince was personally involved in the
design. Nowadays the Prussian reconstruction on the Rhine, which combines
medieval and Biedermeier features,
is regarded as a historical monument
to German Romanticism.

With its picturesque view over the
Rhine, the exterior is modelled on
English stately homes. The first sight
on entering the gate is a surprising
pergola garden with vistas opening up
along the lines of vision. The garden
and the inner courtyard are connected
by a narrow Gothic arcade, a triple
portico with three bays reminiscent
of Queen Luise's tomb in the grounds
of Charlottenburg, designed by Schinkel
in 1810. In front of the *sala terrena*
summerhouse is a terrace with magnificent views of the countryside. In fact,
the whole setting was conceived by its
royal owner as a mixture of artificial and
natural effects. The contents also form a
remarkable collection, the historical-style
wall paintings on medieval themes and
the weapons and armour representing
the 19th-century idea of a picturesque
chivalrous Romanticism.

Opposite top: The large knights' hall with weapon collection at Schloss Stolzenfels, Koblenz.
Opposite bottom: The small knights' hall at Schloss Stolzenfels, Koblenz, with wall paintings by Hermann Stilke, 1841.

St Kastor, Koblenz, from the southeast.

St Kastor

The first collegiate church is recorded as being consecrated by Archbishop Hetti of Trier in the presence of Ludwig the Pious in 836 after the relics of its patron saint had been brought over. In 1100 the west end was turned into a twin-tower façade and the east end with the chancel and flanking towers was renovated between 1147 and 1159. The present building originates largely from the renovation of the Carolingian basilica by Archbishop Johann I of Trier (1190–1212). The nave and side aisles (with the central nave still unvaulted) and the transept were probably completed in 1208, the year the church was consecrated.

The west block with its twin towers (their lower storeys dating from the Carolingian period) is somewhat irregular in appearance, whereas the east end is a typical example of Rhenish architecture around 1200 (for example, St Gereon in Cologne, Bonn Minster, St Klemens in Schwarzrheindorf). A tiered chancel on three levels, it has a blind division in the socle area, with trefoil arches between half-pillars, above that a row of seven windows framed by columns and round arches and at the very top a dwarf gallery of triple arches. Although the wall is broken up, its proportions are still totally Romanesque in their solidity.

Inside, by contrast, radical changes have been made. The Romanesque design of the triple wall structure has been retained, with a false biforate gallery between arches and clearstorey windows and rectangular piers with three-quarter columns in front of them on all sides. Yet the blind division of the upper wall as far as the beginning of the pilaster-strips above the pier abutments was lost when a Gothic star vault was added in the nave and crossing in 1496.

The furnishings include the elaborate Gothic wall tomb of Archbishop Kuno von Falkenstein (died 1388) on the north wall of the chancel. Above the tomb with his recumbent figure is a profiled arch, enclosing the niche with a painted Crucifixion (next to St John on the right is St Castor with a model of the church).

Maria Laach

The monastery church of Maria Laach, from the northwest.

Opposite: The nave of Maria Laach, looking towards the chancel.

Former Benedictine monastery church

The church was started after Count Palatine Heinrich II of Laach and his wife Adelheid founded the monastery in 1093. What distinguishes it from other buildings on the Rhine is its uniformly Romanesque appearance, which remained more or less unchanged despite the fairly long construction period. It is a cruciform pier basilica with a groined vault and a five-bay nave in which the piers are reinforced by wall abutments with engaged columns supporting the reinforcing arches of the groined vaulting. In the cross-arms to the east the projecting transept forms semicircular side apses. The chancel raised above a crypt also ends in a semicircular apse. Square stair turrets articulating the east end with the octagonal crossing tower have been added between the cross-arms and the chancel. Opposite is the massive west section with its raised central part and flanking round towers, also terminating in an apse and separated from the nave by a gallery with double arches.

The largest parts of the surrounding walls were built in the first phase, which suggests that the work progressed in horizontal layers. The consecration in 1156 must have been for the second construction phase under Abbot Gilbert (1127–52) in which the east crossing tower, the nave (not yet vaulted) and lower parts of the westwork were built.

268

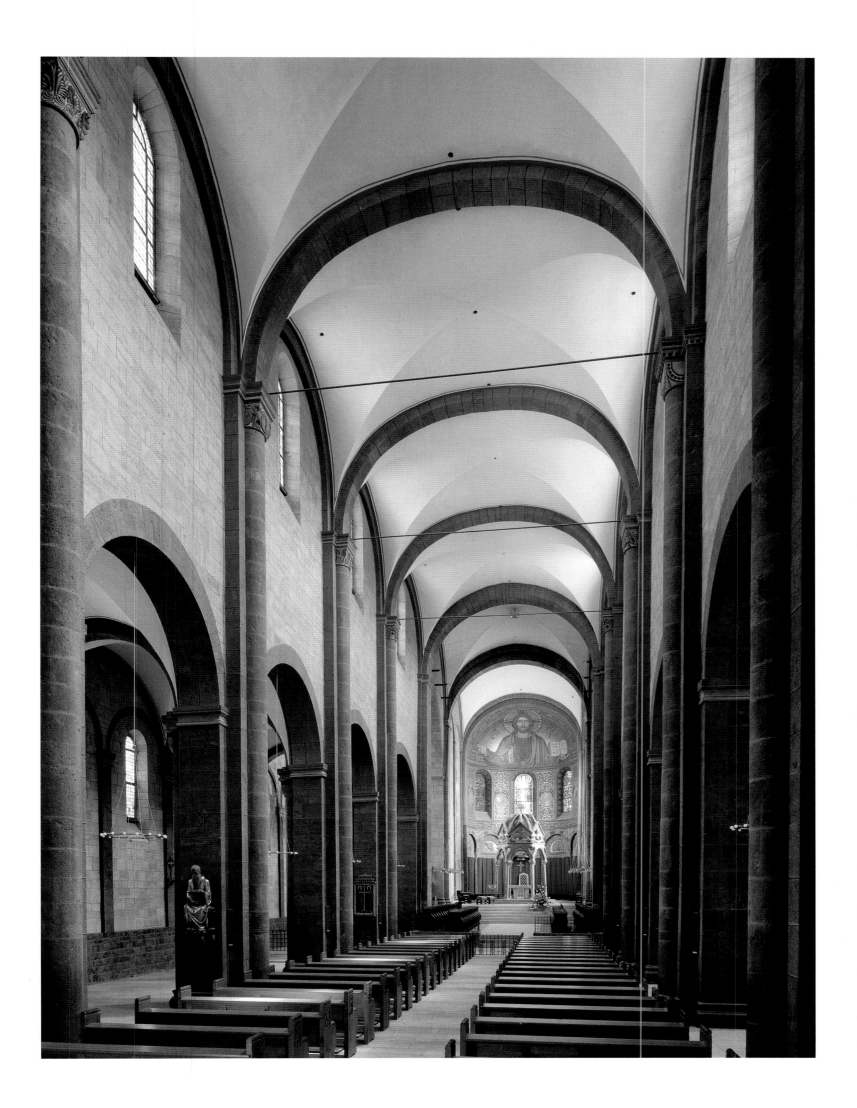

The upper parts of the westwork and the east chancel with the flanking towers were then built under Abbot Fulbert (1152–77). Thus the church had been

largely completed by 1200. However, the paradise in front of the west section, an atrium with a covered walk open on two sides, was not built until 1220.

The monastery church of Maria Laach is a textbook example of the contribution of Romanesque architecture to the Rhineland. Its diversity, expressed both in the division of the tracery by pilaster-strips and blind arcading and in the different shapes of the towers, reflects the regional taste for artistic effect, which is especially pronounced in this building and gives the whole exterior a harmonious and cheerful appearance. The interior, by contrast, is more austere and solemn, just like Speyer Cathedral and many of the buildings in Cologne. The exception is the vaulting system above individual rectangular bays. As the careful treatment of the tracery and the ingenious shape of the imposts show, it is clearly a very elaborate design.

Some of the medieval furnishings have been preserved, including the mid-13th-century hexagonal baldachin on the high altar, an unusual piece reminiscent of ciboria in Italy, and the founder's tomb in the west chancel built in 1270, with the recumbent wooden figure of the palatine count on top holding a model of the church in his right hand. The arrangement of the apses with mosaics in the style of contemporary Byzantine-Norman buildings in Sicily is an early 19th-century addition.

The paradise is notable for the exceptionally delicate and original carvings on the capital, generally attributed to the Master of Samson, the craftsman who made the torso of Samson owned

by the monastery dating from around 1225. However, none of the works mentioned in the same context can equal this masterpiece (see p. 40). What links these sculptures is a progressive style that breaks with local tradition and assimilates the Gothic influence of cathedrals in northern France.

The crypt, the oldest part of the church, is reminiscent of Speyer with its columns and cushion capitals. It contains the mosaic tombstone of Abbot Gilbert and the portrait showing three-quarters of him with his insignia and an inscription (Ill. p. 41).

270

Andernach

The fortified appearance of the imposing Round Tower is counterbalanced by its artistic shape. Built by Master Philipp in 1448, it has been preserved from the medieval walls enclosing the Roman fort.

Mariä Himmelfahrt

Another of the city's landmarks is the parish church of the Assumption of the Virgin, one of the most striking examples of Rhineland Romanesque architecture. Archbishop Johann of Trier (1189–1212) is considered to be the founder of the present building, although there was an earlier building (the northeast tower survived). In 1198 the town was devastated as Otto IV and Philip of Swabia fought for the throne. The new building, in the form of a galleried basilica with an alternating system, no transept and three double bays, was probably built from east to west between 1200 and 1220. Wall abutments reinforcing every second square pillar support the high vaulting in the central nave, which has pointed transverse arches and moulded ribs. The vaulting in the aisles is groined. The square chancel has a semicircular two-storey apse and is noticeably darker than the central nave, which is lit by the paired clearstorey windows. The exterior silhouette is emphasized by the two square flanking towers of the chancel and the dominating twin towers of the west façade, which are divided by numerous blind arches and Lombard friezes. A dwarf gallery runs round the apse, a common motif in Rhineland Romanesque architecture around 1200. Remnants of the old painting outside have been preserved; the coloured decoration inside was marred by 19th-century restoration work. Like the capital frieze on the west portal, the south portal, which has a medallion with the Lamb of God held by angels on the tympanum, is associated with the circle of the Master of Samson.

Schwarzrheindorf

St Klemens

On his family's country estate Arnold von Wied, chancellor to King Konrad III and later archbishop of Cologne, built a private chapel that was consecrated in 1151. The founder was buried in the chapel in 1156 and his sister Hedwig then founded an abbey for Benedictine nuns and extended the family chapel to the west with a nave-like annex for the nuns. The estate buildings used to adjoin the church on the northwest side.

The church is fairly small and stands in a picturesque position on the bank of the Rhine. Its nucleus is a central structure on a cruciform ground plan with an apse on the east side. The two storeys are linked by an opening in the centre. It is therefore similar to the double chapels common in the Romanesque period, in which the upper floor was reserved for the gentry and the lower part was used for the services attended by servants (see Speyer and Mainz cathedrals). A dwarf gallery resting on delicate small columns with different shaped capitals runs round the outside. Above the crossing is a striking square tower with a Gothic spire.

Inside, the complex structure is further enhanced by the fresco decoration, one of the most important sets of Romanesque wall paintings to have survived. By the middle of the 12th century the vaults and walls on the lower floor were probably already covered with a complete set of paintings. The four panels of the vault intersections show Old Testament scenes of the visions of the prophet Ezekiel, the destruction of the Old and the construction of the New Jerusalem. In the apses are scenes from the New Testament (Jesus driving the Moneychangers out of the Temple, the Transfiguration on the Mountain, the Crucifixion). In the wall niches are four symbolic figures of rulers.

Although the surface of the paintings has been damaged by 19th- and 20th-

Below: Transfiguration of Christ (detail), wall painting in the south niche of the undercroft at St Klemens, Schwarzrheindorf.
Bottom: Christ as Pantocrator (detail), wall painting in the apse of the undercroft at St Klemens, Schwarzrheindorf.
Below right: Ground floor of the double chapel at St Klemens, Schwarzrheindorf, facing east.

century restoration, they are still representative of the style of important painters from the Rhenish School.

On the upper floor the original painting is concentrated around the altar. It was carried out in a second phase of work and is related to the monastic life. In the apse is Christ in Judgment in the mandorla, surrounded by the symbols of the Evangelists and figures of the two founders, Arnold von Wied and his sister, Abbess Hedwig.

Siegburg

Painting of the St Anno shrine, 1764. St Pankratius, Belecke (Westphalia).

Opposite: The St Anno shrine at the monastery of St Michael, Siegburg, after 1180.

Benedictine monastery of St Michael

Only the outer walls of the crypt have survived from the church founded by Archbishop Anno II of Cologne in 1064. They were rebuilt after being destroyed in the Second World War. As the centre for the 'Siegburg observance', a Cluniac monastic reform that spread to other parts of Germany, the church enjoyed the special favour of its founder. After Emperor Henry III died, Anno, as tutor to the minor Henry IV (whom he had forcibly abducted from Kaiserswerth to Cologne by boat in 1062 with his imperial insignia), became a key figure in imperial politics. The veneration at his tomb and the miracles recorded in *Vita Annonis* by a Siegburg monk in 1100 eventually led to his canonization in 1183. Anno's bones were placed in a shrine that is one of the most artistically impressive of the Rhine reliquaries.

The St Anno shrine consists of a large oak casket 1.57 metres (over 5 feet) long in a magnificent casing in which various materials and goldsmith's techniques (copper embossing, stamping, engraving, enamelling and gilding, bronze cast gilding, filigree and jewelled trimming) are blended together in a highly imaginative synthesis of architectonic and ornamental forms to make a work of art of great iconographic and aesthetic importance. The long sides are divided by six niches supported on small double piers with trefoil arches. Corresponding to them on the sloping sides of the top are square panels framed with decorative strips containing medallion portraits. The top ridge and gable are embellished with an artistic gilded bronze crest with entwined tendrils and fabulous creatures, topped with large filigree and *champlevé* enamel balls.

Important parts of the furnishings – the silver embossed infilling of the niches and roof panels – were lost in the years after the abbey was dissolved in 1803, but it has been possible to reconstruct the iconography from drawings made before 1764, now in the Bibliothèque Nationale in Paris, and paintings in Belecke parish church in Westphalia. They show that the niches on the long sides originally contained twelve enthroned figures whose names appear in the inscriptions on the arches. They were St Maternus, St Severin, St Evergislus, St Kunibert, St Agilulph and St Heribert (six bishops of Cologne) and on the other side St Demetrius, St Vitalis, St Victor, St Benignus, St Innocent and St Maurice, who were especially venerated because Siegburg owned their relics. The roof panels depicted scenes from St Anno's life: the education of Henry IV, the foundation of St Maria ad Gradus in Cologne, the foundation of St Georg in Cologne, the foundation of St Michael in Siegburg, the fire miracle at the dedication of the rood altar, the rescue of two hanged men, the healing of the blind, the endowment of St Anno's shrine by Abbot Gerhard and Custos Heinrich, the saint's death and burial. At the sides of the gable St Michael, patron saint of the church and empire, stood with a fiery sword and the imperial orb opposite St Anno flanked by angels, presenting three models of the churches he had founded. A small figure of Custos Heinrich was kneeling in front of St Michael.

Although large parts are missing, there are strong indications that this splendid piece was the work of Master Nicholas of Verdun. The architectonic motifs in particular link the Siegburg shrine to his other two major pieces, the Klosterneuburg altar near Vienna (dedicated in 1181) and the shrine of the Three Magi in Cologne Cathedral (Ill. p. 295) made between the other two works. However, some of the small bronze busts in the spandrels of the arches are in the earlier style of the shrine of St Heribert (before 1170).

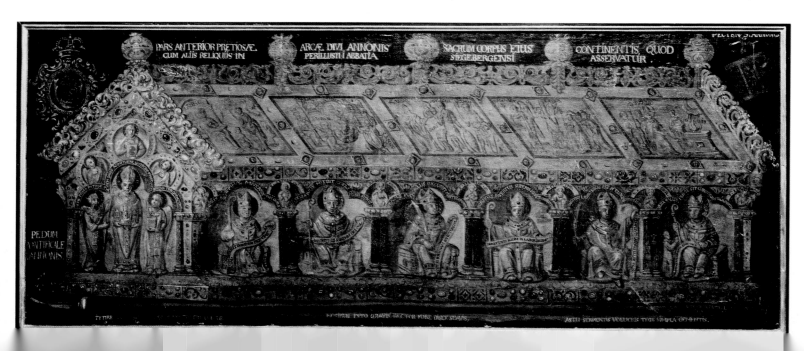

Bonn

View of Bonn Minster from the southeast.

Bonn Minster

The origins of Bonn Minster lie in an early Christian place of worship outside the Roman camp *Castrum Bonnensia* for the veneration of St Cassius and St Florentius, soldiers in the Theban Legion, who were martyred there before the end of the 3rd century. In the 4th century the first hall church was built over this *cella memoriae* under the crypt of the present cathedral, forming the nucleus of the medieval settlement. The Roman sarcophaguses found in the west part of the crypt are believed to be the tombs of the martyred saints.

Under Anno II, Archbishop of Cologne from 1056 to 1075 (see also Siegburg, p. 274), work began on a new structure replacing the Carolingian hall church, which was essentially similar in layout to the present building. The 11th-century building was a flat-roofed basilica with a nave and two aisles, a transept and raised long chancel. The apse was semicircular. On the west side a semicircular apse, straight on the outside with two flanking stair turrets, adjoined the nave. Arranged in three aisles divided by three paired piers and four paired columns with massive cushion capitals, the crypt on the east side has similarities with two other Anno buildings, St Michael in Siegburg and St Gereon in Cologne.

Around 1150 Prior Gerhard von Are (1126–69) had the chancel extended by a square vaulted bay with a square tower on either side. The elaborately divided chevet is pierced by seven round-arched windows. The original crypt was extended to the east in the Late Romanesque style. In 1166 the relics of the martyred saints were removed from the tomb and displayed in shrines on the high altar.

At the end of the 12th century a ribbed vault was erected above the front chancel. After that the transept was built, with a crossing tower and cross-arms ending in polygons. This trefoil chancel design gave the east end the appearance of a central room, following a trend in Cologne churches of the same period. Around 1120–30 the nave took on its present form, a mixture of Romanesque and Gothic influences. The four bays are spanned by ribbed vaults with an ogee moulding profile. The elevation has three storeys. A triforium runs above the

276

The nave of Bonn Minster, looking towards the east chancel.

stepped arches supported on clustered piers. The inner walls in the third section are broken up by five graduated windows with a passageway in front. The nave is supported from outside by arched buttresses, which, with those of St Gereon in Cologne, are the tallest in the Rhineland. Another storey was added to the original single storey of the crossing tower after the nave was completed. The 90 metre (295-foot) high pointed spire was added when the church was renovated in the late 17th century.

The eastern view of the cathedral is another example of a monumental façade on a Romanesque religious building on the Rhine modelled on Speyer Cathedral. The apse, gable, cross-arms, stair turrets and crossing towers form an imposing structure of varied shapes, rhythmically articulated by decorative motifs such as pilaster-strips, blind arches, niches and a dwarf gallery.

The arrangement of the west part, with the apse enclosed in the rectangular chevet, dates back to the 11th-century Anno building. Its present appearance – the structure of the portal, the shape of the gable and the upper storeys of the tower – is the result of renovation work by the architect Franz Schmitz between 1883 and 1889.

The sculptural decoration of the east part shows the influence of the northern French Gothic style, particularly in the plant motifs. Two early 13th-century fragments showing an angel and a devil writing on a banner (Ill. p. 40), probably from stone choir stalls, are particularly interesting in this respect. They are by the group associated with the Maria Laach Master of Samson (see p. 270), although their original appearance has been seriously impaired by more recent retouching of the surface.

Three wings of the cloister with the collegiate buildings built under Provost Gerhard von Are around 1145 have

been preserved. The two-storey St Cyriacus Chapel, erected on the east wing around 1160, was used as a burial place for the prior, whose tomb, previously on the lower floor and connected with the chapel by an opening, was destroyed in 1788.

The church used to contain important wall paintings, but they were damaged in the restoration work at the end of the 19th century. On the triumphal arch is a painting of the Assumption of the Virgin, dating from the first half of the 13th century. The 1619 tabernacle

still has Gothic touches. In the north transept is the tomb of Ruprecht von der Pfalz, Archbishop of Cologne (died 1480), with his recumbent figure. On the St Mary Magdalene altar in the south transept is an Entombment of Christ painted around 1600 and attributed to Hans von Aachen. The windows in the crypt were made by the Blaue Reiter painter Heinrich Campendonk in 1930. When the church was rebuilt in 1951, after it was ruined in the Second World War, they were restored from the cartoons that had been preserved.

Brühl

Schloss Augustusburg

This jewel of Late Baroque Schloss architecture was created in the 18th century by Elector Clemens August, last of the Bavarian Wittelsbachs, who ruled the archdiocese of Cologne as spiritual princes for five generations.

After the archbishops had been driven out of the town and their medieval castle pillaged by Louis XIV's troops in 1689, Elector Joseph Clemens had already planned a new Schloss in the style of Versailles and consulted the first royal architect, Robert de Cotte (see p. 64). However, Clemens August had other ideas. The initial plan was that the hunting lodge designed by the Westphalian architect Johann Konrad Schlaun, for which the elector laid the foundation stone in 1725, should be another moated castle of a type common in Westphalia and on the Lower Rhine, which would incorporate the medieval walls. However, this project was soon radically revised and it was decided to build an imposing residence in the French style, which was the model for both the strict court ceremonial and its translation into an appropriate architectonic setting. On the advice of his brother, the Bavarian Elector Charles Albrecht, Clemens commissioned the Munich court architect François Cuvilliés the Elder in 1728 to update the plans in the Regency and Early Rococo style. Cuvilliés moved the reception rooms to the south wing, which was connected to a French garden parterre by a large terrace in front designed by Dominique Girard, a student of Le Nôtre, who was also sent from Munich. The building works were supervised on site by Michael Leveilly, who built the yellow apartment in the north wing and the summer apartment on the ground floor of the south wing

View of the garden across the parterre
at Schloss Augustusburg, Brühl.

and brought in the Italians Pietro
Morsegno and Pietro Castelli for the
stuccowork.

The magnificent design of the staircase built in the west wing between
1743 and 1748 resulted from a further
change of plan and was the work of the
brilliant French court architect Balthasar
Neumann. From a light-filled entrance
hall a central staircase, dividing into
two and reversing direction at the top of
the first flight, leads to the staterooms
and reception rooms on the upper floor:
the garden room and music room followed by the 'large new apartment' in

the south wing. The double Ionic
columns on the triumphal structure
above the landing, balancing the central
portal of the garden room opposite,
correspond to the two-storey division
of the magnificent area and at the same
time provide the setting for the dominant allegorical theme: the glorification,
or rather mysticization, of the ruler,
whose gold bust is the eye-catching
central feature. As the visitor mounts the
stairs, the physical confines of the architecture seem to disappear and the ceiling
fresco by Carlo Carlone looks as though
it is hovering airily above the ornamental

staircase. The painting personifies the
ruler's virtues, continuing the sculptural
theme of the pictures on the staircase.
Magnanimity and magnificence spread
their generosity over the arts, whose
adversaries, in the forms of envy and
debauchery, are hurled into the depths
in a cascade of figures – a parable of
flight and fall, a typical view of the
world in the Age of Enlightenment.
The significance of this unique setting
derives from the functional integration
of the architecture and decoration into
a strictly hierarchical court ceremonial,
in which every element had its special

279

Opposite: View of the staircase by Balthasar Neumann from the vestibule at Schloss Augustusburg, Brühl.

Right: Detail of decoration on one of the cabinets at Schloss Augustusburg, Brühl.
Below: Garden room with painted ceiling by Carlo Carlone.

meaning and was part of a perfectly regulated ritual in keeping with the occasion and the rank of the guests.

The ceiling fresco in the garden room, also by Carlone, celebrates Clemens August's brother, the Emperor Charles VII (r. 1742–45). In the music room next door, which was used as a vestibule for large receptions, Carlone glorified the owners of the Schloss in a cosmological setting. In the ceiling mirror, framed with a stucco decoration, Apollo appears with the nine Muses, personified as times of day and seasons, the elements, the arts and the virtues of the rulers.

The ornamental garden, turned into a landscaped park in the 19th century, has now been restored from the original design with straight visual axes, geometrical avenues of lime trees and a *parterre de broderie*.

Schloss Falkenlust

The summer palace linked to Schloss Augustusburg by an avenue was designed by François Cuvilliés the Elder and built under the supervision of Michael Leveilly. Clemens August laid the foundation stone in 1729. Cuvilliés had already carried out a similar, very successful commission for the Amalienburg in the grounds of Schloss Nymphenburg.

The court used the rectangular two-storey building with a *cour d'honneur* in front for falconry, a very popular sport with the electors. The plans therefore included outbuildings with stables for

Hall of Mirrors, Schloss Falkenlust, Brühl.

the horses, an aviary and a training ground for the falconers. A belvedere was built on the roof of the Schloss, from which visitors could watch the hunt for herons, which were the falcons' prey.

The staircase, by the genius François Cuvillés, is lined with blue-and-white Rotterdam tiles with falconry and Bavarian lozenge motifs. The highlight of the interior decor is the room lined

with mirrors. With its gilded carvings on blue panels and its ingenious reflections it is one of the finest works of its kind, a gem of the Rococo style in the Rhineland.

Cologne

North of Bonn, the Rhine landscape broadens
out into the Cologne bay bordered by the
Bergisches Land to the east and the Eifel
foothills to the west, which forms the southern
part of the Lower Rhine lowland plain.
Because of the topography of the high river
bank to the left of a wide bend to the west the
Romans founded a town on the site and this
developed into a Rhine capital and centre for
the arts. Many monuments and art treasures
have been preserved from the city's heyday in
the Middle Ages.

The panorama of Cologne across the Rhine
is dominated by the silhouettes of the Gothic
cathedral and the Romanesque Great
St Martin church.

Cologne

The importance of Roman Cologne can be seen from the right-angled street plan, remains of Roman fortifications and archaeological structures of public buildings still visible in the townscape and the many examples of Roman and Germanic art and culture on show in the Römisch-Germanisches Museum.

Cologne has been in existence for two thousand years. It developed from an *oppidum* on the left bank of the Rhine in the shelter of an island where, after the conquest of Gaul, Roman forces settled Celtic Ubii from the right bank of the

Rhine and set up a legionaries' camp with a naval base from which they could protect the Rhine border and launch future campaigns in Germania. In 50 BC Agrippina, daughter of Germanicus and wife and co-regent of the Emperor Claudius, promoted the *Oppidum Ubiorum* to a veterans' colony with the official title *Colonia Claudia Ara Agrippensis*. As the seat of the provincial governor of *Germania Inferior*, Roman Cologne went through a period of political stability and economic expansion. The glass produced at the time was particularly impressive.

In the Constantinian period the town was linked by a bridge to the *Divitiacum* (Deutz) military fort on the right bank. Records refer to a bishop's seat as early as 313. At the same time early Christian places of worship for the veneration of martyrs, the nuclei of later monumental churches such as St Gereon, St Ursula and St Severin, grew up in the burial grounds developed outside the ring of walls.

After several attacks by Germanic tribes, the Franks took the Roman town in 456. In the 6th and 7th centuries

Below left: Gold medallion with seated figure of St Severin, 2nd half of 11th century. St Severin, Cologne.
Below right: Cologne city seal, early 12th century. Historisches Archiv, Cologne.
Bottom: Martyrdom of St Ursula and her companions in Cologne. From the Little Ursula cycle, *c.* 1450. Wallraf-Richartz-Museum, Cologne (see Ill. p. 19).

Frankish mayors of the palace lived on the former Capitol and Plectrude, wife of Pepin of Heristal, founded a convent there. Charlemagne upgraded Cologne to an archbishopric and placed the suffragan bishoprics of Liège, Utrecht, Münster, Osnabrück and Minden under its jurisdiction. In 881 the Normans destroyed the town. The town wall was rebuilt in 948.

In the Middle Ages the establishment of the Ottonian Empire marked the beginning of a new era and a new political status for Cologne, accompanied by a resurgence of creative activity. Otto I's

brother Bruno, archbishop from 953 to 965, founded the series of great medieval buildings and left money in his will for the enlargement of churches such as St Pantaleon, St Maria im Kapitol and St Cäcilien. As chancellor and adviser to Otto III, Archbishop Heribert (999–1021) was the most powerful man in the empire after the emperor. From Archbishop Pilgrim's time (1021–36) the chancellery for Italy and the privilege of crowning kings in Aachen were associated with the archbishopric of Cologne. Archbishop Anno II (r. 1056–75), who set up the Cologne foundations of St Georg and St Mariengraden (in front of the east chancel of the old cathedral, demolished in 1817) and the Benedictine monastery of St Michael in Siegburg, was tutor to the minor Henry IV and played an active role in imperial politics. As ruler of the city, he won the struggle against the rebellious burghers.

On the city seal the 'Holy Cologne' of the High Middle Ages is referred to as *Sancta Colonia Dei Gratia Romanae Ecclesiae Fidelis Filia*. It was a historic moment for the city when in 1164 it came into possession of the bones of the Three Magi, transferred from Milan to Cologne by Archbishop Rainald von Dassel. Even

the relics of great religious figures in Cologne's history such as Archbishop Heribert and Archbishop Anno were now housed in splendid shrines, masterpieces made by Cologne goldsmiths. Those by Nicholas of Verdun, who made the shrines for the Three Magi (Ill. p. 295) and Anno (Ill. p. 275), are outstanding.

This Hohenstaufen period was the pinnacle of church architecture in Cologne. The large collegiate churches, monumental buildings redesigned and altered in a distinctive Rhineland Romanesque style, were erected to

View of Cologne Cathedral from the east, with the Museum Ludwig in front (architects Busmann and Haberer, opened 1986).

commemorate saints and local martyrs (St Gereon, St Ursula). Having been rebuilt since the Second World War, these Romanesque churches are once again a reminder of the creativity of medieval Cologne. The work begun on the new cathedral modelled on French cathedrals marked an abrupt change of style to High Gothic in 1248.

As the territory expanded and the population grew, Archbishop Philipp von Heinsberg (1167–91) built semicircular walls shutting the city off from the Rhine. When the Emperor Frederick (Barbarossa) divided up Henry the Lion's estates in 1180, the Archbishop of Cologne was invested with Westphalia and became prince of the territory. Yet

even in Cologne, the largest and most important city in the empire, the rule of the archbishops conflicted with the citizens' desire for freedom. The burghers won this power struggle in a battle in Worringen in 1288 and from then on the archbishops resided in Bonn and Brühl.

In addition to the traditional monasteries, religious centres and seats of learning for the arts in the early Middle Ages, the new mendicant orders gave fresh impetus to spiritual life in the 13th century. Great theologians like Thomas Aquinas and John Duns Scotus taught at the Dominican *studium generale* founded by Albertus Magnus in 1248. In 1388 local burghers set up Germany's first university.

In the 14th century the civil liberties wrested from the archbishop and the city's economic prosperity found expression in secular buildings like the town hall and the Gürzenich 'dance hall'. Cologne was a leading member of the Hanseatic League. The 1396 *Verbundbrief* set the seal on the rivalry between patricians and guilds with the first democratic constitution.

In the 'autumn of the Middle Ages' arts and crafts and Late Gothic panel painting flourished again in Cologne. The local painting of the 15th and early 16th centuries, known as the School of Cologne, reached its peak with Stefan Lochner (died 1451), whose international status was comparable to that of his great Dutch contemporaries (see Ills. pp. 292 and 293).

The economic decline that began in 1500 was accompanied by a decline in artistic activity. Work on the cathedral came to a standstill around 1560. The city resisted the Reformation and became a stronghold of the Counter-Reformation after the War of Cologne, in which Archbishop Gebhard Truchsess von Waldburg's attempt to go over to the Protestant side was successfully thwarted. When Ernst of Bavaria was elected in 1586, the Cologne archdiocese was made a demesne of the Bavarian Wittelsbachs.

The weakness of the economy precluded any major building work in the city and the medieval churches were largely preserved. Meanwhile, the archbishops gave free rein to their enthusiasm for the Baroque at Schloss Bonn and Schloss Brühl. In the autumn of 1794 the city surrendered to French revolutionary troops without a struggle. The French occupation also spelt the end of the archdiocese. The cathedral was first secularized and then, in 1804, downgraded to a city church. Churches and monasteries were pulled down one

The St Peter Portal at Cologne Cathedral.

after the other and Christian works of art sold off cheap. After becoming part of the Prussian territories on the Rhine in 1816, Cologne entered a new era. In 1821 the cathedral was reinstated as an episcopal church and, with the medieval building work completed, it became a symbol of national recovery (see Ill. p. 70). When the city centre was destroyed in the Second World War, the cathedral was the only building to escape.

Cologne Cathedral

The cathedral hill on the bank of the Rhine is the northeast corner of the old Roman town. In ancient times the temple of Mercurius Augustus used to stand on the site of the present Gothic cathedral. The first early Christian religious building on that site was a basilica with a long atrium and a baptistery adjoining it on the west side. The font has been preserved. The building was extended in the Frankish period but it was only under Archbishop Hildebold, a confidant of Charlemagne, that the Cologne metropolitan church began to take on an ambitious architectonic form based on the large Early Christian basilicas in Rome. The Carolingian cathedral, a three-aisle basilica with two transepts, had a double chancel structure, similar to the famous St Gall monastery plan (Ill. p. 30), which was thus traced back to this particular Cologne model. The west chancel was dedicated to the Virgin Mary, the east chancel to St Peter. Both were built above a crypt with an ambulatory. The church was not consecrated until September 870, although the work must already have been finished before 858.

In the 10th century Archbishop Bruno had the cathedral extended to a five-aisle basilica. His successor Gero (969–76) donated the wooden crucifix named after him (Ill. p. 296).

The acquisition of the bones of the Three Magi in 1164 gave the episcopal

The nave of Cologne Cathedral, facing east.

Opposite: The inner chancel of Cologne Cathedral, with the canons' chancel and painted choir-screens in foreground (see Ill. p. 293).

Stefan Lochner, *The Virgin of the Rose Garden*,
c. 1450. Wallraf-Richartz-Museum, Cologne.

Opposite top: Stefan Lochner, altarpiece of the
patron saints of Cologne Cathedral in the Lady
Chapel, c. 1440–45.
Opposite bottom: Rood-screen painting in canons'
chancel, 1332–40.

end of the Middle Ages, before coming
to a complete standstill in 1560.

It was not until the restoration after
the Napoleonic period that the situation
changed. In the Romantic age enthusiasm for the project revived, encouraged
by the work of Sulpiz Boisserée who
campaigned tirelessly for the building to
be completed. The reconstruction based
on the medieval plans (for the façade),
in the Neo-Gothic style (for the transept),
was promoted by King Frederick William
IV, Prussian ruler of the Rhineland, and
by his architect Karl Friedrich Schinkel,
who appointed Ernst Friedrich Zwirner
to oversee the project. By 1863 the nave
had progressed so far that the temporary
walls built at the end of the chancel
around 1300 could be demolished and
in 1869 the wooden crane that had
been left on the stump of the south
tower since 1560 was finally dismantled
(Ill. p. 70). The work was completed on
15 October 1880.

The new building, inspired by the
Francophile archbishop Konrad von
Hochstaden, rivalled the classic Gothic
cathedrals in France. At 43.35 metres
(142 feet) high the upper chancel is even
higher than its model, Amiens. The cycle
of wall figures on the chancel pillars with
Christ and Mary in the circle of Apostles,
a sculptural masterpiece dating from
around 1300, is modelled on Louis IX's
Ste-Chapelle in Paris and Paris sculpture
of around 1280–1290. The Cologne
design is also more evolved than Amiens,
for instance in the way the elevation of
the long chancel and chevet is elegantly
balanced by the uniform height of the
windows in the arcade and upper floors,
with the pierced triforium between them,
and by the central engaged shafts of the
pillars soaring up to the vaults. So the High
Gothic style of the French cathedrals
was brought to perfection in Cologne.
In its architectonic uniformity the chancel, with its original furnishings largely

church an enormous boost. Pilgrims soon
began flocking to see these highly venerated relics in their magnificent shrine
and a new building was clearly needed,
although initially there was some delay.
The demolition of the old basilica began
after the cathedral chapter had organized
funds in April 1248 and on 15 August
that year Archbishop Konrad von
Hochstaden laid the foundation stone
for the new High Gothic cathedral.

The names of most of the architects
are recorded (the first was Gerhard, who
was responsible for the creative design)
and the medieval plans have largely been
preserved in the form of ground plans
and elevations on parchment. Work
began in the east with the chancel, based
on Amiens Cathedral, and came to a
temporary halt with the consecration in

1322. The next stage was the west front
with its symmetrical towers, starting with
the south tower. The St Peter Portal was
built under the supervision of the cathedral architect Michael (1353–after 1387).
Its sculptures, especially the remarkably
lifelike statuettes in the intrados, show
the influence of the Parlers, the Swabian
family of architects and sculptors to
which the senior architect of Prague
Cathedral was also related (see p. 51).
While the south side of the nave was
under construction from 1325, work
on the north side did not start until
the 15th century (under the architects Nikolaus von Bueren and Konrad
Kuyn), following the original plan
closely, apart from a few decorative
features in Late Gothic style. However,
the project started to flag towards the

Nicholas of Verdun, shrine of the Three Magi at
Cologne Cathedral, 1181–91.

Opposite: Nicholas of Verdun, two of the Three
Magi on the front of the shrine at Cologne
Cathedral, 1181–91.

preserved, is a complete medieval work
of art of supreme quality (Ill. p. 291).

The liturgical focus of the cathedral is
the inner chancel consisting of four rectangular bays and the polygonal chevet,
which, as befits its importance, contains
the most valuable furnishings. The
canons' chancel is in the front three bays,
separated by another bay from the actual
sanctuary in the chevet.

The Three Magi shrine is behind
the high altar, which has white marble
sculptures dating from the time the chancel was consecrated. It is a magnificent
creation by the goldsmith Nicholas

of Verdun from Meuse, who made the
seated figures of the Old Testament
prophets and kings on the lower part
of the long sides and the row of Apostles
above them between 1181 and 1191.
The pictures on the front end wall –
dated between 1198 and 1216 (the
Three Magi and the Emperor Otto IV
in front of the Madonna enthroned and
Child, the Baptism of Christ and the
Second Coming on the gable) – and
those on the back – dated between
1220 and 1230 (the Scourging and
Crucifixion, Christ with St Felix and
St Nabor and the bust of Archbishop

Rainald von Dassel) – were by Cologne
goldsmiths after the master. In addition
to the figures the shrine is decorated
with *champlevé* and *cloisonné* enamel, filigree, precious and semi-precious stones,
antique cameos and intaglios and chased
silver and gilded copper foils.

The canons' chancel is closed off from
the ambulatory by high stone screens.
On the insides of these, above the choir
stalls, is a cycle of tempera paintings
completed between 1332 and 1340,
which can be regarded as a key work
in High Gothic painting in Germany
(Ill. p. 293). However, it is difficult to

define the style of the series of pictures above a bishops' gallery, remarkable for its distinctive architectural forms and elegant figures. It shows scenes from

the legends of the saints, including the translation of the Three Magi relics (Ill. p. 43). Painting was still a relatively new genre and this work was right up to the minute. The inspiration for the cycle might have been masters from Siena in the early part of the century, or possibly the French illuminated manuscripts of Jean Pucelle or northern French or English models.

The stained-glass windows in the clearstorey, made before 1311, contain a kings' gallery similar to the sculpture cycles on the façades of French cathedrals. The twenty-four Elders of the Apocalypse, in high tabernacles against alternating blue and red backgrounds, and twenty-four Judaean kings appear in an apotheosis of light, turning the chancel into a monumental shrine.

The cross chapel on the north side of the chancel ambulatory houses the Gero Cross from the old cathedral, named after its founder. The gold halo setting somewhat detracts from the effectiveness of this exceptional Ottonian work of art. The cross not only is a unique example of an early medieval figurative image, but it also represents a peak in medieval sculpture. This oldest and most venerable of the monumental Rhine crucifixes is the first of a genre that produced magnificent work, particularly in Cologne (see Ill. p. 305).

In its position in the Lady Chapel on the south side of the chancel ambulatory, opposite the cross chapel, the Madonna of Milan, as a counterpart to the Gero Cross, also played an important role in religious ritual for several centuries, befitting its artistic quality. Stylistically the affected stance of this life-sized freely sculpted figure and its elegant arrangement of the drapery show that it is contemporary with the courtly stone pillar figures in the chancel, even though the completely restored paint gives it an artificial Neo-Gothic look.

The altarpiece, with the city's patron saints attributed to Stefan Lochner (Ill. p. 293), now has pride of place in the Lady Chapel. Commissioned by the city council for the town hall around 1440, this monumental work was not installed in the cathedral until 1809. The centre panel and the insides of the wings form a uniform composition, set against the background of a meadow. The Three Magi presenting their gifts are gathered around the enthroned Virgin and Child. Their retinue includes St Ursula with her Virgins on the left and St Gereon with martyrs of the Theban Legion on the right. The closed wings depict the Annunciation. The figures are painted in glowing colours and stand out three-dimensionally against the uniform gold background.

St Pantaleon

In 957 Archbishop Bruno of Cologne, brother of the Emperor Otto the Great, founded a monastery on the site of a Roman villa outside the city walls to which he called Benedictines from the St Maximin reform monastery in Trier. After the original church dedicated to

St Pantaleon had collapsed during rebuilding work, a new building was erected with money left by the founder, who was buried there in 965. It was completed and consecrated in 980. The emperor's widow Theophanu also supported the church. Her donations included the relics of St Albinus and she was buried in front of his altar in 991 (modern tomb in right cross-arm). Otto III, who also endowed the church generously in memory of his mother, lay in state here during his funeral procession from Italy to Aachen in 1002.

The Ottonian building is a magnificent example of its period and a memorial to the imperial claims of the Saxon ruling house. An aisleless nave, originally flat roofed (see St Patrokli in Soest, also founded by Bruno), ends in the east in a semicircular apse. Instead of a transept, cross-arms adjoin the nave in the north and south, opening into an apse on the east side (the vaulting in the south arm was added during renovation work around 1216). On each side of the chancel, steps lead down to the

297

crypt, which at this time took on a new function as a funerary chapel for the founder (see Otto the Great's tomb in Magdeburg Cathedral). On the oppo-

site side the church terminates in a monumental westwork consisting of a transept divided into three and an entrance hall with two square stair

turrets (largely rebuilt during extensive restoration work in 1890). The central area is steep and square with a flat roof and is separated from the nave by a large pillar arcade. In the north and south are adjoining two-storey chapel areas, opening on to the centre with double round arches and flanking the triple arcading leading to the entrance hall on the upper floor. The alternating layers of the archstones and the contrasting red and white colouring create an unusual effect. This architectonic pattern is similar to the design of the Carolingian westwork, which has a square ground plan (such as Corvey monastery church) but no crypt floor (such as the collegiate church in Münstereifel, virtually a replica of St Pantaleon). This westwork, in the form of an antechurch, also contained altars that were probably dedicated to the archangels. The side galleries were used as tribunes for the singers, while the west gallery was probably reserved for the ruler and the imperial family.

In the nave, traces of the old blind arches that divided the wall of the Ottonian building have been preserved. The semicircular arches on square piers with fitted imposts were broken through between 1170 and 1180 to extend the hall church to three aisles. The windows are a relic of the renovation work from 1619 to 1622, when Christoph Wamser, architect of the Jesuit church in Cologne, roofed the nave with a Gothic-style net vault. It was removed when the church was restored after the Second World War. The present coffered ceiling in the nave is a modern – and not a particularly successful – addition. The original Ottonian appearance has been drastically altered by features such as the rood screens, organ and windows. The aisleless nave makes the westwork appear much more monumental. The post-Gothic east chancel was also designed by Wamser.

Below: Shrine of St Albinus on the main gable side of St Pantaleon, Cologne.
Right: A cherub on the shrine of St Maurinus at St Pantaleon, Cologne (detail).

Externally the church is dominated by the Ottonian westwork which gives the church its unmistakable silhouette, although the porch has now been shortened by more than half. The size of the building reflects the ambitious ideas of its imperial patron, Archbishop Bruno, whose concept of a new monumental style had Classical inspiration. This influence is clear if the blind arcades dividing the aisleless Ottonian church are compared with the Constantinian 'basilica' in Trier. It is also evident from the (rebuilt) façade of the westwork with its two-storey structure and gable, articulated by pilaster-strips and Lombard arched mouldings, and the clear structure of the walls, divided into large areas pierced by windows. All these motifs show the influence of the ancient world from which the architects drew their inspiration.

The fine Late Gothic rood screen commissioned by Abbot Johann Lünninck in 1503 was moved to the west side of the nave in 1696 to be used as an organ gallery. It was returned to its original position on the east side in 1959. Above the central basket arches are St Pantaleon and St Maurinus next to the Virgin Mary. A late 14th-century crucifix hangs above the rood screen altar. In the stucco marble high altar in the form of an aedicule there is a statue of the church's patron (1749).

The treasury contains some valuable works, such as the reliquaries of St Maurinus (set up near St Heribert's shrine in 1170) and St Albinus (*c.* 1186, influenced by St Anno's shrine in Siegburg), as well as the Albertus cross dating from around 1170 with the founder's name on it. The fragments of ornamental sculpture from the westwork, made around 1000 and amongst the earliest examples of medieval sculpture (in the lapidarium and the Erzbischöfliches Diözesan-Museum, Cologne), are of unique historical importance.

The Romanesque tympanum on the north transept portal dating from *c.* 1170 to 1175 is now in the Schnütgen-Museum (Ill. p. 39). It shows five standing figures (with faces obliterated), decreasing in size from inside to outside. In the centre is a full-sized figure of Christ with the Book of Life and beside him Mary and John the Baptist as intercessor (deesis). Outside on the left is a saint, probably St Pantaleon, and on the right a bishop, probably the founder.

View of the rood-screen along the nave of St Maria im Kapitol, Cologne.

Opposite: This aerial view shows the magnificent design of the three-conch chancel of St Maria im Kapitol, Cologne.

remains of an Ottonian structure have been found under the west tower. The church in its present form dates from the time of Abbess Ida, granddaughter of Otto II, and the Empress Theophanu (1015–60). The whole church was consecrated by Archbishop Anno II in 1065 but the east part with the triconch must already have been completed by 1049 when Pope Leo IX dedicated the rood altar. The walls surrounding the three apses were extended in 1150 and between 1200 and 1210 and the ribbed vault of the central nave around 1240.

The church was destroyed down to the crypt by bombing during the Second World War and the collapse of the east conch in 1948. Unfortunately, some of the conservation work carried out during the lengthy rebuilding process was fairly haphazard, with a mixture of different periods and styles in the nave and the addition of an overpowering ornamental wooden ceiling.

The Ottonian west end consists of a projecting square central section flanked by two square stair turrets aligned with the side aisles. The upper storeys of the tower were originally round, as in St Pantaleon. In the 12th century the middle section was extended into a massive tower which was only partly rebuilt after it collapsed in the 17th century. The flanking towers were also reduced in size. The upper floor of the porch used as a nuns' gallery and opening on to the nave in a (rebuilt) arcaded wall was based on the Palatine Chapel in Aachen and has parallels in the west chancel of Essen Cathedral and Ottmarsheim (see Ill. p. 155).

The west bays of the aisles still have the blind arcading from the Ottonian period. The round arches in the nave are supported on wall-like piers with profiled imposts. The engaged shafts of the six-part vaulting added in the 13th century have been left directly on the originally

St Maria im Kapitol

According to a 13th-century source the Benedictine abbey was founded around 690 by Plectrude, wife of Pepin of Heristal, the Frankish mayor of the palace. However, no architectonic traces of a Merovingian building have been found and it must be assumed that a mid-1st-century Roman temple, whose foundation walls were uncovered beneath the present church, was originally used as a place of worship. The temple was dedicated to the Capitoline triad Jupiter, Juno and Minerva, hence the name St Maria im Kapitol, although it is certain that the bequest by Archbishop Bruno (died 965) for the decoration of the church was used, because the

undivided wall between the arch and window areas. The square bays in the aisles have ribbed vaults whose solid reinforcing arches are supported on semicircular pier abutments with cushion capitals (see Speyer, p. 232). This system continues seamlessly into the conches and so covers the whole of the church.

The most striking feature is undoubtedly the triconch in the east section. Its harmonious effect derives from its strictly symmetrical layout, with conches of the same size in the chancel and cross-arms and a systematic arrangement on the elevation. The five semicircular arches in the ambulatory, with monolithic columns on Attic bases and profileless cube capitals, are balanced on the upper floor by five window axes divided by half-columns in a similar pattern.

The crypt of Abbess Ida's building, which was buried in the Second World War, is a fine example of Ottonian architecture: a complete underground hall church, larger than in St Pantaleon and similar to the slightly older crypt in Speyer Cathedral (Ill. p. 229).

Combining a cruciform basilica and the central triconch plan, St Maria im Kapitol is an important work of 11th-century western architecture that has had a far-reaching influence. None of the triconch layouts in other Cologne churches can compare with the uniform arrangement of the space and its individual architectural components (see Holy Apostles and Great St Martin).

The two leaves of the walnut door now in the south aisle were once in the portal of the north conch. They were part of the furnishings of Abbess Ida's church and were probably finished for the consecration in 1065. The original arrangement of the relief, in a frame of guilloches, whorled bars and ornamental capitals, together with captions, has been altered. On the left are scenes from the childhood of Christ, on the right scenes

Double pictorial door of St Maria im Kapitol,
Cologne. Walnut wood on oak boards, pre-1065
(see Ill. p. 36).

from the Passion. This unique 11th-
century door is a major work of early
medieval sculpture, similar in style to the
Gero crucifix (Ill. p. 296). The pictures
are in a graphic and vivid narrative style
and have a didactic function as a kind
of pictorial Bible to be read by illiterate
believers at the entrance to the church.

The founder, Plectrude, is commemorated in two pictures. She is shown in
the late 13th-century Gothic memorial
plaque holding a model of the church
and on the Romanesque tombstone
built from 1180 to 1190 with a banner
bearing an inscription from Psalm 26: 8,
Domine dilexi decorem domus tue (Lord, I
have loved the habitation of thy house,
and the place where thine honour
dwelleth). The style is similar to the
abbesses' tombs in Quedlinburg dating
from around 1160.

The 1304 gable cross that used to
be under the rood altar in the crossing
(Ill. p. 49) is an early and important
example of a devotional image (also
known as a plague cross) that was common in the Rhineland and Westphalia.
The stark naturalism and moving
depiction of the Passion is in keeping
with the spirit of mysticism.

The Renaissance style imported from
Flanders made its first appearance in
Cologne with the rood screen separating
the nave from the conch chancel commissioned by several Cologne families
and made in 1523 from designs by the
Mechelen court artist Jan van Romme.
The two Late Gothic chapels in the
spandrels of the cross-arms were also
donated by local burghers. The
Hardenrath Chapel to the south, built in
1466, contains statues of Mary as intercessor and the Redeemer of the World
by Strasbourg artists after Nicolaus
Gerhaert von Leyden (1466). The spon-
taneity of the figure of Mary is typical of
the new lively style that was superseding
the 'Dark Age' of Late Gothic sculpture.

View of the nave of St Cäcilien, Cologne, from the gallery, facing east. Schnütgen Museum, Cologne.

Opposite: Crucifix from St Georg, Cologne. Walnut wood, 2nd half of the 11th century (see Ill. p. 37). Schnütgen Museum, Cologne.

St Cäcilien (Schnütgen Museum)

A convent had existed on the edge of the Roman baths from the second half of the 9th century. Its church was rebuilt after an attack by the Normans in 888. St Cäcilien was another of the churches to which Archbishop Bruno left money in his will (see St Pantaleon, p. 297, and St Maria im Kapitol, p. 300). The present layout of the church dates from building work between 1130 and 1160, which incorporated the old fabric. After the convent was dissolved in 1802 the complex was owned by the local hospital, which later took over the convent buildings and the Gothic cloister. Since being rebuilt after the Second World War, the church has housed the Schnütgen Museum. The two-aisle basilica has no transept and terminates in a rectangular vaulted chancel bay (with important remnants of late 13th-century wall paintings) and a semicircular apse. The round arches in the flat-roofed nave are divided by square piers with profiled imposts. The side aisles have groined vaults and reinforcing arches with semicircular wall abutments. The Gothic vaulting that had been incorporated in the central nave when the community of gentlewomen became an Augustine convent in 1479 was not restored when the church was rebuilt after the Second World War. Instead a wooden ceiling was added, as in the 12th century. The west end of the nave terminates in a gallery for the Divine Office of the canonesses. Underneath is the crypt; the west section is 19th century, while the front part is from the original Ottonian building.

The north portal tympanum dating from between 1150 and 1175 is now on display inside the church. It shows a half-length figure of St Cecilia between her betrothed, Valerian, and her brother, Tiburtius, with an angel swooping down on her. All three figures are named. An inscription referring to St Cecilia runs around the arches: *vos qui spectatis hec premia virginitatis/expectate pari pariter virtute beari* (You who are seeing this honour of virginity expect to be rewarded equally for the same virtue). The panel with the

figure of Tiburtius on it has a Roman epitaph on the back, showing that it has been reused. The composition is from an Italian prototype (see tympanum from the Benedictine abbey of San Leno, Brescia museum).

In 1866 Alexander Schnütgen (1843–1918), curate and (from 1887)

canon of Cologne Cathedral, started collecting medieval works of art, mainly from the Cologne area but also from other parts of the Rhineland, Westphalia and Lower Saxony. In 1906 he presented these treasures to the city of Cologne. They were originally housed in an annex to the Kunstgewerbemuseum, Cologne, in the Hansaring and then, from 1932, in St Heribert's monastery in Deutz, but in 1956 the collection found a home in an appropriately religious setting in the former St Cäcilien basilica.

The ivory comb of St Heribert is a work of exceptional aesthetic and artistic quality. Its source and original purpose are not certain, but liturgical combs are known to have been common in the Middle Ages, for instance on ceremonial occasions such as the anointing of a bishop or king. The strictly symmetrical composition of the front is a relief of the Crucifixion with Longinus and Stephaton, the Virgin and John the Baptist, Sol and Luna on either side. Two angels are leaning down from above over artistically pierced rosettes. The style of the figures and the leaf decoration are characteristic of the highly sophisticated ivory art at the court of Charles the Bald in the late 9th century.

The larger than lifesize crucifix from St Georg (Ills. pp. 37, 305), which originally had relics and possibly also hosts in the back, probably stood above the high altar. It is similar to the Gero crucifix (Ills. pp. 32, 296), although it has been modified and refined to make the

organic forms more strictly geometrical. It is, therefore, typical of the style around 1067 – contemporary with the pictorial doors at St Maria im Kapitol (Ills. pp. 36, 303) – but interpreted in a quite distinct, non-anecdotal manner that might be described as aristocratic.

One of the most famous works in the Schnütgen Museum is the console figure with the Parler mark in the late 14th-century soft style. The figure, wearing a crown of foliage on its head, is fascinating in the way it combines both anthropomorphic and plant motifs. The polychromy is more recent, although traces of colour show that it was originally painted. This original sculpture is believed to be by Heinrich Parler.

View of the chancel of St Gereon, Cologne.

St Gereon

The French chronicler Gregory of Tours, who first referred to 'the church of the golden saints' (*ad aureos sanctos*) around 590, was probably remarking upon its gold mosaic decoration. Records show that a martyrium was built towards the end of the 4th century in the middle of a Roman burial ground outside the city walls. It consisted of an oval central structure about 23 metres (75 feet) long with four radial conches, a larger conch in the east and a rectangular narthex with side niches and an atrium in front in the west. The conches were lined with yellow marble slabs and the floor was covered with mosaic. The architectonic design suggests that it was based on models in Rome (for example, the Constantinian temple of Minerva Medica). The Late Classical building forms the core of the Hohenstaufen decagon.

Records for 839 mention a collegiate chapter that had probably existed since Merovingian times. Hildebold, the first archbishop of Cologne, who was appointed by Charlemagne, was buried in the church (which ranked next to Cologne cathedral) in 818. Archbishop Anno II extended the Romanesque building to the east with a long chancel above a crypt consecrated between 1067 and 1069. In the mid-12th century a square bay was added to the chancel, flanked by two tall square towers and ending in an elaborately divided semicircular apse (the extended chancel and crypt were consecrated by Archbishop Arnold von Wied in 1156). Between 1219 and 1227 the four-storey projecting decagon with a domed vault and a vestibule on the west side was built above the classical oval, which was incorporated in the new building as the bottom floor. The church was furnished with new vaulting and windows in the chancel at the end of the 14th century. The convent buildings and transept were demolished after the

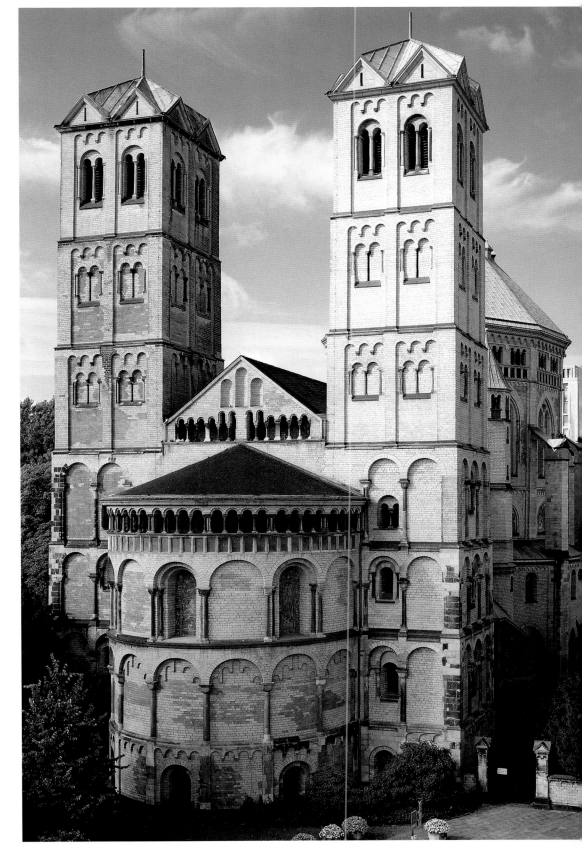

Opposite: Wall elevation of St Gereon, Cologne.

The dome of the decagon at St Gereon, Cologne.

foundation was dissolved in 1802 and the church became a parish church, which was restored at the end of the 19th century. The present church is the result of lengthy rebuilding work after the massive damage caused during the Second World War, particularly to the chancel and decagon.

The Hohenstaufen decagon encloses the side conches of the Early Christian martyrium in a ten-sided bay-like shell in which the small paired columns in front of the Romanesque partition walls are replaced by a system of clustered engaged shafts, the stronger ones

supporting the ten ribs of the dome, the weaker ones the pointed arches. Below them the three lower floors – conches, triforium with double and triple rows of columns and a passageway floor with trefoil window – are optically linked. The top part of the wall also has a passageway and is filled with tall lancet windows with tiny trefoils. Although the influence of the Reims School or of northern French Gothic in general is noticeable, the St Gereon decagon is an original example of Rhenish architecture from the late Hohenstaufen period.

On the outside of the decagon, which is edged with unadorned abutments with narrow arched buttresses, is a clear sequence of storeys, emphasized by an elaborate system of blind arches. A dwarf gallery with a moulding of framed

The nave of Holy Apostles, Cologne, facing east.

squares running round under the base of the roof forms an additional fifth storey. The motif is repeated in the chancel apse. The seven storeys of the towers flanking the chancel are decorated with distinctive Lombard arcading.

Below the east chancel is the crypt, which has three aisles and groined vaults. The five lower bays on the west side were put in during Anno's building work, the higher bays to the east added in the mid-12th century. West of the crypt, immediately under the high altar, is a confessio with the tombs of the martyr St Gereon and his comrades in the Theban Legion.

Around 1230 a baptistery in the form of an irregular central room was built on the south side of the decagon. In 1315 the Cologne Cathedral architect Johannes added a sacristy south of the chancel. The delicate tracery in the quadruple lancet windows matches that in the Lady Chapel in the cathedral.

The unique fragments of floor mosaics from the Hohenstaufen chancel with pictures from the Old Testament (Samson and David as Christ's predecessors) were moved to the crypt in the 19th century and restored. Not only do they show the high artistic quality of the furnishings, they are also tangible evidence of the classical tradition that has lived on in this church.

The fresco fragment in the Schnütgen Museum found on the gallery floor of the decagon in 1970 is similar in style to Roman and Umbrian work around 1100 and it has therefore been dated to the early part of the 12th century. The shapes and colours have remained fresh.

The modern stained glass in the decagon is by Georg Meistermann (upper floor) and Wilhelm Bauschulte (gallery floor). The stained glass in the crypt was created by Alfred Manessier in 1964.

Holy Apostles

The double-chancel ground plan of the former canons' collegiate church founded by Archbishop Pilgrim in the 11th century is unmistakably in the tradition of Cologne church buildings based on the double-chancel layout of the old cathedral. The nave and

west transept were built in this early construction phase, in particular the stepped round arches on rectangular piers still visible under the grey trachyte facing that was added when the vaulting was put in around 1220. Between 1150 and 1175 the original structure of the west chancel was modified by the

construction of the massive five-storey tower (flanked by stair turrets) in the extension of a rectangular connecting bay and the Romanesque crypt was laid out below. The transept consists of three equal-sized squares with the vaulting in the side sections divided by seven ribs rising above delicate clusters of pillars. The trefoil chancel in the east, obviously modelled on Great St Martin, was started after a fire in 1192. As with Great St Martin, the three-conch structure with the towers above is most impressive on the east side, which has been extended as a frontage on to the Neumarkt. The striking and elaborately structured design and harmonious proportions make Holy Apostles one of the most successful examples of Cologne church architecture.

The church's treasures include a gilded silver chalice which, according to legend, belonged to Archbishop Heribert in the early 11th century and is therefore known as the Heribert chalice. However, it is more likely to have come from a set of liturgical objects donated to the church by Prior Heinrich von Heinsberg around 1230. The proportions have been spoilt by the part added between the cup and the knop in the 19th century. The base is decorated with chased medallions showing the Visitation, the Nativity, the Crucifixion and the women at the tomb.

Opposite left: View of the chancel of Holy Apostles, Cologne, from Neumarkt.
Opposite right: The Heribert chalice in the Holy Apostles treasury.

East view of Great St Martin, Cologne, looking towards the Rhine.

On the cup is an engraved band with half-length figures of the Apostles under trefoil arches. The knop, which was probably made in a Cologne goldsmith's workshop, is in filigree.

Great St Martin

The church is on the bank of the Rhine, above the foundations of a Roman storehouse on a former island that was fortified in the early Middle Ages. The Lorsch Chronicle refers to building work by Archbishop Bruno in the mid-10th century and Benedictine monks from the St Veit monastery in Mönchengladbach came here before 1000. Archbishop Anno II built two towers *a fronte sanctuarii.* According to the records, the church (probably the east end) was consecrated in 1172. In 1185 it was damaged by fire.

The existing church was built in several phases in the 12th and 13th centuries. Its cruciform ground plan forms a tri-conch around the square crossing with cross-arms and chancel, the first to be modelled on St Maria im Kapitol, in a simplified form without the columnar ambulatory, but with a double-shell divided wall on the upper floor. The nave and two aisles extend across four bays built at different times. While the barrel-vaulted bay to the east is still part of the central structure of the trefoil chancel, suggesting a change of plan, the three west bays, originally flat roofed, were rebuilt and vaulted between 1235 and 1240 in the Early Gothic style, with a blind triforium and pointed triple arches on small double columns. The west wall with the two-storey arcading and the portal were built from 1220 to 1225.

What particularly distinguishes Great St Martin from other Cologne churches is the picturesque effect of the east side aligned with the Rhine. The massive bulk of the square crossing tower and the four satellite towers rise from the symmetrical

trefoil chancel, with its distinctive two-storey blind division and the moulding of framed squares and dwarf gallery, and the front gable. It is a masterpiece of the detailed and elaborate Rhineland Romanesque style, which, with the Gothic towers of the cathedral, gives Cologne its distinctive skyline (see Ill. pp. 284–85). By 1963 the tower had already been rebuilt after the devastation of the Second World War, although it was another twenty years before the church itself was restored.

St Ursula

The church dedicated to St Ursula and her companions was built on a Roman burial ground above a 4th-century memorial. The Latin inscription on the plaque in the south chancel wall of the existing church, referring to the Roman senator Clematius as founder of a basilica in honour of the saintly virgins, is evidence of the early veneration on this site. The cult of St Ursula has been documented since the 10th century and was a popular subject for Late Gothic painting (Ills. pp. 2, 19, 287). In the north transept is a 1456 St Ursula cycle consisting of 31 panels by the Lochner School.

The church, a galleried basilica with two aisles and side apses to the east of the cross-arms, dates mainly from the early 12th century, although the Gothic chancel and the aisle extended to the south were not built until the late 13th century, after which the nave was vaulted. The interior was extensively rebuilt in 1642 and 1657 and the galleries in the transepts were removed. As so often in Cologne, a number of modifications were made when the church was rebuilt after the destruction in the Second World War. The original Gothic vaults have been replaced by a wooden coffered ceiling with concave vaults and the 17th-century Gothic style vaulting in the transept by a flat wooden ceiling.

The galleries in the nave – their first appearance in Lower Rhine architecture – open into triple arches resting on small columns with cushion capitals. At the top of the wall the pilasters rising from the imposts of the square pillars with carved consoles supporting the Gothic vaulting and the 12th-century Romanesque blind arch frieze have been preserved. In the west the nave ends in a gallery. It used to open on to the 'virgins' gallery' on the top storey of the west section, which had a groined vault. A central column divides the square entrance hall into four bays.

The chancel is an elegant Gothic structure terminating in a 5/8 polygon on the east side. The tall lancet windows fill the whole wall and their jambs go down to the lower part of the wall, from which the engaged shafts of the vaulting starts. In the wall below the windows are small latticework niches containing the relics of the 11,000 virgins. Like the chancel in the Palatine Chapel of Aachen, the chancel at St Ursula is modelled on the Ste-Chapelle in Paris, while stylistically it shows the influence of the Cologne Cathedral lodge.

In 1643 the *Goldene Kammer* was built in the corner of the west end and the extended south aisle. With its curious decoration of human bones on the walls and the niches in the wall panelling framed with gilded acanthus carving and displaying reliquary busts from the

13th to the 18th centuries, the double-bayed chapel is a showpiece of Baroque veneration of the saints and the popular cult of St Ursula.

St Kunibert

St Kunibert stands on the site of a church dedicated to St Clement founded by Bishop Kunibert (*c.* 640–48) on the

bank of the Rhine north of Cologne, first mentioned in 866 as a collegiate chapter. The existing building, a vaulted three-aisle basilica with a wide transept on the west side and a rectangular chancel bay with a semicircular apse towards the Rhine, was built from east to west between 1215 and 1247. The Gothic cathedral, started only a year later, introduced a radical change of style, the full extent of which becomes clear when it is compared with this last example of the great Romanesque tradition on the Rhine.

The main features of St Kunibert are still completely Romanesque, but signs of a new aesthetic are already evident in the imposing proportions and the juxtaposition of round and pointed arches. The chancel apse is similar in shape to the Cologne triconch structures. Five rhythmic blind arches one above the other divide the wall and frame the windows filling the whole area on the upper storey. The double-shell wall inside forms narrow ambulatories. The striking central tower of the west transept restored in 1992 balances the square towers at the east end of the nave, a similar arrangement to Holy Apostles.

Opposite left: The nave and chancel of St Kunibert, Cologne.
Opposite right: The baptistery of St Kunibert, Cologne, with a Gothic painting, 1260–70.

The nave and chancel of the Minorite church of St Mariä Empfängnis, Cologne.

In the baptistery, magnificent wall paintings have been preserved in a niche on the south arm of the chancel. The Crucifixion painting dates from 1260 to 1270. On the west pillars of the chancel bay Mary and the angel are standing opposite a monumental stone Annunciation group. According to the inscription on the angel console, it was donated by Canon Hermanus de Arcka (1439). Attributed to Konrad Kuyn, a Cologne Cathedral architect, the work dates from a period of radical change in the development of German sculptural style known as 'the Dark Age', when the elegance of the soft style evolved into a new naturalistic concept of the human form, here still interpreted with a certain lack of confidence.

The church's treasures include stained glass dating from the time it was built (around 1230), in particular the picture of the Tree of Jesse in the middle window of the chancel with its complex ornamentation and iconography. The side windows are dedicated to the church's two patron saints with scenes from their legends, St Clement on the left and St Kunibert on the right. The smaller windows on the lower floor contain full-length portraits of saints surrounded by a decorative border. In the east window of the south transept arm is John the Baptist with the founder at his feet (Ill. p. 42). The style of this window is similar to the miniatures of the Gospel Book from Great St Martin and still shows the influence of Nicholas of Verdun's goldwork.

St Mariä Empfängnis (church of the Immaculate Conception)

Between 1244 and 1245 the Franciscans, who had been established in Cologne since 1229, settled in the parish of St Columba not far from the cathedral and started building a church. The chancel was consecrated in 1260. The ground

plan followed the usual layout for the mendicant order churches: a nave with two aisles and eight bays and a chancel with a rectangular bay and 7/12 polygon extending from the nave. The church had no transept or towers. Architectural research has shown that the nave was originally built with the nave and aisles the same height, but the plan for a hall church must have been abandoned in favour of the basilican structure while the building work was in progress. This was no doubt due to the influence of the cathedral lodge, which can be seen in the use of open flying buttresses, while the chancel is similar to the chancel in St Ursula built soon afterwards. As the work progressed from east to west, however, the style became much plainer, in keeping with the architectural aesthetic of the Franciscan order and uninfluenced by the Gothic cathedral. Only the large windows in the west gable wall dating from 1350 and the south portal have tracery; the other double lancet windows in the nave and chancel have simple oculi or lozenge-shaped openings.

The church's treasures include a monumental gilded copper cross from Brauweiler abbey donated by Countess Palatine Mathilde in 1024, similar to the Bishop Bernward von Hildesheim cross made in 1007–8. The style of the beautiful crucifix – silver, partly gilded, 66 centimetres (26 inches) high – suggests that it was made around 1330 and it probably replaced the original Ottonian figure of Christ. In contrast to most Cologne crucifixes of the time, which are of the *crucifixus dolorosus* type, this figure of Christ is in the 'courtly' style of chancel pillar figures and the Madonna of Milan in Cologne Cathedral (Ill. p. 296).

A carved winged altarpiece dating from around 1480 is now the most prominent feature of the chancel. In the middle is the Virgin with a halo, in the panels scenes from the life of Jesus and St Catherine and St Nicholas.

St Mariä Himmelfahrt (church of the Assumption of the Virgin)

In 1618 the Jesuits, who had been established in Cologne since 1544,

started building a church that can be regarded as the order's most important building in northwest Germany. The church was consecrated in 1678, although the monastery complex was not finished until 1715. The architect, Christoph Wamser from Aschaffenburg, also designed the Jesuit church in Molsheim, a centre of the Counter-Reformation in Alsace, on which St Mariä Himmelfahrt is largely modelled.

It is a two-aisle vaulted gallery basilica with an almost undifferentiated transept, a long chancel closed on three sides and side chancels in the shape of a 5/8 polygon. The square tower added to the chevet balances the two towers flanking the west front, which has three axes. The net star-ribbed vault in the central nave and the chancel is reminiscent of the Gothic style. In the unique assimilation and fusion of elements of Romanesque, Gothic and Baroque style, the architecture is in keeping with the Jesuits' Counter-Reformation policy, which emphasized the unity and historical continuity of the Church. In that sense

Opposite: View from the south of the Minorite church of St Mariä Empfängnis, Cologne.

Below: The nave and chancel of St Mariä Himmelfahrt, Cologne.
Right: The west front of St Mariä Himmelfahrt, Cologne.

the construction of such an ambitious building in the middle of the Thirty Years' War was also a religious and political statement.

It is therefore not surprising that the coat of arms of Elector Maximilian of Bavaria appears on the columned portal of the west front. As head of the Catholic League in the empire, he assisted the archbishop of Cologne, his brother the Elector Ferdinand (1596–1650), in the construction of the Jesuit church. This influence is also evident from the choice of south German artists (for instance, many of the magnificent furnishings were made by the Augsburg sculptor Jeremias Geisselbrunn between 1594 and 1596). The rebuilt three-storey high altar is a fine example of an Augsburg altarpiece in which the artist made the transition from Late Renaissance Mannerism to the Baroque.

The church was heavily damaged in the Second World War. Although the structure has since been completely rebuilt, the interior decor has only been partly restored.

The Lower Rhine
and the Delta

The Lower Rhine, as the river is called when
it emerges from the highlands on to the plain,
runs about 210 kilometres (130 miles) to the
Dutch border. The Erft flows into it from the
left and the Wupper, Ruhr, Emscher and
Lippe from the right. Along its changeable
course are flat banks lined with willows and
poplars, flood meadows and oxbows. The old
Roman towns of Neuss and Xanten were
originally right on the river.

   Immediately beyond the Dutch border
the Rhine divides into several branches in
a complex system of waterways. To the south
the largest river, the Waal, forms a wide
delta with the Maas. Beyond Rotterdam the
northern arm, at first called the Nederrijn and
then the Lek, joins a branch of the Waal
and the Maas and flows into the North Sea
in the Nieuwe Waterweg at the Hook of
Holland. A third arm, the Kromme Rijn
(which becomes the Oude Rijn in Utrecht),
flows into the sea at Katwijk.

The illustration shows the desolate landscape
of the Lower Rhine with the silhouette of
Xanten Cathedral.

Brauweiler

Below left: Marian altarpiece from Brauweiler, depicting St Nikolaus und St Medardus, late 12th century.
Below: Daniel in the lion's den (detail). A Romanesque ceiling painting in the chapter house of the old abbey, mid 12th century.

Former Benedictine abbey church of St Nikolaus and St Medardus

In 1024 Count Palatine Ezzo-Ehrenfried of Lorraine and his wife Mathilde, daughter of the Emperor Otto II, founded a monastery occupied by Gorze reform Benedictine nuns on a Frankish imperial estate, with a private church dedicated to St Medardus as a family burial place. An ambitious church building was quickly erected after Richezza Queen of Poland, daughter of the two founders and sister of Abbess Ida of St Maria im Capitol in Cologne, had donated her wealth to the convent in 1048 (the crypt was consecrated in 1051 and the east end in 1061 by Archbishop Anno of Cologne). It was modelled on St Maria im Capitol, which was under construction at the same time; the ground plan of the hall crypt, with three radial chapels in the walls of the east apse, was a smaller version of the Cologne church. Between 1136 and 1220 the Richezza building was replaced in several stages by a new building of similar dimensions, one of the earliest examples of a groined vault basilica with an alternating system. Above the pier arches of the two square nave bays is a blind triforium on three-quarter columns. The present ribbed vault with its Late Gothic floral painting and the clerestorey window were built in a later phase, around 1514.

The mid-12th century west towers – a square central tower the same width as the nave (the spire was added in 1629) and two separate stair turrets, also square – are harmoniously and effectively divided with pilaster-strips and blind arches, Lombard friezes, faced columns and pilasters and bifora openings sunk into the wall. The east end with the transept and chancel, started between 1190 and 1196, is in the Ottonian tradition of churches such as St Georg in Cologne. The three-part groined vault in the chancel with a rectangular bay, adjoined at the side by narrow rectangular side choirs, opens in the top of the semicircular apse with a double-shell upper floor and passage into the rectangular chapel of St Bernard commemorating the visit by St Bernard of Clairvaux in 1147. During rebuilding work before 1200 the number of aisles in the 11th-century crypt was reduced from seven to five.

The church still has many remnants of fine sculpture from the Hohenstaufen period. The chancel in particular contains magnificent figurative capital decorations. On the tympanum on the portals of the side chancels are the seated figures of the two founders, Mathilde on the right and Ezzo on the left. The Romanesque limestone Marian altarpiece from the crypt altar is in the south side chancel, where the founders are now buried. It shows the Virgin

The east view of the abbey church of Brauweiler.

enthroned with the Child under a shell baldachin with four bearded saints approaching on a bank of cloud at the side. The two inside appear from their ecclesiastical robes to be St Nicholas and St Medardus, accompanied by two laymen with banners. The figures are almost completely in the round, indicating that they were made in the Cologne area in the late 12th century. The frame and setting were restored around 1870.

The eleven limestone reliefs of Christ enthroned, two cherubim, the risen Christ and seven Apostles in basin-shaped niches in the lapidarium are from the west end of the church. Although still in the Ottonian style, they were not made until the late 11th or early 12th centuries. Other reliefs from the stair turrets at the west end with signs of the zodiac are now in the Landesmuseum in Bonn and the Schnütgen Museum in Cologne. The reliefs outside have been replaced by copies.

After the abbey was dissolved and the parish founded in 1806, the unfinished east end was extended with the two flanking towers and the crossing tower in the course of extensive construction and renovation work in the High Romanesque style by the Cologne Cathedral architect Heinrich Wiethase between 1866 and 1876. As a result the east view of the church now represents the ideal of Rhineland Romanesque.

In the Baroque abbey buildings, now occupied by the Rheinisches Landesamt für Denkmalpflege (the regional office for the preservation of monuments), the two-aisle chapter house on the east cloister wing dating from 1149 has been preserved. Its groined vault was painted by the same workshop that worked in Schwarzrheindorf shortly afterwards (Ill. p. 273).

Düsseldorf

Schloss Benrath

The Elector Palatine Karl Theodor had a country house and hunting lodge designed by his architect Nicolas de Pigage south of Düsseldorf to replace a 17th-century Baroque summer palace. It was intended to be a royal residence in the new style, in idyllic rural surroundings. Pigage's plan for a symmetrical building arranged round a lake, consisting of a rectangular pavilion raised on a terrace flanked by two polygonal subsidiary wings and two gatehouses was a highly original interpretation of the rules for a *maison de plaisance* formulated by the French architect and theoretician Jacques-François Blondel (1618–86). The centrepiece of Schloss Benrath is a magnificent circular domed room flanked by two rectangular garden rooms and opening on to the park. Behind it the royal apartments are grouped around two light wells in a labyrinthine multi-storey arrangement

Marble and stucco cupola room at Schloss Benrath
on the garden frontage of the main building.

(Ill. p. 67). The sculptures outside
(designed by Peter Anton Verschaffelt,
director of the Mannheim Academy)
are of mythological subjects connected
with nature and hunting, underlining
the Arcadian character of the palace.
Most of the interior furnishings based on
Pigage's designs were also by court artists
from Mannheim. The ceiling frescoes in
the garden rooms, which seem to open
up to the heavens, are by Lambert Krahe,
director of the Düsseldorf Academy.
The ideal in the Age of Enlightenment
was to achieve a harmonious synthesis of
architecture and nature in the transition
from Rococo to Classicism. In Benrath
this aim has been realized in a complete
work of art that is one of the finest and
most dazzling examples of European
palace architecture.

Late Ottonian crucifix from St Margareta, Gerresheim, early 11th century.

Opposite left: View of St Margareta, Gerresheim, from the south.
Opposite right: The interior of St Margareta, Gerresheim, looking towards the chancel.

St Margareta (former nunnery church)

The community of secular canonesses was founded at the end of the 9th century and survived for over 800 years. After the foundation was dissolved, the church was taken over by the Catholic parish in 1809. According to records, a previous church was consecrated by Archbishop Gero of Cologne in 970. The monumental Late Ottonian crucifix is believed to have come from that building. The present Hohenstaufen church was built between 1210 and 1236. A cruciform basilica with an alternating system and a projecting transept, it is one of the group of Late Romanesque churches in the transitional Rhineland style from Cologne, characterized by its varied decorative forms. In the three-bay nave, cruciform main piers alternate with inset round engaged shafts supporting the baldachin-like raised vaulting and rectangular intermediate pillars. The horizontal ledge running above the pointed arches forms the base of a triforium, whose quadruple row of arches on small coupled columns breaks up the wall in a double shell. The inner walls above are pierced by round arched windows arranged in pairs. The semicircular chancel apse opens out into five narrow semicircular windows. The present garish-looking painted decoration in the apse, consisting of ornamental decorative strips, a painted curtain in the socle area and a representation of the Trinity in the calotte, is a late 19th-century and 20th-century Neo-Romanesque addition to the remnants of the medieval furnishings discovered in 1896. In the south side aisle is the tomb of Gerrich, the church's founder, made from a single block of trachyte with an architectonic division around it in the shape of Gothic pointed arches and finials (*c.* 1270–80).

The structure and system of decoration outside are clearly defined. Lombard

blind arches in a contrasting colour
decorate the eaves and gable and the
side aisles are pierced by rosette
windows. The two-storey octagonal
crossing tower, modelled on the tower
of St Andreas in Cologne, was rebuilt
in 1874 during restoration work supervised by Heinrich Wiethase, a Cologne
Cathedral architect.

The larger than lifesize oak cross,
now in the chevet, is a rare example of
high-quality Late Ottonian sculpture.
Compared with the crucifix from
St Georg in Cologne (Ills. pp. 37, 305)
as a moving representation of Christ's
Passion, this gentle crucified figure with
arms extended and head bowed as if
suspended in front of the cross appears
as a symbol of mercy and redemption.
The plastic effect of the flat body's internal forms, which are merely suggested,
was originally enhanced by a coloured
frame. The opening at the back of the
head was, as usual, used for relics.

The market place at Düsseldorf, with the town hall and the statue of the Palatine Elector Johann Wilhelm on horseback by Gabriel de Grupello, 1711.

Market place

On a high Classical plinth in the middle of the market square is a statue of Elector Johann Wilhelm, Duke of Jülich-Berg, on horseback. He commissioned the statue himself from the court sculptor Gabriel de Grupello and it was completed in 1711. Next to Andreas Schlüter's equestrian statue of the Great Elector in Berlin it is the most famous Baroque work of its kind in Germany. Behind the monument is the town hall with its three-storey gable façades on either side of a Late Gothic style projecting stair turret, built by Heinrich Tussmann, a master mason from Duisburg, between 1570 and 1573.

The Rococo portal and balcony were added when the building was renovated in 1749.

Kunstsammlung Nordrhein-Westfalen

In 1975 tenders were invited for a museum building to house North Rhine-Westphalia's collection of 20th-century paintings, which until then had been in the Late Baroque Jägerhof palace in the Hofgarten. The commission was awarded to the Copenhagen architects Dissing and Weitling and the new museum in the Grabbeplatz was opened in 1986. The wide sweep of its dynamically soaring façade in dark Bornholm granite introduces a modern architectural note on the edge of Düsseldorf's old town, the polished surface reflecting the Baroque façade of the old Jesuit church of St Andreas or the changing landscape of the sky, depending on the light and the weather.

The three-storey interior of the gallery is designed to maximize the use of the daylight from above (except in the rooms for the special Paul Klee and Julius Bissier collections, which contain light-sensitive works on paper). The Classical Modern rooms on the top floor, the rooms for larger post-war works on

Kunstsammlung Nordrhein-Westfalen, Düsseldorf, in the Grabbeplatz, from the southeast.

the two-storey middle level and the large area for temporary exhibitions on the ground floor are all lit from the top. Each area is designed for the specific conditions and requirements of the collection and an additional top-lighting system of translucent glass screens produces a uniform and neutral daylight effect with few shadows, at the same time lending an architectonic emphasis.

The Kunstsammlung foundation, established in 1961 after the acquisition of eighty-eight works by Klee, built up its collection of 20th-century painting steadily from 1962 with funds from

the state and donations. The museum's policy was to acquire major individual works of an internationally high standard that would have long-term historical value, rather than to aim at historical completeness. The collection focused on Fauvism, Cubism and Expressionism, with major works by Kandinsky, Gris, Léger, Picasso, Kirchner, Chirico, Schwitters, Beckmann, Mondrian and Max Ernst. The American-dominated post-war period is represented by Tachisme, Abstract Expressionism, Minimal and Pop Art, with artists such as Pollock, Rauschenberg, Warhol and Stella.

Werner Schmalenbach, director of the museum for many years, used his expertise and judgment to build up a collection of exceptional originality and quality and set the standard for the future. Since 1990 his successor Armin Zweite has extended the range to contemporary sculptures, installations and projections. The Beuys collection also gives an internationally renowned Lower Rhine artist a place amongst the 20th-century masterpieces.

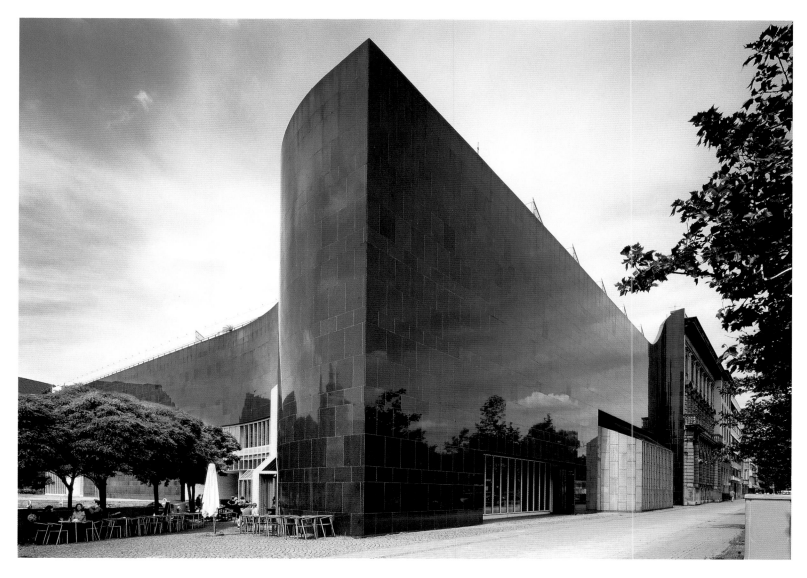

Düsseldorf-Kaiserswerth

Imperial palace

Around 700 the Anglo-Saxon missionary Bishop Suitbert founded a monastic settlement on one of the islands in the oxbows of the Rhine close to the Rinbusen royal court. He had been given it by Pepin of Heristal, the Merovingian mayor of the palace, and his wife Plectrude (the islands were silted up in the 13th century). The bishop was buried in the church there in 713. In the Salian period, emperors and kings often stayed in the castle built on the south of the island to protect the monastery. It was here that Archbishop Anno of Cologne abducted the minor King Henry IV (see p. 274). Between 1174 and 1184 the Emperor Frederick Barbarossa replaced the castle with an imposing Hohenstaufen palace with a great hall facing the Rhine, a keep and a forebuilding on the land side. It played an important role as an imperial customs post for several centuries. At the same time the market settlement was granted the status of a free imperial town. In the 17th century a ring of fortresses and bastions were built right round the castle, the town and the immune area of the foundation. After the palace had been destroyed in 1689 and again in 1702 in the War of the Spanish Succession, the ruins were allowed to decay and used for quarrying until they were explored and preserved from 1908 to 1909.

St Suitbert basilica

The changes of style between the different construction phases are visible both outside and inside. The basilican nave has broad semicircular arches on massive square piers. The undivided upper wall with clearstorey windows and separate crossing with a projecting transept are flat-roofed and still in the Early Romanesque style of the Salian building supported by imperial endowments, which was consecrated in 1078. By contrast, the chancel, consecrated in 1237, is another example

of the varied transitional style in the final Romanesque phase on the Lower Rhine. It has three polygonal apses and a five-part ribbed vault resting on elegant clusters of engaged shafts with crocketed capitals in the polygon.

The church's treasures include the shrine of the monastery's founder St Suitbert, already canonized by 796. His bones were placed in the wooden casket in 1264, but the magnificent casing in gilded copper and silver, mixed with *champlevé* and *cloisonné* enamel, gold filigree and semi-precious stones, was only made in the late 13th century – the last great shrine on the Rhine and Maas in the High Middle Ages. Under the trefoil arches on the long sides, supported by double columns, are the Apostles on thrones, on the sloping sides of the roof eight reliefs with scenes from the lives of Mary and Jesus and on the ends the Virgin and Child and two female saints. Opposite them are St Suitbert and his benefactors Pepin and Plectrude.

Examples of 18th-century buildings in Lower Rhine brickwork have been preserved in the Stiftsplatz and market place.

Neuss

Neuss Cathedral from the northwest.

Neuss Cathedral

Traces of several earlier buildings have been found during excavations underneath the church. A funerary chapel (*cella memoriae*) was built on a Roman burial area in the first half of the 5th century. A basilican Carolingian nave was followed in the Ottonian period by a nave and two aisle layout with a transept and straight-ended chancel above a five-aisle crypt, whose structure has been largely preserved (and extensively restored in the 19th and 20th century). The Ottonian building was probably built around 1050 when Abbess Gepa, sister of the Alsatian Pope Leo IX, transported St Quirin's relics from Rome. Work began on the Late Romanesque galleried basilica after the Benedictine nunnery that had existed since the 9th century became a community of gentlewomen in 1179. The lower part of the monumental west end with its socle area divided by blind arches and a type of gallery floor with quatrefoil and blind arch decoration was probably built at the end of the 12th century. The gable storey and lofty two-storey square tower were added at a later stage. The inscription set into the right side aisle, with the year a foundation stone was laid (1209) and the names of the Emperor Otto, Bishop Adolf, Abbess Sophia and the architect, *magister* Wolbero, is a reliable indication of when the church was built. Progressing from west to east, the work was completed from around 1230 to 1240.

The interior is lofty and imposing, the nave and two aisles with an alternating system extending across three double bays and spanned by baldachin-style groined vaults. The wall elevation has three sections and consists of pilaster arches arranged in pairs with a ceiling joist, the gallery floor on the same axis and large fan-shaped windows in the clearstorey, a motif in the transitional Rhineland style repeated in the side

332

aisles. In front of every second square pillar is a slender round engaged shaft going up to the base of the reinforcing arches and ribs. Around the crossing in the centre, which is vaulted with a high eight-section ribbed dome that lets in the light, is a trefoil chancel based on Cologne models with a barrel-vaulted front bay in each section. On the upper floor the double-shell wall of the conches, pierced by round-arched windows, forms an ambulatory with tall coupled columns, again emphasizing the vertical orientation. The two-storey structure of the conches is balanced outside by a high round-arched blind division ending in a dwarf gallery, linking the trefoil chancel optically and incorporating the stair turrets and wall areas of the front bays (although they have a triple elevation). The dome and spire of the crossing tower were rebuilt after a fire in 1741.

Xanten

Berendonck Crucifixion group on the south side of
Xanten Cathedral, 1525–36.

Opposite: The nave of Xanten Cathedral, facing east.

Xanten Cathedral

Xanten Cathedral, the most monumental and important church building on the Lower Rhine next to Cologne, has had a long history. Under the chancel a wooden *cella memoriae* dated after 383 was built above the grave of the martyred St Viktor and his comrades in the Theban Legion, followed by a stone building around 450. A hall church with a rectangular chancel was built in the middle of the 8th century. It was replaced by a basilican structure in the Carolingian period. The present church is of similar dimensions to the Ottonian pier two-aisle basilica consecrated between 967 and 969.

The three lower storeys on the monumental west side of the Romanesque collegiate church built between 1180 or 1190 and 1213 have been preserved and are clearly distinguishable from the upper floors of the tower. Friedrich of Hochstaden, brother of the Archbishop Konrad who initiated the Gothic Cologne Cathedral in 1248, started building the new High Gothic building in 1263, beginning with the chancel. The high altar was consecrated in 1311. The east end was completed as far as the rood screen in 1437, after which the Romanesque nave was laid out. Between 1483 and 1535 the four-aisle basilica was built and the Romanesque west block extended. The cathedral was seriously damaged in the Second World War and the reconstruction was not finished until 1966.

Built on a basilican ground plan, Xanten Cathedral has no transept. The nave and four aisles lead straight into the main apse and the diagonal side apses. While this graduated chancel layout is modelled on the northern French style (see St Yves-de-Braisne, church of Our Lady in Trier), the structure of the basilican nave was inspired by Cologne Cathedral (see also Utrecht Cathedral,

p. 343). Above the raised arches the upper wall in each of the bays is completely broken up by windows set back behind a passageway with a balustrade, similar to the division of the walls in the chancel. The chronological sequence of the construction can be seen from the shapes of the tracery. Outside, piers surmounted by pinnacles with finials and openwork arched buttresses accentuate the Gothic structure of the nave, whose unusual connection with the massive paired towers at the Romanesque west end makes it a dominant feature in the Lower Rhine landscape (Ill. p. 320–1).

The furnishings are particularly magnificent. On the pillars in the nave and chancel is a cycle of twenty-eight stone statues on consoles under baldachins, similar to those in the upper chancel in Cologne Cathedral. The Annunciation and Visitation groups dating from around 1270–80 and eleven Apostles are particularly fine. Like the figures in Naumburg and Bamberg cathedrals they are not as remote as the Cologne sculptures and are therefore easier to see. The figures of St Helena and St Viktor, made somewhat later, show the influence of Lorraine.

The high altar, built between 1529 and 1549, is a late example of a Gothic carved altar with painted wings. The Renaissance-style housing carved by Wilhelm von Roermondt of Cologne has the shrine of St Viktor in its centre niche. The 12th-century casket 1.42 metres (4½ feet) long, covered with gilded silver plate and decorated with precious stones and enamel, is one of the oldest in the Rhineland, although it has been altered several times (first in 1391, most recently in 1904). On the long sides are six sheet gold Apostle figures, similar in style to those on the Eilbertus portable altar (c. 1150, in the Kunstgewerbemuseum in Berlin). On the sloping sides of the top are reliefs of the Wise and Foolish Virgins. Around

the shrine, in the niches on the façade, are twelve carved wood bust reliquaries, six of them by Henrik Douvermann (1533–44). The Renaissance triptych set into the façade of the altarpiece under the reliquary, with a central picture of the Virgin, is a copy after Jan Gossaert (1470–1541), replacing the 'Jewel of the Golden Altarpiece' donated by Archbishop Bruno of Cologne (d. 965), which was lost during the French Revolution. The wings are in three parts and illustrate the legends of St Helena (the legendary founder of the church) and the church's patron saint. Influenced by the Dutch Renaissance (1529–34), they are a major work by Barthel Bruyn, the last great representative of the Cologne School. The Crucifixion in the semicircular tympanum of the altarpiece

(c. 1540) is by the same painter. The altarpiece is topped by carved figures of St Helena and St Viktor in baldachins instead of a Gothic superstructure.

The altar of Our Lady, a major work by Henrik Douvermann carved from 1535 to 1536, has the Virgin in the centre surrounded by eight symmetrically arranged scenes from her life. The motif of the sleeping Jesse in the predella, from which an artistic decoration of intertwined foliage emerges to frame the shrine, is a counterpart to the older altarpiece of the Seven Sorrows of the Virgin by the same artist in St Nikolai in Kalkar (Ill. p. 58).

The carved choir stalls – the oldest in the Rhineland, dating from the late 13th century – are also worthy of note.

Kalkar

St Nikolai

In the early 15th century the present hall church replaced the first church built by Count Dietrich V of Cleves when the town was founded in 1230, although it was unfinished when it was consecrated in 1450. The building work continued under several architects until the beginning of the 16th century. The elevation of the church to an independent parish in 1441 prompted ambitious local initiatives to bring its furnishings up to the standard of those in the monastic and episcopal churches. The town authorities and brotherhoods organized donations and commissioned the major work on

the altar. In fact, the church still had over fifteen altarpieces in 1818. Many of the furnishings were sold at that time to finance repairs, but the church still has a sizeable collection of late medieval sculptures.

Several people in succession worked on the monumental altarpiece. The overall design was by the prominent Lower Rhine craftsman Arnt von Zwolle, who was commissioned to carve the altar in 1488, but died in 1492 before finishing it. Shortly before that year, the housing of the shrine (without the painted wings) had been completed in Kalkar on the master's instructions. Arnt was initially

succeeded by his pupil Jan van Halderen, but Ludwig Jupan from Marburg completed the work by 1500. The central block underneath the Crucifixion was largely made by Arnt. The composition and host of animated figures show his artistic superiority; the groups at the side, which are Jupan's work, are much less impressive. The oak carvings were not polychromed, as was increasingly common towards the end of the century after Tilman Riemenschneider's Münnerstadt altar and the even earlier Lorch altar (Ill. p. 257). The predella shows – as a kind of prelude to the Passion – the Entry into Jerusalem, the

Last Supper and Jesus washing the Disciples' feet. The painted wings were made by Jan Joest of Wesel between 1506 and 1508.

The scenes in a panoramic landscape on the St George altar dating from about 1480 are also the work of Arnt. Delicately turned small pillars divide the saint's shrine into three sections. The main scene from the St George legend, which again is remarkable for its diversity and the narrative flow of the composition, shows St George fighting the dragon in the centre at the front (not part of the two predellas). In this case the carving was polychromed and it has largely been preserved in that form. On the insides

of the painted wings are scenes from the legend of St Ursula, on the left the departure from Britain, on the right the martyrdom of St Ursula and her companions in Cologne (Ill. p. 2). Here again the painter, who has not been identified but was probably from the Cologne School, has given the scene historical authenticity by the artistic depiction of the panorama of Cologne with the striking outline of the Gothic cathedral.

The ogee arch-shaped contoured altarpiece of the Seven Sorrows of the Virgin, made between 1519 and 1522 by the sculptor Henrik Douvermann who had settled in Kalkar in 1517, is a major work from the next generation.

The scenes, in which the wood is left visible, are grouped symmetrically in seven niches around a pietà that was originally probably older (replaced by Ferdinand Langenberg's Neo-Gothic group in 1902). The Tree of Jesse in the predella (Ill. p. 58), which continues in the arabesques on the hollow mouldings of the shrine and leads on to the figure of the Woman of the Apocalypse in the superstructure (see the altar of the Virgin in Xanten Cathedral) is particularly artistic and original. The paintings on the insides of the wings are later, dating from 1636.

It was the Dutch master Arnt van Tricht who made the transition from Late

Opposite: The St George altar at St Nikolai, Kalkar, with sculptures by Master Arnt , *c.* 1480. Scenes of the legend of St Ursula on the painted wings by an unknown master from the Cologne School (see Ill. p. 2).

Below: The nave of St Nikolai, Kalkar, facing east.
Right: Arnt van Tricht, St Mary Magdalene on the Holy Trinity altar, 1541–43.

Gothic to Renaissance around 1535–40, when he worked on the Holy Trinity altar. The capricious face of Mary Magdalene, who appears under a baldachin in the centre of the shrine flanked by St Peter and St Paul, is a perfect embodiment of the contemporary spirit of humanism and the new nature-orientated concept of human beings. Facing the spectator self-confidently in her fashionable clothes, she is not a spiritual saint but an image of flesh and blood beauty. In the columns of the baldachin the artist has used the Renaissance repertoire of Classical forms, a common motif at the time in graphic works.

Among the most moving works in this church are the figures of the Virgin and the John the Apostle from a triumphal cross dated 1469, which used to be above the rood screen.

Nijmegen

St Nicholas Chapel, Nijmegen, in the grounds of
the Valkhof, early 19th century.

Opposite top: The Grote Markt and the Waag, 1612.
Opposite bottom: Herman van Herensgraves, Latin
school, 1545.

Nijmegen, in the south of the province
of Gelderland, is only seven kilometres (four miles) from the German
border. Situated on the left bank of the
Waal, the southern branch of the Rhine
estuary, it is a strategic border and
bridging point for traffic and inland
navigation between the Lower Rhine
and Rotterdam. Under the Emperor
Trajan the Celtic settlement *Noviomagus
Batavorum* was developed into a military
and administrative base for the province
of *Germania inferior*. In 768 Charlemagne
had a palace built on a hill above the
river in the grounds of the Valkhof, now
parkland. It was often used as a temporary imperial residence under the Saxon,
Salian and Hohenstaufen emperors. The
Empress Theophanu died there in 991
and Frederick Barbarossa's son, the future
Emperor Henry VI, was born there in
1165. The St Nicholas Chapel, probably
dating from the early 10th century, is
an indication of how important the site
once was. The chapel is a brick building
similar in design to the Palatine Chapel
in Aachen, with a sixteen-cornered
ground plan and a central tower whose
octagonal shape corresponds to the piers
inside. An imperial and Hanseatic town
in the Middle Ages, Nijmegen joined
the Protestant Union of Utrecht in
1579. From 1678 to 1679 the Peace of
Nijmegen set the seal on the independent existence of the States General,
threatened by Louis XIV's expansion policy in the Dutch war of 1672–78. In the
Second World War the town was badly
damaged in Allied and German attacks.

The old brick Waag (weighhouse) on
the triangular Grote Markt in the centre
of the old town is a striking example of
Dutch Renaissance architecture, with its
two gate arches on the ground floor and
an outside staircase to the upper floor
(a common feature in the Netherlands).
It is a classically influenced Renaissance
building similar to those designed by

Hendrik de Keyser in the same period (see Delft). From the market square a double gate arch (the Kerkboog) leads to the Gothic St Stevenskerk through one of the houses. The church was built around 1600, although the carillon is 18th century, and has a massive four-cornered tower topped with a picturesque

octagon. Next to it is the Latin school designed by the city architect Herman van Herensgraves (1545), its façade divided by a harmonious arrangement of basket arches in which the Renaissance influence is already apparent. In the window axes on the upper floor are carvings of the twelve Apostles and in the frieze below the words of the Ten Commandments.

Records show that there has been a town hall here since the 14th century. The two-storey brick *stadhuis* was built in 1554 by Herman van Herensgraves and rebuilt in 1953. The statues between the windows on the ground floor commemorate the city's imperial benefactors. Heads on the gables and medallions in the window axes complement the sculptures on the handsome façade.

Utrecht

Since the nave collapsed in 1674, leaving only the body of the chancel and transept, the 112 metre (367 foot) tower built between 1321 to 1382 has been isolated. With its square brick lower floors topped by an octagonal super-structure, it became the prototype for many Dutch church towers and belfries.

Utrecht Cathedral

The influence of northern French Gothic architecture on the Lower Rhine extended as far as Utrecht. The former Roman military camp, *Trajectum ad Rhenum*, became a bishop's seat from shortly before 700. The chancel of the cathedral church, started in 1254, shows the influence of Tournai (started 1243), but the model for both is Soissons Cathedral. The vaulting of the chancel ambulatory also covers the five radial chapels.

The long chancel, not built until 1300, is supported by profiled clustered piers unbroken by capitals, while the carved keystones of the chancel vault point to a connection with the art of Claus Sluter in the Burgundian capital, Dijon, around 1400.

Rotterdam

Left: Ossip Zadkine, *The Destroyed City*. Bronze sculpture in Rotterdam, 1951.
Below: The Kunsthal in the Museumpark. Architect Rem Koolhaas, 1992.

Rotterdam in the Rhine-Maas delta is the largest port in the world, owing its economic importance largely to its connection with Europe's biggest waterway, the Rhine. In 1872 the Nieuwe Waterweg, a direct link to the North Sea, was built to accommodate modern shipping. The city has had a turbulent history, but its reconstruction and the building of the Europoort since the Second World War have given it a new lease of life. *The Destroyed City*, a bronze sculpture by the Russian-born Ossip Zadkine (1890–1967) on the Leuwehaven, is a vivid Surrealist expression of fear and despair commemorating the war, when German air attacks reduced the whole city centre to rubble.

Named after a small river called the Rotte, Rotterdam developed from a medieval settlement and was granted a town charter in 1340. The great humanist Geert Geertsz, known as Erasmus of Rotterdam, was born there in 1469 (Ill. p. 24). The city honoured its famous son not long after his death with the bronze statue in front of the Late Gothic St Laurenskerk cast by Hendrik de Keyser in 1622, which survived the bombing during the Second World War. Immigrants from the Spanish Netherlands and French Huguenots contributed to the city's prosperity at the start of the modern era.

One of the countless buildings that represent the modern face of the city and

Hendrik de Keyser, bronze statue of Erasmus in Rotterdam, 1622.

have made an architectural contribution to its economic and cultural revival is the art gallery (Kunsthal), designed by the local architect Rem Koolhaas (born 1945) and built between 1987 and 1992. At first sight the building seems to have been modelled on Ludwig Mies van der Rohe's Neue Nationalgalerie in Berlin. However, it is clear, when the visitor goes inside, that the architecture is not an organic whole, a ready-made structure that the visitor merely has to 'accept'. Instead the visitor is invited to 'reconstruct' the interior from various features that seriously challenge traditional architectural forms, such as the slanting columns. Koolhaas's design is part of a tradition of architecture and town planning shaped by a Utopian vision going back to the Renaissance, here interpreted in a modern or postmodern way and ironically counteracted. The work of art on the roof is also to be seen in that light: the passing camel driver, a symbol of the timeless and the transitory, is an allusion to the building being used for temporary exhibitions.

By contrast, the Boymans-van Beuningen Museum on the other side of the Museumpark is a traditional institution, world famous for its remarkable collections of painting, sculpture, crafts, drawings and graphics. Amongst the old masters, both the Early Netherlandish artists and the Dutch interior and landscape painters are well represented.

Besides being a modern industrial city, Rotterdam has a thriving cultural life and has been nominated European City of Culture for 2001.

Delft

A settlement grew up on the Oude Delft canal (*delf* means moat) in the northern part of the Rhine-Maas delta in or before the 10th century. It was granted a town charter in 1246 and in the 13th and 14th centuries enjoyed an economic boom from its cloth weaving and brewing industries, helped by the construction of a canal link with the Maas, which provided direct access to the sea. The historic and picturesque city of Delft, one of the most beautiful in the Netherlands, is still shaped by its canals.

Delft became internationally famous as the most important centre in the Netherlands for the production of earthenware. In the 17th century the tin-glazed fine earthenware in the characteristic Delft blue on a white background in local and oriental patterns even competed with the porcelain imported from China in large quantities at the time. After 1720 Delftware was eclipsed by European porcelain and inexpensive English stoneware and Delft's heyday was over.

Oude Kerk

The parish church (dedicated to St Hippolytus) that already stood on the site of what is now the Oude Kerk in the 13th century was renovated and enlarged several times over the next few centuries. The aisles and a chancel were built around 1400, the nave in 1430. Further alterations in the Flamboyant style were made in the early 16th century. The lofty pyramidal spire and four small corner towers now to be seen on the massive, heavily tilted square brick tower were added around 1450.

Many famous people are buried in the church. In the chancel there is a monument to Admiral Tromp by Rombout Verhulst and Pieter and Willem de Keyser dating from 1658. The statue of the admiral in front of a niche with

Right: Delft tile mural of a sea battle. Museum Lambert van Meerten, Delft.
Below: The Prinsenhof, with the tower of the Oude Kerk behind it.

weapons and trophies is also by Willem de Keyser and his brother Pieter made the monument to Admiral Piet Hein (1629). Above the admiral's recumbent figure is a baldachin supported by Doric columns.

Prinsenhof

Opposite the Oude Kerk, separated from it by the Oude Delft canal, is the brick complex of the Prinsenhof, grouped around two courtyards. The Prinsenhof has played an important role in Dutch history. In 1575 William I of Orange, who fought for the independence of the United Netherlands and founded the dynasty, built the first seat of the House of Orange in St Agatha's convent, which had existed since 1400 and was secularized during the Reformation (the seat was later moved to The Hague). The seven northern provinces broke away from Spanish rule in 1581 and proclaimed the Republic of the United Provinces. Their leader William of Orange was then assassinated in the Prinsenhof in 1584 on the orders of Philip II. The Prinsenhof is now a

Hendrik de Keyser, the town hall of Delft, 1620.

Opposite: The Nieuwe Kerk and the Markt.

museum commemorating the fight for
independence and the House of Orange-
Nassau.

Stadhuis (town hall)

The large main square in Delft is dominated by two important buildings of
different periods and styles facing one
another. On one side is the town hall, on
the other a church, the Brabant Gothic
Nieuwe Kerk with its high 108 metre
(354 foot) façade tower. In the middle of
the square is F. Stracké's bronze statue of
the eminent jurist Hugo Grotius (1886).

The old 15th-century town hall was
destroyed in a fire in 1618 and only the
belfry survived. Around this massive
Gothic relic the architect Hendrik de
Keyser built a two-storey stone building
in the contemporary style on a square
ground plan with a three-dimensionally
divided façade. An elegant row of
pilasters on pedestals on the upper floor
connects with rusticated pilasters on the
ground floor. The central axis is emphasized by the portal under a baldachin-
style porch with a stepped ramp, a projecting balcony ending in a segmental

arch and the statue of Justice on a raised
gable, with the old belfry towering
above. Like De Keyser's buildings in
Amsterdam, particularly the Beurs (stock
exchange) modelled on the London
building (1608–11) and the weighhouse
in Haarlem (1598, by the architect
Lieven de Key), Delft town hall is
notable as an outstanding example of
Dutch Renaissance architecture in which
Classical influences are already apparent.

Nieuwe Kerk

The Nieuwe Kerk, dedicated to
St Ursula, was built after a miraculous
apparition by the Virgin and ranks as
one of the finest Gothic churches in the
northern Netherlands. The transept and
lower part of the tower are 14th century,
the chancel and nave 15th century. The
impression of lightness and space in
the nave and two side aisles is enhanced
by the clear rhythm of the bays, with
pointed arches supported by solid
columns, a blind triforium with lancet-
type openings and the latticework of the
large clearstorey window. By contrast,
the ogee arched wooden ceiling is dark,
with the struts fitting into engaged shafts
resting on the slabs of the columns. The
ambulatory chancel, built between 1453
and 1476, also surrounded by a ring of
columns, originally had tracery in the
lower (closed) part of the top window
as well.

The most important work of art in
the church is the splendid monument of
Prince William I of Orange (r. 1553–84),
known as William the Silent, in the
chevet. Commissioned from the Utrecht
sculptor and city architect Hendrik de
Keyser by the States General in 1614,
the monument was completed by his son
Pieter in 1622 after his death. The figure
of the dead prince lying on his death bed
and the baldachin-style cover on black
columns are in white marble, while the
statue of the hero on the front, in armour

Gerard Houckgeest, the chancel ambulatory in the Nieuwe Kerk, Delft, with the tomb of William I. Painting, *c.* 1651.

Overleaf: Jan Vermeer, *View of Delft.* Painting, *c.* 1660. Mauritshuis, The Hague.

and seated in a triumphal pose, is made of bronze. The personification of Glory at the feet of the recumbent figure and the female statues of the Virtues at the corners of the baldachin inspired by Cesare Ripa's *Iconologia* are also bronze. The obelisks on top of the baldachin symbolize the prince's glory. The dual portrayal of the deceased (here, unusu-

ally, on the same level) is copied from a type of monument much admired in the 16th century, especially in France (see the tombs of Henri II and Louis XII in St-Denis). William the Silent is shown both in his lifetime, deified as a national hero in the bronze seated figure, and on his death bed, touchingly frail, with real-istic signs of age and clothing in disarray,

giving the observer a feeling of intimacy and involvement.

Virtually all the members of the House of Orange are buried in the royal vault below. The monument to Prince Frederick William of Orange, made by the prominent Classical sculptor Antonio Canova in 1806, can also be seen in the choir ambulatory.

The Delft School

In the 17th century a school of painting flourished in Delft. Its most eminent representative, Jan Vermeer (1632–75), lived in the city all his life. Others, like Pieter de Hooch, Carel Fabritius and Emanuel de Witte, were only there temporarily. Their paintings are in the Dutch tradition of portraying daily life realistically and are notable for their subtle and atmospheric treatment of light and masterly depictions of domestic interiors and genre scenes. In his use of colour to convey a naturalistic impression of light Vermeer in particular was far ahead of his time.

Vermeer only transposed his visual experience with interiors to an outdoor setting in two of his paintings. His *View of Delft* (in the Mauritshuis Museum in The Hague) shows a real-life scene from a window, which here is widened out into a panoramic view. The effect of space is created by the contrasts between the light and the transparent shadows. The town, depicted with topographical accuracy, is spread out in the middle between the shifting expanse of the sky and the reflecting surface of the water. In this *veduta* of Delft the painter has captured the character and atmosphere of the Dutch landscape with total realism.

APPENDICES

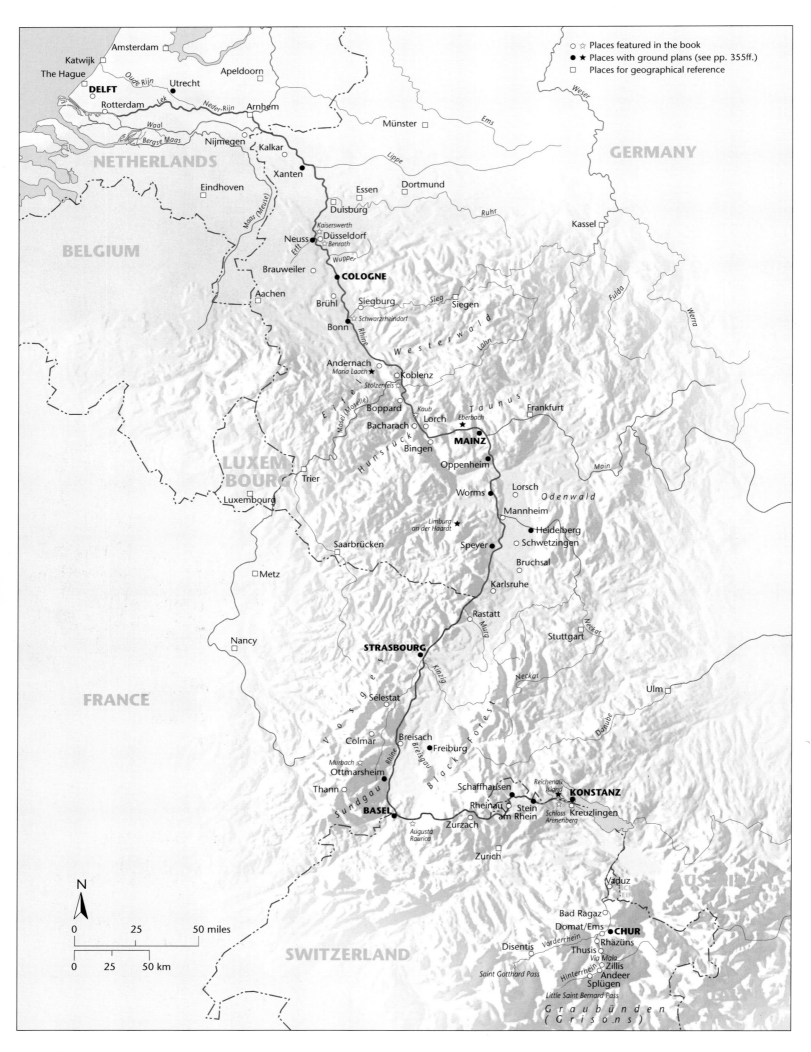

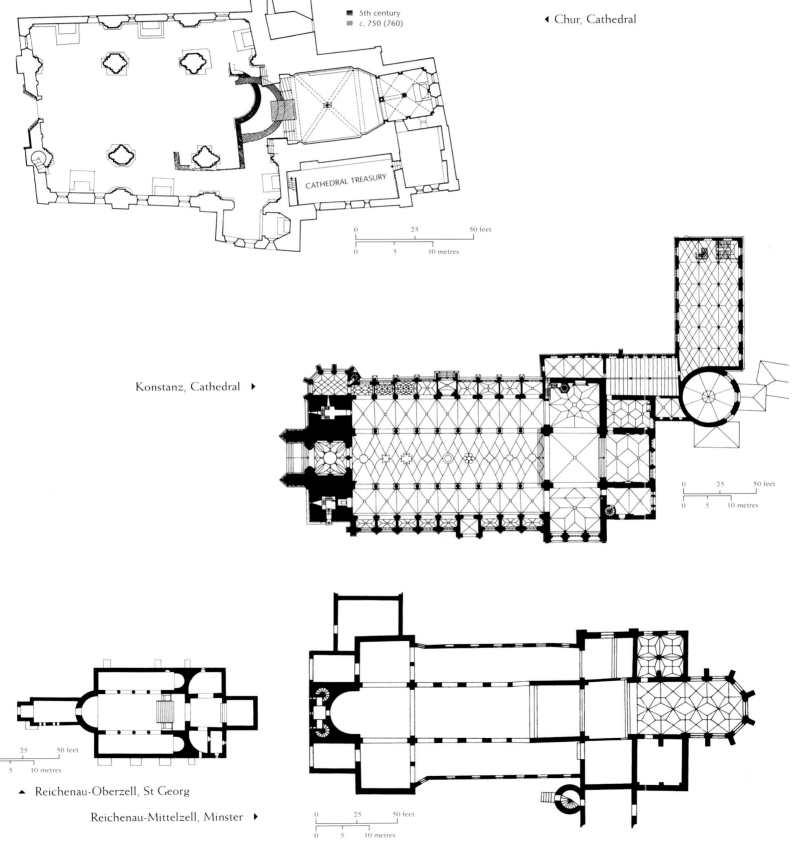

Ground Plans

◄ Chur, Cathedral

■ 5th century
▨ c. 750 (760)

CATHEDRAL TREASURY

0   25   50 feet
0   5   10 metres

Konstanz, Cathedral ►

0   25   50 feet
0   5   10 metres

0   25   50 feet
0   5   10 metres

▲ Reichenau-Oberzell, St Georg

Reichenau-Mittelzell, Minster ►

0   25   50 feet
0   5   10 metres

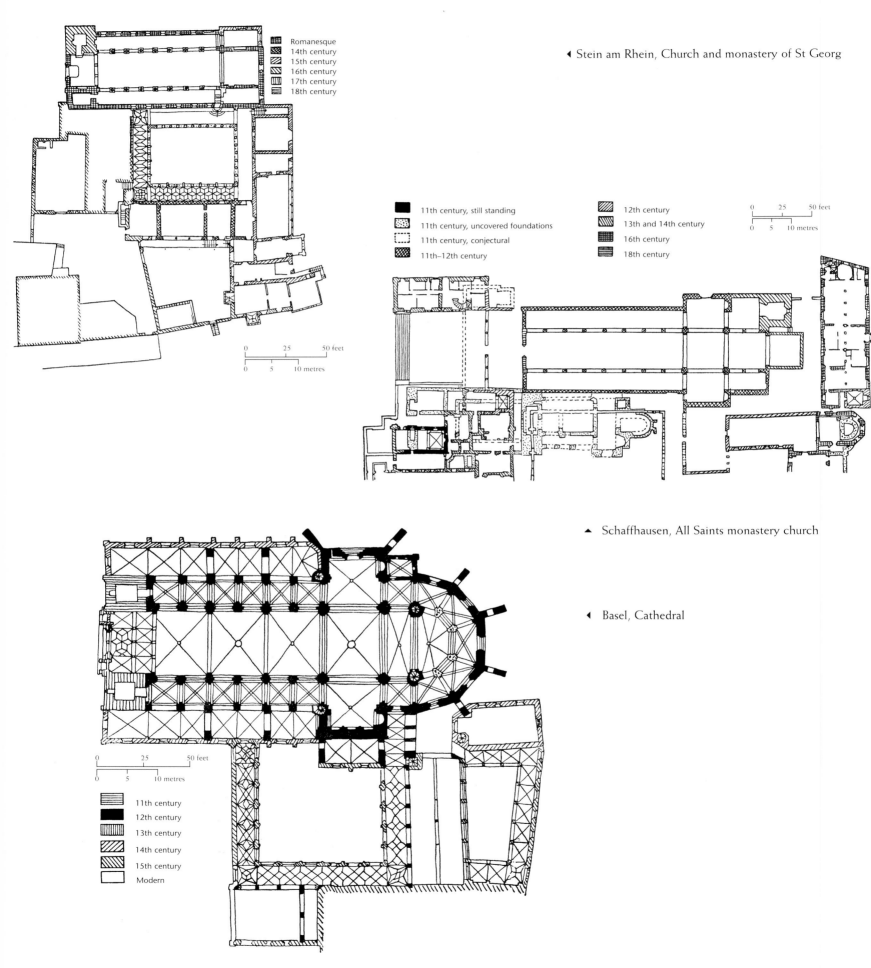

Romanesque
14th century
15th century
16th century
17th century
18th century

◀ Stein am Rhein, Church and monastery of St Georg

11th century, still standing
11th century, uncovered foundations
11th century, conjectural
11th–12th century

12th century
13th and 14th century
16th century
18th century

0   25   50 feet
0   5   10 metres

0   25   50 feet
0   5   10 metres

▲ Schaffhausen, All Saints monastery church

◀ Basel, Cathedral

0   25   50 feet
0   5   10 metres

11th century
12th century
13th century
14th century
15th century
Modern

Ottmarsheim, Nunnery church ▶

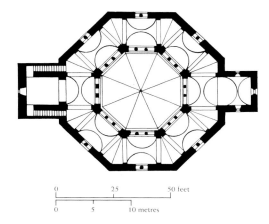

0   25   50 feet

0   5   10 metres

◀ Freiburg, Cathedral

■ Late Romanesque

▥ Early Gothic

▨ Middle Gothic

▧ Late Gothic

▦ Later additions

0   25   50 feet

0   5   10 metres

Strasbourg, Cathedral ▶

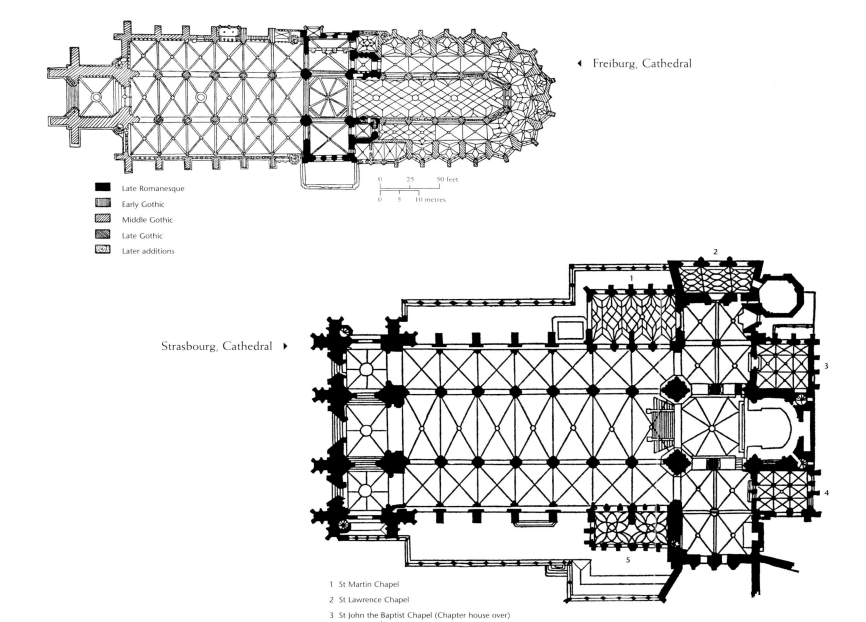

1   St Martin Chapel

2   St Lawrence Chapel

3   St John the Baptist Chapel (Chapter house over)

4   St Andrew Chapel

5   St Catherine Chapel

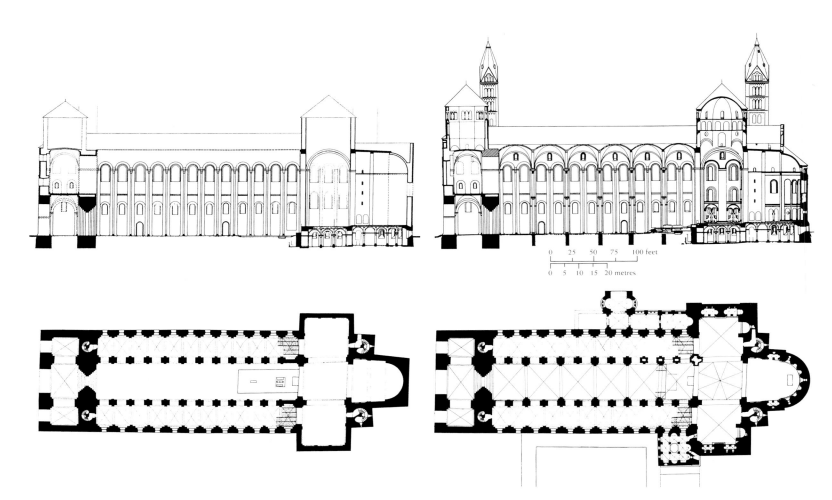

▲ Speyer, Cathedral, first building
(section and ground plan)

▲ Speyer, Cathedral, remodelled building
(section and ground plan)

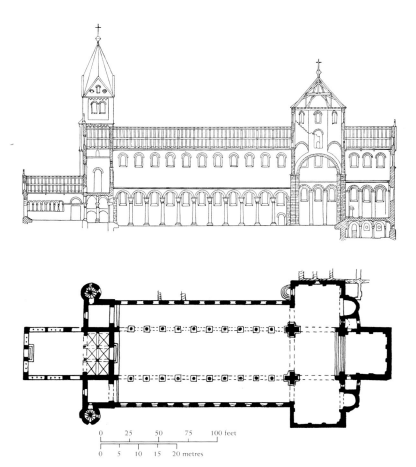

◀ Limburg an der Haardt, Monastery church (section and ground plan)

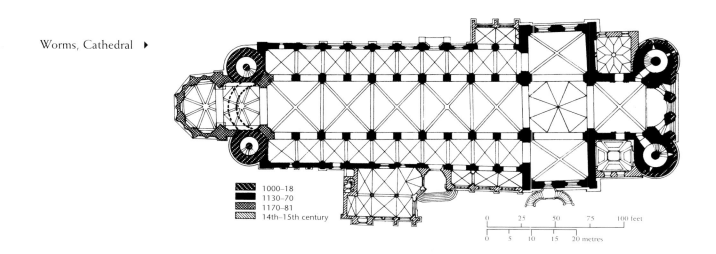

Worms, Cathedral ▸

▨	1000–18
■	1130–70
▨	1170–81
▨	14th–15th century

0   25   50   75   100 feet

0   5   10   15   20 metres

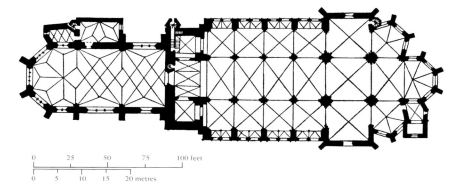

◀ Oppenheim, St Catherine's church

0   25   50   75   100 feet

0   5   10   15   20 metres

Mainz, Cathedral ▸

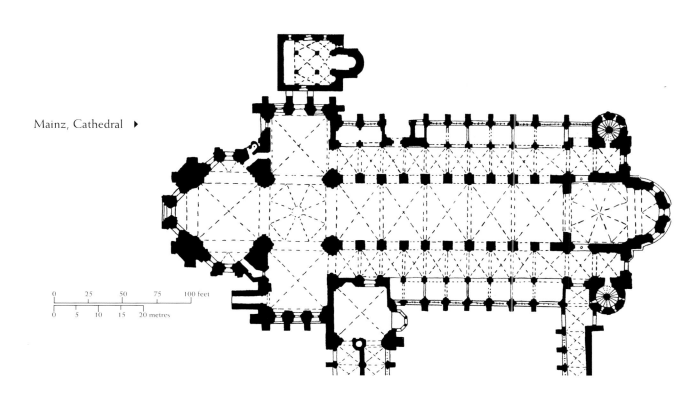

0   25   50   75   100 feet

0   5   10   15   20 metres

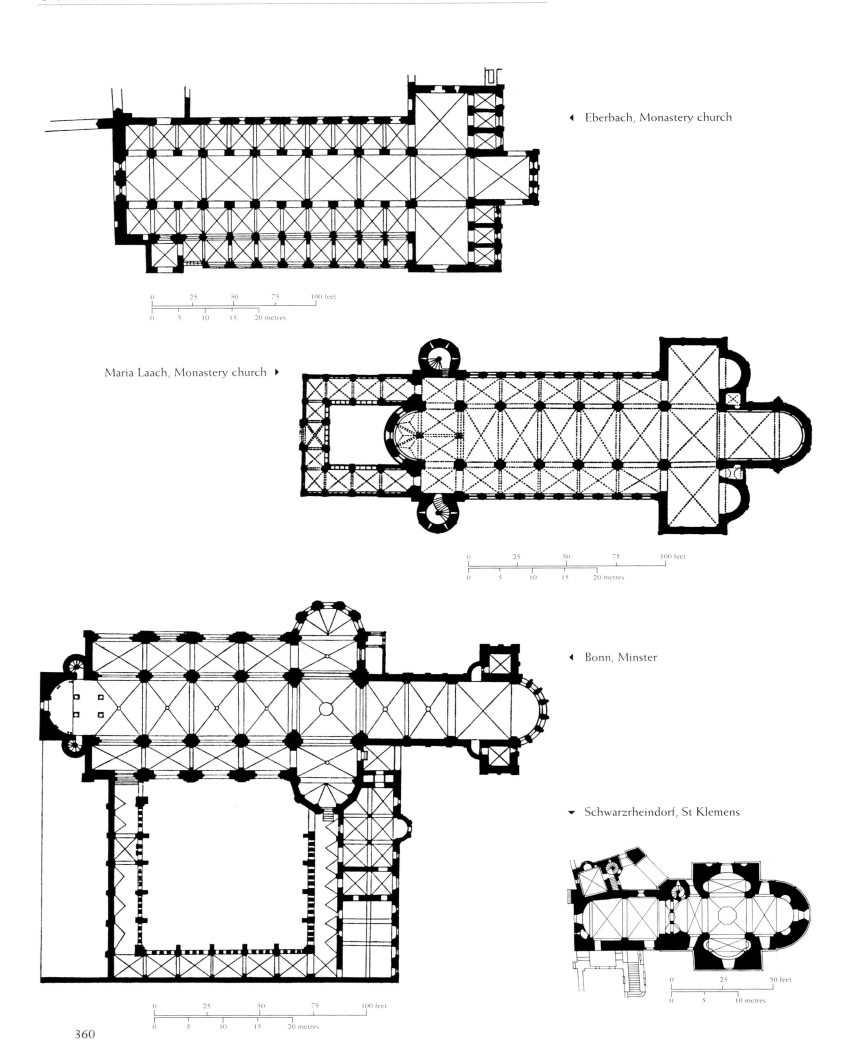

◀ Eberbach, Monastery church

Maria Laach, Monastery church ▶

◀ Bonn, Minster

▾ Schwarzrheindorf, St Klemens

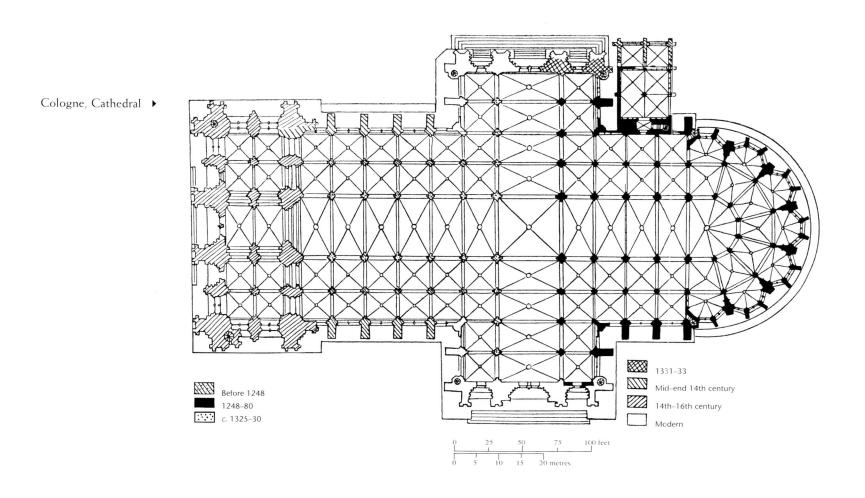

Cologne, Cathedral ▶

Before 1248

1248–80

c. 1325–30

1331–33

Mid–end 14th century

14th–16th century

Modern

0   25   50   75   100 feet

0   5   10   15   20 metres

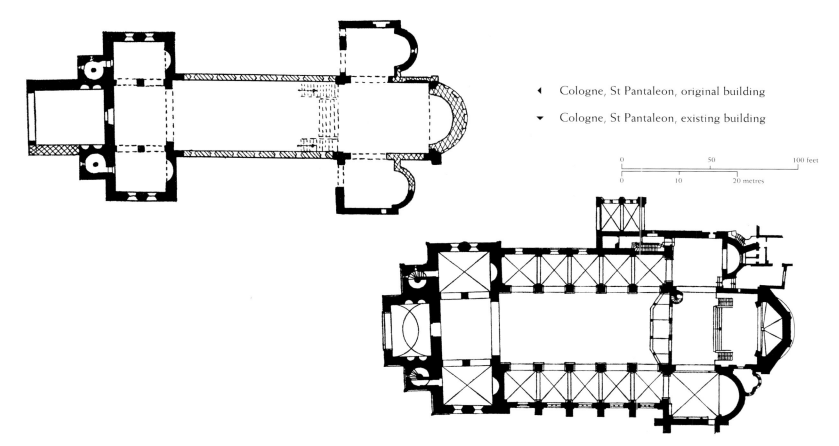

◀ Cologne, St Pantaleon, original building

▼ Cologne, St Pantaleon, existing building

0   50   100 feet

0   10   20 metres

361

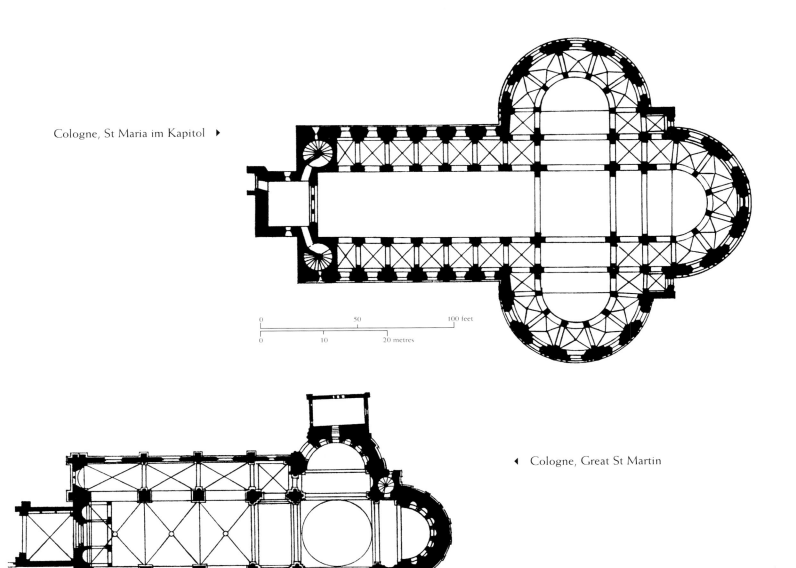

Cologne, St Maria im Kapitol ▶

◀ Cologne, Great St Martin

▼ Cologne, St Gereon; on the left, the plan of the 4th-century Roman building (After A. von Gerkan)

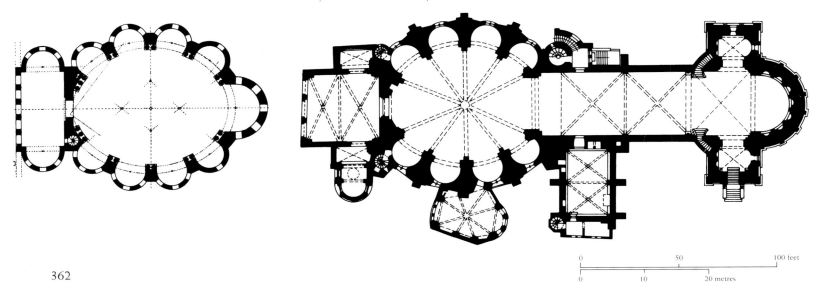

Cologne, Holy Apostles ▶

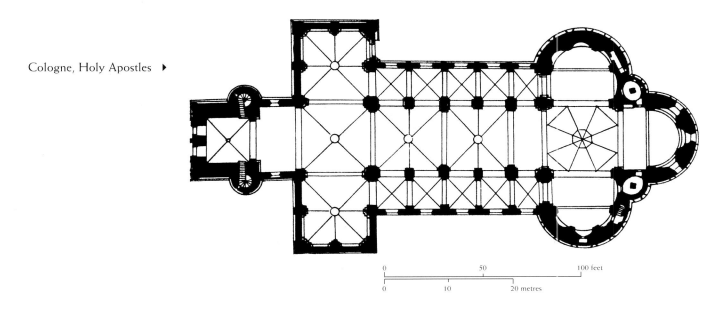

Cologne, St Mariä Himmelfahrt
(Church of the Assumption of the Virgin) ◀

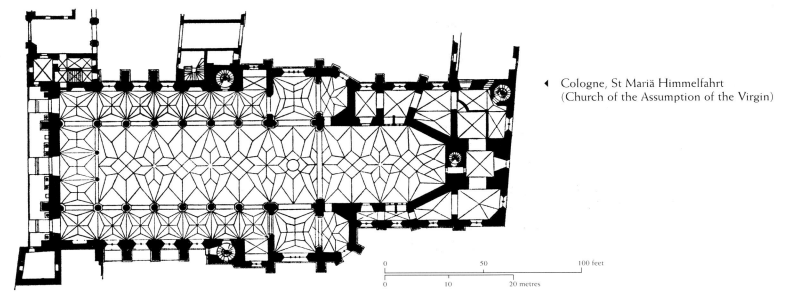

Neuss Cathedral ▶

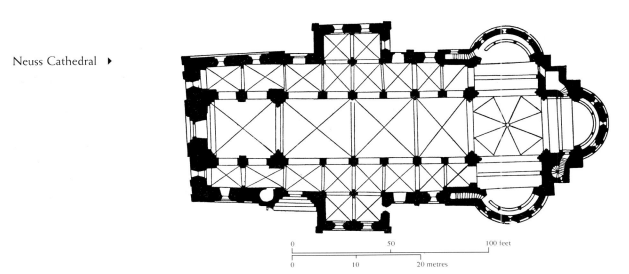

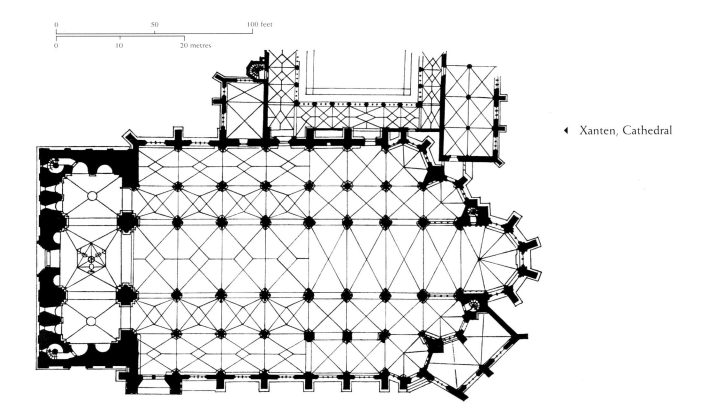

◀ Xanten, Cathedral

Utrecht, Cathedral, choir and transepts ▶
(nave destroyed in the 17th century)

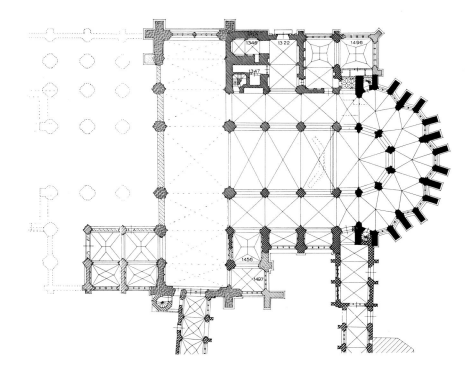

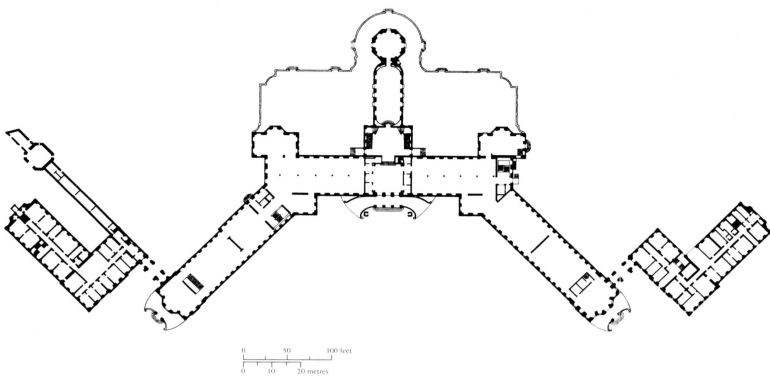

0   50   100 feet

0   10   20 metres

▲ Karlsruhe, Schloss

▼ Bruchsal, Schloss, ground floor and first floor

Heidelberg, Schloss ▼

0   50   100 feet

0   10   20 metres

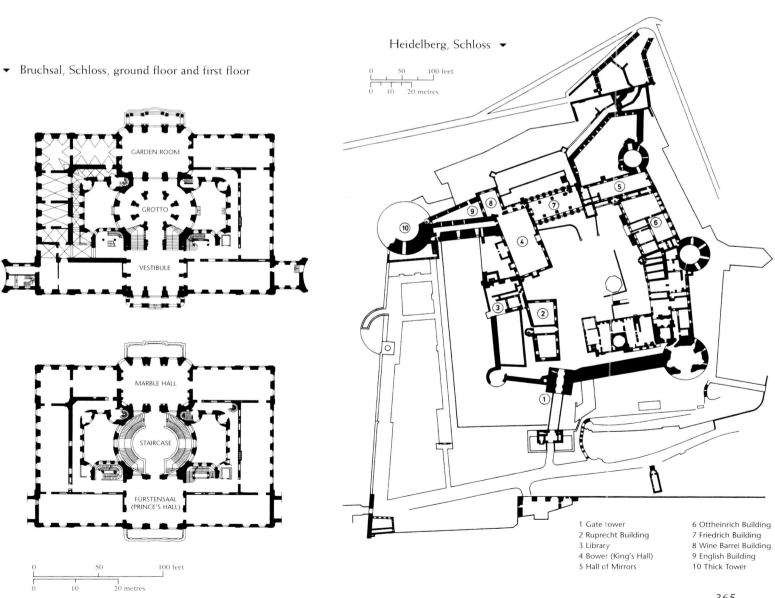

GARDEN ROOM

GROTTO

VESTIBULE

MARBLE HALL

STAIRCASE

FÜRSTENSAAL
(PRINCE'S HALL)

0   50   100 feet

0   10   20 metres

1 Gate tower
2 Ruprecht Building
3 Library
4 Bower (King's Hall)
5 Hall of Mirrors
6 Ottheinrich Building
7 Friedrich Building
8 Wine Barrel Building
9 English Building
10 Thick Tower

Bibliography

General

Ayçoberry, Pierre, and Marc Ferro (ed.), *Une histoire du Rhin* (Des fleuves et des hommes), Paris, 1981

Baum, Julius, *German Cathedrals*, London, 1956

Baxandall, Michael, *The Limewood Sculptors of Renaissance Germany*, New Haven and London, 1980

Bodt, Hans, Peter Hüttenberger et al., *Der Rhein. Mythos und Realität eines europäischen Stromes*, Cologne, 1988

Boehner, Kurt (ed.), *Das erste Jahrtausend. Kultur und Kunst im werdenden Abendland an Rhein und Ruhr*, 3 vols, Düsseldorf, 1962–64

Brenk, Beat, *Die romanische Wandmalerei in der Schweiz* (Basler Studien zur Kunstgeschichte, new series, vol. V), Bern, 1963

Colombier, Pierre du, *L'architecture française en Allemagne au XVIIIe siècle* (Travaux et Mémoires des Instituts français en Allemagne, 4–5), 2 vols, Paris, 1956

Colombier, Pierre du, *L'art français dans les cours rhénanes* (L'art français à l'étranger), Paris, 1930

Conant, Kenneth, *Carolingian and Romanesque Architecture*, Harmondsworth, 1959

Congrès archéologique de France. 85e Session en Rhénanie, Société française d'archéologie, Paris, 1924

Connaissance du Rhin, Saisons d'Alsace (special number), Strasbourg, 1966

Espagne, Michel, and Michael Werner (ed.), *Transferts. Les relations interculturelles dans l'espace franco-allemand* (XVIIIe–XIXe siècles), Paris, 1988

Febvre, Lucien, *Le Rhin. Histoire, mythes et réalités*, Paris, 1997 (1st edn, 1935)

Frankl, Paul, *Gothic Architecture*, Harmondsworth, 1962. (Rev. edn, New Haven and London, 2001)

Gachot, Edouard, *La Dispute du Rhin. De l'Antiquité à nos jours*, Paris, 1952

Gall, Ernst, *Cathedrals and Abbey Churches of the Rhine*, London and New York, 1963

Gantner, Joseph, *Kunstgeschichte der Schweiz*, Frauenfeld, 1936 (vol. 1), 1947 (vol. 2)

Geisler, Irmingard, *Oberrheinische Plastik um 1400* (Forschungen zur Geschichte der Kunst am Oberrhein, 7), Berlin, 1957

Geschichtlicher Atlas der Rheinlande, Cologne, 1982–

Grodecki, Louis, *L'architecture ottonienne au seuil de l'art roman*, Paris, 1958

Guichonnet, P. (ed.), *Histoire et civilisation des Alpes*, Toulouse and Lausanne, 1980

Hässling, Johann Jakob (ed.), *Rheinfahrt*, 2 vols, Munich, 1980

Heuser, Hans-Jörgen, *Oberrheinische Goldschmiedekunst im Hochmittelalter*, Berlin, 1974

Hitchcock, Henry-Russell, *German Renaissance Architecture*, Princeton, 1981

Hüttenberger, Peter, and Hansgeorg Molitor (ed.), *Franzosen und Deutsche am Rhein 1789–1918–1945*, Essen, 1990

Juillard, Etienne, *L'Europe rhénane. Géographie d'un grand espace*, Paris, 1968

Julier, Jürgen, *Studien zur spätgotischen Baukunst am Oberrhein* (Heidelberger Kunstgeschichtliche Abhandlungen, new series, vol. 13), Heidelberg, 1978

Kirschbaum, Engelbert, *Deutsche Nachgotik*, Augsburg, 1930

Knoepfli, Albert, *Kunstgeschichte des Bodenseeraumes, I: Von der Karolingerzeit bis zur Mitte des 14. Jahrhunderts* (Bodensee-Bibliothek, 6), Konstanz and Lindau, 1961

Konow, Helma, *Die Baukunst der Bettelorden am Oberrhein* (Forschungen zur Geschichte der Kunst am Oberrhein, 6), Berlin, 1954

Lasko, Peter, *Ars Sacra, 800–1200*, Harmondsworth, 1972

Legner, Anton, Albert and Irmgard Hirmer, *Romanische Kunst in Deutschland*, Munich, 1982, 2nd edn, 1998

Meckseper, Cord, *Kleine Kunstgeschichte der deutschen Stadt im Mittelalter*, Darmstadt, 1982

Mémorial d'un voyage d'études de la Société Nationale des Antiquaires de France en Rhénanie (juillet 1951), Paris, 1953

Merten, Klaus (ed.), and Paolo Marton, *German Castles and Palaces*, London, 1999

Minder, Robert, *Allemagnes et Allemands*, vol. 1, *Vues d'ensemble. La Rhénanie*, Paris, 1948

La Mystique rhénane. Colloque de Strasbourg 1961, Paris, 1963

Nussbaum, Norbert, *German Gothic Chruch Architecture*, New Haven and London, 2000

Réau Louis, *L'Europe française au Siècle des Lumières*, 2nd edn, Paris, 1971

Recht, Roland, *L'Alsace gothique de 1300 à 1365. Etude d'architecture religieuse*, Colmar, 1974

Reichelt, Günther, *Lasst den Rhein leben! Strom im Spannungsfeld zwischen Ökologie und Ökonomie*, Berlin, 1986

Reiners, Heribert, *Tausend Jahre rheinischer Kunst*, Bonn, 1925

Ruland, Wilhelm, *Rheinisches Sagenbuch*, Cologne, 1921

Suckale, Robert, *Die Hofkunst Kaiser Ludwigs des Bayern*, Munich, 1993

Suckale, Robert, *Kunst in Deutschland. Von Karl dem Grossen bis Heute*, Cologne, 1998

Swarzenski, Hanns, *Monuments of Romanesque Art. The Art of Church Treasures in North-Western Europe*, London and Chicago, 1954

Ternes, Charles-Marie, *La vie quotidienne en Rhénanie romaine*, Paris, 1972

Tümmers, Horst Johannes, *Der Rhein. Ein europäischer Fluss und seine Geschichte*, Munich, 1994

Tümmers, Horst Johannes, *Rheinromantik. Romantik und Reisen am Rhein*, Cologne, 1968

Verbeek, Albert, *Kölner Kirchen. Die kirchliche Baukunst in Köln von den Anfängen bis zur Gegenwart*, Cologne, 1959

Vorromanische Kirchenbauten. Katalog der Denkmäler bis zum Ausgang der Ottonen, pub. Zentralinstitut für Kunstgeschichte, ed. F. Oswald et al., 3 vols, Munich, 1966–1971

Watkin, David, and Tilman Mellinghoff, *German Architecture and the Classical Ideal*, London, 1987

Will, Robert, *Alsace romane* (La Nuit des Temps, 22), St-Léger-Vauban, 1965

Williamson, Paul, *Gothic Sculpture 1140–1300* (Pelican History of Art), New Haven and London, 1995

Art-historical series

Corpus Vitrearum Medii Aevi, Berlin, etc., 1961–2000

Dehio, Georg, *Handbuch der deutschen Kunstdenkmäler*, begun 1900, rev. edn Dehio-Vereinigung, Munich and Berlin, 1976–

Hootz, Reinhard (ed.), *Deutsche Kunstdenkmäler – Ein Bildhandbuch*, Darmstadt, 1958–1981

Die Kunstdenkmäler der Schweiz – Les Monuments d'art et d'histoire de la Suisse, pub. Gesellschaft für Schweizerische Kunstgeschichte, Basel, 1927–1982

Exhibition catalogues

Herbst des Mittelalters. Spätgotik in Köln und am Niederrhein, Cologne, 1970

Lebenslust und Frömmigkeit. Kurfürst Carl Theodor (1724–1799) zwischen Barock und Aufklärung, 2 vols, Regensburg, 1999

Marianne und Germania 1789–1889. Frankreich und Deutschland. Zwei Welten – Eine Revue, Berlin, 1996

Middeleeuwse Kunst der Nordelijke Nederlanden, Amsterdam, 1958

Monumenta Annonis, Köln und Siegburg. Weltbild und Kunst im hohen Mittelalter, Cologne, 1975

Mystik am Oberrhein und in benachbarten Gebieten, Freiburg im Breisgau, 1978

Ornamenta Ecclesiae. Kunst und Künstler der Romanik, 3 vols, Cologne, 1985

Die Parler und der schöne Stil 1350–1400. Europäische Kunst unter den Luxemburgern, 5 vols, Cologne, 1978

Das Reich der Salier 1024–1125, Sigmaringen, 1992

Die Renaissance im deutschen Südwesten zwischen Reformation und Dreissigjährigem Krieg, 2 vols, Karlsruhe, 1986

Rhein und Maas. Kunst und Kultur 800–1400, 2 vols, Cologne, 1972/73

Spätgotik am Oberrhein. Meisterwerke der Plastik und des Kunsthandwerks 1450–1530, Karlsruhe, 1970

Vom Zauber des Rheins ergriffen…Zur Entdeckung der Rheinlandschaft, Munich, 1992

Die Zeit der Staufer. Geschichte–Kunst–Kultur, 5 vols, Stuttgart, 1977

Geographical and General Index

Works of art are listed by location.

Numerals in *italics* refer to illustrations.

Strasbourg *continued*
  St Thomas 46, 204–206, *204, 205, 206*
    Maurice of Saxony tomb 205, *206*
  Schloss Rohan 64, 65, 206–207, *207*
  Spiegel guildhall 69
  windows 55
Stuttgart 216
Sundgau (southern Alsace) 142
Swabia 28, 55
Switzerland 16, 28
synod of Milan (451) 86

Tamins, parish church 83
Tennenbach, Cistercian monastery 164
textiles 55, *150, 152*
Thann 16, 20, 46, 50, 51, 54, 55, 156
  Collégiale-St Thiébault 20, 49, 51, 156–58,
    156, 157, 158
Thirty Years' War (1618–48) 61, 63, 96, 220, 224,
  243, 319
Thusis, Church of Our Lady 81, *81*
tombs 30, 32, 38, *39*, 48, 48–50, *49, 54*, 56, *56*,
  61, 68, 130, 149, 200, *200*, 204, 205–206, *206*,
  232, *232, 248*, 249–50, *263*, 263, 267, 270, *270*,
  346–47, 350–51, *350*
Tournai Cathedral 343
Tours, abbey 33
trade and transport routes 14, 15, 16, 17–19, 78,
  154, 156
travel guides 22
treasury art 32, 33, 34, *34*, 36, 40, *41*, 60, 112,
  129, 131, 137, *138*, 139, *150*, 171, *172*, 274,
  274, 299, *299, 313, 315*
Trier 15, 20, 30, 34
  basilica 299
  church of Our Lady 43, 258
  elector of 65
  St Maximin 297
  Stadtbibliothek, *Egbert Codex* 33, *33*

Troyes Cathedral 193
Turckheim 16

Überlingen 68
  St Nikolaus, high altar 63
  town hall 60
Ulm 46
  Cathedral/cathedral lodge 28, 147
universities 16, 24–25, 191, 288
Untersee *see* Lower Lake
Utrecht 15, 16, 20, 24, 287
  Cathedral 343, *343*
  Union of (1579) 340

Vaduz, Schloss 93, *93*
Venice 18, 21, 27, 30, 61
  Frari church, choir stalls 56
  Scuola di San Orsola 20
Verona 39
Versailles 64
  palace of 64, 212, 278
  Treaty of (1919) 17
Vézelay 70
Via Mala 11, 18, 78, 80, *80*
Vicherey, church 187
Vienna 46
  Congress of (1815) 17, 19
Vieux-Thann 50, 55
Vorarlberg 30
  school of architecture 68–69, 77, 96, 135
Vorderrhein (anterior Rhine) 13, 18, 75, 76, 84
Vosges 13, 16, 156

Wagenhausen, provost parish 125
wall/ceiling paintings 34, 36, 54, 55, 60, 65, 79,
  82–83, *82*, 92, *92*, *104*, 107, 108, *109*, 112, *113*,
  121, *121, 122, 123, 124*, 125, *130, 136, 153*,
  155, 168, *168*, 179, 208, 212, *213, 219*, 265,
  272, 273, 277, *293*, 304, *310*, 317, 322, 323

Wars of Liberation 17
Weingarten, Benedictine abbey 68
Weltenburg, monastery 68
Wessobrunn school 135
Westerwald 16, 253
Westphalia 17, 278, 288, 306
  Treaty of (1648) 16, 19
westwork 32, 229, 298–99, *297, 298*
windows/stained glass 27, 31, 37, 41, 42, *42*, 43,
  47, 51–52, *52*, 54, 55, *57*, 60, 121, 157, *165*,
  176–78, *178*, 189, *199*, 209, *209*, 262, 296, 302,
  310, 317
wine growing/wine trade 13, 14, 16, 18, 23
Wise and Foolish Virgins 149, *192*, 199, 334
Worms 15, 16, 19, 24, 25, 234–38, 260
  bishopric/diocese 242
  Cathedral 37, 49, 160, 234–37, *234, 235, 236*
    west chancel 37, *235*, 236–37
  Concordat of (1122) 15, 234
  Dominican church 238, *238*
  synagogue 237–38, *237*
Würzburg, residence 67

Xanten 30, 55, 321
  altar of Our Lady 58, 336, *336*
  Cathedral 334–35, *334, 335*
  high altar with shrine of St Viktor 334,
    336

Zähringen, imperial fortress 16, 161
zigzag style 51
Zillis, St Martin 41, 78–79, *78, 79*
Zülpich-Hoven, Madonna 39, *39*
Zurich 25, 27, 49
  Cathedral, portal 37
Zurzach 20, 136–37
  former collegiate church of St Verena *136*, 137,
    137
Zurzacher Messe 136

Index of People

Numerals in *italics* refer to illustrations.

Illustration Credits

The following abbreviations have been used: a above; b below; l left; r right.